Lecture Notes in Computer Science 10090

Commenced Publication in 1973
Founding and Former Series Editors:
Gerhard Goos, Juris Hartmanis, and Jan van Leeuwen

More information about this series at http://www.springer.com/series/7408

Leila Ribeiro · Thierry Lecomte (Eds.)

Formal Methods: Foundations and Applications

19th Brazilian Symposium, SBMF 2016
Natal, Brazil, November 23–25, 2016
Proceedings

 Springer

Editors
Leila Ribeiro
Universidad Federal do Rio Grande do Sul
Porto Alegre
Brazil

Thierry Lecomte
ClearSy
Aix en Provence
France

ISSN 0302-9743   ISSN 1611-3349   (electronic)
Lecture Notes in Computer Science
ISBN 978-3-319-49814-0   ISBN 978-3-319-49815-7   (eBook)
DOI 10.1007/978-3-319-49815-7

Library of Congress Control Number: 2016958976

LNCS Sublibrary: SL2 – Programming and Software Engineering

Printed on acid-free paper

This Springer imprint is published by Springer Nature
The registered company is Springer International Publishing AG
The registered company address is: Gewerbestrasse 11, 6330 Cham, Switzerland

Preface

This volume contains the papers presented at SBMF 2016: the 19th Brazilian Symposium on Formal Methods. The conference was held in Natal, Brazil, during November 23–25, 2016. The Brazilian Symposium on Formal Methods (SBMF) is an event devoted to the dissemination of the development and use of formal methods for the construction of high-quality computational systems, aiming to promote opportunities for researchers with interests in formal methods to discuss the recent advances in this area. SBMF is a consolidated scientific-technical event in the software area. Its first edition took place in 1998, reaching the 19th edition in 2016. The proceedings of the last editions have been published in Springer's *Lecture Notes in Computer Science* series as volumes 5902 (2009), 6527 (2010), 7021 (2011), 7498 (2012), 8195 (2013), 8941 (2014), and 9526 (2015).

The conference included two invited talks, given by Augusto Sampaio (UFPE, Brazil) and Michael Leuschel (University of Düsseldorf, Germany), and a tutorial, given by Ana Cristina Vieira Melo (USP, Brazil). A total of 12 papers were presented at the conference and are included in this volume. They were selected from 22 submissions that came from ten different countries: Algeria, Argentina, Brazil, Canada, Equador, Estonia, Finland, Italia, Portugal, South Africa, and Venezuela. The Program Committee comprised 47 members from the national and international community of formal methods. Each submission was reviewed by three Program Committee members. The process of submissions by the authors, paper reviews, deliberations of the Program Committee, as well as proceedings elaboration were all assisted by EasyChair, which provided excellent support for these tasks.

We are grateful to the Program Committee, and to the additional reviewers, for their hard work in evaluating submissions and suggesting improvements. We are very thankful to the general chair of SBMF 2016, Marcel Oliveira (UFRN), and the local organization team, who made everything possible for the conference to run smoothly, and to IMD (Instituto Metrópole Digital) that kindly hosted the event. SBMF 2016 was organized by Federal University of Rio Grande do Norte (UFRN), promoted by the Brazilian Computer Society (SBC), and sponsored by the following organizations, which we thank for their generous support: CAPES, CNPq, UFRN, and ClearSy System Engineering. Finally, we would like to thank Springer for agreeing to publish the proceedings as a volume of *Lecture Notes in Computer Science*.

November 2016

Leila Ribeiro
Thierry Lecomte

Organization

Program Committee

Aline Andrade	Federal University of Bahia, Brazil
Luis Barbosa	Universidade do Minho, Portugal
Christiano Braga	Fluminense Federal University, Brazil
Michael Butler	University of Southampton, UK
Sergio Campos	Federal University of Minas Gerais, Brazil
Ana Cavalcanti	University of York, UK
Simone André Da Costa Cavalheiro	Federal University of Pelotas, Brazil
Márcio Cornélio	Federal University of Pernambuco, Brazil
Andrea Corradini	Università di Pisa, Italy
Jim Davies	University of Oxford, UK
Ana De Melo	University of Sao Paulo, Brazil
Leonardo de Moura	Microsoft Research
David Deharbe	ClearSy, Aix-en-Provence, France
Ewen Denney	SGT/NASA Ames, USA
Clare Dixon	University of Liverpool, UK
Rachid Echahed	CNRS and University of Grenoble, France
Rohit Gheyi	Federal University of Campina Grande, Brazil
Stefan Hallerstede	Aarhus University, Denmark
Reiko Heckel	University of Leicester, UK
Rolf Hennicker	Ludwig-Maximilians-Universität München, Germany
Juliano Iyoda	Federal University of Pernambuco, Brazil
Peter Gorm Larsen	Aarhus University, Denmark
Thierry Lecomte	ClearSy, Aix-en-Provence, France
Michael Leuschel	University of Düsseldorf, Germany
Patricia Machado	Federal University of Campina Grande, Brazil
Marcelo Maia	Federal University of Uberlândia, Brazil
Narciso Marti-Oliet	Universidad Complutense de Madrid, Spain
Anamaria Martins Moreira	Federal University of Rio de Janeiro, Brazil
Tiago Massoni	Federal University of Campina Grande, Brazil
Alvaro Moreira	Federal University of Rio Grande do Sul, Brazil
Alexandre Mota	Federal University of Pernambuco, Brazil
Arnaldo Moura	IC/UNICAMP
David Naumann	Stevens Institute of Technology, USA
Daltro Jose Nunes	Federal University of Rio Grande do Sul, Brazil
Jose Oliveira	Universidade do Minho, Portugal
Marcel Vinicius Medeiros Oliveira	Federal University of Rio Grande do Norte, Brazil

Fernando Orejas	UPC, Spain
Arend Rensink	University of Twente, The Netherlands
Leila Ribeiro	Federal University of Rio Grande do Sul, Brazil
Augusto Sampaio	Federal University of Pernambuco, Brazil
Leila Silva	Federal University of Sergipe, Brazil
Adenilso Simao	ICMC/USP, Brazil
Neeraj Singh	McMaster University, Canada
Gabriele Taentzer	Philipps-Universität Marburg, Germany
Sofiene Tahar	Concordia University, Canada
Matthias Tichy	University of Ulm, Germany
Jim Woodcock	University of York, UK

Additional Reviewers

Julia, Stéphane
Lopes, Bruno
Lucero, Giovanny
Siddique, Umair

Contents

Invited Talks

Formal Model-Based Constraint Solving and Document Generation

Michael Leuschel[✉]

Institut Für Informatik, Universität Düsseldorf,
Universitätsstr. 1, 40225 Düsseldorf, Germany
leuschel@cs.uni-duesseldorf.de

Abstract. Constraint solving technology for formal models has made considerable progress in the last years, and has lead to many applications such as animation of high-level specifications, test case generation, or symbolic model checking. In this article we discuss the idea to use formal models themselves to express constraint satisfaction problems and to embed formal models as executable artefacts at runtime. As part of our work, we have developed a document generation feature, whose output is derived from such executable models. This present article has been generated using this feature, and we use the feature to showcase the suitability of formal modelling to express and solve various constraint solving benchmark examples. We conclude with current limitations and open challenges of formal model-based constraint solving.

1 Animation and Constraint Solving for B

The B-Method [2] is a formal method rooted in predicate logic and set theory, supporting the generation of code "correct by construction" via successive refinement. Initially, the B-method was supported by two tools, BToolkit [4] and Atelier B [7], which both provided automatic and interactive proving environments, as well as code generators. To be able to apply the code generators, one has to *refine* an initial high-level specifications into lower-level B (called B0). It is of course vital that the initial high-level specification correctly covers the requirements of the application being developed. To some extent suitability of the high-level specification can be ensured by stating and proving invariants and assertions. In addition, the BToolkit provided an interactive animator, where the user had to provide values for parameters and existentially quantified variables, the validity of which was checked by the BToolkit prover. However, quite often these techniques are far from satisfactory and sufficient. The PROB validation tool [24,25] was developed to satisfy this need in the tooling landscape, and provide a more convenient and extensive validation of high-level specifications. The first problem that PROB set out to solve was to provide automatic animation, freeing up the user from providing values for parameters and quantified variables. This was achieved by providing a constraint solver for the B language. On top of the animator, a model checker was developed, in order to automatically construct the state space of a formal B model and check temporal properties.

© Springer International Publishing AG 2016
L. Ribeiro and T. Lecomte (Eds.): SBMF 2016, LNCS 10090, pp. 3–20, 2016.
DOI: 10.1007/978-3-319-49815-7_1

Constraint Solving, Execution and Proof

What distinguishes constraint solving from proof and execution (e.g., of generated code) in the context of B:

- the expression $\{2, 3, 5\} \cap 4..6$ can be executed, yielding the value $\{5\}$. The characteristics of execution for B are: no non-determinism arises, no search is required, and there is a clear procedure on how to obtain the result. An example for execution is the running of code generated from B0.
- The sequent or proof obligation $x \geq 0 \land n > 0 \vdash x + n > 0$ can be proven. The characteristics of proof for B are: usually a non-deterministic search for a proof is required; human intervention is also often required. Proof can deal with infinite values and infinitely many possibilities; e.g., the above sequent holds for infinitely many values for x and n. A proof attempt either yields a proof or it does not. In the latter case, we do not know the status of the proof obligation and in either case no values are obtained.
- The predicate $x \geq 0 \land n > 0 \land x + n \in \{2, 3\}$ can be solved yielding a solution $x = 0, n = 2$. The characteristics of constraint solving are that, in contrast to execution and just like for proof, a non deterministic search for possible solutions is required. In contrast to proof, the process is fully automatic and provides concrete values. On the downside, constraint solving usually can only deal with a bounded number of finite values for the variables.

Challenge. The major challenge of animating or validating B is the expressiveness of its underlying language. B is based on predicate logic, augmented with arithmetic (over integers), (typed) set theory, as well as operators for relations, functions and sequences. (A similar point can be made for other formal methods who share a similar foundation, such as TLA+ [21] or Z [38].) As such, B provides a very expressive foundation which is familiar to many mathematicians and computer scientists. For example, Fermat's Last Theorem can be written in B as follows:

$$\forall n.(n > 2 \Rightarrow \neg(\exists(a, b, c).(a^n + b^n = c^n)))$$

In B's ASCII syntax (AMN or Abstract Machine Notation) this is written as follows:

```
!n.(n>2 => not(#(a,b,c).(a**n + b**n = c**n)))
```

A more typical example in an industrial formal specifications would be the integer square root function, which can be expressed in B as follows:

$$isqrt = \lambda n.(n \in \mathbb{N} \mid max(\{i \mid i^2 \leq n\}))$$

Here, the λ operator allows us to construct an infinite function, whose domain are the natural numbers and whose result is the largest integer whose square is less or equal to the function parameter n.

Due to arithmetic and the inclusion of higher-order functions, the satisfiability of B formulas is obviously undecidable. As such, animation is also undecidable, as operation preconditions or guards in high-level models can be arbitrarily complex. We cannot expect to be able to determine the truth value of Fermat's Last Theorem automatically, but PROB *is* capable of computing with the integer square root function above, e.g., determining that $isqrt(101) = 10$ or $isqrt(1234567890) = 35136$.[1] The relational composition operator ";" can actually be used as the higher-order "map" function in functional programming, and PROB can compute $([99, 100, 101]; isqrt) = [9, 10, 10]$.

In essence, the challenge and ultimate goal of PROB is to solve constraints, for an undecidable formal method with existential and universal quantification, higher-order functions and relations, unbounded variables. Ideally, infinite functions should be dealt with symbolically, while large finite relations should be stored efficiently. Moreover, we generally need not just to find one solution for a predicate, but all solutions. For example, when evaluating a set comprehension, all solutions must be found. Similarly, when using model checking we need to find all solutions for the guard predicates, to ensure that the complete state space gets constructed.

Applications of Constraint Solving

Over the years the constraint solving kernel of PROB has been improved, e.g., making use of the CLP(FD) library of SICStus Prolog [6] or using CHR [12]. This opened up many additional applications:

- Constraint-based invariant or deadlock checking [14].
  E.g., for deadlock checking, we ask the constraint solver to find a state of a B model satisfying the invariant, such that no event or operation is enabled.
- Model-based testing [16,31,34].
  Here we ask the constraint solver to find values for constants and operation parameters to construct test cases.
- Disproving and proving [17].
  Here we ask the constraint solver to find counter examples to proof obligations. Sometimes, when no counter example is found, the constraint solver can return a proof, e.g., when only finite domain variables occur.
- Enabling analysis [10].
  Here the constraint solver determines whether an event can disable or enable other events. The result is used for model comprehension, inferring control flow and for optimising the model checking process.
- Symbolic model checking [18].
  Here the constraint solver is used to find counter example traces for invariance properties.

---

[1] This is one of the specifications which is given as an example of a non-executable specification in [15].

2   Model-Based Constraint Solving

We now want to turn our focus from constraint solving technology for validating B models towards using B models to express constraint satisfaction problems.

The idea is to use the expressivity of the B language and logic to express practical problems, and to use constraint solving technology on these high level models. In other words, the B model is not refined in order to generate code but is "executed" directly.

Data validation in the railway domain [1,5,22,26,27] was a first practical application where B was used in this way, i.e., properties where expressed in B and checked directly by a tool such as PROB, PredicateB or Ovado. Here the B language was particularly well suited, e.g., to express reachability in railway networks. The constraint solving requirements are typically relatively limited and could still be solved by naive enumeration.

In the article [28] we later argued that B is well suited for expressing constraint satisfaction problems in other domains as well. This was illustrated on the Jobs puzzle challenge [37] and we are now using this approach at the University of Düsseldorf to solve various time tabling problems [35], e.g., determine whether a student can study a particular combination of course within a given timeframe.

A question is of course, why not encode these constraint satisfaction problems in a dedicated programming language such as CLP(FD) [6] or Zinc [29]. Some possible answers to this question are:

- By using B we obtain constraint programming with proof support B. For example, we can add assertions about our problem formulation and discharge them using proof. We also hope that optimisation rules can be written in B and proven for all possible values.
- B is a very expressive language, many problems can be encoded more elegantly in B than in other languages [28].
- we want to use a formal model not just as a design artefact but also at runtime; B can also be a very expressive query language, thereby enabling introspection, monitoring and analysis capabilities at runtime.
- We also wanted to stress test the constraint solver of PROB, identify weaknesses and improve the tool in the process.
- Finally, we hope to use B in this way for teaching mathematics, theoretical computer science and obviously B itself.

In the SlotTool project [35] we will compare the formal model based approach with a traditional constraint programming implementation, but it is still to early in the project to draw any conclusions.

In Sect. 4 we will present a few more constraint satisfaction benchmarks and problems which can be stated in the logic of the B notation. To this end, we will use another new feature of PROB: being able to generate "executable" Latex documentation. This feature was developed out of the necessity to understand complex models and complex situations in [35], as well as out of the need to generate validation reports and summaries for data validation. This new feature is described in the following section.

3   Model-Based Document Generation

In this section we present a new feature of PROB, allowing one to generate readable documents from formal models. PROB can be used to process Latex [20] files, i.e., PROB scans a given "raw" Latex file and replaces certain PROB Latex commands by processed results, yielding a "proper" Latex file with all PROB commands replaced by evaluated results.

```
probcli FILE -init -latex RawLatex.tex FinalLatex.tex
```

The `FILE` and `-init` parameters are optional; they are required in case one wants to process the commands in the context of a certain model. Currently the PROB Latex commands mainly support B and Event-B models, TLA+ and Z models can also be processed but all commands currently expect B syntax. You can add more commands if you wish, e.g., set preferences using `-p PREF VAL` or run model checking `--model-check`. The Latex processing will take place after most other commands, such as model checking.

To some extent this feature was inspired by Z, where models are written in Latex format from the start. The Z Word Tools [13] were later developed to enable one to write Z models in Microsoft Word. A difference with our approach is that the B model is still kept separate from the Latex document, and that the Latex document may also contain commands to derive additional data, tables or figures. Moreover, multiple Latex documents can be attached to a B model and can also be re-used for the same model, with varying data inputs.

Applications. We hope that some of the future applications of this Latex package are:

– **Model documentation**: generate an executable documentation for a formal model, that shows how to operate on the model. Moreover, provided PROB's Latex processing runs without errors, the documentation is guaranteed to be up-to-date with the current version of the model.
– **Worksheets**: for certain tasks the Latex document can replace a separate formal B model, the model is built-up incrementally by Latex commands and the are results shown in the final Latex output. This is probably most appropriate for smaller, isolated mathematical problems in teaching.
– **Validation reports**: on can automatically construct a summary of a validation task such as model checking or assertion checking.
– **Model debugging or information extraction**: here the processing of the executable document extracts and derives relevant information from a formal model, and presents it in a user friendly way. We use this feature regularly for our time tabling application [35] to depict conflicts either graphically or in a tabular fashion.
– Finally, we also plan to use the Latex package to produce documentation for some of PROB's features (such as this latex package or PROB's external functions).

Some Commands. The `\probexpr` command takes a B expression as argument and evaluates it. By default it shows the B expression and the value of the expression, for example:

- `\probexpr{{1}\/{2**100}}` in the raw Latex file will yield:
  $\{1\} \cup \{2^{100}\} = \{1, 1267650600228229401496703205376\}$

The `\probrepl` command takes a REPL command and executes it. By default it shows only the output of the execution, e.g., in case it is a predicate TRUE or FALSE.

- `\probrepl{2**10>1000}` in the raw Latex file will yield:
  TRUE
- `\probrepl{let DOM = 1..3}` outputs a value and will define the variable `DOM` for the remainder of the Latex run:
  $\{1, 2, 3\}$
- there is a special form for the let command: `\problet{DOM}{1..3}`, it has the same effect as the command above, but also prints out the let predicate itself:
  let DOM $= 1..3 \rightsquigarrow \{1, 2, 3\}$

The `\probprint` command takes an expression or predicate and pretty prints it, for example:

- `\probprint{bool({1|->2,2|->3}|>>{4}:NATURAL+->INTEGER)}` yields:
  $bool(\{(1 \mapsto 2), (2 \mapsto 3)\} \triangleright \{4\} \in \mathbb{N} \nrightarrow \mathbb{Z})$

The `\probif` command takes an expression or predicate and two Latex texts. If the expression evaluates to TRUE the first branch is processed, otherwise the other one is processed. Here is an example:

- `\probif{2**10>1000}{$\top$}{$\bot$}` in the raw Latex file will yield:
  $\top$

The `\probfor` command takes an identifier, a set expression and a Latex text, and processes the Latex text for every element of the set expression, setting the identifier to a value of the set. For example, below we embed the command:
`\probfor{i}{2..3}{\item square of$\probexpr{i}$: $\probexpr{i*i}$}`
within an itemize environment to generate a list of entries:

- square of $i = 2$: $i * i = 4$
- square of $i = 3$: $i * i = 9$

The `\probtable` command takes a B expression as argument, evaluates it and shows it as a table. For example, the command:
`\probtable{{i,cube|i:2..3 & cube=i*i*i}}{no-row-numbers}` in the raw Latex file will yield:

Finally, the `\probdot` command takes a B expression or predicate as argument, evaluates it and translates it into a graph rendered by dot [3].

i	$Cube$
2	8
3	27

4   A Portfolio of Constraint Solving Examples in B

The following examples were generated (on $1/10/2016 - 11h383s$) using the Latex package described in Sect. 3 with PROB version $1.6.1 - beta4$.

4.1   Graph Colouring

The graph colouring problem consists in assigning colours to nodes of a graph, such that any two neighbours have different colours. Let us first define some arbitrary directed graph $gr = \{(1 \mapsto 3), (2 \mapsto 4), (3 \mapsto 5), (5 \mapsto 6)\}$ (using integers as nodes). Suppose we want to color this graph using the colours $cols = \{red, green\}$. We now simply set up a total function from nodes to $cols$ and require that neighbours in gr have a different colour:

$$\exists col.(col \in 1..6 \rightarrow cols \wedge \forall(x, y).(x \mapsto y \in gr \Rightarrow col(x) \neq col(y)))$$

The graph and the first solution found by PROB for col are shown in Fig. 1 using the \probdot command.

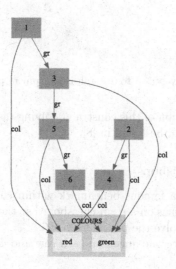

Fig. 1. A solution to a graph colouring problem

4.2   Graph Isomorphism

Let us define two directed graphs $g1 = \{(v1 \mapsto v2), (v1 \mapsto v3), (v2 \mapsto v3)\}$ and $g2 = \{(n1 \mapsto n2), (n3 \mapsto n1), (n3 \mapsto n2)\}$. The nodes of $g1$ are $V = \{v1, v2, v3\}$

and of $g2$ are $N = \{n1, n2, n3\}$. These two graphs are isomorphic if we can find a bijection between V and N, such that the successor relation is preserved. We can compute the successors of a node by using the relational image operator $[.]$, e.g., the successors of $v1$ in $g1$ are $g1[\{v1\}] = \{v2, v3\}$. In B we can thus check $g1$ and $g2$ for isomporhism by trying to find a solution for:

$$\exists iso.(iso \in V \rightarrowtail\!\!\!\!\rightarrow N \land \forall v.(v \in V \Rightarrow iso[g1[\{v\}]] = g2[iso[\{v\}]]))$$

The graph and the first solution found by PROB for iso are shown in Fig. 2 using the \probdot command.

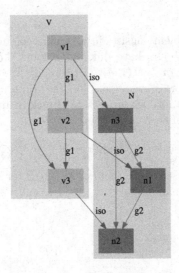

Fig. 2. A solution to a graph isomorphism problem

An industrial application of this constraint solving task — expressed in B — for reverse engineering can be found in [8].

4.3   N-Queens and Bishops

The N-Queens puzzle is a famous benchmark within constraint programming. The task is to place n queens on a $n \times n$ chessboard so that no two queens attack each other. Initially, we solve the puzzle for $n = 6$.

In a first step, we place one queen on each row and column by using a total injection constraint:

$$\exists queens.(queens \in 1..n \rightarrowtail 1..n)$$

Here, $queens$ is a function which for every queen stipulates the column it is placed on. By stipulating that the function is injective, we ensure that no two queens can be on the same column. By numbering queens from 1 to n, we have implicitly placed one queen on each row.

We still need to ensure that queens cannot attack each other on the diagonals, above we have actually described the N-Rook problem. The first solution found by PROB is shown below \probfor command and the skak package.[2]

Dealing with the diagonals requires a more involved universal quantification:

$queens \in 1..n \rightarrowtail 1..n \land \forall(q1, q2).(q1 \in 1..n \land q2 \in 2..n \land q2 > q1 \Rightarrow queens(q1) + (q2 - q1) \neq queens(q2) \land queens(q1) + (q1 - q2) \neq queens(q2))$

The first solution found by PROB is

$$queens = \{(1 \mapsto 5), (2 \mapsto 3), (3 \mapsto 1), (4 \mapsto 6), (5 \mapsto 4), (6 \mapsto 2)\}$$

which can be depicted graphically as follows:

For $n = 17$ we obtain the following first solution (after about 20 ms):

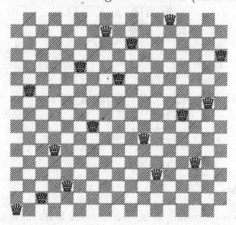

---

[2] See https://www.ctan.org/pkg/skak.

Related to the N-Queens puzzle is the Bishops problem: how many bishops can one place on an n by n chess board without any bishop attacking another bishop. In this case one can place multiple bishops on the same row and column; hence our encoding in B must be slightly different. Below we represent the placement of the bishops as a subset of $(1..n) \times (1..n)$ and solve the puzzle for $n = 8$. The following constraint encodes the proper placement of the bishops:

$$\exists bshp.(bshp \subseteq (1..n) \times (1..n) \wedge \forall(i,j).(\{i,j\} \subseteq 1..n \Rightarrow (i \mapsto j \in bshp \Rightarrow \forall k.(k \in i+1..n \Rightarrow (k \mapsto (j+k)-i) \notin bshp \wedge (k \mapsto (j-k)+i) \notin bshp))))$$

To find the optimal solution one can solve the above predicate with an additional constraints about the cardinality of $bshp$, and continuously use the size of the previous solution as a strict lower bound for the next solution. Below is solution of the above with 14 bishops (found in about half a second); there is no solution with 15 bishops.

We can also try to solve these various puzzles together, e.g., place 8 queens, 8 rooks and 13 bishops on the same eight by eight board. For this, we simply conjoin the four problems above and add constraints linking them, to ensure that a square is occupied by one piece at most. This is a simplified version of the crowded chess board problem from [11].

A solution found after about 0.4 s is shown below. Note, that while PROB can solve the problem quite efficiently for 13 bishops, solving time for the optimal 14 bishops together with 8 queens and rooks is dramatically higher (about 560 s). Here, a custom low-level encoding will probably be much more efficient than the B version (but also more tedious to write).

4.4   Golomb Ruler

Another well-known constraint solving benchmark is the Golomb ruler. The task is to set marks on a ruler of a given length so that no two marks have the same distance. The marks have to be put at integer positions and the ruler is also of integer length.

We now solve this puzzle for $n = 7$ marks and a length $len = 25$.

The following expresses the problem in B:

$\exists a.(a \in 1..n \rightarrow 0..len \wedge \forall i.(i \in 2..n \Rightarrow a(i-1) < a(i)) \wedge \forall(i1, j1, i2, j2).(i1 > 0 \wedge i2 > 0 \wedge j1 \leq n \wedge j2 \leq n \wedge i1 < j1 \wedge i2 < j2 \wedge (i1 \mapsto j1) \neq (i2 \mapsto j2) \Rightarrow a(j1) - a(i1) \neq a(j2) - a(i2)))$

The first solution found by PROB (in about 130 ms) is the following one:

$$a = \{(1 \mapsto 0), (2 \mapsto 2), (3 \mapsto 6), (4 \mapsto 9), (5 \mapsto 14), (6 \mapsto 24), (7 \mapsto 25)\}$$

The solution is depicted graphically below, using the \probfor command within a Latex picture environment.

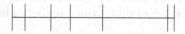

It takes 320 ms to compute all 10 solutions using a set comprehension. Note that some of the rulers can be obtained from the other rules by reversing the order of the marks.

We can filter out these rulers using the B function $\lambda r.(r \in seq(\mathbb{Z}) | rev((r; \lambda i.(i \in \mathbb{Z} | 25 - i))))$ yielding the table below:

a
[0, 2, 6, 9, 14, 24, 25]
[0, 1, 4, 10, 18, 23, 25]
[0, 2, 3, 10, 16, 21, 25]
[0, 1, 7, 11, 20, 23, 25]
[0, 3, 4, 12, 18, 23, 25]

4.5 Sudoku and Latin Squares

Sudoku is a popular puzzle in constraint programming circles. We first define the domain for our numbers: $let\ D = 1..9$. Let us first construct a 9×9 square containing numbers in D, such that on all rows and columns we have different numbers, i.e., we just construct a **Latin square** of order 9.

We first compute the pairs of positions on columns that need to be different:

$$let\ Diff1 = \{x1, x2, y1, y2 | \{x1, x2, y1\} \subseteq D \wedge x1 < x2 \wedge y1 = y2\}$$

This gives rise to $card(Diff1) = 324$ pairs of positions. Now we do the same for rows:

$$let\ Diff2 = \{x1, x2, y1, y2 | \{x1, y1, y2\} \subseteq D \wedge x1 = x2 \wedge y1 < y2\}$$

A solution to the constraint $\exists Board.(Board \in D \rightarrow (D \rightarrow D) \wedge \forall(x1, x2, y1, y2).(x1 \mapsto x2 \mapsto y1 \mapsto y2 \in Diff1 \cup Diff2 \Rightarrow Board(x1)(y1) \neq Board(x2)(y2)))$ is depicted below, again using the \probfor command:

2	5	4	1	3	6	7	8	9
1	4	2	3	6	5	9	7	8
4	9	3	2	1	8	5	6	7
3	1	8	7	9	2	4	5	6
6	3	9	8	7	1	2	4	5
5	2	1	9	8	7	6	3	4
7	6	5	4	2	9	8	1	3
8	7	6	5	4	3	1	9	2
9	8	7	6	5	4	3	2	1

Now we take into account difference constraints on the nine relevant 3×3 sub squares. We define a set containing three sets of indices:

$$let \; Sub = \{\{1,2,3\}, \{4,5,6\}, \{7,8,9\}\}$$

Observe that this is a set of sets. We can now compute the pairs of positions that need to be different within each sub square:

$let \; Diff3 \; = \; \{x1, x2, y1, y2 | x1 \; \geq \; x2 \wedge (x1 \; \mapsto \; y1) \; \neq \; (x2 \; \mapsto \; y2) \wedge \exists(s1, s2).(s1 \in Sub \wedge s2 \in Sub \wedge \{x1, x2\} \subseteq s1 \wedge \{y1, y2\} \subseteq s2)\}$

Observe that above we have quantified over sets (for $s1$ and $s2$). The constraint $x1 \geq x2$ is not strictly necessary; it just reduces the number of conflict positions to be checked. As a further improvement, one could add the additional symmetry breaking constraint that $x1 = x2 \Rightarrow y1 > y2$.

To conclude, we simply combine all position pairs into a single set:

$$let \; Diff = Diff1 \cup Diff2 \cup Diff3$$

To generate a valid Sudoku solution we now need to solve the following constraint:

$\exists Board.(Board \in D \to (D \to D) \wedge \forall(x1, x2, y1, y2).(x1 \mapsto x2 \mapsto y1 \mapsto y2 \in Diff \Rightarrow Board(x1)(y1) \neq Board(x2)(y2)))$

The first solution found in about 50 ms is shown below:

2	7	5	1	4	3	8	6	9
1	3	6	7	9	8	2	4	5
8	4	9	5	6	2	7	1	3
7	1	2	8	3	5	4	9	6
4	6	3	2	1	9	5	7	8
5	9	8	4	7	6	1	3	2
6	5	4	3	2	1	9	8	7
3	2	1	9	8	7	6	5	4
9	8	7	6	5	4	3	2	1

4.6   Coins Puzzle

This is a puzzle from chap. 7 of [32]. One interesting aspect is the use of an aggregate constraint (Σ) and the fact that decision variables are in principle unbounded.

The puzzle is as follows. A bank has various bags of money, each containing differing number of coins $coins = \{16, 17, 23, 24, 39, 40\}$. In total 100 coins are stolen; how many bags are stolen for each type of bag?

We can express this puzzle in B as the solution to the following predicate:

$$\exists stolen.(stolen \in coins \rightarrow \mathbb{N} \wedge \Sigma(x).(x \in coins | x * stolen(x)) = 100)$$

A solution found by PROB is: $stolen = \{(16 \mapsto 2), (17 \mapsto 4), (23 \mapsto 0), (24 \mapsto 0), (39 \mapsto 0), (40 \mapsto 0)\}$, also depicted as a table as follows:

Coins	16	17	23	24	39	40
Stolen	2	4	0	0	0	0

All solutions can be found by computing the following set comprehension:

$$\{s | s \in coins \rightarrow \mathbb{N} \wedge \Sigma(x).(x \in coins | x * s(x)) = 100\}$$

The solution computed by PROB contains just the single solution already shown above: $\{\{(16 \mapsto 2), (17 \mapsto 4), (23 \mapsto 0), (24 \mapsto 0), (39 \mapsto 0), (40 \mapsto 0)\}\}$. Observe that here the constraint solver needs to find all solutions the predicate inside the set comprehension. This is made more difficult by the fact that the range of the *coins* variable is not bounded explicitly, and only bounded implicitly by the summation constraint. The bounds on *coins* can only be inferred during the constraint solving process itself.

5   External Data Sources and Data Validation

The core B language does not provide any features for input and output. Moreover, the operations for data types such as strings are quite limited (only equality and inequality are provided). This has lead us to extend the B language via so-called **external functions**. Basically, these are B DEFINITIONS which get mapped to code in the PROB kernel. Some of these functions have been taken over and implemented by ClearSy in their PredicateB secondary toolchain. Here we briefly showcase these features, in particular in the context of data validation.

5.1   External Data Sources

PROB can read in XML and CSV files using various external functions. In this section we read in a CSV file called "elementdata.csv" containing data about chemical elements:

$$let\ data = READ\_CSV\_STRINGS(\text{``elementdata.csv''})$$

The read in data is of type $seq(STRING \nrightarrow STRING)$ and contains $size(data) = 118$ entries.

The first entry has $card(data(1)) = 20$ fields in total, for example the fields ("Atomic_Number" $\mapsto$ "1"), ("Atomic_Weight" $\mapsto$ "1.00794"), as well as the fields ("Name" $\mapsto$ "Hydrogen") or ("Symbol" $\mapsto$ "H").

Note that the external read function is generic: it works for any CSV file where the field names are stored in the first row; empty cells lead to undefined fields in the B data.

5.2 Data Validation Example

Data validation is one area where B's expressivity is very useful, and we illustrate this on the data we have read in above. We can check that the index in the data sequence correspond to the atomic number using the following predicate:

$$\forall i.(i \in dom(data) \Rightarrow i = STRING\_TO\_INT(data(i)(\text{"Atomic\_Number"})))$$

This property is $TRUE$. STRING_TO_INT is another external function, converting strings to integer. DEC_STRING_TO_INT is a variation thereof, also dealing with decimal numbers and expects a precision as argument. It is often useful for a user to define other auxiliary functions. In that respect, B is almost like a functional programming language:

$$let\ aw = \lambda i.(i \in dom(data)|DEC\_STRING\_TO\_INT(data(i)(\text{"Atomic\_Weight"}), 4))$$

The above function can now be applied, e.g., $aw(1) = 10079$.

We can check if the atomic weights are ordered by atomic number:

$$\forall (i,j).(i \in dom(aw) \wedge j \in dom(aw) \wedge i < j \Rightarrow aw(i) \leq aw(j)) \rightsquigarrow FALSE$$

Maybe surprisingly, this property has been evaluated to false. One counter example is $i = 18 \wedge j = 19 \wedge awi = 399480 \wedge awj = 390983 \wedge namei = $ "Argon" $\wedge$ $namej = $ "Potassium". All counter examples are shown in the table below:

$Element1$	$aw1$	$Element2$	$aw2$
"Argon"	"39.948"	"Potassium"	"39.0983"
"Cobalt"	"58.9332"	"Nickel"	"58.6934"
"Plutonium"	"244.0642"	"Americium"	"243.0614"
"Tellurium"	"127.6"	"Iodine"	"126.90447"
"Thorium"	"232.0381"	"Protactinium"	"231.03588"
"Uranium"	"238.0289"	"Neptunium"	"237.048"

In summary, in this section we have shown how to read in and manipulate data in B, how to validate properties in the data and how validation reports with counter example tables can be generated.

6   Discussion

Above we have shown the promises of using the B language to express constraint satisfaction problems. In practice, there are of course still limitations to this approach. The B approach will often engender a computational overhead compared to a direct encoding in a lower-level constraint programming language. Future research will try to minimise this overhead.

A crucial aspect of the constraint solving is the treatment of quantifiers and (nested) set comprehensions. PROB has techniques to expand quantifiers of bounded scope, or some special forms such as $\forall x.(x \in S \Rightarrow ...)$.[3] When these cannot be applied, the quantifiers will delay until all relevant variables are known: this can lead to performance degradations.

Debugging is another issue, which is problematic for constraint programming in general and B is no exception here. We have added external functions for debugging, e.g., to print values or observe how values are instantiated. PROB can now also provide performance warning messages, e.g., when universal or existential quantifiers cannot be dealt with efficiently.

Below we discuss some related approaches (and repeat some of the points made in the not easily accessible article [23]).

Comparison with Non-constraint Solving Tools. We have already discussed the proof-based BToolkit animator. A variety of other tools have been developed for animating or model checking high-level specifications: Brama [36] and AnimB [30] for Event-B or TLC [40] for TLA+. These tools rely on naive enumeration and can be used if the models are relatively concrete. However, there is little chance in using such tools for more challenging constraint solving tasks. For example, TLC takes hours to find an isomorphism for two graphs with 9 nodes (see [27]). TLC on the other hand can be very efficient for concrete models, where the overhead of constraint solving provides no practical advantage.

Comparison with Other Technologies. In the past years we have also investigated a variety of alternative technologies to replace or complement the constraint solver of PROB: BDD-Datalog based approaches, SAT- and SMT-solving techniques. For SAT, we have implemented an alternative backend for first-order B in [33] using the Kodkod interface [39]. For certain complicated constraints, in particular those involving relational operators, this approach fared very well. The power of clause learning and intelligent backtracking are a distinct advantage here over classical constraint solvers. However, for arithmetic the SAT approach usually has problems scaling to larger integers.

Quite often, the SAT approach is better for inconsistent predicates, while the PROB constraint solver fared better when the predicates were satisfiable. Also, the SAT approach typically has problems dealing with large data and cannot

---

[3] See, https://www3.hhu.de/stups/prob/index.php/Tips:_Writing_Models_for_ProB for more details.

deal with unbounded values or with infinite or higher-order functions. Here, an SMT-based approach could be more promising. We have also experimented with SMT-solvers, in particular a SMT-plugin for Event-B [9] and now also provide a Z3 backend for PROB[19]. For proof, SMT solving has proven very useful for B. In [18] have also used SMT to complement PROB for symbolic model checking. But for constraint solving, the results are thus far still rather disappointing.

In conclusion, constraint solving has provided the foundation for many novel tools and techniques to validate formal models. While SAT and SMT-based techniques also have played an increasingly important role in this area, constraint solving approaches have advantages when dealing with large data. In future, we are striving for an approach which can reconcile the advantages of all of these approaches.

Acknowledgements. I would like to thank all those people who have contributed towards the development of PROB and without whom the tool would not be where it is now: Jens Bendisposto, Michael Butler, Ivaylo Dobrikov, Marc Fontaine, Fabian Fritz, Dominik Hansen, Philipp Körner, Sebastian Krings, Lukas Ladenberger, Daniel Plagge, David Schneider, Corinna Spermann, and many more. I also thank Stefan Hallerstede for feedback and discussions about this article.

References

1. Abo, R., Voisin, L.: Formal implementation of data validation for railway safety-related systems with OVADO. In: Counsell, S., Núñez, M. (eds.) SEFM 2013. LNCS, vol. 8368, pp. 221–236. Springer, Heidelberg (2014). doi:10.1007/978-3-319-05032-4_17
2. Abrial, J.-R.: The B-Book. Cambridge University Press, Cambridge (1996)
3. AT&T Labs-Research. Graphviz - open source graph drawing software. http://www.research.att.com/sw/tools/graphviz/
4. B-Core (UK) Ltd, Oxon, UK. B-Toolkit. https://github.com/edwardcrichton/BToolkit
5. Badeau, F., Doche-Petit, M.: Formal data validation with Event-B. CoRR, abs/1210.7039 (2012). Proceedings of DS-Event-B 2012, Kyoto
6. Carlsson, M., Ottosson, G., Carlson, B.: An open-ended finite domain constraint solver. In: Glaser, H., Hartel, P., Kuchen, H. (eds.) PLILP 1997. LNCS, vol. 1292, pp. 191–206. Springer, Heidelberg (1997). doi:10.1007/BFb0033845
7. ClearSy: Atelier B, User, Reference Manuals. Aix-en-Provence, France (2009). http://www.atelierb.eu/
8. ClearSy: Data Validation & Reverse Engineering, June 2013. http://www.data-validation.fr/data-validation-reverse-engineering/
9. Déharbe, D., Fontaine, P., Guyot, Y., Voisin, L.: SMT solvers for rodin. In: Derrick, J., Fitzgerald, J., Gnesi, S., Khurshid, S., Leuschel, M., Reeves, S., Riccobene, E. (eds.) ABZ 2012. LNCS, vol. 7316, pp. 194–207. Springer, Heidelberg (2012). doi:10.1007/978-3-642-30885-7_14
10. Dobrikov, I., Leuschel, M.: Enabling analysis for event-B. In: Butler, M., Schewe, K.-D., Mashkoor, A., Biro, M. (eds.) ABZ 2016. LNCS, vol. 9675, pp. 102–118. Springer, Heidelberg (2016). doi:10.1007/978-3-319-33600-8_6

11. Dudeney, H.E.: Amusements in Mathematics (1917). https://www.gutenberg.org/ebooks/16713

12. Frhwirth, T.: Constraint Handling Rules. Cambridge University Press, Cambridge (2009)

13. Hall, A.: Integrating Z into large projects tools and techniques. In: Börger, E., Butler, M., Bowen, J.P., Boca, P. (eds.) ABZ 2008. LNCS, vol. 5238, pp. 337–337. Springer, Heidelberg (2008). doi:10.1007/978-3-540-87603-8_26

14. Hallerstede, S., Leuschel, M.: Constraint-based deadlock checking of high-level specifications. TPLP **11**(4–5), 767–782 (2011)

15. Hayes, I., Jones, C.B.: Specifications are not (necessarily) executable. Softw. Eng. J. **4**(6), 330–338 (1989)

16. Idani, A., Ledru, Y.: B for modeling secure information systems. In: Butler, M., Conchon, S., Zaïdi, F. (eds.) ICFEM 2015. LNCS, vol. 9407, pp. 312–318. Springer, Heidelberg (2015). doi:10.1007/978-3-319-25423-4_20

17. Krings, S., Bendisposto, J., Leuschel, M.: From failure to proof: the PROB disprover for B and Event-B. In: Calinescu, R., Rumpe, B. (eds.) SEFM 2015. LNCS, vol. 9276, pp. 199–214. Springer, Heidelberg (2015). doi:10.1007/978-3-319-22969-0_15

18. Krings, S., Leuschel, M.: Proof assisted symbolic model checking for B and Event-B. In: Butler, M., Schewe, K.-D., Mashkoor, A., Biro, M. (eds.) ABZ 2016. LNCS, vol. 9675, pp. 135–150. Springer, Heidelberg (2016). doi:10.1007/978-3-319-33600-8_8

19. Krings, S., Leuschel, M.: SMT solvers for validation of B and Event-B models. In: Ábrahám, E., Huisman, M. (eds.) IFM 2016. LNCS, vol. 9681, pp. 361–375. Springer, Heidelberg (2016). doi:10.1007/978-3-319-33693-0_23

20. Lamport, L.: Latex: A Document Preparation System. Addison-Wesley Longman Publishing Co., Inc., Boston (1986)

21. Lamport, L.: Specifying Systems, The TLA+ Language and Tools for Hardware and Software Engineers. Addison-Wesley, Salt Lake City (2002)

22. Lecomte, T., Burdy, L., Leuschel, M.: Formally checking large data sets in the railways. CoRR, abs/1210.6815. Proceedings of DS-Event-B 2012, Kyoto (2012)

23. Leuschel, M., Bendisposto, J., Dobrikov, I., Krings, S., Plagge, D.: From animation to data validation: the ProB constraint solver 10 years on. In: Boulanger, J.-L. (ed.) Formal Methods Applied to Complex Systems: Implementation of the B Method, chap. 14, pp. 427–446. Wiley ISTE, Hoboken (2014)

24. Leuschel, M., Butler, M.: ProB: a model checker for B. In: Araki, K., Gnesi, S., Mandrioli, D. (eds.) FME 2003. LNCS, vol. 2805, pp. 855–874. Springer, Heidelberg (2003). doi:10.1007/978-3-540-45236-2_46

25. Leuschel, M., Butler, M.J.: ProB: an automated analysis toolset for the B method. STTT **10**(2), 185–203 (2008)

26. Leuschel, M., Falampin, J., Fritz, F., Plagge, D.: Automated property verification for large scale B models. In: Cavalcanti, A., Dams, D.R. (eds.) FM 2009. LNCS, vol. 5850, pp. 708–723. Springer, Heidelberg (2009). doi:10.1007/978-3-642-05089-3_45

27. Leuschel, M., Falampin, J., Fritz, F., Plagge, D.: Automated property verification for large scale B models with ProB. Formal Asp. Comput. **23**(6), 683–709 (2011)

28. Leuschel, M., Schneider, D.: Towards B as a high-level constraint modelling language. In: Ait Ameur, Y., Schewe, K.-D. (eds.) ABZ 2014. LNCS, vol. 8477, pp. 101–116. Springer, Heidelberg (2014)

29. Marriott, K., Nethercote, N., Rafeh, R., Stuckey, P.J., de la Banda, M.G., Wallace, M.: The design of the Zinc modelling language. Constraints **13**(3), 229–267 (2008)

30. Métayer, C.: AnimB: Animator of B system model in the Rodin platform (2010). http://wiki.event-b.org/index.php/AnimB

31. Moreira, A.M., Hentz, C., Déharbe, D., Matos, E.C.B., Neto, J.B.S., Medeiros, V.: Verifying code generation tools for the B-method using tests: a case study. In: Blanchette, J.C., Kosmatov, N. (eds.) TAP 2015. LNCS, vol. 9154, pp. 76–91. Springer, Heidelberg (2015). doi:10.1007/978-3-319-21215-9_5

32. Murty, K.G.: Optimization Models For Decision Making, vol. 1 (2005). http://www-personal.umich.edu//~murty/books/opti_model/

33. Plagge, D., Leuschel, M.: Validating B, Z and TLA$^+$ Using PROB and Kodkod. In: Giannakopoulou, D., Méry, D. (eds.) FM 2012. LNCS, vol. 7436, pp. 372–386. Springer, Heidelberg (2012). doi:10.1007/978-3-642-32759-9_31

34. Savary, A., Frappier, M., Leuschel, M., Lanet, J.-L.: Model-based robustness testing in EVENT-B using mutation. In: Calinescu, R., Rumpe, B. (eds.) SEFM 2015. LNCS, vol. 9276, pp. 132–147. Springer, Heidelberg (2015). doi:10.1007/978-3-319-22969-0_10

35. Schneider, D., Leuschel, M., Witt, T.: Model-based problem solving for university timetable validation and improvement. In: Bjørner, N., de Boer, F. (eds.) FM 2015. LNCS, vol. 9109, pp. 487–495. Springer, Heidelberg (2015). doi:10.1007/978-3-319-19249-9_30

36. Servat, T.: BRAMA: a new graphic animation tool for B models. In: Julliand, J., Kouchnarenko, O. (eds.) B 2007. LNCS, vol. 4355, pp. 274–276. Springer, Heidelberg (2006). doi:10.1007/11955757_28

37. Shapiro, S.C.: The jobs puzzle: a challenge for logical expressibility and automated reasoning. In: AAAI Spring Symposium: Logical Formalizations of Commonsense Reasoning (2011)

38. Spivey, J.M., Notation, T.Z.: A Reference Manual. Prentice-Hall, Upper Saddle River (1992)

39. Torlak, E., Jackson, D.: Kodkod: a relational model finder. In: Grumberg, O., Huth, M. (eds.) TACAS 2007. LNCS, vol. 4424, pp. 632–647. Springer, Heidelberg (2007). doi:10.1007/978-3-540-71209-1_49

40. Yu, Y., Manolios, P., Lamport, L.: Model checking TLA$^+$ specifications. In: Pierre, L., Kropf, T. (eds.) CHARME 1999. LNCS, vol. 1703, pp. 54–66. Springer, Heidelberg (1999). doi:10.1007/3-540-48153-2_6

Formal Testing from Natural Language in an Industrial Context

Augusto Sampaio[✉] and Filipe Arruda

Centro de Informática, Universidade Federal de Pernambuco, Recife, Brazil
acas@cin.ufpe.br

1 Overview

We present some results on developing formal testing strategies and tools for mobile applications, in the context of a partnership with Motorola, a Lenovo company. Actually, the overall scope is much larger, encompassing image processing, optimisation algorithms, sentiment analysis, energy-aware software design, and other research areas.

Our focus here is on testing. The input to the process are text documents written in natural language. There are two major scenarios. In the first one (see Fig. 1), the text documents specify requirements written in a (controlled) natural language, with well-defined syntax and semantics. A formal model is automatically derived from these requirements, from which test cases are automatically generated. These test cases can be expressed in natural language (for manual execution) or as scripts of an automation framework, like UIAutomator [7].

The second scenario is more challenging: the text documents are test cases written in natural language following no standard whatsoever (Fig. 2). There is no independent requirements specification; the test cases are the requirements. In this case, for the purpose of automation, we use natural language processing techniques to match test steps in natural language with test actions already automated in a database. When there is no match, we adopt capture & replay techniques to carry out automation and execute the test cases in the mobile phone; these actions with their respective scripts are then included in the database for further reuse.

Our major, medium-term, objective is to build a single and integrated framework to support the generation, selection automation and execution of test cases from natural language requirements, as displayed in Fig. 3. In this framework, the input to the automation step might be automatically generated as in the first scenario, Test Cases (CNL) in the figure, or input by a tester: Textual Test Cases, in the figure. In the first case, the test case descriptions follow a standard and the automation can be fully mechanised. Nevertheless, the option for the tester to use the framework to automate textual test cases coming from other sources must be available, as test cases for manual execution are also produced without requirements, based on the test designer expertise.

In the next section, we present the current status of the tools (Sect. 2) that independently mechanise these two scenarios. The underlying formalisms are

© Springer International Publishing AG 2016
L. Ribeiro and T. Lecomte (Eds.): SBMF 2016, LNCS 10090, pp. 21–38, 2016.
DOI: 10.1007/978-3-319-49815-7_2

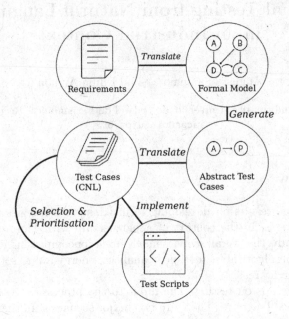

Fig. 1. First scenario

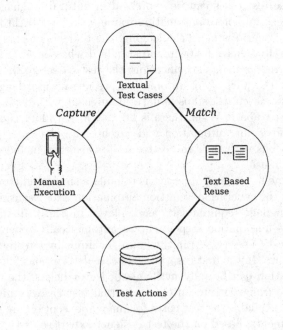

Fig. 2. Second scenario

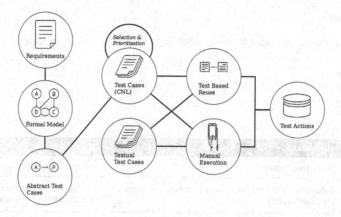

Fig. 3. Proposed framework

considered in Sect. 3. In Sect. 3.1 we show how the CSP process algebra is used as a basis to the test generation strategy; we emphasise the modularity of the approach. In Sect. 3.2 we propose a notion of test step consistency and show how it can be automated in Alloy. In the final section we discuss ongoing work and the remaining steps to the full development of the proposed framework.

2   Tools

The two scenarios introduced in the previous section are supported by practical tools, although at present they are not integrated. These tools are briefly described below.

2.1   Test Generation with TaRGeT

This section is based on material presented in [12,14]; particularly, we use a simplified version of the illustrative example given in [14]. Our focus is on the generation of black-box (functional) test cases. The input to the process are use case templates, which describe interaction of a user with the system through natural language sentences of three kinds: user actions, system states and system responses. All these sentences must follow a writing standard defined in terms of a controlled natural language (CNL). An example is presented in Fig. 4, which describes a use case to move a message to an important folder.

A template, as the one in Fig. 4, describes a use case that is part of the specification of a feature (mobile device functionality). A use case defines several execution flows (main, alternative or exception flows) each one representing a relevant scenario. The main one describes the *happy path*. In our example, the main flow successfully captures moving a message to the important folder.

An alternative flow involves a choice; during the execution of a flow it might be relevant to engage in an alternative behaviour. If an event from an alternative flow happens, the execution proceeds behaving according to the specified

Description

This use case moves messages from Inbox folder to Important Messages folder.

Main Flow
Description: Moving Messages with success
From Step: START
To Step: END

Step Id	User Action	System State	System Response
1M	Scroll to a message		Message is highlighted.
2M	Select "Move to Important Messages" option.	Message storage has enough space.	"Message moved to Important Messages folder" is displayed.

Alternative Flow
Description: Cannot move messages
From Step: 2M
To Step: END

Step Id	User Action	System State	System Response
1A	Clean up messages	Message storage has not enough space.	Clean up is performed.

Fig. 4. Use case template

alternative behaviour. In our example, the alternative flow captures the situation when a message cannot be moved because there is no more storage space.

Templates like this one are the input to the TaRGeT tool [8,12], whose purpose is to mechanise a test case generation strategy that supports the steps presented in the first scenario discussed in the previous section. The tool generates test cases, also written in CNL, which include the test procedure, a description and related requirements. Moreover, the tool can exhibit traceability information relating test cases, use cases and requirements.

TaRGeT inputs and processes information in use case templates, first checking adherence to the CNL and, if the sentences obey the CNL, it generates test suites. An overview of the input and output artifacts is presented in Fig. 5, which shows a use case template as the input to the tool, and the output is a test suite with CNL test cases for manual execution, in the form of an excel file. The tool also implements several selection mechanisms, based on similarity algorithms and test purposes; this latter selection criteria is discussed in Sect. 3.1.

2.2 Test Automation with Zygon

As mentioned before, there is a challenging testing scenario in which the text documents provided as input are test cases written in natural language. Because

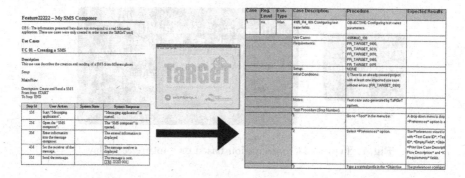

Fig. 5. The TaRGeT tool

there is no formal standard to write these test cases, it becomes difficult to define a meaningful mapping between the text descriptions and an automation code script. Thus, code scripts become scattered because there is no straightforward means to match and reuse test cases already automated.

Therefore, we proposed an intermediate-layer notation called *test action* to fill this gap and implemented it in a tool called Zygon; the description presented in this section (including the figures) is closely based on [2]. A test action, based upon the composite pattern, is a recursive structure that supports several abstraction layers, composition and code-level interpretation for the atomic actions (Fig. 6).

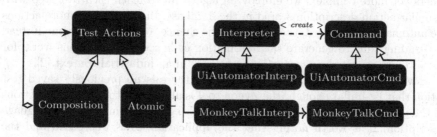

Fig. 6. Overall architecture

The idea behind this proposition is to represent every piece of information (that ranges from a simple test step to a complete TC or even a test suite) uniformly, allowing their retrieval or execution regardless the artifact category. In short, we have shifted from a monolithic (Fig. 7) to a hierarchical (Fig. 8) mapping between natural language descriptions and GUI operations.

The test action representing the TC illustrated in Fig. 7, that checks whether an email can be sent, could be composed by several actions, which in turn could also be a composition of other atomic actions (screen interactions), as shown in Fig. 8. This potentialises the reuse and reduces effort by only mapping code scripts to atomic actions.

```
@Test
public void testSendEmail(){
    UiDevice device = UiDevice
        .getInstance(instrumentation);
    device.pressHome();
    UiObject2 apps=device.findObject(
        By.description("Apps"));
    apps.click();
    [...]
}
```

TC - Check
if a email can
be sent

Fig. 7. Typical TC automation based on capture & replay

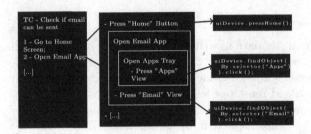

Fig. 8. Test case automation using hierarchical test actions

Because test actions may be organized and composed in any order to create others yet more complex, we employ an algorithm to mach each test step with a similar action description stored in the database. In this way, as more actions are automated and stored, the greater is the chance to find a similar one instead of spending time to generate the automation code script. In previous work, for instance, we reported a reuse ratio up to 71% in an industrial context [2].

However, in order to assist testers when there is no previously saved test action that is similar enough, the Zygon tool is able to capture user interactions on the phone and store them as test actions, also giving them a natural language description. It is worth noting that the application UI is web-based and the process is transparent to the user (Fig. 9). In summary, we developed a full-stack solution by which a tester is able to automate an entire test suite without any programming skills during her common activities, reducing both time and effort to automate tests.

Similar to traditional Capture & Replay tools, Zygon also captures user inputs to reproduce them later. However, instead of capturing low-level events in order to strictly reproduce them, the tool listens to the Android accessibility events[1], yielding high-level descriptions of what was performed on the device, mitigating issues with different screen sizes, besides being more meaningful to the

---

[1] http://developer.android.com/intl/en-us/reference/android/view/accessibility/
AccessibilityEvent.html.

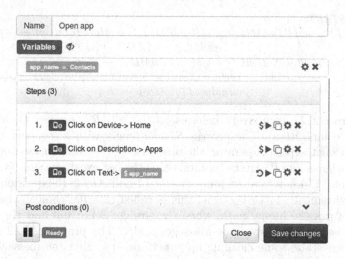

Fig. 9. Capture screen (Zygon)

end user. For instance, instead of "Press the screen at the coordinate (100,250)", Zygon captures "Click the button with description 'Apps'".

A custom keyboard is also installed during the capturing in order to get what the user is typing. However, the user can transform the text typed in a variable to reuse the same action in other situations, as shown in Fig. 9.

3 Underlying Formalisms

In this section we discuss how the underlying formalism (particularly, the process algebra CSP) supports an incremental strategy for test generation (first scenario), and how contracts and Alloy models support a consistent automation strategy for the second scenario; we propose a new notion of test step concistency, and its mechanisation, in the context of test automation.

3.1 Process Algebraic Approach to Test Generation

In this section we briefly introduce an approach to test case generation based on the CSP process algebra. The details can be found in [14]; the purpose here is to emphasise the modularity supported by this approach, and particularly the fact that it has been conservatively extended to capture several facets of test generation, like control behavior, data, quiescence and time. We explain the CSP notation and the test case generation strategy on demand.

As previously explained, the first step is to translate the (input) use case template into CSP. For the example presented in Fig. 4, the corresponding CSP model is given below.

$I1 = START;\ I1$
$START1 = scrollToAMsg \rightarrow msgHighlighted \rightarrow selMoveToIMOpt \rightarrow$
$\qquad reqStoInfo \rightarrow (ALT1 \ \Box \ ALT2)$
$ALT1 = msgStoIsNotFull \rightarrow msgMovedToIMDisp \rightarrow Skip$
$ALT2 = msgStoIsFull \rightarrow performCleanUp \rightarrow reqCleanUp \rightarrow cleanUpOk \rightarrow$
$\qquad msgMovedToIMDisp \rightarrow Skip$

The process $I1$ recursively behaves as the $START$ process (semicolon is sequential composition). The process $START$ engages in a sequence of events captured using the prefix operator; the process $a \rightarrow P$ communicates the event a and then behaves like P. After communicating the last event, $reqStoInfo$, $START$ offers a choice ($\Box$) between the processes $ALT1$ and $ALT2$; the decision is taken by the environment; in CSP terms, this is called external choice. The process $ALT1$ captures the happy path, when the storage is not full and the message can be moved to the Important Messages folder. The process $ALT2$ captures a full storage state; some cleaning up is performed so that the message can be moved to the same folder. These two processes terminate successfully (behaving like $Skip$); when any of them terminates, $I1$ recurses.

As a rich process algebra, CSP offers several additional operators for combining processes; here we use only parallelism and hiding. The process $P \ [[\ X\ ]]\ Q$ is the generalised parallel composition of the processes P and Q with synchronisation set X. This means that, regarding events in X, P and Q can only communicate when both are ready to engage in the same events; for the events not in X, each one behaves independently. The interleaved composition $P \ |||\ Q$ is a particular case of parallel composition when the synchronisation set is empty. In this case, both processes can evolve totally independently. The process $P \setminus X$ behaves as P, but hides all events in X, making them internal.

The test case generation strategy under consideration is based on the CSP traces model and traces refinement. A process Q refines another process, say P, in the traces model, denoted $P \sqsubseteq_T Q$, if, and only if, $traces[\![Q]\!] \subseteq traces[\![P]\!]$. Traces refinement can be automatically verified using, for instance, the FDR tool [9]. If the refinement does not hold, the tool produces a trace (the shortest counter-example), say ce, such that $ce \in traces[\![Q]\!]$ but $ce \notin traces[\![P]\!]$. Some facilities are available to make FDR generate subsequent counterexamples, if there are any can be obtained. Two other classical and more elaborate semantic models of CSP are the failures and the failures-divergences models. The first one captures deadlock situations, whereas the latter captures livelock traces as well. Further details can be found, for example, in [16].

Selection criteria can be used to guide the test case generation. The main selection mechanism is via the definition of a test purpose, which allows marking certain traces of the specification; this is also specified as a process in CSP. The effect of marking the relevant traces is achieved by parallel composition of the specification with the test purpose. Consider that a given test purpose, say TP, is defined to select some test scenarios from a specification S. The parallel composition of S and TP (denoted parallel product), with synchronisation set α_S, is $STP = S \,|[\,\alpha_S\,]|\, TP$.

Note that, with this synchronisation set (the entire alphabet of S), the test purpose TP synchronises in all events of S until there are no further events to synchronise, when TP communicates an event $mark \in MARKS$, and then both S and TP deadlock. As a result, the parallel product will have the traces of the form $ts = t \frown \langle mark \rangle$, for $t \in tracesS$, where each ts is a test scenario of interest. Because $ts \notin traces[\![S]\!]$ (due to the $mark$ event), then the shortest counterexample of the refinement $S \sqsubseteq_T STP$, say ts_1, is generated. If TP does not select any scenario from S, no $mark$ is included in the parallel product STP, and so this will be the same as S; in this case no counterexample is generated.

In the context of our example, the shortest scenario for moving a message is:

$\langle scrollToAMsg, msgHighlighted, selMoveToIMOpt, msgStoreHasSpace,$
$msgMovedToIMDisp, accept \rangle$

The conformance notion adopted in this approach is the relation **cspio**, intended to capture the **ioco** [21] relation in the CSP setting. As an informal intuition, consider an arbitrary trace σ of the specification. Then I **cspio** S holds provided, for all such traces, the set of output events of the implementation, after performing σ, is a subset of the outputs performed by S after σ. The standard semantic models of CSP do not distinguish between inputs and outputs, but this is essential in testing. Here we assume that the alphabet of a process is split into disjoint input and output sets of events. In the formulation, it is enough to reference the set of output events, which we denote $\mathcal{O}$. The relation **cspio** is formalised by the following definition.

Definition 1 (CSP input-output conformance).

$$I \textbf{ cspio } S \,\hat{=}\, \forall \sigma : traces[\![S]\!] \bullet out(I, \sigma) \subseteq out(S, \sigma)$$

where $out(R, \sigma) = \{a : \mathcal{O} \mid \sigma \frown \langle a \rangle \in traces[\![R]\!]\,\}$

cspio fully captures **ioco** if the CSP processes (S and I) are annotated with quiescence (δ).

Theorem 1 [14] below captures **cspio** using process refinement.

Theorem 1 (Verification of cspio).

$$I \textbf{ cspio } S \Leftrightarrow S \sqsubseteq_T (S \mathbin{\triangle} ANY(\mathcal{O}, STOP)) \,|[\, \Sigma \,]|\, I$$

where $ANY(X, R) = \square\, a : X \bullet a \rightarrow R$.

With the result established by Theorem 1, it is possible to mechanically verify I **cspio** S using a tool like FDR, provided, of course, there is an implementation model I.

The relation **ioco** is defined in a model called Straces [21]. This model explicitly includes a special event to represent quiescence (δ). Although there is no implementation of suspension traces in any refinement checker for CSP, it is possible to automate verification via an encoding as standard traces refinement. As shown in [17], if all quiescences are identified in the traces as the special output δ, then the relations **cspio** and **ioco** coincide.

Although the refinement assertion in Theorem 1 captures **cspio** conformance, it does not show how quiescent states (δ) of S and I are effectively signaled. To take advantage of Theorem 1 in a mechanisation of conformance verification for **ioco**, we use a notion of priority for CSP processes in [15]. We define, for a process P, a corresponding process P_δ that outputs δ in all quiescent states of P [5].

Definition 2.

$$P_\delta \mathrel{\widehat{=}} \mathrm{prioritise}(P \mathbin{|||} RUN(\{\delta\}), \langle \mathcal{O}, \{\delta\} \rangle)$$

The behaviour of $\mathrm{prioritise}(P, R)$ is similar to that of P, but it prevents any event in X_i in the relation R (represented as an ordered sequence), for $i > 1$, from taking place when τ (an internal event), $\checkmark$ (termination) or an event in some X_j, with $j < i$, is possible. The events in X_1 have the same priority as that of τ and $\checkmark$. Events not in R are incomparable to all other members of R.

The fact that the event δ happens only in the absence of output is captured by the order of the sets $\langle \mathcal{O}_{UT}, \{\delta\} \rangle$ in the prioritise operator, which prioritises output events over δ.

The following theorem [5] captures our proposed strategy for **cspio** taking quiescence into account. We use $\mathcal{O}_\delta$ as an abbreviation of $\mathcal{O} \cup \{\delta\}$. Similarly, Σ_δ stands for $\Sigma \cup \{\delta\}$.

Theorem 2 (Verification of cspio).

$$I \textbf{ cspio } S \Leftrightarrow S_\delta \sqsubseteq_T (S_\delta \mathbin{\triangle} ANY(\mathcal{O}_\delta, STOP)) \mathbin{\|[\Sigma_\delta]\|} I_\delta$$

Regarding soundness, initially, we proved that the encoding in the traces model captures ioco [14]. Currently, we are defining a new Straces model for CSP, including the definition of all operators and the relevant healthiness conditions. Some initial results are presented in [5].

The mechanised verification of conformance, captured as a refinement expression, is an important advantage of a formalisation using a process algebra like CSP. Unlike an explicit algorithm for checking conformance, as presented in [22] for **ioco**, we benefit from the expressive power of the refinement notions and the model checker for CSP to verify conformance in a simple way.

An example of the modularity of this approach is that quiescence is handled in an orthogonal way, preserving the structure of the conformance verification theorem. Similarly, as shown in [14], state can also be incorporated as a conservative extensions of the presented conformance verification strategy. The model that specifies the control behaviour of a use case is composed in parallel with a process that represents an abstract memory to record the state of variables. Despite this model increment, the test generation strategy is entirely reused.

We have also explored another application domain (timed reactive systems). In [4], we discuss how the test generation strategy can be incrementally evolved to address time aspects (in addition to control and data), in an orthogonal way.

We are currently considering the extension of the strategy to handle hybrid systems; this is very challenging, as there is a shift of paradigm, due to the complexity inherent to dynamic systems. This produces a vertical impact on the overall strategy. For the CNL, the main change is to add structure so that the requirements engineering is able to write differential equations, in addition to the textual presentation. However, the other steps of the strategy require more radical adaptations. We are currently working on the definition of a conformance relation that combines the discreet features of **ioco** with tolerance (output and timed values) margins as is common in relations for dynamic systems [1,6].

3.2   Contract Based Approach to Consistent Automation

Regarding test automation from test cases described in natural language, despite the fact that we were able to uniformly represent every test artifact improving the reuse among them, we still faced some problems concerning consistency and dependency management. There was no way to guarantee, for instance, that a sequence of test actions could actually be correctly executed. It was sorely dependent on the tester or test engineer experience and individual knowledge about the given domain.

Further subtle problems appeared in the execution stage when multiple test cases, although consistently composed, rely upon prior configurations that could also interfere or even cancel other dependencies. For that matter, we had to develop a strategy to automatically check consistency of individual test actions as well as their dependencies, in order to provide a coherent (and possibly optimal) execution order.

The strategy consists on defining: which actions are individually valid; what are their dependencies and behaviors; and how to correctly dispose actions or what actions can be inserted to allow the execution of a set of test cases. The valid actions and their dependencies are represented as a domain model that is automatically translated into Alloy [11] signatures, facts and predicates, see Listing 1.1. Then, for every execution request, a predicate is evaluated to find a valid sequence of test actions including those requested.

Listing 1.1. Alloy model

```
  open util/ordering[State]
2 sig State{conditions: set Action, current: one Action} {
    some this.next implies migrate[this, this.next]
4   dependenciesAreSatisfied[current, conditions]
  }
6 sig Action {operation: Operation, patient: Patient}{
    operationIsValid[operation,patient]
8 }
  abstract sig Operation{ dependsOn: set Operation,
10                         cancels: set Operation }
  abstract sig Patient{}
12 [.] //Placeholder ∀ operations and patients
  //Example
14 one sig Logout extends Operation{}{
                  cancels = Login and dependsOn = Login
16 }
  [.]
18 pred directDependenciesAreSatisfied( action: Action,
                                       conditions: set Action) {
20   let directDependencies = action.operation.dependsOn •
        directDependencies = none or (
22         ∀ directDependency:  directDependencies •
             some condition: conditions •
24              condition.operation in directDependency
                and condition.patient in action.patient
26         )
  }
28 pred extrasDependenciesAreSatisfied(a: Action,
                                      conditions: set Action){
30   let extraRel = extraDependencies[a.operation][a.patient] •
        no extraRel  or some cond: conditions •
32           (cond.operation -> cond.patient) in extraRel
  }
34 pred new(a: Action, o: Operation, patient: Patient){
      a.operation in o and a.patient in patient
36 }
  pred migrate(s: State, s': State) {
38   s.current in s'.conditions
     s'.conditions - s.current in s.conditions
40   removeCanceledActions(s, s')
  }
42 pred dependenciesAreSatisfied( action: Action,
                                 conds: set Action){
44   extrasDependenciesAreSatisfied[action, conds]
     directDependenciesAreSatisfied[action, conds]
46 }
  pred addStep(s: State, action: Action){
48             s.current = action
  }
```

By referring to Listing 1.1 from lines 2 to 5, we define the concept of the state of a system for the purpose of test case execution. A state comprises a set of conditions (actions that were executed in past states) and the current action to be executed. An action, in turn, is an operation over a patient (lines 6–11) such as "Send an Email" or "Press a button". All operations and patients from the domain model would be automatically rendered between lines 12 and 17.

It is worth mentioning that some operations have inherent dependencies: A "logout" operation can only be performed after "login"; similarly, to "delete" a message, one has to have been created before (via Operation.dependsOn). On the other hand, if a "delete" operation is performed, we have to remove the action "create" from the conditions of the next state (via Operation.cancels).

We check these inherent dependencies evaluating the predicate defined between the lines 18 and 27: the direct dependencies are satisfied if a given action has no dependencies or if its dependencies are present in the set of conditions of the current state. Besides these direct dependencies, we have to also check indirect ones, such as: to send an email, one has to ensure first that there is an active connection to the internet. These "extra" dependencies are checked by evaluating the predicate defined between lines 28 and 33. With a valid action and all dependencies satisfied (a valid state of the system), then the migration to the next state happens. This is covered by the predicate defined between lines 37 and 41, by which all conditions plus the current action become the conditions of the next state, but removing the actions from the conditions of the next state that were canceled by the current action.

Example. A very simple example of finding a correct sequence of execution can be illustrated by trying to execute the action "Send an email". Testers with no experience could naively try to build a sequence with "Turn the WiFI on and then Send an email", but considering a default scenario that no action was performed before, and by analysing the dependency graph in Fig. 10, such a test sequence is considered inconsistent. The proposed consistency analysis strategy can easily warn the tester that this sequence cannot be executed, by evaluating the predicate referred in Listing 1.2.

Listing 1.2. Testing consistency

```
   pred test{
2     let s=first , s'=s.next•
          s.conditions = none and
4           some activateWiFi, sendEmail: Action • {
                new[activateWiFi , Activate , WiFi]
6               new[sendEmail, Send , EmailMessage]
                addStep[s, activateWiFi]
8               addStep[ s    , sendEmail]
                }
10 }

12 run test for 10
```

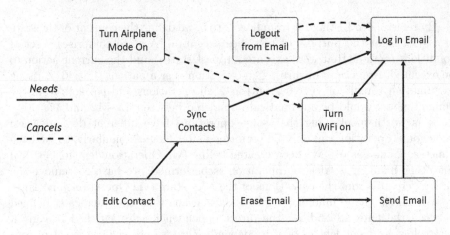

Fig. 10. Dependency graph

Since the given sequence is detected as inconsistent, one can ask the Alloy Analyzer to find a valid one, which is achieved by evaluating the predicate in Listing 1.3. In this predicate, it is first assured that no actions were performed in the initial state and, for every state in the system, a valid action must be performed. Then, we declare that one of these valid actions should be "Send an Email". In this case, the Alloy Analyzer finds an instance of the model that satisfies this predicate: Turn WiFI On –> Login Email –> Send Email, which give us the final state described in Fig. 11.

Listing 1.3. Finding dependencies

```
pred findDependencies{
2    first.conditions = none
     ∀ s: State●
4        some anyAction: Action ● {
                new[anyAction, Operation, Subject]
6           addStep[s, anyAction]
         }
8    some s: State ●
         some sendEmail: Action ●{
10          new[sendEmail, Send, EmailMessage]
            addStep[s, sendEmail]
12       }
}
```

In summary, a simple dependency analysis can both detect inconsistent sequences, as well as automatically insert actions to turn an inconsistent sequence into a consistent one. The main challenge here is scalability; this and other concerns are considered in the next section.

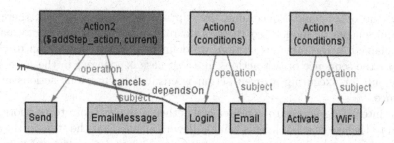

Fig. 11. Instance of our model with a valid sequence to "Send an email"

4   Ongoing Work: Integrated Framework

We are currently working on the integration of the strategies and tools for test case generation and automation, as already summarised in Fig. 3. The main activities involved are discussed below.

Controlled Natural Languages. In order to be able to automate the textual test cases generated by TaRGeT, we need to revise the current use case templates so that the descriptions are presented in sufficient detail to allow Zygon to match all the steps with actions in the database, without requiring capture. Therefore, we need a writing standard common to both TaRGeT and Zygon, which, currently, is not the case. The challenge relies on how to connect both languages since they have different abstraction levels: the former is usually specified in general terms while the latter is tightly coupled to the UI implementation and describe concrete actions in full.

The CNL for representing test actions (as these are stored in a database) is heavily built upon the concept of a frame, which is a structure to store data about a previously known situation [13]. These frames contain prefixed *slots* or *terminals* that, when filled, represent an instance of a specific situation. Therefore, we can automatically build the frames from the use cases, but the frames would still miss some important properties, such as the default values for all possible *slots* (in order to allow generic statements) and rules for valid instances. To fill this gap, we have two choices under analysis: (1) compel users to give sufficient details yet inside use cases or (2) build a detached domain knowledge model to provide a bridge between use case and test action CNLs, with the missing information.

Soundness and Consistency Notions. The approach to test generation is based on a well-defined conformance relation (**cspio**). As usual, this assumes as test hypothesis that both the model and the implementation can be specified in the formal model (in our case, as CSP processes), so that they can be related. Soundness of the generated test cases, in this context, means that if the execution of a test case gives a fail verdict, then the implementation is non-conforming.

On the other hand, concerning the capture & replay approach, there are no requirements or models, so there is no reference for defining conformance. As explained in the previous section, we defined a consistency notion to check whether the sequence of test actions in a test case is coherent in the sense that the set up for executing a given action is ensured by previous actions in the sequence.

An interesting aspect to consider is whether it makes sense to promote this notion to the use case level. This would allow to ensure that the steps of the generated test cases be consistent by construction. This is a complementary notion to that of soundness, already proved. However, as discussed in the previous topic on considerations about the CNL, this consistency notion can be associated with a detailed use case template or with a detached domain knowledge model.

Populating the Database. Assuming that we have a finite number of (non-recursive) frames, it becomes feasible to pre-populate the database with automated actions prior to the test case generation, since the (parametrised) test action will be executed the same way in spite of variations of slot values (similar to the behavior of variables in a program) [13]. In complex systems, however, this approach might not be practical because we would lose too much time trying to automate all the frames at once. As an alternative, we can employ an interactive, on demand approach, as it is currently used in existing projects.

Scalability. The evaluation carried out by the Alloy Analyzer to find a valid sequence of steps may me impractical, specially when the domain model has a huge number of different actions and patients. For a model representing only a specific application, the time to find a valid sequence for an Alloy scope of 10 instances is usually negligible, but that is not the case when testing multiple apps in a mobile platform. For that matter, we are exploring the alternative of partitioning the dependency graph to consider only reachable nodes for particular applications, in order to reduce the Alloy model and consequently the number of combinations to be analysed.

Some Related Approaches. The proposed framework integrates textual test case generation from use case descriptions and an approach to test case automation, based on capture & replay, from textual test case descriptions. A detailed comparison of work related to each strategy can be found in [2,14]. Here we mention just a few examples.

Concerning textual test case generation from use case descriptions, with the aim of GUI testing, some relevant approaches are, for instance, [3,10,19]. The approach described in [19] is closely related to ours, since it uses natural language for the specification of use cases, maps use cases to a formal model (FSM) and generates textual test cases.

The search for an optimal mapping between natural language description and concrete tests has also been an active research area. Some examples are [18,20,23]. Cucumber [18], for instance, assists the writing of acceptance tests in a behavior driven development environment: parameterised scenarios are written in natural language and semi-automatically mapped to a source code or stub, in order to accelerate the process and provide a better tracking. However, besides the implementation being developer-centric, in-depth reuse and consistency/dependency checking are outside the scope of the tool.

The distinguishing feature of the proposed framework is to integrate two promising strategies (and related tools), which have been used in an industrial context; together, they allow a mechanised generation of automated test cases from natural language use cases, benefiting from the extensibility of both strategies, as well as from soundness and consistency notions, as previously explained. Nevertheless, each strategy and tool can still be used in isolation.

Acknowledgments. The work described here had the contribution of several colleagues: Hugo Araujo, Flavia Barros, Ana Cavalcanti, Gustavo Carvalho, Alexandre Mota and Sidney Nogueira, among others.

References

1. Abbas, H., Hoxha, B., Fainekos, G., Deshmukh, J.V., Kapinski, J., Ueda, K.: Conformance testing as falsification for cyber-physical systems (2014). arXiv preprint: arXiv:1401.5200
2. Arruda, F., Sampaio, A., Barros, F.: Capture and replay with text-based reuse and framework agnosticism. In: Proceedings of the 28th International Conference on Software Engineering and Knowledge Engineering. KSI Research Inc. http://dx.doi.org/10.18293/SEKE2016-228
3. Bertolino, A., Gnesi, S.: Use case-based testing of product lines. ACM SIGSOFT Softw. Eng. Notes **28**(5), 355–358 (2003)
4. Carvalho, G., Sampaio, A., Mota, A.: A CSP timed input-output relation and a strategy for mechanised conformance verification. In: Groves, L., Sun, J. (eds.) ICFEM 2013. LNCS, vol. 8144, pp. 148–164. Springer, Heidelberg (2013). doi:10.1007/978-3-642-41202-8_11
5. Cavalcanti, A., Hierons, R.M., Nogueira, S., Sampaio, A.: A suspension-trace semantics for CSP. In: 10th International Symposium on Theoretical Aspects of Software Engineering, TASE 2016, Shanghai, China, 17–19 July 2016, pp. 3–13 (2016). http://dx.doi.org/10.1109/TASE.2016.9
6. Dang, T., Nahhal, T.: Coverage-guided test generation for continuous and hybrid systems. Formal Methods Syst. Des. **34**(2), 183–213 (2009)
7. Android Developers: UiAutomator (2016)
8. Ferreira, F., Neves, L., Silva, M., Borba, P.: TaRGeT: a model based product line testing tool. In: Tools Session of CBSoft (2010)
9. Goldsmith, M., Roscoe, B., Armstrong, P.: Failures-divergence refinement-FDR2 user manual (2005)
10. Hartmann, J., Vieira, M., Foster, H., Ruder, A.: A UML-based approach to system testing. Innov. Syst. Softw. Eng. **1**(1), 12–24 (2005)
11. Jackson, D.: Software Abstractions: Logic, Language, and Analysis. MIT Press, Cambridge (2012)

12. Machado, P., Sampaio, A.: Automatic test-case generation. In: Borba, P., Cavalcanti, A., Sampaio, A., Woodcook, J. (eds.) PSSE 2007. LNCS, vol. 6153, pp. 59–103. Springer, Heidelberg (2010). doi:10.1007/978-3-642-14335-9_3

13. Minsky, M.: A framework for representing knowledge (1975)

14. Nogueira, S., Sampaio, A., Mota, A.: Test generation from state based use case models. Form. Asp. Comput. **26**(3), 441–490 (2014). http://dx.doi.org/10.1007/s00165-012-0258-z

15. Roscoe, A.W.: Understanding Concurrent Systems. Springer Science & Business Media, London (2010)

16. Roscoe, A.: The Theory and Practice of Concurrency. Prentice Hall Series in Computer Science. Prentice-Hall, Englewood Cliffs (1998)

17. Sampaio, A., Nogueira, S., Mota, A., Isobe, Y.: Sound and mechanised compositional verification of input-output conformance. Softw. Test. Verif. Reliab. **24**(4), 289–319 (2014). http://dx.doi.org/10.1002/stvr.1498

18. Soeken, M., Wille, R., Drechsler, R.: Assisted behavior driven development using natural language processing. In: Furia, C.A., Nanz, S. (eds.) TOOLS 2012. LNCS, vol. 7304, pp. 269–287. Springer, Heidelberg (2012). doi:10.1007/978-3-642-30561-0_19

19. Some, S.S., Cheng, X.: An approach for supporting system-level test scenarios generation from textual use cases. In: Proceedings of the 2008 ACM Symposium on Applied Computing, pp. 724–729. ACM (2008)

20. Thummalapenta, S., Sinha, S., Singhania, N., Chandra, S.: Automating test automation. In: 2012 34th International Conference on Software Engineering (ICSE), pp. 881–891. IEEE (2012)

21. Tretmans, J.: Test generation with inputs, outputs and repetitive quiescence. Software—Concepts and Tools (TR-CTIT-96-26) (1996)

22. Weiglhofer, M., Wotawa, F.: On the fly input output conformance verification. In: Proceedings of the IASTED International Conference on Software Engineering, pp. 286–291. ACTA Press (2008)

23. Wong, E., Zhang, L., Wang, S., Liu, T., Tan, L.: Dase: document-assisted symbolic execution for improving automated software testing. In: 2015 IEEE/ACM 37th IEEE International Conference on Software Engineering, vol. 1, pp. 620–631. IEEE (2015)

Analysis and Verification

Application of Formal Methods to Verify Business Processes

Luis E. Mendoza Morales[1,2(✉)], Carlos Monsalve[1], and Mónica Villavicencio[1]

[1] Facultad de Ingeniería Eléctrica y Computación, FIEC, Escuela Superior
Politécnica del Litoral, ESPOL, Campus Gustavo Galindo Km 30.5 Vía Perimetral,
P.O. Box 09-01-5863, Guayaquil, Ecuador
{lemendoza,monsalve,mvillavi}@espol.edu.ec
[2] Processes and Systems Department, Simón Bolívar University, Valle de Sartenejas,
P.O. Box 89000, Caracas, Venezuela
lmendoza@usb.ve

Abstract. Formal specifications and modeling languages can be used to
provide support for *Business Process* (BP) analysts and designers to verify the behavior of BPs with respect to business performance indicators
(i.e., service time, waiting time or queue size). This article presents the
application of the *Timed Automata* (TA) formal language to check BPs
modeled with *Business Process Model and Notation* (BPMN) using the
model checking verification technique. Also, a set of transformation rules
and two algorithms are introduced to obtain TA-networks from BPMN
models, allowing the formal specification of a *BP-task model* equivalent
to the BPMN model. The approach presented here contributes to conduct the qualitative analysis of BPMN models.

Keywords: Qualitative analysis · Business Process · Task model ·
Timed automata · Model checking

1 Introduction

Some approaches [4,8] have been proposed to try to solve the lack of formal
definition of time in *Business Process Model and Notation* (BPMN) [9]. However,
when several participants are involved in a *Business Process* (BP) execution,
BPMN does not deal well enough with temporal and concurrency constraints.
BPMN models do not provide mechanisms to quantify the computational/human
effort required to perform the activities established by a BP, nor the response
time of a BP when resources (e.g., a *BP-worker*) are concurrently shared among
multiple BPs. In previous work presented in [2], it was proposed an approach
to obtain an executable model (i.e., a *BP-task model*) that can be analyzed
qualitatively from a BP conceptual one (i.e., a BPMN model). The analysis is
based on the *model checking* (MC) verification technique, which is the most
suitable in the case of BP diagrams [5].

In this work, we describe an approach to generate a BP-task model as a
timed automata network (TA-network), which conforms with the semantics of the
BPMN standard [9] and the business time and concurrency constraints. Then,
with the support of the model-checker UPPAAL [1], the behavioral aspects and

© Springer International Publishing AG 2016
L. Ribeiro and T. Lecomte (Eds.): SBMF 2016, LNCS 10090, pp. 41–58, 2016.
DOI: 10.1007/978-3-319-49815-7_3

temporal constraints in a BP-task model are simulated and verified. In particular, we can verify safety properties and constraints (stating that no unsafe state can be reached), schedulability properties (stating that a BP will be completed within a given deadline), and response properties (stating that, whenever a task is executed, another task will be executed within a given time). As a result, BP designers and business analysts can verify BPs efficiently through the following steps: (1) description of BPs and their constraints with a formal temporal logic; (2) systematic transformation into *timed automata* (TA) with the transformation rules and algorithms; and (3) running the model-checker UPPAAL. With the verification results, the BP analysts and designers can perform improvements and adjustments to the BPs and their constraints. This helps to solve problems related to temporal constraints and to assure the quality of BPMN models.

Some works are found in the literature related to the specification and verification of the temporal perspective of BPMN. It is worth mentioning the work in [3], which presents a novel approach enabling the formal specification and verification of advanced temporal constraints of BPs, using TA. The authors provided a specification for relative and absolute related temporal constraints while relying on the dependencies that can exist between theses constraints. It is also important to mention the work in [12], which proposes an automatic mapping of the extended BPMN onto TA. This last approach aims at verifying some features, such as deadlocks and bottlenecks; but the scope of this paper is limited to a small subset of BPMN elements and does not consider timed properties related to a set of activities (e,g., inter-activities temporal constraints). Finally, the work in [6] focuses on the application of UPPAAL in order to verify interoperability requirements for a given collaborative BPMN model. However, this last approach is limited to detect interoperability problems without providing solutions to them [6]. In contrast to the works mentioned before, the work presented here allows us to analyze the decisions made at design-time of a BP-task model. That is, performing the qualitative analysis of the behavior of BP-workers as part of a verification approach. In this way, the results about the performance of the workers (e.g., waiting time or queue size) and some business performance indicators (e.g., service time or attention time) of a BP can be evaluated.

The rest of this paper is organized as follows. Section 2 introduces the background that support this work. Section 3 explains our concept of BP-task model. Section 4 presents a set of mapping rules to transform BPMN models into TA and explains the steps to specify and verify BPMN models. Section 5 shows how we use the model-checker UPPAAL [1] to verify the corresponding BP-task model with an instance of a *Customer Relationship Management* (CRM) strategy, while the concluding remarks are presented in Sect. 6.

2   Theoretical Framework

2.1   Timed Automata (TA)

According to the TA theory, a *timed automaton* is a finite directed graph annotated with conditions over states and resets of non-negative integer valued clocks;

and a *system* is modeled as a collection of *finite state machines* and a *finite set of clocks*. In the standard scheme, the clocks are synchronized and can be reset by the transition from one state to another. Clocks are also used as invariants and guards for TA. Let C be a set of clocks, a *temporal constraint* is a conjunction of expressions that compares the value of a clock $c \in C$ to a non-negative integer constant $a \in \mathbb{Z}_{\geq 0}$. The set of *constraints* over C, denoted $\Psi(C)$, is defined by the following BNF notation: $\Psi(C) \ni \theta = a < c \mid a > c \mid a \leq c \mid a \neq c \mid \mathbf{true} \mid \theta \wedge \theta$, where $c \in C$ and $a \in \mathbb{Z}_{\geq 0}$. Transitions are defined to be instantaneous and hence it is possible to model behaviors that are not easily implementable. Where there are two or more possible transitions from a state then each is a valid transition.

For example, according to the in Fig. 1 the transition out of state S cannot be taken before time 3. In this example, T is a clock; it is resetting when the state S is achieve. In a simple model (i.e., the invariant $T < 5$ do not exist) the only exit from the state S is when T is greater than 3; i.e., the example therefore illustrates the imposition of a delay. A state can also have a temporal invariant to force an exit transition. Figure 1 illustrate this because the state S cannot leave before $T = 3$ but must leave before $T = 5$. If for some reason the transition cannot be taken then the automata contains an error condition (deadlock).

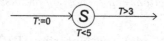

Fig. 1. Example of a TA.

Next are presented the basic definitions for TA, Union of TA, and TA-network, which are important for our purposes.

Definition 1 (Timed Automata). *A timed automaton TA is a tuple $\mathcal{A} = \langle S, \Sigma, C, T, s_0, Inv \rangle$, where S is a finite set of states, Σ is a finite alphabet or set of actions, C is a finite set of clocks, $T \subseteq S \times \Sigma \times \Psi(C) \times 2^C \times S$ is a set of transitions between states with an action, $\Psi(C)$ is the set of Boolean clock constraints involving clocks from C, $s_0 \in S$ is the initial state, and $Inv : S \rightarrow \Psi(C)$ is a function that assigns invariants to states. An edge $\langle s, a, g, r, s' \rangle \in T$ is a transition from state s to s' with action a, guard g and clock resets r.*

In this work, we use UPPAAL [1], a model-checker that supports the graphical representation of TA and allows the user to interact with a window editing program to create and modify models. Then, according with the syntax and semantic of TA in UPPAAL, given $t = \langle s, \lambda, \gamma, r, s' \rangle \in T$, s is the source state, λ is the synchronization action, γ is the guard, r is the set of clocks to reset, and s' is the target state. S^u is used to denote the subset of urgent states in S ($S^u \subseteq S$). An urgent state is a state where no delay is allowed. Expressions in UPPAAL range over clocks and integer variables, and clocks and clock differences are only compared to integer expressions; also, guards over clocks are essentially conjunctions (disjunctions are allowed over integer conditions).

Since each TA (representing the BP-workers) will be constructed iteratively, incorporating—gradually—the tasks that they perform, it is necessary to define the union of TAs.

Definition 2 (Union of TA). *Let $\mathcal{A}$ and $\mathcal{A}'$ be two TA. The* union *of two TA is a tuple* $\mathcal{A}'' = \langle S'', \Sigma'', C'', T'', s_0'', Inv'' \rangle = \langle S, \Sigma, C, T, s_0, Inv \rangle \uplus \langle S', \Sigma', C', T', s_0', Inv' \rangle$ *with* $S'' = S \cup S'$, $\Sigma'' = \Sigma' \cup \Sigma''$, $s_0'' = s_0 \cup s_0'$, $C'' = C \cup C'$, $T'' = T \cup T'$, *and* $Inv'' = Inv \cup Inv'$.

To model concurrent systems (as the BPs), TA can be extended with parallel composition. This algebraic operator can be adopted in TA, which allows interleaving of actions as well as hand-shake synchronization. Essentially, the parallel composition of a set of TA is the product of TA, just called TA-network.

Definition 3 (TA-network). *A TA-network is the parallel composition $TAN = \mathcal{A}_1 \parallel \cdots \parallel \mathcal{A}_n$ of a set of timed automata $\mathcal{A}_1 \ldots \mathcal{A}_n$, called processes, combined into a single system by a parallel composition operator with all internal actions hidden. Synchronous communication between the processes is done by hand-shake synchronization using input and output actions. The action alphabet is assumed to consist of symbols for input actions denoted* $\mathsf{a}?$, *output actions denoted* $\mathsf{a}!$, *and internal actions represented by the distinct symbol* τ.

2.2   Business Process Model and Notation (BPMN)

BPMN provides organizations with the capability of specifying and depicting their BPs using a graphical notation with an emphasis on control-flow. BPMN 2.0 [9] aims to be a graphical notation to communicate BPs in a standard manner. The BPMN models incorporate constructs adequate to BP modeling, such as *events, tasks, gateways* and *flows*, and defines more advanced constructs, such as *task looping, parallel multinstances, inclusive OR decision, subprocesses* and *exception handling*. Hence, a language of this type will include the modeling concepts necessary to describe certain aspects of a BP at a certain abstraction level, as labels to capture temporal constraints of the process.

An *event* is something that happens during the course of a process and affects the flow of the process. The *start event* indicates where a process will start, and *end event* indicates where a process will end. An *activity* is a generic term for work performed in the process; it can be atomic (called *task*) or compound. In this work, the term activity refers to an *atomic activity* or *task*. A *sequence flow* is used to show the order in which activities will be performed. A *gateway* is used to control the divergence and convergence of sequence flows. Gateways can have several behavior controls and each type of control affects both the incoming and outgoing flow: *exclusive, parallel,* and *inclusive gateways*. In a parallel between BPMN objects and the workflow terminology, an *exclusive gateway* corresponds to a *XOR-split/join*, a *parallel gateway* corresponds to an *AND-split/join*, and an *inclusive gateway* corresponds to an *OR-split/join*. A *Pool* typically represents an *organization* or *business entity* and a *Lane* represents a *department* or

BP-worker within that organization, or other modeling entities like functions, applications, and systems. Both, pools and lanes, represent *BP participants*. A *message flow* represents the communication between two asynchronous organizations or business entities; i.e., two asynchronous pools. An *association* is used to link information with graphical elements. *Text annotations* provide additional information for readers of the BPMN diagrams.

Consider, for instance, the BPMN example of the leave application process[1] shown in Fig. 2. There are altogether three participants in this ABC Company, the employee, the manager as well as the human resources (HR). On the diagram, the start event symbol is drawn on the lane labelled *Employee* to indicate that he initiates the process. Then, a sequence flown indicates the process flow direction and shows that the first thing that the employee needs to do is to *Fill in the Leave Application Form*. After that, he has to submit the form to the manager for approval.

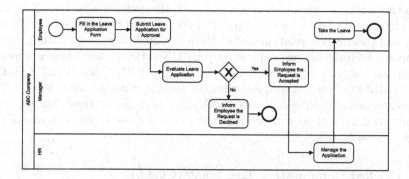

Fig. 2. Example of a BPMN diagram.

The task *Submit Leave Application for Approval* is linked to the task *Evaluate Leave Application* on the *Manager* lane, which is responsible for the process. After the manager will evaluate on it in order to decide whether to approve the leave request or not. At this point, a gateway symbol is drawn on the diagram to diverge the process into two ends. That is, if the application is rejected, the manger will need to inform the employee and the application process terminates. So, the task *Inform Employee the Request is Declined* is connected to an end event symbol. On the other hand, if the application is accepted, the manager will inform the employee and the application process will continue to follow to the lane of *HR* where he needs to manage the application. Finally, what is left in the process is for the employee to take the leave. The end event symbol is connected to the last task *Take the Leave* to indicate the whole process completes.

---

[1] This example was taken from: http://www.visual-paradigm.com/tutorials/bpmn-tutorial-with-example.jsp.

Formally, a structured BPMN model is defined as follows[2]:

Definition 4 (BPMN model or process graph). *Let Γ be a set of types of flow objects, a BPMN model or process graph is a tuple $\mathcal{M} = \langle N, T, \gamma, \mu, \mathcal{N}, \Theta, \tau, P, L \rangle$, where: $N \subseteq A \times E \times G$ is a set of flow objects, where A is a non-empty set of activities and tasks, E is a non-empty set or events, G is a set of gateways; $T \subseteq N \times N$ is the set of sequence flows and defines the control flows; $\gamma : N \to \Gamma$ is a function that maps flow objects to their types; $\mu : A \to \mathcal{N}$ is a function that assigns each activity and task a name, $\mathcal{N}$ is the set of names; $\Theta : A \to \theta$ is a function that assigns temporal constraints (i.e., min and max text annotations) to activities and tasks, θ is the set of temporal constraints labels of the process; $P \subseteq N \times T$ is a non-empty set of pools where process is contained; $L \subseteq P$ is the set of lanes in which the process is organized within each pool (e.g., representing roles, systems, or departments); for all $P_i, P_j \in P : P_i \cap P_j = \emptyset$ and for all $L_i, L_j \in L : L_i \cap L_j = \emptyset$.*

In this work, we assume that a structured BP modeled with BPMN is contained in at least one pool and composed of flow objects (tasks, events, and gateways) and control flow relations; all of them depicted over a set of lanes within the pools. Additionally, we explore only BPMN orchestration-oriented models [9]; this means that we abstract away from other BPMN notational elements such as artifacts, annotations, associations, groups, message flows, sub-process invocations and attributes associated with sub-process invocations. Nonetheless, the proposed algorithms can be applicable, even if these types of elements are present in the model.

2.3 Clocked Computation Tree Logic (CCTL)

Property specification languages are used to obtain a formal specification of the expected BP behavior according to the business requirements. CCTL [11] is a propositional temporal logic that extends *Computation Tree Logic* (CTL) with quantitative time bounds for expressing real time properties (e.g., bounded liveness). CCTL is used to deal with sequences of states, where a state gives a temporal interpretation of a set of *atomic propositions* (AP) within time intervals, and time instants are isomorphic to the set of non-negative integers. CCTL includes the CTL specification language with the operators *until* (U) and *next* (X), and other derived operators in *Linear Temporal Logic* (LTL), such as *release* (R), *weak until* (W), *cancel* (C), *since* (S), and *finally* (F). All of them have proved to be useful for facilitating the definition of the properties included in reactive systems requirements specification [11]. All LTL-like temporal operators are preceded by a run quantifier (A universal, E existential) which determines whether the temporal operator must be interpreted over *one run* (existential quantification) or over *every run* (universal quantification). For this paper, we will only use the semantics

---

[2] We agree with [3] to specify a structured BPMN model as a *process graph* to conduct the transformation (presented in Sect. 4).

for the AG and EF-operators (*Always Globally* and *Eventually*, respectively). For more details about the semantics for every CCTL operator see [11].

3   BP-Task Model

Taking into account that any business comprises several BPs, a BP-task model *is a set of groups of tasks, representing a large number of possible real-world scenarios of a BP expressed in compact form.* A BP-task model associated with a set of BPs combines the behaviors of every BP-worker involved in these BPs. Under the BPMN standard, for modeling completely every BP of a company is required one BPMN model for each BP. Each of these models represents a *scenario* where each BP-worker carries out the tasks set up in the BP. In this work, (1) each task is performed by only one BP-worker at a time, and (2) a BP-worker is either the person that performs tasks or the system that automates tasks. Formally, based on the definition of a (nondeterministic) finite state machine, a BP-task model is defined as follows:

Definition 5 (BP-task model). *A* BP-task model *is a tuple* $\mathcal{B} = \langle A, \Sigma, \delta, A_0, F \rangle$, *where: A is a non-empty set of tasks; Σ is a finite set of input actions; $\delta : A \times (\Sigma \cup \{\lambda\}) \to 2^A$ is the transition function (λ represents the empty string $\Sigma_0 = \{\lambda\}$), which returns for a given task and a given input action, the set of (possible) tasks that can be reached; A_0 is the set of initial states with $A_0 \in A$; and F is the set of final (accepting) tasks with $F \subseteq A$.*

We are focused here on the BP-task model and the set of overlapping *scenarios*, which allow us to obtain a description of the majority of tasks that a BP-task model must take into account [10]. Due to a BP-worker can be concurrently involved in several BPs into a company, the BP-task model is obtained taking into account the behavior of these BP-workers according to each BP. The BP-workers are the ones who execute the tasks and are responsible of BP behavior. Thus, the BP-task model gives us a *cross-BP view* of the business behavior, unlike the partial view showing by the BPMN models. Some non-functional requirements (i.e., deadlock-freeness, reliability) and temporal constraints (i.e., timeliness, deadlines) that the BP-task model must fulfill are modeled using a TA for each BP-worker or business entity. In this sense, the verification carried out here exclusively refers to the BP-task model behavior modeled by the TA-network that describes the behavior of the collaboration among BP-workers to perform the BPs. The TA formal language have proved very useful to describe this behavior [3,4,6].

4   Mapping Rules to Specify and Verify BPMN Models Using TA

By applying our proposal of mapping rules (see Table 1), we can transform an original BPMN model into an equivalent executable BP-task model using TA.

The current BPMN specification (version 2.0) [9] defines at least 34 types of events, 7 kinds of activities or tasks, 8 types of gateways, and 7 types of sequence flows; this list does not include the possible variations that can have each of the flow objects proposed by BPMN. Given the large number of notational elements covered by BPMN and due to space limitations, we are only presenting a sample of 10 mapping rules.

Table 1. Some mapping rules of BPMN into TA.

BPMN	TA	BPMN	TA
Start event:		End event:	The Start event is in same lane: $Nj-1$ Initial
	Initial $Nj+1$		The Start event is in another lane: $Nj-1$ Idle
The sequence flow come from another lane:	Idle akj? Nj	The sequence flow go to another lane:	The Start event is in same lane: Nj ajk! Initial
			The Start event is in another lane: Nj ajk! Idle
Task:	$cij:=0$ $Nj-1$, Nj $cij>=minNj$ $Nj+1$, $cij<=maxNj$	Timer intermediate event:	$cij:=0$ $Nj-1$, Nj $cij>=T$ $Nj+1$, $cij<=T$
Exception flow:	$cij:=0$ $Nj-1$, Nj $cij>=minNj$ && $cij<=T$ $Nj+1$, $cij<=maxNj$ $cij>T$ Ne	Diverge exclusive gateway:	$N1$ $Nj-1$ $a1$ ... ax ... an Nn
Converge exclusive gateway:	$N1$ ... $Nj+1$ ... Nn	Timer start event:	Initial $cij:=0$ S $cij>=T$ Nj $cij<=T$

With the mapping rules, behavioral aspects and temporal constraints of BPMN models are formally specified by using the TA formal specification language. As a result, we obtain a set of detailed TA, to which the BP-task model conforms as a TA-network, and which completely describes the temporal behavior of the BP represented by the BPMN model. After obtaining the BP-task model, we can check its correctness through the model-checker UPPAAL [1]; with respect to formally specified properties of the BP-task model, derived from the business rules and goals usually given by business designers and analysts. To proceed with the transformation, we take into consideration the following:

- A TA should be constructed for each BP-worker (represented by a lane in a BPMN model), which describes how the BP-worker perform the tasks as part of a BP. The events, tasks, and decisions (i.e., gateways) that a BP-worker performs are specified by states in the TA, whereas sequences of tasks (defined by sequence flows) are specified by transitions in the TA (see Table 1).
- The temporal parameters denoted in a BPMN model corresponds to invariants, guards, and assignments in the TA. For instance, to specify the behavior of a BPMN task N_j (within the lane L_i) annotated with the $maxN_j$ and $minN_j$ temporal parameters in the BPMN model (see Task mapping rule in Table 1), we use the following expressions in the corresponding TA: the invariant is `cij <= maxNj` and the guard condition is `cij >= minNj` are defined on the location and the outside edge of the corresponding TA; the assignment or clock reset is `cij:= 0` is defined in the inside edge coming from the location `Nj-1`. Thus, `cij` is a clock variable that holds the elapsed time of the task. The invariant and the guard specify that the transition from the task N_j to any BPMN flow object N_{j+1} (i.e., event, task, gateway) can never occur until the minimum execution time (`minNj`) has elapsed, and must occur before the maximum execution time (`maxNj`) has elapsed. Graphically, this mapping is shown at center-left in Table 1.
- Since a BP-worker can participate in many processes, the TA that brings together all these behaviors will result from the union of all the tasks that the BP-worker perform for each BPMN model in which it participates. For every BP in which a BP-worker is involved, the TA representing the complete behavior of the BP-worker will contain a single path that specifies that participation; i.e., in the TA will be the same number of paths from the initial state representing the number of BPMN models in which the BP-worker participates.
- Always, within a BP, the BP-workers interact with each other to perform completely a BP. In addition, BP-workers can also interact with others outside of the BPs in which they participate to achieve the correct execution of a BP. In any case, this collaboration is specified through the synchronization actions (i.e., `akj?` and `ajk!`) between TAs, as is shown in the second row of Table 1. According to BPMN, this kind of interactions corresponds to those sequence flows that come or go to another lane, or when the BP-worker is part of a choreography [9] via message flows (not yet covered by this work).
- The formal representation of the BP-task model corresponds to the product of the TAs that specifies and deals with behavioral aspects and temporal constraints of the BP-workers involved into the BPMN model. As a result, we obtain a TA-network. Synchronous communication between the BP-workers is

by hand-shake synchronization using input and output actions (as is shown in second row in Table 1). The action alphabet is assumed to consist of symbols for input actions denoted akj?, output actions denoted ajk!, and internal actions represented by the distinct symbol τ.

Given the mapping rules, the steps to perform the specification and verification of BPMN models are the following:

(1) Include Temporal Constraints to BPMN Models. For the verification of temporal properties of BPs, such as response time of business services; and temporal constraints, such as execution time of activities; the temporal properties and constraints must be specified in the BPMN models to carry out their verification. Since there is no attribute for specifying these in BPMN, we use *text annotations* associated to each task to define the *min* and *max* time values representing the minimum and maximum durations of a task N_j. In this way, we incorporate temporal constraints on the BPMN model. For the case of *timer start event, timer intermediate event,* and *timer exception flow,* the business modeler must specify the maximum duration T, as it is established by the BPMN notation. We consider that it is sufficient to use the text annotations defined by BPMN to include temporal constraints to BPMN models.

(2) Obtain the BP-Task Model. By applying the mapping rules introduced in Table 1, the TA-network that corresponds to the BP-task model is obtained. This model specifies and deals with behavioral aspects and temporal constraints of the BP-workers involved into the BP-task model. The CREATE_BP-TASK_MODEL function, described by Algorithm 1, is the main function of this specification step. The objective of this function is to return a TA-network (denoted with the TAN variable in Algorithm 1) from a process graph or BPMN model. The function calls the CREATE_TA_OF_BP-WORKERS function given by Algorithm 2, which constructs the TA of each BP-worker involved in the BPMN model. As a result, the TA-network is composed in an easy way, at an adequate level of formality (see Fig. 5).

Algorithm 1. function CREATE_BP-TASK_MODEL

Require: $\mathcal{M} = \langle N, T, \gamma, \mu, \mathcal{N}, \Theta, \tau, P, L \rangle$
Ensure: $TAN = \mathcal{A}_1 \parallel \cdots \parallel \mathcal{A}_i$
 1: **for all** pool $P_m \in P$ **do**
 2:     **for all** lane $L \in P_m$ **do**
 3:         $Create\_TA\_of\_BP - workers(\mathcal{M}_m = \langle N, T, \gamma, \mu, \mathcal{N}, \Theta, \tau, P_m, L \rangle)$
 4:         $TAN = TAN \parallel \mathcal{A}_i$
 5:     **end for**
 6: **end for**

Throughout the execution of the Algorithm 2, the CREATE_TA_OF_BP-WORKERS function generates a TA for each BP-worker. We differentiate between three major parts of this algorithm. The first one (lines 4–17) is devoted to nodes which are at the beginning of each lane. In case of the first node corresponds to the BPMN *start event* (i.e., $START$) the TA representing the BP-worker is created with this initial state (i.e., $s_0 \leftarrow$ Initial). Otherwise, the TA is created with the state 'Idle' as initial state (i,e., $s_0 \leftarrow$ Idle) and is specified the synchronization transition between the automata $\mathcal{A}_k$ (which corresponds to the BP-worker represented by the lane L_k) and the automata $\mathcal{A}_i$ (which it is being created at the time the algorithm runs), because the sequence flow comes from another lane of the process graph.

Algorithm 2. function CREATE_TA_OF_BP-WORKERS

Require: $\mathcal{M}_m = \langle N, T, \gamma, \mu, \mathcal{N}, \Theta, \tau, P_m, L \rangle$
Ensure: $\mathcal{A}_i = \langle S \cup S^u, \Sigma, C, T, s_0, Inv \rangle$
1: **local** $\mathcal{A} = \langle S, \Sigma, C, T, s_0, Inv \rangle$
2: **for all** lane $L_i \in L$ **do**
3:     Reach the first node $N_j \in L_i$
4:     **if** $\gamma(N_j, \mathcal{M}_m) = START$ **then**
5:         $s_0 \leftarrow$ Initial
6:         $S^u = \{$Initial$\}$
7:         $S \leftarrow N_{j+1}$ where $N_{j+1} \in L_i$ of the sequence flow
8:         $T = T \cup (s_0, \emptyset, \emptyset, \emptyset, S)$
9:         $\mathcal{A}_i = \mathcal{A}_i \uplus \mathcal{A}$
10:        Reach the next node of the sequence flow
11:    **else**
12:        $s_0 \leftarrow$ Idle
13:        $S^u = \{$Idle$\}$
14:        $S \leftarrow N_j$
15:        $T = T \cup (s_0, a_{kj}?, \emptyset, \emptyset, S)$ $\{a_{kj}?$ denotes a synchronisation between $\mathcal{A}_k$ and $\mathcal{A}_i\}$
16:        $\mathcal{A}_i = \mathcal{A}_i \uplus \mathcal{A}$
17:    **end if**
18:    **while** node $N_j \in L_i$ of the sequence flow **do**
19:        **if** $\gamma(N_j, \mathcal{M}_m) = EXC\_FLOW$ **then**
20:            $S \leftarrow N_j$
21:            $S' \leftarrow N_{j+1}$
22:            $S'' \leftarrow N_{j-1}$
23:            $S''' \leftarrow N_e$
24:            $C = C \cup c_{ij}$
25:            $T = T \cup (S'', \emptyset, \emptyset, c_{ij}, S)$
26:            $T = T \cup (S, \emptyset, c_{ij} \geq minN_j \wedge c_{ij} \geq \mathsf{T}, \emptyset, S')$
27:            $T = T \cup (S, \emptyset, c_{ij} > \mathsf{T}, \emptyset, S''')$
28:            $Inv(S) = \{c_{ij} \leq maxN_j\}$
29:            $\mathcal{A}_i = \mathcal{A}_i \uplus \mathcal{A}$
30:        **end if**
31:        Reach the node N_{j+1} of the sequence flow
32:        **if** node $N_{j+1} \notin L_i$ **then**
33:            $S \leftarrow N_j$
34:            $T = T \cup (S, a_{jk}!, \emptyset, \emptyset, s_0)$ $\{a_{jk}!$ denotes a synchronisation between $\mathcal{A}_i$ and $\mathcal{A}_k\}$
35:            $\mathcal{A}_i = \mathcal{A}_i \uplus \mathcal{A}$
36:        **end if**
37:    **end while**
38: **end for**

The second part (lines 18–37) deals, one by one, with the nodes N_j in the sequence flow of each lane L_i of the process graph. Due to space limitations, the presented version of Algorithm 2 here only describes the processing of the BPMN node *exception flow* (i.e., EXC_FLOW, lines 19–30), which is a composition of BPMN nodes *task* and *timer intermediate event* mapping rules (see Table 1). Note the use of the $minN_j$, $maxN_j$, and T time values (attached to the tasks and timer intermediate events in the BPMN model, respectively) as invariants and guards in the construction of TA. Finally, the lines 32–36 are devoted to specify when a process flow goes to another lane L_k; i.e., generates the synchronization action ajk! between the automata $\mathcal{A}_i$ (created at the time the algorithm runs) and the automata $\mathcal{A}_k$, which corresponds to the another BP-worker represented by the lane L_k.

(3) Define the BPs Properties. The requirements and temporal constraints (i.e., timeliness, deadlines) that the target BP must fulfill are specified in a set of CCTL formulas. These formulas comprise the formal specification of the BP *temporal properties* that the BP-task model must fulfill. Concurrent aspects of BPs, such as temporal consistency between tasks and temporal BP rules (including task timeliness and performance) are specified in this step. As a result, the set of temporal logic formulas that will be introduced in UPPAAL [1] is obtained.

(4) Verify the BP-Task Model. Once the TA-network is obtained, we can proceed to the BP-task model verification using UPPAAL. In this way, it is possible to check if a BP-task model satisfies the expected temporal behavior specified with a set of CCTL formulas. We obtained the verification of a BP-task model by the interpretation of boolean expressions (*True, False*), according to the *expected behavior properties* for the model. From the business analysts and designers viewpoint, UPPAAL is easy to use; although for non-trivial models considerable computing power is required by the model checker.

5   CRM Application Example

CRM is a strategy by which a company seeks to establish and maintain relations with its customers [7]. CRM is considered to be a complex combination of business and technical factors that should be aligned according to a strategy [7]. Briefly, the CRM' BP modeling obtained the following set of BPs: *Informing Customer, Customizing Service, Studying behavior Pattern, Product/Service Produce, Product/Service Sell* and *Assisting Customers*, which represents a minimum functionality of the CRM strategy. Due to space limitations, we have mainly focused on two key CRM BPs: *Product/Service Sell* and *Product/Service Produce*. The information needed to perform the BP-task model verification is on the BPMN models depicted on Figs. 3 and 4; these contain the temporal properties and constraints that the BP-task model must comply to meet the CRM business goals.

The *Logistic* worker is located in the execution of both *Product/Service Sell* BP and *Product/Service Produce* BP. This means that the *Logistic* worker must perform tasks associated with the *Product/Service Produce* BP having the responsibility of providing the materials required to create a new product/service. Also, the *Logistic* worker must perform (in collaboration with the

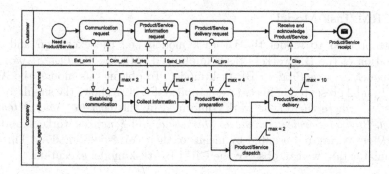

Fig. 3. BPMN model of the Product/Service Sell BP.

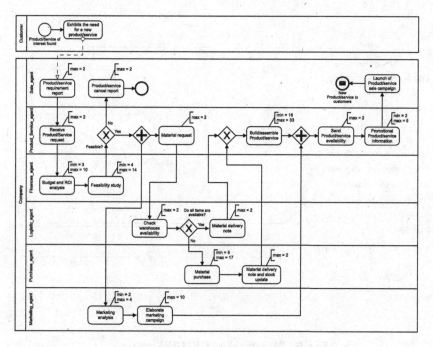

Fig. 4. BPMN model of the Product/Service Produce BP.

Attention Channel worker) the tasks associated with the *Product/Service Sell* BP when he receives a purchase order from a customer. In this sense, the *Logistic* worker should conform the time execution and synchronization established in the BP-task model associated to both BPs. In addition, the *Logistic* worker should work closely with the *Product/Service* and *Purchase* workers to perform the *Product/Service Produce* BP. Hence, he must not be in conflict with other BP-workers as this could cause a *deadlock*; i.e., all BP-workers cannot perform any task.

5.1   CRM Task Model

We now proceed to model the BP-task model; i.e., the execution and synchronization of the BP-workers tasks implicated with the *Product/Service Sell* and *Product/Service Produce* BP-task model. To obtain this model, the Algorithms 1 and 2 presented in Sect. 4 were applied. Figure 5 shows the simulator tab of UPPAAL, where the TA-network conformed by the *Logistic, Sale, Attention Channel, Product/Service, Purchase, Marketing*, and *Finances* workers; and the *StockBD* entity, are represented by means of their corresponding TAs. Through the simulator tab, we can observe the CRM BP-task model execution.

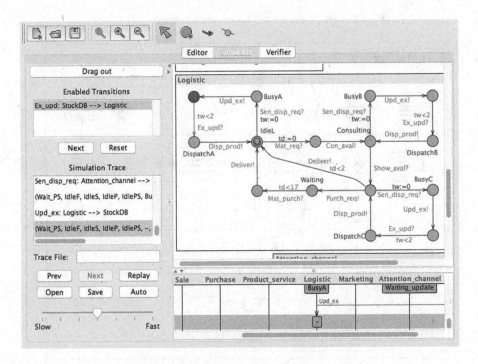

Fig. 5. TA-network of CRM BP-worker.

For the sake of simplicity, we comment only the behavior of the *Logistic* worker tasks (see the TA in Fig. 5), which is the most important for this application, because it is concurrently involved in the execution of both BPs. The most important aspect of the *Logistic* worker execution is that the transitions are modeled to accurately represent the possible execution of the *Logistic* worker tasks; i.e., this worker can attend a request for an available product/service from the *Attention Channel* worker while he is waiting for the *Purchase* worker to acquire the materials that the *Product/Service* worker requires to build/assemble a new product/service. The TA at center-right of Fig. 5 presents the states entered by the *Logistic* worker when he is seeking information from the *StockDB* entity and collaborating with the *Purchase* worker, respectively. The BusyA, BusyB, BusyC states were added to represent the situation when the Logistic worker is updating information in the *StockDB* entity, while the DispatchA, DispatchB, and DispatchC states are reached when it is working with the *Purchase* worker. In Fig. 5, when the *Logistic* worker is in the IdleL state, concurrently requests from the *Attention Channel* and from *Product/Service* workers can both be attended. The *Logistic* worker leaves the IdleL state in the following cases:

1. When it receives the Sen_disp_req? synchronization from the *Attention Channel* worker. In this case, the *Logistic* worker enters the BusyA state and captures the reception time of the request in the tw variable. Then, it sends the Upd_ex! synchronization to the *StockDB* entity. When the *Logistic* worker is in the BusyA state, it may not be able to receive requests from *Product/Service* worker remaining in the current state while: (a) the *Logistic* worker is receiving from *StockDB* entity, within the time interval [tw,tw+2), the Ex_upd? synchronization and dispatching to the *Attention Channel* worker the task execution results (Disp_prod! synchronization) and then passing to the IdleL state; or (b) the *Logistic* worker is in the waiting time for Ex_upd? synchronization defeat; i.e., the time instant [tw+2,tw+2] is reached and a timeout is provoked, returning the *Logistic* worker to the IdleL state.
2. When the *Logistic* worker is addressing the Mat_req? synchronization from the *Product/Service* worker. In this case, the *Logistic* worker passes to the Consulting state, storing in the td variable the time instant at which the request is received and initiates the execution of the action to satisfy it. This latter situation then presents two alternatives: (a) when the items required are available and the Show_aval? synchronization is received; then, the *Logistic* worker delivers the required results (Deliver! synchronization) within the time interval [td,td+2), and again returns to the IdleL state; or (b) when the items required are not available and the Show_aval? synchronization is received; then, the *Logistic* worker sends the material purchase request (Purch_req! synchronization) to the *Purchase* worker and continues waiting within the [td,td+17) time interval to receive the notification of the material purchase.

Note that the temporal constraints, discussed in the previous paragraph and assigned to the TA in Fig. 5, corresponds to the text annotations previously associated to the tasks in the BPMN models depicted on Figs. 3 and 4.

5.2   CRM Properties

We can now define what is expected to be accomplished by the CRM BP-workers when they receive a specific request from the *Customer*. To show an example, a few properties are presented in Table 2, in which an instance of the business rules are specified by CCTL formulas, according to the *Quality of Service* (QoS) contract level set by the CRM business.

The formulas in Table 2 describe the CRM BP-task model timed abstract behavior, which gives a high level of insight into what is expected of a CRM

Table 2. Some CRM properties – BP-task model expected behavior

Property	CCTL specification
The BP-task model satisfies the tasks order and never execute tasks asynchronously	$\phi_1 := \mathsf{AG}(not\ deadlock)$
The BP-task model can always satisfy the creation of a new *Product/Service* in 44 units of time up.	$\phi_2 := \mathsf{EF}_{[44]}(Prom\_inf)$
A new *Product/Service* will be eventually available in 44 units of time up. If the new Product/Service is not feasible, its cancellation will be eventually notified to the *Customer* in 24 units of time up.	$\phi_3 := \mathsf{AG}_{[44]}(Wait\_new\_PS \rightarrow [\mathsf{EF}_{[44]}(Prom\_inf) \wedge \mathsf{EF}_{[24]}(Can\_PS)])$
An available *Product/Service* will be eventually delivered in 23 units of time up.	$\phi_4 := \mathsf{AG}_{[23]}(Wait\_PS \rightarrow Deliv)$

BP-worker to deliver and how long would it take when it receives a *Customer* request. On the other hand, these CCTL formulas specify the task order and the execution time required for each task (or set of tasks) expected from the *Product/Service Sell* and *Product/Service Produce* BP-task model to accomplish the BPs Quality of Service (QoS) contract level.

Note that the deadlock concept is being transferred from the software verification field to the BP world to obtain the ϕ_1 formula. Thus, we say that the BP-task model is deadlock-free if the CRM BP-workers are never blocked; i.e., a time deadlock-freeness reflects that the time constraints of the two composed TA are compatible. In other words, the BP-task model is deadlock-free because the tasks are always executed in order, which is the result of the correctness of the CRM BP-workers synchronization. Thus, when we check that the BP-task model is deadlock-free, we are proving that the BP-task model satisfies tasks timely and orderly, i.e., *the CRM BP-workers do not perform tasks asynchronously*.

5.3 CRM Verification

To proceed to the CRM BP-task model verification, we introduce each one of the CCTL formulas (see Sect. 5.2) in the Query field below Overview (see Fig. 6), using the UPPAAL notation. According to the UPPAAL notation, the CCTL temporal formula $\phi_2 := \mathsf{EF}_{[44]}(Prom\_inf)$ corresponds to the E<>Product_service. Prom_inf imply ta<=44 query, and it should be understood as *it is possible to reach the location* Prom_inf *in process* Product_service *in 44 units of time up*. The bullet in the overview section will turn green indicating that the property indeed is satisfied. In addition, the messages "Property is satisfied" or "Property is not satisfied" will appear in the status section depending on whether the property pass or not the verification.

The most important result to highlight is that the BP-task model passes the verification of the property $\phi_1 := \mathsf{AG}(not\ deadlock)$ (i.e., A[] (not deadlock),

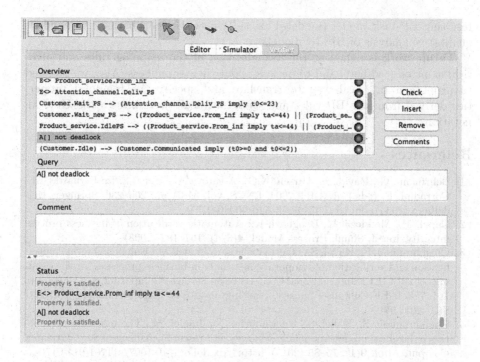

Fig. 6. Screen shot of the CRM BP-task model verification with UPPAAL.

according to the UPPAAL notation). This indicates that the BP-task model is
deadlock-free (i.e., in the BP-task model does not occur a deadlock situation by
which the BP-workers remain waiting indefinitely for communication between
each other). Additionally, the BP-task model has satisfied the ϕ_3 and ϕ_4 (see
Table 2) properties verification, which means the BP-task model always met the
Customer requests within the time stipulated by the QoS contract level for the
Product/Service Sell and *Product/Service Produce* BPs (i.e., the BP-task model
modeled completely satisfied the CRM business rules).

6   Conclusion and Future Work

In this work is introduced a set of mapping rules and two algorithms to transform BPMN models into TA-networks. This transformation is the main step
to conduct the qualitative analysis of a BP. The TA-network generated by the
transformation corresponds to the BP-task model, which can be analyzed with
the model-checker UPPAAL to provide results about some BP performance indicators (e.g., service time, waiting time, or queue size).

Our proposal was applied to a real project related to the CRM business,
showing its usefulness. As it was seen in the application example, our proposal
ensures the preservation of the individual properties associated with independent
task-sets within the BP-task model into which they are integrated; i.e., the

resulting BP-task model (modeled as a TA-network) can be used to conduct qualitative analysis of BPMN models.

Future work is aimed at the formalization of the mapping rules and algorithms introduced here, and to discuss about their soundness. Also, we planned to propose a practical way to translate and specify the temporal properties derived from the BP rules and QoS contracts, according to the UPPAAL notation.

References

1. Behrmann, G., David, A., Larsen, K.G.: A tutorial on UPPAAL. In: Bernardo, M., Corradini, F. (eds.) SFM-RT 2004. LNCS, vol. 3185, pp. 200–236. Springer, Heidelberg (2004). doi:10.1007/978-3-540-30080-9_7
2. Capel, M., Mendoza, L., Benghazi, K.: Automatic verification of business process integrity. Int. J. Simul. Process Model. **4**(3/4), 167–182 (2008)
3. Cheikhrouhou, S., Kallel, S., Guermouche, N., Jmaiel, M.: Enhancing formal specification and verification of temporal constraints in business processes. In: Proceedings of 2014 IEEE International Conference on Services Computing, SCC 2014, pp. 701–708. IEEE Computer Society, Washington (2014). http://dx.doi.org/10.1109/SCC.2014.97
4. Cheikhrouhou, S., Kallel, S., Guermouche, N., Jmaiel, M.: The temporal perspective in business process modeling: a survey and research challenges. Serv. Oriented Comput. Appl. **9**(1), 75–85 (2015). http://dx.doi.org/10.1007/s11761-014-0170-x
5. Kossak, F., et al.: How the semantic model can be used. In: A Rigorous Semantics for BPMN 2.0 Process Diagrams, pp. 153–159. Springer International Publishing, Heidelberg (2014). http://dx.doi.org/10.1007/978-3-319-09931-6_5
6. Mallek, S., Daclin, N., Chapurlat, V., Vallespir, B.: Enabling model checking for collaborative process analysis: from BPMN to 'Network of Timed Automata'. Enterp. Inf. Syst. **9**(3), 279–299 (2015). http://dx.doi.org/10.1080/17517575.2013.879211
7. Mendoza, L., Marius, A., Pérez, M., Grimán, A.: Critical success factors for a customer relationship management strategy. Inf. Softw. Technol. **49**(8), 913–945 (2007)
8. Morimoto, S.: A survey of formal verification for business process modeling. In: Bubak, M., Albada, G.D., Dongarra, J., Sloot, P.M.A. (eds.) ICCS 2008. LNCS, vol. 5102, pp. 514–522. Springer, Heidelberg (2008). doi:10.1007/978-3-540-69387-1_58
9. OMG: Business Process Model and Notation - v2.0. Object Management Group, Massachusetts (2011). http://www.omg.org/spec/BPMN/2.0/PDF
10. Paternò, F.: Task models in interactive software systems. In: Handbook of Software Engineering and Knowledge Engineering: Recent Advances. World Scientific Publishing Co., Inc., River Edge (2001)
11. Rüf, J., Kropf, T.: Symbolic model checking for a discrete clocked temporal logic with intervals. In: Proceedings of IFIP WG 10.5 International Conference on Correct Hardware Design and Verification Methods, pp. 146–163. Chapman & Hall Ltd, London (1997)
12. Watahiki, K., Ishikawa, F., Hiraishi, K.: Formal verification of business processes with temporal and resource constraints. In: 2011 IEEE International Conference on Systems, Man, and Cybernetics (SMC 2011), pp. 1173–1180. IEEE Computer Society, Los Alamitos (2011)

An Approach for Verifying Educational Robots

Sidney Nogueira[1]([⊠]), Taciana Pontual Falcão[1], Alexandre Mota[2],
Emanuel Oliveira[1], Itamar Moraes[1], and Iverson Pereira[1]

[1] Universidade Federal Rural de Pernambuco, Recife, Brazil
sidney.nogueira@ufrpe.br
[2] Universidade Federal de Pernambuco, Recife, Brazil

Abstract. Virtual robot programming environments provide a visual
interface for programming and simulating educational robots. Nowadays,
simulation is the only way to assess the robot behaviour inside such environments, as there is no approach that supports the automatic analysis of
the correctness of robot programs. This paper introduces an automatic
approach for verifying robot programs written in the educational programming language ROBO. We give semantics for ROBO programs in
the setting of CSP process algebra and automatically verify the properties of the programs using the FDR refinement checker. The verification
approach has been defined considering programming exercises proposed
in the literature on educational robotics. We illustrate the approach using
sample programs written in ROBO and discuss how to integrate such an
approach with educational tools.

Keywords: Educational robotics · Program verification · CSP

1 Introduction

Educational robotics had its origins in the 80's, with the launch of LOGO, a
computer language for children, associated with a physical turtle robot which
moved according to simple algorithmic commands [13]. Nowadays, more than
30 years later, many Brazilian schools have included programs of educational
robotics as extra-curricular activities and a lot of research is being performed
in the area [1]. The benefits of engaging students in robotics include promoting
autonomy and creativity within constructionist learning environments [12]; and
developing computational thinking, i.e. problem solving strategies through formal logical reasoning [18]. Furthermore, robot programming environments provide a clear mapping between abstract concepts represented by programming
languages and concrete outcomes represented by the robot's movement, helping
students to understand computer programming logic [6].

Traditionally, educational robotics consists in controlling a physical robot
through software commands. Virtual environments that provide simulations of
the robot's movement — replacing the actual physical robot — have emerged
as viable alternatives that decrease cost and complexity of physical robots, thus

© Springer International Publishing AG 2016
L. Ribeiro and T. Lecomte (Eds.): SBMF 2016, LNCS 10090, pp. 59–77, 2016.
DOI: 10.1007/978-3-319-49815-7_4

broadening the reach of educational robotics. Robomind [3,5] is an example of a virtual robotic environment, used in the present research, and where the digital representation of a robot moves across a bi-dimensional grid according to commands written in the educational scripting language named ROBO.

Observing the effect of executing ROBO programs using simulation has high pedagogical value, although the final result of the execution is only known after the completion of commands. This means that the only way to verify a robot behaviour is throughout observation: there is no automatic way to state whether the robot behaves as expected.

This paper introduces an automatic approach for verifying robot programs written in a subset of ROBO. We give semantics for the ROBO language by defining a mapping from the specification of the robot environment and the robot program source code to elements in the notation of CSP [14,15]. The notation of CSP was chosen since it has a rich set of operators for combining processes that facilitated the definition of the mapping from ROBO to CSP, moreover, it has mature tools like the FDR [4] refinement checker. The robot formal specification is characterised by a CSP process that is input by the FDR refinement checker that performs automatic analysis of refinement between processes. We formalise as CSP refinement expressions the properties of robot programs that are valid solutions for exercises proposed in the literature for teaching robotics. Thus, the correctness of a robot with respect to the exercises can be automatically verified using FDR. The outputs of the refinement checker are used to give feedback to the learner about the robot behaviour. Moreover, using FDR we can analyse deadlock behaviour, whose presence in the specification indicates that the robot programs do not loop forever (terminates). Finally, we discuss how the proposed verification approach can be used as backend solution for the verification of ROBO programs in the context of educational tools.

The next section presents the problem of verifying robots using simulation in the RoboMind environment, and overviews the proposed verification approach. Section 3 shows the concepts of CSP used in this work and the CSP specification for the robot's program and environment. Section 4 presents the characterisation of the properties of the programs as CSP refinements expressions and how to analyse then using FDR. Possible ways to integrate the verification approach within educational tools are discussed in Sect. 5. Finally, Sect. 6 presents the conclusions, related and future work.

2   Simulating Robot Programs

The RoboMind (www.robomind.net) environment enables programming and simulating a virtual robot in a map for learning programming logic and developing computational thinking. Figure 1 shows a screenshot of RoboMind software for desktops. The left-hand side of the figure depicts a program with thirteen lines of code written in the ROBO language. An arrow is pointing to the next command (line 4) to be executed by the simulation. The right-hand side of the same figure shows a bi-dimensional map and the robot's position and orientation for the current step of the simulation. The bottom of the figure shows the

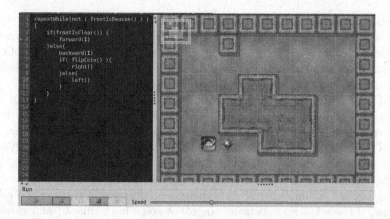

Fig. 1. RoboMind programming environment

main simulation controls: a button to start the simulation, a button to advance a single step, two buttons to pause and stop, a button to restart the simulation and a scroll to set the simulation speed. The software has predefined maps and also enables loading maps defined by the user.

Figure 2 shows screenshots of the initial state of two different simulations. Those maps are used to test robot programs that do not know the location of a simulation object called beacon, and aim at exploring the environment until the robot faces the beacon. In Fig. 2, beacons are displayed as round objects surrounded with spikes.

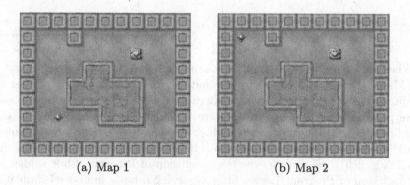

(a) Map 1   (b) Map 2

Fig. 2. Initial state of simulations

We introduce the elements of the ROBO language considered in this paper through sample programs. Programming a robot to find an object in a map is a typical exercise proposed in the literature on educational robotics [3,5]. Listing 1.1 shows a program written in ROBO [5] to move the robot in the map until it faces a beacon. Such a program uses predefined functions and commands of the ROBO language. The boolean function frontIsBeacon() evaluates to true if the robot faces a beacon; otherwise, it evaluates to false. The boolean function frontIsClear() returns true if the robot faces an empty cell. The function flipCoin() represents the toss of a coin; it yields a random boolean value as the result of an internal choice of the robot. The commands forward(n), backward(n), right() and left() make the robot move forward (and backward) the number of cells specified as parameter, and change the robot orientation to its left (and to its right), respectively. Like any imperative language, the syntax of ROBO has conditionals (for instance, if/else) and looping structures (for instance, repeatWhile) for controlling the program flow. The program in Listing 1.1 repeats the loop while the robot is not in front of a beacon (line 1). Inside the loop, the program calls the forward command (line 4) if there is no obstacle in front of the robot; otherwise, if there is some obstacle, the robot steps back (line 6) and turns its direction to the right (or left) depending on the result of "flipping the coin" (line 7) (true or false) (lines 8 and 10). The expected behaviour for this program is that the robot stops in front of the beacon, when executed considering the two maps in Fig. 2.

Listing 1.1. Program 1

```
repeatWhile ( not ( frontIsBeacon ()))
{
    if ( frontIsClear ()) {
        forward (1)
    } else {
        backward (1)
        if ( flipCoin () ) {
            right ()
        } else {
            left ()
        }
    }
}
```

Listing 1.2. Program 2

```
repeatWhile ( not ( frontIsBeacon ()))
{
    if ( frontIsClear ()) {
        forward (1)
    } else {
        if ( flipCoin () ) {
            right ()
        } else {
            left ()
        }
    }
}
```

When executing the programs in Listings 1.1 and 1.2 (Programs 1 and 2) with Map 1 (Fig. 2(a)), we can observe that the robot moves until it reaches the beacon, then the programs conclude. Because flipCoin() is an internal decision of the program, the time required to reach the program conclusion can vary according to these internal results, which depends on the implementation of RoboMind that is programmed in Java [11]. If the same programs are run with Map 2 (Fig. 2(b)), we can observe the conclusion of Program 2 but cannot see the conclusion of Program 1, even after observing a huge number of simulation steps (more than 100). One way to ensure Program 1 terminates is to perform an exhaustive and systematic analysis of this program, however there is no approach that automatically verifies termination or other properties of the robot program.

Program 1 and Program 2 present the core of the ROBO language. Additionally, the language includes commands for moving the robot according to the cardinal directions, for painting the floor in black or white, and for grabbing and releasing beacons. The language has further functions that simulate the usage of robot sensors for detecting beacons, walls and colours. Moreover, the language allows the definition of constants, procedures parameterised by constants, and global integer variables. For a complete definition of ROBO please consult [5].

2.1 Overview of the Verification Approach

The approach proposed in this paper uses refinement checking to exhaustively verify the states of a ROBO program that runs in a specific map. For instance, we can verify that Program 1 never terminates in Map 2, i.e. the robot does not find the beacon. We are also able to verify that Program 2 (Listing 1.2) terminates, i.e. the robot eventually finds the beacon in the two maps displayed in Fig. 2. In this approach, a program never terminates if its simulation model satisfies the property of deadlock-freedom.

Figure 3 overviews the verification approach. Its inputs are ROBO programs, maps in the RoboMind format and the properties to be verified. A program is manually translated into a CSP process following translation rules; the map is automatically translated into a data structure and the properties are manually specified as assertions to be verified by FDR. The formal specification is the composition of the CSP processes that represent predefined commands and functions of ROBO, the robot program itself and the map. The specification and the properties are inputs to the FDR refinement checker that performs the automatic analysis of the program properties. The results of the verification are used by the programmer to confirm the program works as expected or for debugging.

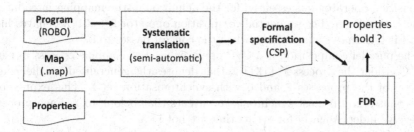

Fig. 3. Approach workflow

3   Formalising the Robot

This section presents the CSP formalisation of the robot and its environment. We start showing the main elements of CSP and next the robot's formal specification.

3.1   Communicating Sequential Processes

In this paper we define the semantics of the ROBO language in terms of the process algebra CSP [14]. CSP is a formal language mainly designed to specify and verify concurrent and distributed systems. It is composed of events, processes, and operators. We present CSP using the notation of CSP_M, the machine readable version of CSP used in FDR [17].

Events are used to abstract the occurrence of facts. For instance, the event right could mean the fact that a robot has turned right. Events in CSP are atomic and instantaneous. That is, they cannot be broken after being started and they do not consume time. When an event can communicate values, it is named a channel and has an associated type. For instance, the syntax channel forward : { 1,2 } defines a channel that is able to communicate the events forward.1 and forward.2. The CSP syntax forward?x specifies that the process can communicate an event forward.x such that the value of x is selected by the process environment. The set of all events present in a CSP specification is denoted by the set Events.

The CSP primitive process STOP specifies a broken process (deadlock), and the primitive SKIP a process that terminates successfully. Prefix, external choice and conditional are basic CSP operators. The CSP prefix operator P = ev -> Q specifies that event ev can be communicated by P, and upon its occurrence the process behaves as the process Q. The external choice operator, as in P = Q [] R, indicates that the process P can behave as the processes Q or R; the choice is made by the environment. The process if exp then P else Q uses the conditional operator to express it is equivalent to P if the boolean expression exp holds, and behaves as Q otherwise.

The mapping from ROBO programs into CSP presented in this work is very concise due to the compositionality of CSP operators. Particularly, the sequential composition operator was essential for the definition of the mapping introduced in the next section. The sequential composition operator P = Q; R behaves like Q until it terminates successfully, when the control passes to R.

The parallel composition is a CSP operator used to combine process in parallel. Consider the process P [|X|] Q that denotes the generalised parallel composition of the processes P and Q with synchronisation set X. This expression states that P and Q must synchronise on events that belong to X. Each process can evolve independently for events that are not in X.

The CSP notation P \ X defines a process that behaves like P, communicating all its events, except the events that belong to X, which become internal (invisible). The operator \ stands for the hiding operator.

Moreover, consider the replicated external choice construction of CSP [] x:X @ F(x), where x ranges over the values in the set X, and F(x) is any process expression involving x. This construction behaves as the process F(x_1) [] ...[] F(x_k), for X = {x_1,...,x_k}.

Finally, consider the process RUN(A) = [] ev:A @ ev -> RUN(A) that continuously offers the events from the set A, and P /\ Q which indicates that Q can interrupt the behaviour of P if an event offered by Q is communicated.

The formal semantics of a CSP processes is given in terms of three main semantic models: traces ($\mathcal{T}$), failures ($\mathcal{F}$), and failures-divergences ($\mathcal{FD}$). In this paper it is enough to work with the traces model. The traces of a process P, say $\mathcal{T}$(P), records the sequences of events that can be communicated by P.

For example, $\mathcal{T}(\text{STOP}) = \{\langle\rangle\}$ and $\mathcal{T}(\text{forward.1 -> right -> STOP}) = \{\langle\rangle, \langle$ forward.1$\rangle, \langle$ forward.1, right $\rangle\}$.

CSP processes can be verified using the FDR refinement checker [4]. A refinement checker is a variant of a model checker where verifications are performed by means of refinements. A CSP refinement is defined by behaviour containment. Thus a process Q trace refines a process P iff $\mathcal{T}(\text{Q}) \subseteq \mathcal{T}(\text{P})$. In FDR, refinement is denoted as the expression P [T= Q. If a refinement checking fails, FDR yields the shortest trace (counterexample) produced by Q that cannot be observed in P. We can also ask FDR to check whether a process P can exhibit deadlock, livelock or non-determinism.

3.2 Robot Formal Specification

We show how to translate the robot program and the map into the respective elements in CSP. Translating the map into its CSP representation is a very straightforward process. Listing 1.3 shows the RoboMind representation for the map displayed in Fig. 2(a), which has eleven columns and nine lines. Letters represent the different formats of walls displayed in the RoboMind interface. The character @ (line 3) represents the initial position of the robot, and the character * (line 7) indicates the initial position of the beacon. In [9], one can find the textual representation for Map 2 (Fig. 2(b)), as well as the complete CSP specification for the examples in this paper.

Consider the constants Start, Obs and Beacon, which are members of a CSP datatype named Things. This datatype represents the elements of a map. In CSP, the map is represented by a constant named MAP, which is bound to a set of triples in the form (x,y,element), associating one element to its position in the map. The value for x (y) belongs to the set of values between 0 and XMAX (YMAX), which is a constant in the CSP model that denotes the maximum value for x (y). The map in Listing 1.3 has XMAX (YMAX) equals to ten (eight). For instance, the map in Listing 1.3 shows the robot in position (7,2), i.e. column number 7 (eighth column) and line number 2 (third line). Hence, (7,2,Start) is a triple that belongs to the set MAP. Other examples are the triples (0,2,Obs) and (2,6,Beacon) that represent a wall (letter A) and the initial position for the beacon. Regardless of its format, every wall is semantically identical in the specification so all walls are represented by the same constant (Obs).

Listing 1.3. Textual representation for Map 1

```
  AAAAAAAAAAA
2 A   A       A
  A       @   A
4 A    CD     A
  A    CKLHD  A
6 A    BFJNI  A
  A *   BFE   A
8 A   .       A
  AAAAAAAAAAA
```

Beacons and the robot can change their state. So they should be represented as variables. CSP does not have variables but they can be emulated through recursive processes that represent memory, as presented in [8]. A memory process binds values to identifiers and uses get and set channels to simulate reading and writing values to the variables. The declaration of such channels is as follows.

```
nametype TX = {1..XMAX-1}
nametype TY = {1..YMAX-1}
nametype TO = {NORTH_,EAST_,SOUTH_,WEST_}
datatype VarType = X.TX | Y.TY | ORIENTATION.TO | BX.TX | BY.TY
channel get,set : VarType
```

The types TX, TY and TO define the range for column and line indexes, and for the robot orientation, respectively. The notation {1..XMAX-1} represents a set whose members are integers between 1 and XMAX-1. The ranges of TX and TY exclude 0 and XMAX (YMAX) because these indexes are only occupied by obstacles. The constants NORTH_,EAST_,SOUTH_,WEST_ encode the robot orientation; they are aliases for the numbers 0, 1, 2 and 3. The datatype VarType is the type for the values communicated by channels get and set. It is a set whose members have the form VarName.Binding, where VarName is a variable name and Binding is a possible value bound to the variable. The variables X, Y and ORIENTATION represent the current position and orientation of the robot. The variables BX and BY are the current position of the beacon. The CSP process MEMORY is presented in the sequel. It is the interleaving of memory cells, which are recursive processes parameterised by the name of a variable and its current binding. Such a process offers the choice of events produced by channels get and set. It uses the get channel to communicate the current value of the variable to the environment, and the channel set to receive from the environment a new value for the variable; the new value is carried as a parameter of the process. The initial state of the process MEMORY considers the initial position of the robot and the beacon in the map. The robot initial orientation is always NORTH_.

```
Mcel(v,val) = get!v!val -> Mcel(v,val)
              [] set!v?val_ -> Mcel(v,val_)

MEMORY = Mcel(X,7) ||| Mcel(Y,2) ||| Mcel(ORIENTATION,NORTH_)
         ||| Mcel(BX,2) ||| Mcel(BY,5)
```

Painting is a dynamic element of the specification. However, in the current specification we deal only with programs that do not paint the floor. So paintings are represented as members of the set MAP.

Each command of ROBO is directly represented as a CSP process with the same name and parameters. For instance, the ROBO command right() is characterised by the CSP process RIGHT.

```
channel right
RIGHT = right -> get!ORIENTATION?o -> set!ORIENTATION!(o+1)%4 ->
        SKIP
```

The behaviour of the process RIGHT starts by trying to communicate the event right, which indicates the robot has turned to the right and that the robot orientation is to the right as well. Formally, this process uses the get channel to read the current value for the orientation, which is bound to the variable o. Then, the channel set communicates the new value for the orientation: an increment in the value of o module 4 (recall the robot orientation are values between 0 and 3). Finally, the process terminates successfully. As another example, the ROBO command forward(n) is represented as CSP process FORWARD(n).

```
FORWARD(n) = get!ORIENTATION?o -> MOVE_STEPS(n,o)
```

The behaviour of the process FORWARD(n) is to read the current robot orientation using the get channel and behaving as the process MOVE_STEPS(n,o), which receives as parameters the number of steps (n) to move and the current robot orientation (o). The partial description for this process is as follows.

```
channel forward : {1}
MOVE_STEPS(0,o) = SKIP
MOVE_STEPS(n,o) =
  get!X?x -> get!Y?y -> get!BX?bx -> get!BY?by ->
  if(o == NORTH_) then (
    if(frontIsClear(x,y,o,bx,by)) then
      forward!1 -> set.Y!(y - 1) -> MOVE_STEPS(n-1, o)
    else
      forward!1 -> MOVE_STEPS(0, o)
  ) else if(o == EAST_) then (
  ...
  ) else if(o == SOUTH_) then (
  ...
  ) else (
  ...
  )
```

In the description of MOVE_STEPS, consider frontIsClear(x,y,o,bx,by) is a boolean function that inputs the current robot position and orientation, and, the current position for the beacon. Such a function consults the tuples in MAP and evaluates to true if there is no impediment for the robot moving forward. The process MOVE_STEPS terminates successfully if there are no steps to go forward, otherwise, it reads the current position for the robot and updates the position of the robot considering the existence of obstacles that may block the robot movement. For instance, if the robot points towards north, this process verifies whether the next position in the map is free from obstacles. If it is true, the event forward.1 is communicated, the robot line is decreased by one, and the process behaves as MOVE_STEPS(n-1,o). Otherwise, if there is an obstacle in front of the robot its position is not updated, the event forward.1 is communicated and the process behaves as MOVE_STEPS(n-1,o). The event forward.1 represents the calling of the command to go forward, so it is communicated if the robot is able to move forward or not. The behaviour is analogous if the robot points to other directions, hence the details of the process MOVE_STEPS are omitted.

The behaviour of a robot program, say PROGRAM_DEBUG, is formalised as the parallel composition of the CSP process that represents the robot program control (COMMANDS) flow with the memory process (MEMORY). The synchronisation set contains all the events communicated by channels get and set. The notation {|get,set|} represents the union of the extensions of the channels get and set. For instance, the element get.X.5 is a member of the extensions of the channel get, and the element set.ORIENTATION.0 is a member of the extensions of the channel set.

PROGRAM_DEBUG = COMMANDS [|{|get,set|}|] MEMORY

The CSP process COMMANDS formalises the flow of commands of the robot program. The translation of the flow of commands to CSP follows a compositional mapping that is presented in Table 1. Such a mapping inputs a sequence of ROBO commands and outputs CSP processes. In Table 1, consider that cmd represents a ROBO command, and seq, seq_1 and seq_2 sequences of ROBO commands. Moreover, consider the notation exp represents a boolean expression in ROBO, and $TE(exp)$ the respective representation of exp in CSP. Additionally, consider that $T(seq)$ denotes a transformation function that inputs a sequence of commands and outputs its CSP representation. Finally, consider R is a robot program written in ROBO. Thus the definition COMMANDS is the result of $T(R)$.

Table 1. Mapping from ROBO to CSP

ROBO syntax	CSP syntax
$\langle\rangle$	SKIP
repeatWhile(exp) {seq}	WHILE =
	get.X?x -> get.Y?y ->
	get.ORIENTATION?o ->
	get.BX?bx -> get.BY?by ->
	if ($TE(exp)$) then ($T(seq)$; WHILE)
	else (SKIP)
if(exp) {seq_1} else {seq_2}	get.X?x -> get.Y?y ->
	get.ORIENTATION?o ->
	get.BX?bx -> get.BY?by ->
	if ($TE(exp)$) then $T(seq_1)$
	else $T(seq_2)$
$\langle cmd\rangle\widehat{\ } seq$	$T(\langle cmd\rangle)$; $T(seq)$

Each line in Table 1 represents a possible input for the function (column ROBO syntax) and the function output (column CSP syntax). The CSP representation for an empty sequence of commands is the process SKIP. The mapping of a command (sequence with size one) that is neither a conditional (i.e. if/else) nor a loop (i.e. repeatWhile) is very straightforward and is omitted in the table. For instance, the expression $T(\langle \text{forward}(1) \rangle)$ yields the process FORWARD(1). Similarly, the CSP representation for boolean expressions is very direct so is omitted. As an illustration, the expression $TE(\text{frontIsBeacon}())$ yields the CSP expression frontIsBeacon(x,y,o,bx,by).

As exhibited in Table 1, the CSP representation for the ROBO command repeatWhile is a recursive process whose initial behaviour is to read the variables in the memory and to evaluate the loop enter condition. If the loop condition holds, the process behaviour is the CSP representation for the commands in the body of the loop sequential composition with the process that represents the loop. If the condition does not hold, the behaviour is equivalent to SKIP. The CSP representation for a conditional command in ROBO is a process that initially reads the variables from the memory and subsequently evaluates the if condition. If the condition holds, the process behaves as the CSP specification for the commands in the body of the if. Otherwise, the behaviour is equivalent to the specification for the commands in the body of the else. Finally, the CSP specification for a non-empty sequence of commands is the mapping of the first command, sequential composition with the mapping of the subsequent commands in the sequence.

As an example of applying the mapping in Table 1, the function T applied to Program 1 (Listing 1.1) yields a CSP process that is equivalent to the process WHILE specified as follows.

```
WHILE =
  get.X?x -> get.Y?y -> get.ORIENTATION?o ->
  get.BX?bx -> get.BY?by ->
  if( not( frontIsBeacon(x,y,o,bx,by) ) ) then (
    IF1; WHILE
  ) else (
    SKIP
  );SKIP
```

The process WHILE represents the program loop. Thus, COMMANDS = WHILE represents the flow of the Program 1. If the loop condition holds, this process behaves as the process IF1, which is the CSP representation obtained using the mapping in Table 1 to the if/else in Program 1 (lines 3 to 12). Otherwise, the process behaves as SKIP. The specification for the process IF1 is as follows.

```
IF1 =
  get.X?x -> get:Y?y -> get.ORIENTATION?o -> get.BX?bx ->
  get.BY?by ->
  if( frontIsClear(x,y,o,bx,by) ) then
    FORWARD(1); SKIP
  else
    BACKWARD(1); IF2
```

In IF1, if the evaluation of the function frontIsClear(.) holds the process behaves as FORWARD(1); SKIP. Otherwise, behaves as the process BACKWARD(1) sequential composition the process IF2. This last process has been obtained using the mapping in Table 1 to the lines 7 to 12 of the Program 1. The CSP representation for BACKWARD(1) is very similar to that for the process FORWARD so is omitted. The process IF2 shows how to represent in CSP the call of the function flipCoin() in the context of Program 1. In IF2, the boolean expression c represents the calling of flipCoin(). The channel coin communicates events in the form coin.c, such that c belongs to the set {true,false}. The environment defines the value bind to c in the communication coin?c. Thus, in IF2, if(c) is the CSP representation for if(flipCoin()). If c equals true, IF2 behaves as the process RIGHT; SKIP. Otherwise, behaves as LEFT; SKIP. The CSP representation for LEFT is very similar to that for the process RIGHT and it is omitted.

```
channel coin : Bool
IF2 =
  get.X?x -> get.Y?y -> get.ORIENTATION?o -> get.BX?bx ->
  get.BY?by ->  coin?c ->
  if( c ) then
    RIGHT; SKIP
  else
    LEFT; SKIP
```

In the general case, consider exp a boolean expression in ROBO that contains k occurrences of flipCoin(), and $TE(exp)$ the representation for exp in CSP. Moreover, consider there are channels channel coin_i, such that i belongs to $\{1,\ldots,k\}$. So the ith occurrence of flipCoin() in exp is represented in $TE(exp)$ as c_i, which is communicated by the environment in coin_i?c_i.

Finally, we show the complete CSP specification for the Program 1 that is represented by the process PROGRAM defined as follows.

```
PROGRAM = PROGRAM_DEBUG \ {|get,set,coin|}
```

In the process PROGRAM, the communications of the channels get, set and coin are hidden and only the events that represent the robot actions are kept visible. For instance, the events forward.1 and right. Moreover, due to the hiding, the choice for the value for a coin flip becomes an internal choice.

4   Verifying Robot Programs

We show how to verify robot programs using their CSP specifications. Table 2 presents the exercises proposed for the learners of RoboMind collected from [3,5] that we are able to formalise and verify. We have assigned ids to the exercises and organised them in categories. The ids follow the format source_level_name, where source identifies the source from which the exercise has been collected (rmn stands for [5] and furb for [3]); level identifies the student level (es stands for elementary school, hs for high school and he for high education) and name is an abbreviation for the exercise name. Moreover, in Table 2 exercises are classified in five categories: moving the beacon to a target location (Move beacon), moving the robot trough predefined navigation paths (Navigator), following trails using robot colour sensor (Follow trails), searching the beacon location (Finder), and, avoiding obstacles while following a path (Avoid obstacles). Following this classification, Program 1 introduced in Sect. 2 belongs to the category Finder and is a possible solution for the exercise rmn_hs_findBeacon considering the maps provided by the exercise (Maps 1 and 2 in Fig. 2). The complete description for the exercises and their respective maps can be downloaded in [9].

Table 2. Categories of exercises in RoboMind

Category	Exercises
Move beacon	furb_es_foodChain, furb_es_mathPuzzle, furb_es_recycling
Navigator	furb_es_cardinalPoints,
	furb_hs_concordiaBlumenauBus,
	furb_he_studentInstruction, rmn_hs_mazeSolving
Follow trails	furb_es_cartesianCoordinates, rmn_hs_lineFollowing,
	rmn_roboExercises
Finder	rmn_hs_findBeacon
Avoid obstacles	furb_hs_dodgingBoxes, furb_he_contouringBoxes1,
	furb_he_contouringBoxes2, furb_he_contouringBoxes3

The exercises that we are not able to formalise and verify are those whose solution manipulates variables or the robot needs to paint the floor. Fortunately, a variety of exercises does not require variables and painting, so the approach can be used for verifying exercises similar to those displayed in Table 2. We discuss how to verify the exercises in Table 2.

All the exercises implicitly expect that the robot program terminates after completing some tasks. Thus a basic property for every robot program is that it eventually ends. This is equivalent to check the existence of deadlock behaviour in the process PROGRAM introduced in the previous section. For instance, consider the exercise rmn_hs_findBeacon in Table 2 (category Finder). As explained in Sect. 2, in this exercise, the robot must find the beacon in the maps displayed in Fig. 2. Listings 1.1 and 1.2 show two candidate solutions, Program 1 and Program 2, which are expected to terminate only if the robot faces the beacon. Remember these programs contain a loop. Such a loop reduces to SKIP (the program terminates) if the function frontIsBeacon() evaluates to true. Otherwise, the loop executes again, potentially forever. Consider that PROGRAM represents the specification of Program 1 in Map 1. The verification of the FDR assertion assert PROGRAM :[deadlock free [F]] yields false as the result. This indicates the program is not deadlock

free (it contains a deadlock) so terminates. The counterexample provided by
FDR in this verification is the shortest execution path that leads the robot to
find the beacon forward.1, backward.1, left, forward.1, forward.1,
forward.1, forward.1, forward.1, forward.1, backward.1, left,
forward.1, forward.1, forward.1, say ce. Consider that PROGRAM_2 is the
specification for Program 1 in Map 2. Checking the assertion assert PROGRAM_2
:[deadlock free [F]], the result given by FDR is true, which indicates the
CSP specification for the program does not contain a deadlock. Thus, the program does not exit the loop and does not find the beacon. We can observe a
different behaviour for Program 2. Consider PROGRAM2_1 and PROGRAM2_2 are
the specifications for Program 2 in Map 1 and Map 2, respectively. Using FDR
we can check that Program 2 terminates (so is able to find the beacon) when
run in Maps 1 and 2 by checking the assertions assert PROGRAM2_1 :[deadlock
free [F]] and assert PROGRAM2_2 :[deadlock free [F]] that yield false as
result.

Program termination is a useful property but it is not strong enough to
assess the correctness of robot programs with respect to the exercises requirements. On the other hand, checking whether the specification reaches specific
states can check whether programs conform (or not) to the exercises in Table 2.
For instance, an alternative form to verify if Program 1 finds the beacon located
in position (2,6) in Map 1 is to check the existence of a specification state such
that the robot faces the beacon. In Map 1, (2,5) is a possible position for the
robot to face the beacon pointing southbound. Recall that the CSP specification communicates get events like get.X.2, which represents the reading of the
current variable binding from memory. If we can find a specification state for
which the memory communicates the sequence of events get.X.2, get.Y.5,
get.ORIENTATION.2 (recall that 2 represents south in the model) then we are
sure the robot eventually reaches the beacon.

We perform the verification of the eventual states reached by the CSP specification using CSP test purposes [8,10]. A CSP test purpose is a CSP process that
describes the property of the traces that we want to automatically select from
a CSP process. For instance, we can describe a CSP test purpose that selects
the traces of the specification for Program 1 in Map 1, such that the traces
communicate the sequence of events get.X.2, get.Y.5, get.ORIENTATION.2.
In order the test purpose can read the memory states, we have to create a copy
of the channel get in the memory, say get2. The process MEMORY_GET2 is the
adaptation of the process MEMORY to include get2 events. The definitions of the
channel get2, the process MEMORY_GET2 and the process PROGRAM_DEBUG_GET2 are
as follows. The last process represents the specification adapted for test selection.

```
channel get2 : VarType
MEMORY_GET2 = MEMORY [[ get.x <- get.x,
                        get.x <- get2.x | x <- {|get|} ]]
PROGRAM_DEBUG_GET2 = (COMMANDS
                       [|{|get,set|}|]
                      MEMORY_GET2) \ {|get,set,coin|}
```

The channel get2 has the type of the channel get. The process MEMORY_GET2 is defined using the CSP renaming operator applied on the process MEMORY. The renaming defines a mapping of the events in the form get.x into themselves and into events in the form get2.x, such that x belongs to the extensions of get. Hence, the process MEMORY_GET2 communicates the same events of MEMORY; additionally, it communicates get2.x events whenever the process MEMORY communicates get.x events. The process PROGRAM_DEBUG_GET2 is defined as the parallel composition of the program control flow (COMMANDS) with the process MEMORY_GET2. The events that belong to the channels get, set and coin are hidden, so only events that represent commands (for instance, backward.1) and get2 events are visible.

A CSP test purpose is a process, say TP, that is constructed using the auxiliary CSP processes that follow. Such processes are a simplification of the primitive processes introduced in [8]. The process ACCEPT communicates the event accept and deadlocks. The behaviour of the process MATCH(ev, NEXT) is to communicate ev and to behave as the process NEXT. Consider the function diff(s1,s2) yields the difference between the sets s1 and s2. The process NOT(ev, NEXT) offers the choice of the events that belong to the alphabet of the specification (represented by the set Events) that are different from ev and accept. After communicating an event the process behaves as NEXT. The process UNTIL(ev,NEXT) behaves as the process RUN(diff(Events,{ev,accept})) interrupted by the process MATCH(ev, NEXT). This process can communicate the events that belong to the set diff(Events,{ev,accept}) until the event ev is communicated, then it behaves as NEXT.

```
channel accept
ACCEPT = accept -> STOP
MATCH(ev, NEXT) = ev -> NEXT
NOT(ev, NEXT) = [] ev_ : diff(Events,{ev,accept}) @ ev_ -> NEXT
UNTIL(ev,NEXT) = RUN(diff(Events,{ev,accept})) /\ MATCH(ev,NEXT)
```

The test purpose TP specified in the sequel is used to verify if specification communicates the sequence of events get.X.2, get.Y.5, get.ORIENTATION.2. If this sequence is found this process behaves as ACCEPT.

```
. TP = UNTIL(get2.X.2, (MATCH(get2.Y.5, TP_) [] NOT(get2.Y.5, TP)))
TP_ = MATCH(get2.ORIENTATION.SOUTH_, ACCEPT) []
      NOT(get2.ORIENTATION.SOUTH_, TP)

PP = PROGRAM_DEBUG_GET2 [|diff(Events,{accept})|] TP
assert RUN(diff(Events,{accept})) [T= PP
```

The initial behaviour of the process TP it to wait for the communication of the event get2.X.2. Then it behaves as the choice between the processes MATCH(get2.Y.5, TP_) and NOT(get2.Y.5, TP). The test purpose behaves as the process MATCH(get2.Y.5, TP_) if the event get2.Y.5 is communicated. Then, the process behaves as the process TP_. The test purpose behaves as the process NOT(get2.Y.5, TP) if an event different to get2.Y.5 is communicated. Next, the test purpose behave as TP. The behaviour of TP_ is the choice between the processes MATCH(get2.ORIENTATION.SOUTH_, ACCEPT) and NOT(get2.ORIENTATION.SOUTH_, TP). The process TP_ behaves as the process MATCH(get2.ORIENTATION.SOUTH_, ACCEPT) if get2.ORIENTATION.SOUTH_ is communicated. In the sequel, it behaves as ACCEPT. Finally, the test purpose behaves as the process NOT(get2.ORIENTATION.SOUTH_, TP) if an event different to get2.ORIENTATION.SOUTH_ is communicated. Afterwards, it behaves as TP.

The parallel product, say PP, is the CSP process defined as the parallel composition of the process TP with the process PROGRAM_DEBUG_GET2 with a synchronisation set that includes all events except accept. This process communicates an accept event only if the the test purpose finds a trace in the specification that matches the test purpose specification. Since RUN(diff(Events,{accept})) communicates every event except accept, the refinement assertion assert RUN(diff(Events,{accept})) [T= PP does not hold iff the specification presents a trace that matches the test purpose description. If the refinement does not hold, the counterexample is the shortest trace of PP that ends with accept. Running in FDR this refinement expression yields a false result and a counterexample trace that equals ce concatenated with the sequence get.X.2, get.Y.5, get.ORIENTATION.2,accept. This ensures Program 1 moves the robot until it faces the beacon in Map 1.

5   Integrating the Approach with Educational Tools

This section discusses how the proposed verification approach can be used as a backend solution for the verification of ROBO programs in the context of educational tools.

First of all, the mechanisation of the translation from ROBO to CSP, as well as the complete abstraction of the CSP notation (i.e., hiding all formal details) is required for the adoption of the approach. One way to hide the CSP notation for the definition of the CSP test purposes (presented in previous section) is to implement a graphical interface that allows the teacher to specify points of the map that are expected for the robot to pass through and the expected orientation for the robot in each point. This information would consist of the specification for the robot's expected behaviour for a given map and would be automatically translated into CSP test purposes. Another alternative is to develop a Controlled Natural Language (CNL) for abstracting CSP test purposes inspired in the CNL introduced in [10]. The teacher then could describe the properties for the expected ROBO solutions using such a CNL that would be translated into CSP test purposes similarly to the translation approach presented in [10].

Another action towards the integration of the approach within educational processes is the development of graphical user interfaces. One possibility is to integrate the automatic verification as an option in the interface of Robomind (Fig. 1). The expected properties for each map would be included as additional information in the map specification (Listing 1.3) and loaded together with the map. New interface elements would be added into Robomind to allow the execution of the approach's steps in background. Upon the conclusion of the verification, Robomind would show whether the program conforms (or not) to the expected properties. Another possibility is to create a tool, independent of Robomind, with a web interface following the style of Online Judge Systems [2], which are used for testing programs submitted during programming contests. Possibly, there would be two different interfaces, for tutors and students. The tutors' interface would enable the inclusion of new problems, maps and expected properties for programs written in ROBO (or, as an extension of this work, in other similar educational programming languages for robots). The students' interface would enable the submission of programs to be automatically verified using the proposed approach. Feedback about submitted programs would be given to the students, allowing resubmissions until the program meets the expected properties.

6 Conclusions

This paper has presented an approach for the verification of educational robots programmed using the ROBO language. We have shown how to systematically translate maps and the syntactical elements of the robot program into CSP using a well defined set of compositional transformation rules. Moreover, we show how to use the FDR tool to automatically verify program properties as termination as well as safety properties expressed as CSP test purposes. We have presented a catalogue of exercises collected from the literature for teaching robot programming that we are able to verify using the approach. Finally, we have discussed how the approach can be integrated with educational tools.

Verification approaches have been used for providing automatic feedback about the correctness of programs for educational purpose. However, neither there is a formalisation of languages for programming robots nor approaches for model checking robot programs. Nonetheless, our approach is very similar to the approach of the SVA tool [16] that supports the teaching of concurrent programming. SVA compiles shared variables programs written in an imperative language into CSP processes, and uses FDR to verify the properties of the programs. The LTSA tool [7] is another educational tool that supports the teaching of concurrency programming and uses model checking. However, while our approach hides the formal specification from the programmer, in LTSA the programs are directly expressed in a process algebra.

The main limitation of dealing with a subset of the ROBO language is that programs that use variables and commands for painting the floor are not considered. Such a drawback will disappear with the formalization of variables and painting, which are left as future work.

A classical drawback of using refinement checking is the exponential growth in the number of states of the model (the state-space explosion problem). In our context, the number of states to be analysed by FDR increases very fast with the size of the maps. A future work is to perform a detailed analysis on the efficiency of the approach and study ways to make it more efficient.

The proposed approach is a complement to robot simulation environments. It would represent a relevant support for the apprentices of robot programming if the translation approach is fully automated and the approach becomes integrated with educational tools, as discussed in Sect. 5. Future works include the mechanisation of the translation from ROBO to CSP, implementation of tools and performing controlled experiments to assess the educational contribution.

The notation of CSP was very useful for the definition of the compositional mapping from ROBO to CSP. Nonetheless, another potential advantage of using CSP is the possibility to use the CSP refinement notions for establishing notions of equivalence between ROBO programs, and explore refinement notions between robots for educational purposes. This research is left as future work as well.

Acknowledgements. This research project is supported by CNPq under grant 442859/2014-7.

References

1. Anais do XXVI Simpósio Brasileiro de Informática na Educação (SBIE 2015) (2015)
2. Online judge, February 2016. https://en.wikipedia.org/wiki/Online_judge
3. RoboMind FURB (2016). http://robolab.inf.furb.br/
4. Gibson-Robinson, T., Armstrong, P., Boulgakov, A., Roscoe, A.W.: FDR3 — a modern refinement checker for CSP. In: Ábrahám, E., Havelund, K. (eds.) TACAS 2014. LNCS, vol. 8413, pp. 187–201. Springer, Heidelberg (2014). doi:10.1007/978-3-642-54862-8_13
5. Kitchen, R., Amsterdam, U.V.: RoboMind. http://robomind.net/
6. Lessa, V., Forigo, F., Teixeira, A., Licks, G.P.: Programação de computadores e robótica educativa na escola: tendências evidenciadas nas produções do workshop de informática na escola. In: Anais do Workshop de Informática na Escola, vol. 21, p. 92 (2015)
7. Magee, J., Kramer, J.: Concurrency: State Models & Java Programs. Wiley, New York (1999)
8. Nogueira, S., Sampaio, A., Mota, A.: Test generation from state based use case models. Formal Aspects Comput. **26**(3), 441–490 (2014)
9. Nogueira, S., et al.: Exercises Catalog and Paper Samples, August 2016. http://bit.ly/2aYR2Q4
10. Nogueira, S., Araujo, H.L.S., Araujo, R.B.S., Iyoda, J., Sampaio, A.: Automatic generation of test cases and test purposes from natural language. In: Cornélio, M., Roscoe, B. (eds.) SBMF 2015. LNCS, vol. 9526, pp. 145–161. Springer, Heidelberg (2016). doi:10.1007/978-3-319-29473-5_9
11. Oracle: Java JSE, August 2016. http://www.oracle.com/
12. Papert, S.: A máquina das crianças. Artmed, Porto Alegre (1994)
13. Papert, S., Valente, J.A., Bitelman, B.: Logo: computadores e educação. Brasiliense (1980)
14. Roscoe, A.W.: The Theory and Practice of Concurrency. Prentice Hall PTR, Upper Saddle River (1998)

15. Roscoe, A.W.: Understanding Concurrent System. Springer, Heidelberg (2011)
16. Roscoe, A.W., Hopkins, D.: SVA, a tool for analysing shared-variable programs. Proc. AVoCS **2007**, 177–183 (2007)
17. University of Oxford: FDR3 Web Site, May 2015
18. Wing, J.M.: Computational thinking. Commun. ACM **49**(3), 33–35 (2006)

Verigraph: A System for Specification and Analysis of Graph Grammars

Andrei Costa[✉], Jonas Bezerra, Guilherme Azzi, Leonardo Rodrigues,
Thiago Rafael Becker, Ricardo Gabriel Herdt, and Rodrigo Machado

Universidade Federal do Rio Grande do Sul (UFRGS), Porto Alegre, Brazil
{acosta,jsbezerra,ggazzi,lmrodrigues,trbecker,rgherdt,rma}@inf.ufrgs.br

Abstract. Graph grammars are models that allow for a visual representation of both static and dynamic aspects of a system. There are several tools that allow the edition, simulation and analysis of graph grammars, each of them focusing on one kind of analysis technique or graph model. In this paper we present a new tool for simulation and analysis of graph grammars, called Verigraph, built with the following design principles: an implementation as direct as possible of formal concepts (to ease correctness arguments), a generic implementation of core algorithms (to allow its application for several graph models), and a reasonable running time. In this paper we present architectural aspects of Verigraph, together with a comparison with other similar tools in terms of available features.

1 Introduction

Graph grammars are a rule-based framework, suitable for modelling both static and dynamic aspects of complex systems in an intuitive yet formal manner [3,14]. They arose from the observation that graphs are well-suited for specifying the states of a system, describing the entities currently present and their current relations. In order to specify the transitions between such states, *rewriting rules*, also called *productions*, are employed. Besides having an intuitive and visual representation, graph grammars have a solid formal background, which enables several analysis techniques.

The theory of graph transformation is still an active field of research, with more expressive notions of rewriting being explored [1]. The algebraic approach to graph transformation [3] uses notions of category theory to describe graph transformation rules and rule application. One of the advantages of this approach is that these definitions and the underlying theory are applicable not only to graphs, but also to other kinds of high-level structures such as labelled graphs, typed graphs, attributed graphs [3] and even transformation rules themselves [11].

This formalism has found multiple applications. The spread of model-based software development, where transformation of visual models is an important part of the process, provides a natural application for graph grammars. Being rule-based, data-driven and non-deterministic, graph grammars are also a good match for modelling concurrent and distributed systems.

L. Ribeiro and T. Lecomte (Eds.): SBMF 2016, LNCS 10090, pp. 78–94, 2016.
DOI: 10.1007/978-3-319-49815-7_5

In order to support the use of graph grammars for modelling, however, appropriate tools are necessary. Many such tools exist (AGG [16], Groove [13], among others), nonetheless they are generally focused on a particular kind of analysis. Also, the lack of interoperability between them hinders the integration of the complementary analysis techniques that they provide. On top of that, research on variations of Graph Transformation, such as Second-Order Graph Grammars [11] and AGREE [1] may often benefit from tools that are easy to extend.

Furthermore, existent tools are generally tied to a particular high-level structure and implemented at a concrete rather than categorical level, making their extension to deal with novel approaches quite difficult. The Verigraph tool we will present in this paper was constructed to address these issues.

This paper is organized as follows: Sect. 2 presents the basic theory of algebraic graph transformations using the Double Pushout, Sect. 3 gives an overview of the architecture and some basic implementation details of Verigraph, Sect. 4 presents the analysis techniques that were implemented in the tool, Sect. 5 shows an overview of related work and tools, Sect. 6 presents the conclusions and finally the references.

2   Algebraic Graph Transformation

In this section, we review the basic definitions of algebraic graph transformation according to the double pushout approach [4]. These definitions are standard in the area, and more details can be found in [3].

A **graph** $G = (V, E, s, t)$ consists of a set V of nodes (vertices), a set E of edges, and two functions, $s, t : E \to V$, the source and target functions.

Given two graphs, $G_1 = (V_1, E_1, s_1, t_1)$ and $G_2 = (V_2, E_2, s_2, t_2)$, a **graph morphism** $f : G_1 \to G_2$ is a pair $f = (f_V, f_E)$ where $f_V : V_1 \to V_2$ and $f_E : E_1 \to E_2$ are total functions such that $f_V \circ s_1 = s_2 \circ f_E$ and $f_V \circ t_1 = t_2 \circ f_E$.

A pair (G, t) where G is a graph and $t : G \to T$ is a graph morphism is a **T-typed graph**. Nodes (resp. edges) of T are considered node types (resp. edge types). The morphism t associates to each node and edge in G (instance graph) a corresponding node type and edge type in T (type graph). Notice that any graph morphisms $f : G_1 \to G_2$ can be viewed as a G_2-typed graph G_1.

Given two T-typed graphs $t_1 : G_1 \to T$ and $t_2 : G_2 \to T$, a **T-typed graph morphism** $f : t_1 \to t_2$ is a graph morphism $f : G_1 \to G_2$ such that $t_2 \circ f = t_1$. This condition establishes that nodes/edges of G_1 can only be mapped by f to nodes/edges of the same type in G_2. The category with T-typed graphs as objects and T-typed graph morphisms as morphisms is known as **Graphs$_T$**.

A *graph production* (also referred as a *graph transformation rule* or simply *graph rule*) describes a local modification over a portion of a graph. In the DPO approach, a (T-typed) **graph production** is defined as a pair $p = (l, r)$ where $l : K \to L$ and $r : K \to R$ are (T-typed) graph monomorphisms (injective morphisms) with the same source K. The typed graphs L, K and R are known as left-hand (deleted and preserved elements), interface (preserved elements) and right-hand (preserved and created elements) graphs, respectively.

Productions can be applied over typed graphs at certain places, inducing local modifications. These modifications are called *graph transformations*, *graph rewritings* or *rule/production applications*. The definition of transformation is based on the categorical operation called *pushout* [4]. Given a production $p = L \xleftarrow{l} K \xrightarrow{r} R$ and a (T-typed) graph G, a **match** $m : L \to G$ is an arbitrary T-typed graph morphism from L to G. A **graph transformation** $G \overset{p,m}{\Longrightarrow} H$ from G to H via production p and match m exists if the diagram below can be constructed in the category $\mathbf{Graphs}_T$, where squares (1) and (2) are *pushouts*.

Intuitively, the graph D is obtained from G by removing all elements marked for deletion by p, and the graph H is obtained from D by adding elements according to p. The rewriting induced by production p and match m depends on the existence of the pushout (1), which is not guaranteed for all possible matches: there are two additional conditions (named *gluing conditions*) that must be satisfied in order to be able to construct pushout (1). The *dangling* condition ensures that the graph D does not have dangling edges, which occurs when the match deletes a node and does not delete some incident edge to this node. The *identification* condition only applies to non-injective matches and ensures that the match does not identify a deleted element with a preserved one.

$$
\begin{array}{ccccc}
L & \xleftarrow{\;l\;} & K & \xrightarrow{\;r\;} & R \\
\downarrow m & (1) & \downarrow & (2) & \downarrow m' \\
G & \xleftarrow{\;l'\;} & D & \xrightarrow{\;r'\;} & H
\end{array}
$$

Besides the structural gluing conditions, productions can also be enriched with a set of negative application conditions (NAC) [7]. These negative application conditions act as guards, disabling a rewriting $G \overset{p,m}{\Longrightarrow} H$ in the presence of

$$
\begin{array}{ccccc}
 & & N & & \\
q \nearrow & & \uparrow n & & \\
G & \xleftarrow{\;m\;} & L & \xleftarrow{\quad} K & \xrightarrow{\quad} R
\end{array}
$$

a pattern in G and m. Let $p = L \leftarrow K \to R$ be a production. A negative application condition (NAC) n is an arbitrary typed graph morphism $n : L \to N$. A match $m : L \to G$ satisfies NAC $n : L \to N$, written $G \vDash n$, if and only if $\nexists q : N \to G$ such that q is injective and $q \circ n = g$. A production with NACs is a pair $(p, \mathcal{N})$ where p is a production and $\mathcal{N}$ is a set of NACs for p. A match $m : L \to G$ satisfies $\mathcal{N}$ if and only if $m \vDash n$ for all $n \in \mathcal{N}$.

A **typed graph grammar with NACs** is a tuple $\mathcal{G} = (T, G_0, P, \pi)$ where T is a (type) graph, G_0 is a T-typed graph, P is a set of *rule names* and π is a function that associates each rule name to a T-typed graph production.

2.1   Example

We present an example of a Graph Grammar (with NACs) for transforming a binary tree into a list: The binary trees are modelled with a single node type and two possible edges types that represent, respectively, a tree *node* and the *left* and *right* relationship of nodes, which results in the following type graph:

l $\circlearrowleft$ $\bullet$ $\circlearrowright$ r

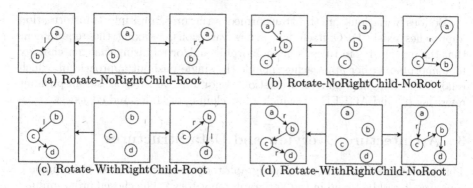

(a) Rotate-NoRightChild-Root   (b) Rotate-NoRightChild-NoRoot

(c) Rotate-WithRightChild-Root   (d) Rotate-WithRightChild-NoRoot

Fig. 1. Set of productions

The productions in Fig. 1 represent the possible cases for the right rotations on a tree, so that after applying successive transformations, the binary trees become lists[1].

As stated in their names, there are certain conditions under which these productions must not be applied, i.e. the production in 1(a) may only be applied if its node a is a root (it does not have incident edges), and the node b does not have a right child. These negative conditions are modelled as NACs, such as the one shown in Fig. 2 forbidding the application when node b has a right child. The remaining NACs are omitted due to lack of space[2].

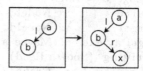

Fig. 2. NAC for the production in Fig. 1(a)

This graph grammar is used in the next sections to exemplify some concepts, therefore we leave the choice of initial graph open in this section. Note that any binary tree represented as a typed graph may be used as initial graph.

2.2 Generalization and Other Approaches

Although the definitions presented in the previous sections are restricted to graphs, they are generalizable to categories that satisfy certain properties. This has led to the theory of High-Level Rewriting (HLR), which was linked with the notion of adhesive categories [5]. Examples of structures that fit into this framework include variations on graphs (e.g. typed, attributed, labelled), Petri nets and algebraic specifications [3]. Another particularly interesting example are Second-Order Graph Grammars [11], where graph rewriting rules are themselves transformed in a rule-based manner. This is a promising approach for modelling the *evolution* of systems.

---

[1] For simplicity, lists are modelled as right degenerate trees.

[2] The complete grammar of the example is available along with the Verigraph source code.

Besides variations on the transformed structures, multiple transformation approaches exist. DPO itself has a few variations, relaxing the requirement that the morphisms in rules be monomorphic and/or requiring that matches are monomorphic. Other approaches include the single-pushout approach [6], which relaxes the dangling and identification conditions, as well as sesqui-pushout rewriting [2] and AGREE [1], which allow cloning of nodes and edges.

3   Architecture Overview and Data Structures

This section introduces how the Verigraph tool was implemented, the complete source code can be found in the Verigraph repository[3]. The chosen programming language was Haskell, aiming especially to have as little mismatch as possible between theory and code.

```
data Node a = Node
  { nodePayload :: Maybe a
  } deriving (Show, Read)
data Edge a = Edge
  { source      :: NodeId
  , target      :: NodeId
  , edgePayload :: Maybe a
  } deriving (Show, Read)
data Graph a b =  Graph
  { nodeMap :: [(NodeId, Node a)]
  , edgeMap :: [(EdgeId, Edge b)]
  } deriving (Read)
```

Fig. 3. Implementation of graphs

The simplest structure implemented in Verigraph is the Graph type, which consists of association lists for nodes and edges. Its definition may be seen in Fig. 3. Nodes and edges have numeric identifiers that are unique within a graph, and they may also carry a *payload*. The whole structure is polymorphic on the types of payloads, allowing graphs to be easily extended by adding additional information to nodes and edges, which should be used in the future to implement attributed graphs, for example. We intentionally omit the declaration and implementation of many basic functions for manipulating graphs, such as insertNode, insertEdge, removeNode, removeEdge, incidentEdges, neighbourNodes, among others.

The next fundamental building blocks for graph transformation are graph morphisms. The corresponding type GraphMorphism, whose definition may be seen in Fig. 4, closely matches the formal definition. It consists of domain and codomain graphs, as well as two relations for nodes and edges.

```
data GraphMorphism a b =
  GraphMorphism {
    domain       :: Graph a b
  , codomain     :: Graph a b
  , nodeRelation :: Relation NodeId
  , edgeRelation :: Relation EdgeId
  } deriving (Read)
```

Fig. 4. Implementation of graph morphisms

In order to efficiently represent and manipulate mappings, the polymorphic Relation type was implemented, as well as utility functions such as compose, inverse, domain, image and apply. The choice of implementing relations rather

---

[3] Link to Verigraph repository https://github.com/verites/verigraph.

```
type TypedGraph a b = GraphMorphism a b

data TypedGraphMorphism a b =
    TypedGraphMorphism {
        domain    :: TypedGraph a b
      , codomain  :: TypedGraph a b
      , mapping   :: GraphMorphism a b
    } deriving (Show, Read)
```

Fig. 5. Implementation of typed graphs and their morphisms

than just functions is due to many algorithms needing the inverse relation of a non-injective function.

Typed graphs are implemented exactly as their formal definition: a graph morphism whose codomain is the type graph. Indeed, TypedGraph is just a type synonym for GraphMorphism, as may be seen in Fig. 5. Typed graph morphisms (TGMs) also follow the formal definition: they consist of a domain and codomain typed graphs, as well as an untyped graph morphism.

```
class (Eq m) => Morphism m where
    type Obj m :: *

    compose   :: m -> m -> m
    domain    :: m -> Obj m
    codomain  :: m -> Obj m
    id        :: Obj m -> m

    monomorphism :: m -> Bool
    epimorphism  :: m -> Bool
    isomorphism  :: m -> Bool
```

Fig. 6. Type class for morphisms

We have presented the implementation of morphisms of two different categories, **Graphs** (graphs as objects and their morphisms as arrows) and **Graphs**$_T$ (introduced in the Sect. 2). Therefore, a whole class of operations relative to morphisms is relevant for both data types. In order to uniformly deal with both

```
class (Morphism m) => AdhesiveHLR m where
    -- Assumes one of the morphisms is mono
    pushout :: m -> m -> (m, m)

    -- Tests if a pushout complement exists
    hasPushoutComplement :: m -> m -> Bool

    -- Assumes a pushout complement exists
    pushoutComplement :: m -> m -> (m, m)

    -- Assumes both morphisms are mono
    injectivePullback :: m -> m -> (m, m)
```

Fig. 7. AdhesiveHLR class

morphism types, the type class `Morphism` was defined. It may be seen in Fig. 6. Since every morphism type has an associated type for representing objects of that category, standard Haskell would not suffice to express these ideas. We therefore employed the GHC extension allowing type families, which are essentially functions at the type level [15].

Besides the basic operations for morphisms of general categories, many of the algorithms implemented in Verigraph depend on operations available in Adhesive High-Level Replacement (HLR) categories [5], such as pushouts and pullbacks. Morphisms of such categories must therefore implement the operations of the `AdhesiveHLR` type class, which may be seen in Fig. 7. These type classes decouple the implementation of DPO rewriting from the implementation of the category in which it occurs.

```
data Production m =
  Production
  { left  :: m
  , right :: m
  , nacs  :: [m]
  }
```

Fig. 8. Data production

Having an abstract notion of morphism, the implementation of *productions* may be polymorphic on the morphism type, as may be seen in Fig. 8. The operations related to productions, such as checking the applicability of a match (existence of gluing condition and satisfiability of NACs) and doing the actual transformation, are implemented in terms of the `AdhesiveHLR` class.

Also, two different notions for checking the NAC satisfiability were implemented: the classical one (as presented earlier in this paper) and the partial injective version as defined in [9] and implemented in AGG.

The last type is `DPO`. This abstract class has two functions: `inverse` to invert a production, and `shiftNac` to shift a set of NACs over a production.

Note that the `Graph`, `GraphMorphism`, `TypedGraph` and `Production` types allow malformed instances (e.g. a `Graph` with an edge that references an undefined node as source or target). Therefore, a *well-formedness* condition must be implemented, which was done by defining the type class `Valid`, instantiated for those types, providing a single predicate `valid` for its verification. In order to reduce the runtime overhead of such checks, the algorithms implemented in Verigraph are designed to construct and preserve well-formedness. Thus, it must only be checked when values are obtained from external sources.

The implementation explained in this section suffices for performing graph transformations. Although this functionality is not new, we aimed to create an architecture were the transformation logic is cleanly separated from the category in which it is performed. This allows us to easily adapt Verigraph for transformation on other Adhesive HLR categories, which is done in Sect. 4.5.

4 Implemented Analysis Techniques

A few analysis techniques are implemented in Verigraph. The focus is on static analysis, such as Critical Pair/Sequence Analysis and the calculation of Concurrent Rules. A proof-of-concept implementation of model checking is also included. Given that Verigraph was extended to support second-order graph grammars, conflict analysis specific to this model was also implemented.

4.1 Critical Pair Analysis

A common static analysis technique is checking whether rewriting rules are in conflict: intuitively, when the application of one disables the application of the other. More formally, two productions are in conflict if there is a valid match for each of the productions into the same graph, but after transforming with one of those matches, the other match is invalidated. Note that it is possible for a pair of rules to have multiple conflicts. The complete definitions and main results for conflicts are found in [9,10].

Since there may be an infinite amount of conflicts between any two productions, generating all possible conflicts is not feasible. The notion of critical pairs, however, allows the detection of canonical forms for every possible conflict [10], and the number of critical pairs is guaranteed to be finite when dealing with finite graphs. The implemented approach for finding all critical pairs consists of generating all possible overlappings between two graphs, then checking if such pairs configure a conflict. Such overlappings are specified categorically as jointly epimorphic pairs of morphisms [10].

When checking if two transformations are in conflict, we consider asymmetry between the pairs of productions. Because of this, there are three possible causes for a conflict: (1) one transformation deletes an element used by the other (*delete-use*); (2) one transformation enables some NAC of the other (*produce-forbid*); (3) one transformation invalidates the gluing conditions for the other (*produce-dangling*). The first two kinds of conflict are well known in the literature, and we implement their calculation based on the traditional algorithms for such. The third kind appears only when considering asymmetric conflicts, since it always occurs together with a *delete-use* conflict in the reverse direction. We need to account for *produce-dangling* conflicts since we count critical pairs considering direction (i.e. the number of critical pairs between p_1 and p_2 may differ from the number of critical pairs between p_2 and p_1 in our implementation). For this reason we propose next a characterization for this conflict and show the respective algorithm to calculate it.

Produce-Dangling Conflict Characterization. Let $p_1 = (l_1, r_1, [n_1])$ and $p_2 = (l_2, r_2, [n_2])$ be productions, as shown in the diagrams below. Note that p_1 is presented from right to left. The starting point is the object G^4, obtained by the combination of the L_1 and L_2. The existence of a morphism $h_{21} : L_2 \rightarrow D_1$ is required (in the case of non existence it is a delete-use conflict), which means that after deleting the elements of p_1, the production p_2 still is applicable. Through h_{21} we come (by composition) to the m_2' morphism, that is the object after the creation step of p_1. Even if m_2' exists, it may not be an applicable match for p_2, and this case is called produce-dangling. The following two conditions characterize a (produce-dangling) conflict between $G \xrightarrow{p_1, m_1} P_1$ and $G \xrightarrow{p_2, m_2} P_2$.

---

[4] The $\frown$ indicates that m_1 and m_2 are jointly surjective, i.e. $m_1(L_1) \cup m_2(L_2) = G$.

Definition 1 (Produce-Dangling). *Two conditions determine the existence of the Produce-Dangling:*
(i) There exists $h_{21} : L_2 \to D_1 : d_1 \circ h_{21} = m_2$, and $m'_2 : L_2 \to P_1 : h_{21} \circ e_1 = m'_2$.

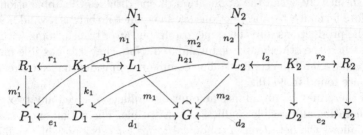

(ii)Morphism m'_2 is a match where all NACs are satisfied ($\nexists q : N_2 \to P_1$, with q injective), but other application conditions do not hold: let (1) the initial pushout of m'_2, there is no $b^*_2 : B_2 \to K_2 : l_2 \circ b^*_2 = b_2$, and (m_1, m_2) jointly surjective.

The simplest case of this conflict in DPO is when p_1 deletes a particular node, and p_2 creates an incident edge on the same node. After the application of p_2, p_1 is unable to delete the node. An example is shown in Fig. 9, where p_1 is the right and p_2 the left productions. In DPO, this conflict follows from the requirement that deleted nodes have no incident edges outside the match.

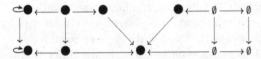

The implementation of these algorithms was done entirely in terms of categorical operations, and is therefore polymorphic on the types of objects and mor-

Fig. 9. Example of produce-dangling conflict   phisms, as long as they are instances of the appropriate type classes. The proximity of implementation and theory may be seen in Fig. 10, which shows a function that checks if a particular overlapping induces delete-use or produce-dangling conflicts. Variables are named consistently with the previously presented diagrams.

The matrix M in Fig. 11(a) summarizes the results of Critical Pair Analysis for the graph grammar presented in Fig. 1. This matrix has dimensions $N \times N$, where N is the number of rules of the specification, which we name $R_1, \ldots, R_N$. Each entry $M_{i,j}$ shows the number of potential conflicts between rules R_i and R_j for all pairs of productions in the given graph grammar. Notice that this matrix is not symmetric because we consider the direction of the conflicts between rules. Also notice that there is at least one critical pair between almost all pairs of rules (R_i, R_j) in this particular example. When analysing the individual conflicts, however, we observe that some of the conflicts occur only when a node has two right children, which does not correspond to a valid binary tree. This is due the static aspect of this analysis, since it does not consider the initial conditions.

```
deleteUseDangling :: DPO m =>
  Production m -> Production m -> (m, m) -> Maybe ConflictType
deleteUseDangling p1 p2 (m1,m2) =
  case (null h21, dang) of
    (True, _)      -> Just DeleteUse
    (False, True)  -> Just ProduceDangling
    _              -> Nothing
  where
    l1 = left p1
    r1 = right p1
    (k1,d1) = pushoutComplement m1 l1
    h21Candidates = findMorphisms (domain m2) (domain d1)
    h21 = filter (\x -> m2 == compose x d1) h21Candidates
    (_,e1) = pushout k1 r1
    m2' = compose (head h21) e1 —if h21 exists, it is unique
    dang = (not (satsGluing p2 m2')) && (satsNacs p2 m2')
```

Fig. 10. Delete-use and produce-dangling verification algorithms

\	R1	R2	R3	R4
R1	3	1	1	0
R2	5	10	7	5
R3	4	5	10	5
R4	5	13	17	42

(a) Critical Pairs Analysis

\	R1	R2	R3	R4
R1	1	6	6	9
R2	3	12	13	32
R3	4	13	13	28
R4	5	28	24	74

(b) Critical Sequences Analysis

R1: Rotate-NoRightChild-Root; R2: Rotate-NoRightChild-NoRoot;
R3: Rotate-WithRightChild-Root; R4: Rotate-WithRightChild-NoRoot

Fig. 11. Results of critical pair analysis and critical sequence analysis

4.2 Critical Sequence Analysis

Dependency analysis is analogous to conflict analysis, considering sequential rather than parallel transformations. Given two productions t_1 and t_2 (applied in this order), the possible dependencies are divided in two kinds, which intuitively are: *triggered*, where t_2 is not applicable before t_1 is applied; and *irreversible*, where after the sequential application of t_1 and t_2, the transformation t_1 can not be undone [9].

Dependencies are also tied to a notion of critical sequence, analogous to critical pairs, which captures all sources of dependencies in a finite number of canonical forms. The definition and characterization of critical sequences is very similar to that of critical pairs [10], enabling the same implementation strategy. In fact, the diagrams for dependencies are mostly the same as those for conflicts, except that the overlappings are created between the left-side of one production and the right-side of the other.

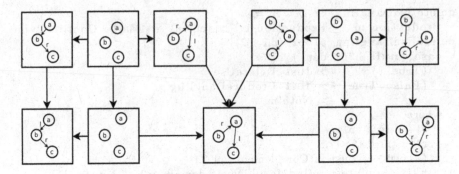

Fig. 12. Example of dependent transformations

Figure 11(b) shows the results of Critical Sequence Analysis for the graph grammar presented in Fig. 1. One such dependency is presented in Fig. 12, involving the productions Rotate-WithRightChild-Root and Rotate-NoRightChild-NoRoot, respectively. This dependency indicates a case when the first production enables the second (produce-use type).

4.3   Calculation of Concurrent Rules

Another common technique for static analysis may be used when the behaviour of individual rewriting rules is less important than the overall effect of applying multiple rules. In order to capture this notion, one may calculate a single rule (named concurrent rule) which summarizes the combined effect of a complete derivation whose individual transformations are induced by the ordered list of productions (rule sequence) $p_0, \ldots, p_{n-1}, p_n$ [3,9]. The construction of such rules is done by recursively combining pairs of subsequent rules, where the pairwise combination is defined as follows:

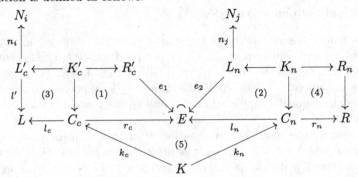

For $n = 0$: The *concurrent rule* p_c for the single rule p_0 is p_0 itself. If p_0 has a set of NACs it will be preserved.

For $n \geqslant 1$: A concurrent rule $p_c = p'_c *_E p_n$ with NACs for the rule sequence $p_0, \ldots, p_{n-1}, p_n$ is defined as $p_c = (l_c \circ k_c : K \to L, r_n \circ k_n : K \to R)$ where:

- $p'_c : L'_c \leftarrow K'_c \rightarrow R'_c$ is a concurrent rule for the sequence $p_0, \ldots, p_{n-1}$
- E is an overlapping of R'_c and L_n with (e'_c, e_n) jointly surjective
- (1)-(3) and (2)-(4) are valid double-pushout rewritings
- (5) is a pullback
- All the NACs N_i of the production p'_c are shifted over the morphism l', resulting in a set of NACs $n'_i : L \rightarrow N'_i$
- All the NACs N_j of the production p_n are shifted over the morphism e_2 and then over the span $q'_c = l_c : C_c \rightarrow L, r_c : C_c \rightarrow E$, resulting in a set of NACs $n'_j : L \rightarrow N'^5_j$

As an example, Fig. 13 shows one of the concurrent rules generated from the rule sequence [Rotate-WithRightChild-Root,Rotate-NoRightChild-NoRoot]. This particular concurrent rule represents the overall effect of the derivation shown in Fig. 12.

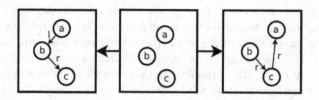

Fig. 13. Example of concurrent rule

Presently, AGG is the main tool for calculating the concurrent rules of a Graph Grammar. It does not, however, produce all possible concurrent rules for a particular rule sequence, considering only the cases where dependencies exist between all subsequent transformations. Verigraph does calculate all possible concurrent rules. Nonetheless, this is an expensive operation, since there exists a concurrent rule for each different overlapping between a R'_c and a L_n in each step of the induction, which may result in a combinatorial explosion. Also, the shifting of NACs adds considerably to this cost. We also implement the calculation based on dependencies, as it is done in AGG.

The number of possible overlappings may also be significantly reduced when non-injective matches are forbidden. Using the least disjoint overlappings for each step may also provide enough information for analysis, while greatly reducing the number of concurrent rules. Both options are already available in Verigraph.

4.4 State Space Exploration and Model Checking

Although static analysis helps understanding the interactions between productions, dynamic analysis is often useful as a complementary technique. Manual

---

[5] Both the algorithms for shifting NACs over a morphism and over a span are omitted here due to lack of space, but can be found in [9].

exploration of the state space induced by an initial graph and by a set of transformation rules helps build an intuitive understanding of the modelled system. Another important technique is model checking, which may provide guarantees that are not ensured by static analysis, since it only considers *potential* interactions.

A practical tool for graph transformation should, therefore, provide both static and dynamic analysis techniques. Even though the current focus of Verigraph is on static analysis, its architecture should also be suitable for the implementation of dynamic analysis. In order to ensure this, a preliminary implementation of these techniques is provided in Verigraph.

The core of dynamic analysis techniques is the generation of a state space from an initial graph and a set of productions. Therefore, a depth-limited search on the state space was implemented in Verigraph, collapsing isomorphic graphs as a single state. Both the transition system and the individual states are exported as .dot files, allowing their visualization. Since this implementation is only intended as a proof of concept, the efforts to optimize this exploration, such as improving the search for isomorphic graphs, are left for future work.

Having the exploration of the state space, Verigraph also implements model checking of CTL expressions. The atomic predicates are defined is a similar approach to GROOVE [13]: productions that don't change the instance graph are considered predicates, and such predicates hold in a graph if and only if the production is applicable. The model checking itself is completely decoupled from the generation of the state space, using the algorithm described in [8].

An example application is checking that the grammar presented in Fig. 1 eventually linearises the tree (AF *noLeftChildren*) and terminates if and only if that is the case (AG($\neg$EX true $\leftrightarrow$ *noLeftChildren*)). Given the little effort invested in optimizing this analysis, running times of the tool are prohibitively large. Checking the aforementioned properties, with a full binary tree of depth three as starting graph, took over 3 min (as shown in Table 3) in an Intel i5-3330 processor, running at 3 GHz with 16GiB of RAM.

4.5   Inter-Level Conflict Analysis

Second-Order Graph Grammars (SOGG) were proposed and studied in [11,12]. This new kind of transformation can be seen as modelling the evolution of typed graph grammars. Due to the fact that SOGG form an adhesive HLR category, the analysis proposed in the sections above are also valid for this type. Besides usual analysis techniques, two kinds of Inter-Level Conflicts were proposed in [12] to analyse the interaction between first- and second-order rules. Particularly, two new analysis come from the Inter-Level layer. The first is named *critical pair evolution*, it defines how match overlaps in the original system behave after an evolution (application of second-order production). The second is named *second-order critical pairs analysis*, it captures all situations where a transformation by a second-order production inserts a conflict in the system.

Formal definitions and implementation will be omitted due to lack of space, but they can be found in [11] and in the Verigraph repository, respectively. Both analysis techniques are implemented, however the process of generating all situations that are relevant to analyse requires a large computational effort, which causes a combinatorial explosion. However, to our knowledge, no implementation of SOGG and their analysis has been reported in the literature.

5   Related Work

The known graph transformation tools published so far differ widely on their features, due mainly to the different fields of research that they come from. We selected two tools to compare with Verigraph based on the transformation system and analysis they perform. These tools employ approaches related to ours as well as some reconcilable features with our tool.

A more detailed comparison between the tools is shown in Table 1.

5.1   AGG

The Attributed Graph Grammar System (AGG) [16] is a graph transformation tool that supports the development of typed graph grammars. The rewriting system is based on the SPO approach, but the user can configure the application to run a simulated version of the DPO approach. AGG supports attributed graphs, which means that elements of a graph can be enriched with algebraic types, provided mainly by the Java types. This tool is focused on static analysis having some features mentioned in this paper, such as critical pair/sequence analysis and concurrent rules, but also several others like termination and consistency checking.

5.2   GROOVE

The Graphs for Object-Oriented Verification (GROOVE) Tool Set [13] aims for modelling graph grammars, its rewriting engine also implements the SPO approach. The focus of this tool is generation and exploration of state space, implementing many exploration strategies as well as an efficient search for isomorphic states. Graphs in GROOVE are untyped, however the tool does support labelling to simulate types in complex systems.

5.3   Preliminary Performance Evaluation

Besides the comparison of features, we performed basic performance evaluations. In Verigraph, the execution time was not the central point of the implementation. However, many of the analysis performed are intractable in theory, they are only made possible due to the use of some restrictions, such as graph typing. Therefore, the algorithms implemented need to be at least comparable to the existing tools.

We compared the execution time of Critical Pairs/Sequences Analysis between AGG and Verigraph. Two graph grammars were used: *treeToList*

Table 1. Comparison between tools

Feature	AGG	GROOVE	Verigraph
Rewriting	SPO/DPO simulation	SPO	DPO
NAC strategy	Partial injective	Arbitrary injectivity	Partial or total injective
Transformation objects	Typed attributed graphs	Typed attributed graphs	Typed graphs or typed graph rules
Critical pair analysis	Yes	No	Yes
Model-checking	No	Yes	Work in progress
GUI	Yes	Yes	No: import from and export to AGG
Attributes	Yes	Yes	No
Second order	No	No	Yes
Language	Java	Java	Haskell

defined in the Fig. 1), and *mutex*, a grammar with 16 productions that was used as a benchmark in [17]. The same entry files were used for testing both tools[6].

Table 2 shows the results of the comparison. The timed execution of Verigraph involved reading the grammar from a file, computing the analysis and saving the conflict matrix to a file. The execution time of AGG, on the other hand, involves the analysis of an already loaded grammar and displaying the computed matrix on the GUI. The results were obtained averaging the running time of ten executions in an Intel i5-3330 processor, running at 3 GHz with 16 GiB of RAM.

Table 2. Critical pairs and sequences analysis performance

Tool	treeToList		mutex	
	Critical Pairs Time (s)	Critical Sequences Time (s)	Critical Pairs Time (s)	Critical Sequences Time (s)
AGG	1.704	6.156	10.874	47.717
Verigraph	0.822	3.489	1.036	3.224

There are two major issues that can affect the fairness of these evaluations. First, the execution process in the tools is not equal: while in Verigraph the grammar is read, processed and written in a file, in AGG the GUI already has the grammar loaded and only has to show a matrix of conflicts after they are processed. Second, AGG supports attributed graphs, which may lead to an overhead in the critical pair analysis algorithm due to the handling of attributes.

---

[6] `treeToList.ggx` and `mutex.ggx` are available on Verigraph Repository.

Table 3. Model checking performance

Initial graph	Number of states	Time (s)	
		GROOVE	Verigraph
Complete binary tree of depth 3	370	1.217	199.957

Since Verigraph does not support attributed graphs, its algorithm is not affected by the same overhead.

6   Conclusions

In this paper, we have introduced Verigraph, a new tool for simulating and verifying graph grammars. The Verigraph tool is implemented in the purely functional programming language Haskell and it currently implements important techniques such as critical pair analysis, construction of concurrent rules from rule sequences, construction of state space from graph grammar and (currently not optimized) model checking using CTL. Important algorithms are implemented in a generic style, inspired by the framework of adhesive HLR systems. Most of the constructions are implemented in a style which is close to the formal definitions, which makes it easier to inspect for correctness. Although formal proofs of correctness are not yet provided, we claim this style of code (purely functional) favours the effort of proving correctness, and we intend to do so for our implementation in the future.

When compared to established tools such as AGG and GROOVE, Verigraph is still lacking in some aspects. Verigraph currently does not have a GUI: it has a Command Line Interface (CLI) and utilizes the .ggx file format, also used by AGG, in order to import and export specifications and to visualize the result of our analysis. Another limitation is that our graph model does not support attributes. To solve these issues is current and future work. On the other hand, as far as we know, Verigraph is the only tool that integrates both static and dynamic analysis and the only one that has support for second-order specifications. Another positive aspect is that our initial evaluation shows that it is competitive with current tools in terms of performance, at least in the realm of static analyses for non-attributed graph grammars.

Acknowledgements. The authors would like to acknowledge the brazilian agencies CNPq, CAPES and FAPERGS for their support in the form of financial aid (VeriTes project/CNPq) and scholarships (CAPES, CNPq and FAPERGS).

References

1. Corradini, A., Duval, D., Echahed, R., Prost, F., Ribeiro, L.: AGREE – algebraic graph rewriting with controlled embedding. In: Parisi-Presicce, F., Westfechtel, B. (eds.) ICGT 2015. LNCS, vol. 9151, pp. 35–51. Springer, Heidelberg (2015). doi:10.1007/978-3-319-21145-9_3

2. Corradini, A., Heindel, T., Hermann, F., König, B.: Sesqui-pushout rewriting. In: Corradini, A., Ehrig, H., Montanari, U., Ribeiro, L., Rozenberg, G. (eds.) ICGT 2006. LNCS, vol. 4178, pp. 30–45. Springer, Heidelberg (2006). doi:10.1007/11841883_4
3. Ehrig, H., Ehrig, K., Prange, U., Taentzer, G.: Fundamentals of Algebraic Graph Transformation. Monographs in Theoretical Computer Science. An EATCS Series. Springer, New York (2006)
4. Ehrig, H., Pfender, M., Schneider, H.J.: Graph-grammars: an algebraic approach. In: IEEE Conference Record of 14th Annual Symposium on Switching and Automata Theory, SWAT '08, pp. 167–180, October 1973
5. Ehrig, H., Habel, A., Padberg, J., Prange, U.: Adhesive high-level replacement categories and systems. In: Ehrig, H., Engels, G., Parisi-Presicce, F., Rozenberg, G. (eds.) ICGT 2004. LNCS, vol. 3256, pp. 144–160. Springer, Heidelberg (2004). doi:10.1007/978-3-540-30203-2_12
6. Ehrig, H., Heckel, R., Korff, M., Löwe, M., Ribeiro, L., Wagner, A., Corradini, A.: Algebraic approaches to graph transformation: part ii: single pushout approach and comparison with double pushout approach. In: Handbook of Graph Grammars, pp. 247–312 (1997)
7. Habel, A., Heckel, R., Taentzer, G.: Graph grammars with negative application conditions. Fundamenta Informaticae 26(3,4), 287–313 (1996)
8. Huth, M.R.A., Ryan, M.: Logic in Computer Science: Modelling and Reasoning about Systems. Cambridge University Press, New York (2000)
9. Lambers, L.: Certifying rule-based models using graph transformation. Ph.D. thesis, Berlin Institute of Technology (2009)
10. Lambers, L., Ehrig, H., Orejas, F.: Conflict detection for graph transformation with negative application conditions. In: Corradini, A., Ehrig, H., Montanari, U., Ribeiro, L., Rozenberg, G. (eds.) ICGT 2006. LNCS, vol. 4178, pp. 61–76. Springer, Heidelberg (2006). doi:10.1007/11841883_6
11. Machado, R.: Higher-order graph rewriting systems. Ph.D. thesis, Instituto de Informática - Universidade Federal do Rio Grande do Sul (2012)
12. Machado, R., Ribeiro, L., Heckel, R.: Rule-based transformation of graph rewriting rules: towards higher-order graph grammars. Theoret. Comput. Sci. 594, 1–23 (2015)
13. Rensink, A.: The GROOVE simulator: a tool for state space generation. In: Pfaltz, J.L., Nagl, M., Böhlen, B. (eds.) AGTIVE 2003. LNCS, vol. 3062, pp. 479–485. Springer, Heidelberg (2004). doi:10.1007/978-3-540-25959-6_40
14. Rozenberg, G. (ed.): Handbook of Graph Grammars and Computing by Graph Transformation: Volume I. Foundations. World Scientific Publishing Co., Inc., River Edge (1997)
15. Schrijvers, T., Jones, S.P., Chakravarty, M., Sulzmann, M.: Type checking with open type functions. In: Proceedings of the 13th ACM SIGPLAN International Conference on Functional Programming, ICFP 2008, pp. 51–62. ACM, New York (2008)
16. Taentzer, G.: AGG: a tool environment for algebraic graph transformation. In: Nagl, M., Schürr, A., Münch, M. (eds.) AGTIVE 1999. LNCS, vol. 1779, pp. 481–488. Springer, Heidelberg (2000). doi:10.1007/3-540-45104-8_41
17. Varro, G., Schurr, A., Varro, D.: Benchmarking for graph transformation. In: 2005 IEEE Symposium on Visual Languages and Human-Centric Computing (VL/HCC'05), pp. 79–88. IEEE (2005)

Modeling and Logic

Modelling 'Operation-Calls' in Event-B with Shared-Event Composition

Andrew Edmunds and Marina Waldén[✉]

Faculty of Science and Engineering,
Åbo Akademi University, Turku, Finland
marina.walden@abo.fi

Abstract. Efficient reuse is a goal of many software engineering strategies and is useful in the safety-critical domain where formal development is required. Event-B can be used to develop safety-critical systems, but could be improved by a component-based reuse strategy. In previous work, we outlined a component-based reuse methodology for Event-B. The methodology provides a means for bottom-up scalability, and can also be used with the existing top-down approach. We developed a process for creating library components, composing them, and for specifying new properties (involving the composed elements). We introduced Event-B component interfaces and propose to use a diagrammatic representation of component instances. However, in that approach, the communication between components is modelled in an abstract manner. In this paper, we describe a more concrete specification approach which includes interfaces with 'callable' *interface events*. These events model operations, and additional syntactic constructs model their invocation.

Keywords: Event-B · Formal modelling · Interface events · Operation calls

1 Introduction

Formal methods can play a useful role in the development of safety-critical systems. Having flexibility in formal approaches will make them more useful in the development process. We are seeking to improve the flexibility and adaptability of Event-B [4] developments by enhancing the methodology and improving the supporting tools [17]. In recent work, we proposed a method of creating a library of components, with interfaces, and a way to assemble them based on shared-event composition [13]. We believe that this approach provides an intuitive abstraction for the encapsulation that is often seen in object-oriented software components. The ideas are facilitated by extending the existing iUML-B class-diagram tool [21,25], and by extending the composition work of [22–24]. iUML-B is a graphical modelling approach, influenced by UML [18], for specifying state-machines and class diagrams. The diagrammatic representations are embedded in a machine and contribute to its content by making use of automatic

© Springer International Publishing AG 2016
L. Ribeiro and T. Lecomte (Eds.): SBMF 2016, LNCS 10090, pp. 97–111, 2016.
DOI: 10.1007/978-3-319-49815-7_6

translators to generate Event-B from the diagrams. State-machine diagrams are used to impose an ordering on the occurrence of a machine's events. They can be animated to improve understanding of a model's behaviour. Class diagrams are used to define data entities and their relationships. The system specification is undertaken at a relatively high level of abstraction, and it uses a notion of event synchronization inspired by the CSP semantics of synchronization [16]. To facilitate component composition, we proposed new diagrammatic representations, enabling us to specify which machines and components are combined, and the (communication) relationships between them.

In order to provide a more concrete description of the interaction between components, we propose to use 'callable' *interface events* which are similar in principle to the callable operations of the modularisation approach [2]. The specification of the *interface events* are at a sufficiently low level of abstraction to allow them to be related, in a clear way, to the normal programming concept of operations and of operation calls.

In the remainder of the paper we describe the *interface events* which model programming operations, and we describe *interface event* calls which model synchronous operation calls. We also show how some types of *interface event* calls can be nested in the terms of Event-B expressions. In Sect. 2 we provide a brief introduction to Event-B, and in Sect. 3 there is an overview of the recent Event-B components work. In Sect. 4 we introduce, using a simple example, the notion of procedure-style *interface events*. In Sect. 5 we expand on this to describe nested event calls, using function-style *interface events* that can be used as terms in expressions. In Sect. 6 we discuss related work, and in Sect. 7 we conclude. This work is being undertaken as part of the ADVICeS project[1] [26].

2   Event-B

Event-B is a specification language and methodology [1,4] with tool support provided by the Rodin tool [17]. Event-B has received interest from industry, for the development of railway, automotive, and other safety-critical systems [20]. In Event-B, the system, and its properties, are specified using set-theory and predicate logic. It uses proof and refinement [19] to show that the properties hold as the development proceeds. Refinement iterations add detail to the development. Event-B tools are designed to reduce the amount of interactive proof required during specification and refinement steps [15]. Proof obligations in the form of sequents are automatically generated by the Rodin tool. The automatic prover can discharge many of the P.O.s, and the remainder can be tackled using the interactive prover. The basic Event-B elements are *contexts*, *machines* and *composed-machines*. Contexts define the static parts of the system using sets, constants and axioms which we denote by s, c, and a. Machines describe the dynamic parts of a system using variables and events: v and e, and use invariant predicates I to describe the properties that should hold. We specify an event in the following way,

---
[1] The ADVICeS Project, funded by Academy of Finland, grant No. 266373.

$$e \triangleq \mathbf{ANY} \ p \ \mathbf{WHERE} \ G(p, s, c, v) \ \mathbf{THEN} \ A(p, s, c, v) \ \mathbf{END},$$

where e has parameter names p; a guarding predicate G; and actions A. State updates (described in the action) can take place only when the guard is true. Guards and actions can refer to the parameters, sets, constants and variables of the machine and seen contexts. For events to occur, the environment non-deterministically chooses an event from the set of enabled events. In the simpler case, where there are no parameters, we write

$$\mathbf{WHEN} \ G(s, c, v) \ \mathbf{THEN} \dots \mathbf{END}$$

If there is no guard clause either, we write,

$$\mathbf{BEGIN} \ A(s, c, v) \ \mathbf{END}$$

As development proceeds, the models can become very detailed. Therefore, complex systems can be broken down into more tractable sub-units using shared-event [23,24] or shared-variable [5] decomposition. With the shared-event composition style [22], variables are distributed between (and encapsulated by) machines. Communication between components is modelled by event synchronization which is inspired by CSP [16]. Synchronizing events are combined in the *combined events* clause of a composed machine. With shared variable composition/decomposition, the events are distributed between machines. Updates to the shared variables models communication between components since variables in one machine can be read and updated by another machine.

3 An Overview of Event-B Components

In our previous work [13], we describe how events and parameters of Event-B components are displayed to other machines and components which allows them to synchronize. We propose a *composed machine diagram*, see Fig. 1, based on [24]. Here, the composed machine CM is represented by the annotated box. The diagram describes the relationships between the included machine(s) M which are under development and the included machines L which are library components that have been developed for reuse. A class-diagram, such as the FIFO component example at the lower left of Fig. 1, can be annotated with interface information. The public part of the *interface machine* is identified using the annotation i, showing which events of a component are allowed to synchronize with other, external, events. The unmarked events are assumed to be hidden and are, therefore, not able to synchronize with other events. Synchronized events have communicating parameters that model the communication between modules. It is an abstraction of what happens during an operation call and is exactly the technique used in [12]. On the right-hand side of the figure, we can see *synch*1, which is a combined event, and an example of synchronization between two machines. This aspect of the diagram captures the fact that there is communication occurring across the component boundaries, but disregards information about the number of component instances.

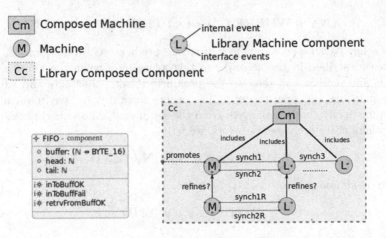

Fig. 1. Composition of library components [13]

In order to describe the component instances, and the communication across their boundaries, we introduce a new component instance diagram. A user will connect components to their callers by linking component instances with connectors as seen in an example from our previous work [13], and reproduced in Fig. 2. Solid, arrowed lines represent instance containment. Dashed lines represent communication across interfaces. Each dashed line can be associated with two, or more, synchronizing events. Using this information, stubs (a programming term for place-holders) for modelling communication can be generated in the caller, if required. We can add input (output) parameters that match output (input) parameters in the component and create typing guards to match. Of course, we can strengthen the guard of any output parameter since the pre-condition-style PO's will still hold. This approach will also work for communication between two pre-existing library components (as indicated in the diagram in Fig. 1).

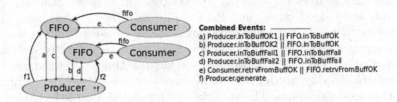

Fig. 2. A component instance diagram [13]

In the modularisation approach [2], module interfaces are specified using an entirely different concept. Firstly, an interface module is defined using a pre- and post-condition syntax. Then a machine that 'implements' the interface is defined which must refine the interface. The approach allows an interface operation to be called and updates to take place. Refinement rules require the generation of proof obligations to show that an interface is correctly implemented. In our approach, since an *interface machine* is just a machine (but with associated interface annotations) any valid refinement of the machine is a valid refinement of the interface. However, we do produce additional proof obligations to show that the event's communicating parameters are within certain constraints; i.e., the set of values of any output parameter should be compatible with the set of values of the corresponding input parameter. A more detailed comparison of the two approaches is provided in Sect. 6.1.

4   Procedure-Style Interface Events

In order to clarify the use of *interface event* calls in guards and actions, we refer to the constraints imposed by Ada [7] on function calls and procedure calls. Ada distinguishes between the two, based on the fact that functions can be used in expressions, whereas procedures cannot. Ada functions are side effect free and return a single value which is substituted for the call on its return. Side effects are updates that persist after the return of a call. Procedures do allow side effects and can return multiple values, therefore, they cannot be used in expressions.

We choose to apply constraints on function- and procedure-style *interface events* in the same way that Ada does. We relate Ada function calls to function-style *interface events* and Ada procedure calls to procedure-style *interface events*. We consider these to be useful abstractions of safe implementations. In addition to this, we consider that it will be useful to add an annotation to describe an *interface event* as either a function-style *interface event* or procedure-style *interface event*. This will help a developer determine how suitable a component is for use in a particular situation.

In the remainder of the section, we describe the new syntax for procedural-style *interface events* and for procedure-style calls. In Sect. 5 we describe function-style *interface events*.

4.1   Procedural Interface Events

We begin by showing the public part of an *interface event*. This simply describes the event name and input and output parameters, in the style of a Java interface [14]. It has no behavioural information associated with it and takes the following form (with syntactic sugared parameters),

$$\textbf{Procedural Interface Event } evt(ip? \cup op!) \triangleq \tag{1}$$
$$\textbf{WHEN } G(ip, op) \textbf{ END}$$

Here, evt is the event name, $ip?$ is the set of input parameters, $op!$ is the set of output parameters, and $ip? \cup op!$ is an ordered set since we will need to match formal parameter names with actual parameter values. G consists only of typing predicates. The annotations "?" and "!", for input and output sets, are not part of the name. They simply inform us about the direction of data flow into, and out of, events. Therefore, they do not appear in guard and action clauses. The annotation might alternatively be written using the Ada parameter mode style '$p : in$' for input, and '$p : out$' for output. We do not have an equivalent of the Ada mode *inout*, which allows a parameter to be used as both input and output parameters. Events may legitimately have parameters without input or output specifiers, these are the local variables of an event, but we ignore them for the purposes of the discussion that follows.

Below, we show a concrete example of Eq. 1, it is an *interface event* called *i_callee* that we will use as a running example.

Procedural Interface Event $i\_callee(fp1?,\ ret!) \triangleq$
    WHEN $fp1 \in \mathbb{N} \wedge ret \in \mathbb{N}$
    END

This interface has two parameters; $fp1?$ is an input parameter, and $ret!$ is an output parameter. Both are typed as natural numbers. The underlying Event-B representation of the interface is shown below,

$$
\begin{aligned}
&i\_callee \triangleq \\
&\quad \textbf{ANY } fp1?\ ret! \\
&\quad \textbf{WHERE } fp1 \in \mathbb{N} \wedge ret \in \mathbb{N} \\
&\quad \textbf{END}
\end{aligned}
\tag{2}
$$

Having defined an interface, we can add a behavioural description, either in the same machine or in a refinement (depending on our adopted strategy). We specify the return behaviour of the component, by adding the guard in a refinement. We also show the increment of a machine variable *count*, in the action clause, as an illustration of a side effect.

$callee \triangleq$
    REFINES i_callee
    ANY $fp1?\ ret!$
    WHERE $fp1 \in \mathbb{N} \wedge ret \in \mathbb{N} \wedge ret \in 10 .. (20 + fp1)$
    THEN $count := count + 1$
    END

The event has a non-deterministic definition of a return value. The output parameter $ret!$ should satisfy the guard $ret \in 10 .. (20 + fp1)$. Notice that we also retain the weaker typing guard (although it may appear to be redundant) since we may wish to apply separate annotations to typing guards, to assist with later processing. This would be the case when using the models to generate code, as in [12] for instance.

A procedure-style *interface event* call can be used anywhere that an assignment expression can appear (that is, an expression involving the := operator).

Thus, calls can be composed in parallel, provided the assigned variables are unique in the composition, but they can not otherwise be nested in an expression. A call takes the following form,

$$iEventName(v)$$

where $iEventName$ is the name of an *interface event*, and v is the list of machine variables that are passed as actual parameters. We show a concrete example, below, where a refinement of the *interface event i_callee*, named *callee*, will be 'invoked' in the *caller* event. Again we use syntactic sugar to hide the underlying Event-B. We can add the call, as an action, in the *caller* event. An iUML-B class diagram would be a suitable place to do this, since we can generate the underlying Event-B representation when the iUML-B translators run.

$$caller \triangleq \textbf{BEGIN} \; callee(var1, var2) \; \textbf{END} \tag{3}$$

The event shown in Eq. 3 shows a call to an event named *callee*, with actual parameters $var1$ and $var2$. Here, $var1$ is a machine variable representing a required input, and $var2$ is a machine variable that holds (or is assigned) the return value. Note that this representation of assignment to $var2$ is like the Ada style *out* parameter, which allows multiple return values. The Java style would be $var2 := callee(var1)$. This Java call style is exactly the one presented in [11]. However, in [12], the single assignment, performed on return, is omitted, with a preference for multiple assignments of return parameters, using Ada style *out* parameters.

4.2 Translation of the Call

The call, described above, is syntactic sugar for the following event which can be generated automatically by translation tools.

$caller \triangleq$
      ANY $fp1!$ $ret?$
      WHERE $fp1 \in \mathbb{N} \wedge ret \in \mathbb{N} \wedge fp1 = var1 \wedge ret = var2$
      END

In the generated *caller* event we introduce input and output parameters that correspond to the input and output parameters of the *i_callee* interface. We can automatically generate the parameter direction annotations, the *i_callee*'s input $fp1?$ is matched to an output in the *caller* $fp1!$, and the return value $ret?$ is matched to $ret!$ in the same way. The guards constraining the input $fp1 = var1$, and the output $var2 = ret$, model the relationship between formal and actual parameters. The parameters' typing guards correspond to the *i_callee* interface.

We propose to make use of the composition semantics of [8] where the call is modelled by a merge of (conjoined) guards and (parallel) actions. The whole caller and callee update is atomic.

4.3   The Combined Event Representation

The complete behaviour of an event call involving the *caller* and *callee* events can be described by a merge, or parallel composition, of the two events. We call this two-way synchronization since it involves two events. We propose to use shared-event composition to model the call, so in practice it is not necessary for the merge to actually take place. The composed machine construct records the composition details using a combined-events clause, and an actual merged machine can be generated from this if required. The merged machine representation, however, provides a useful way for us to describe the result of a composition since all the details are contained in a single event. A combined event, such as *caller* ∥ *callee*, encapsulates the atomic synchronization of the two, separate events.

$$callee \parallel caller \triangleq$$
$$\textbf{ANY } fp1 \; ret$$
$$\textbf{WHERE}$$
$$fp1 \in \mathbb{N} \wedge ret \in \mathbb{N}$$
$$\wedge \, fp1 = var1 \wedge ret = var2$$
$$\wedge \, ret \in 10 \, .. \, (20 + fp1)$$
$$\textbf{THEN } count := count + 1$$
$$\textbf{END}$$

In the combined event, we do not duplicate parameters and guards. Parameters are matched by name, and the direction annotations can be removed, since the event models both the *caller* and *callee*.

5   Function-Style Interface Events for Use in Expressions

In the next step we introduce a functional interface specification. A functional interface specification is restricted to return a single value *op!*. It may have an ordered set of input parameters *ip?* which will be replaced with actual parameters, and any refinement should have no side effects – as explained in Sect. 4.

$$\textbf{Functional Interface Event } op! \leftarrow evt(ip?) \triangleq$$
$$\textbf{WHEN } G(ip, op) \; \textbf{END} \tag{4}$$

5.1   Functional Interface Events

In order to demonstrate how a call is used as a (nested) term we extend our example, introducing a functional interface specification *i_callee2*. The *i_callee2 interface event* is so-named because of its similarity to *i_callee* from the previous example.

$$\textbf{Functional Interface Event } ret2! \leftarrow i\_callee2(fp1?) \triangleq$$
$$\textbf{WHEN } fp1 \in \mathbb{N} \wedge ret2 \in \mathbb{N}$$
$$\textbf{END}$$

We can then introduce a refinement of $i\_callee2$, a new event $callee2$, which is a more concrete version of the *interface event*. In traditional programming terms it might be said to be an implementation of the interface. In the Event-B world it is a refinement of $i\_callee2$, where we provide a more precise definition of the return value (highlighted in bold font).

$$callee2 \triangleq$$
$$\textbf{REFINES } i\_callee2$$
$$\textbf{ANY } fp1?\ ret2!$$
$$\textbf{WHERE } fp1 \in \mathbb{N} \land \boldsymbol{ret2} \in \mathbb{N} \land \boldsymbol{ret2} = \boldsymbol{2 * fp1}$$
$$\textbf{END}$$

Now, to show the use of the call in an expression we introduce the $newCallee$ event of Eq. 5. It refines the i_callee interface that first appeared in Eq. 2. We can see the call, to the $callee2$ event, in the highlighted expression.

$$newCallee \triangleq$$
$$\textbf{REFINES } i\_callee$$
$$\textbf{ANY } fp1?\ ret!$$
$$\textbf{WHERE } fp1 \in \mathbb{N} \land ret \in \mathbb{N}$$
$$\land \boldsymbol{ret} \in \boldsymbol{10 .. callee2(fp1)}$$
$$\textbf{END}$$

(5)

During a call, actual parameters replace formal parameters, and we model this in the guard. As previously mentioned, the *interface event* used in an expression is a function with exactly one return parameter. In the expression, we substitute $callee2(fp1)$ with the return parameter $ret2$, to get $\dots \land ret \in 10 .. ret2$. This will be observable in the final merge of Eq. 6 described later. The flow of data throughout the whole call sequence, via the parameters, is observable in Fig. 3 on Page 11.

5.2 Translation of the Call

We are now at the point where we consider the call of the $newCallee$ *interface event*, itself. We write,

$$caller \triangleq \textbf{BEGIN } var2 := newCallee(var1) \textbf{ END}$$

As in the previous examples, this is syntactic sugar, and a translation will be performed to generate the following Event-B,

$$caller \triangleq$$
$$\textbf{ANY } fp1!\ ret?$$
$$\textbf{WHERE } fp1 \in \mathbb{N} \land ret \in \mathbb{N}$$
$$\land fp1 = var1 \land ret = var2$$
$$\textbf{END}$$

In the caller, the formal and actual parameter assignments are modelled by the constraints in the guard, $fp1 = var1 \land ret = var2$. Once again, we pair input and output parameters. Parameters $fp1!$ and $ret?$ are added to *caller*, to complement the parameters $fp1?$ and $ret!$ in the *i_callee* interface and its implementation, *newCallee*.

5.3   The Combined Event Representation

As in the procedural-style example, when all the callers, and callees are composed, we can represent this as a three-way merge with the following result,

$$caller \parallel callee2 \parallel newCallee \triangleq$$

ANY $fp1\ ret\ ret2$
WHERE

$fp1 \in \mathbb{N}$	— *In Parameter Type*
$\land\ fp1 = var1$	— *Actual parameter subst.*
	on entry to caller
$\land\ ret \in 10 .. ret2$	— *Subst. call for return*
	parameter
$\land\ ret2 \in \mathbb{N}$	— *Out Parameter Type*
$\land\ ret2 = 2 * fp1$	— *Nested return value*
$\land\ ret = var2$	— *Final assignment*

(6)

END

Since we use matching parameter names, with input-output direction annotations, to identify the communication that takes place across interface boundaries, we have to consider a new scenario. With the two-way synchronization, found in the procedural-style, we simply match a pair of parameters "p?" and "p!" and this defines a pair engaging in communication. However, by introducing the three-way synchronization, caused by nesting in function-style calls, we can see that the input parameter $fp1?$ can be used to communicate its value across two component (interface) boundaries. The combined event models two operation calls. However, since input parameters cannot be assigned to, the value of $fp1?$ will always remain the same. This avoids us having to redefine the parameter on 'entry' to the operation, and the value percolates down through successive calls, as can be seen in Fig. 3. For multi-way synchronizations, we can freely pass input parameters across component boundaries by reusing the formal input parameter name. This is not the case for returning output parameters however, as can be seen in Fig. 3. Returning parameters involve assignment, or substitution in expressions. As the 'calls' return, we model the substitutions, and are required to use the return parameters to record the changes. In the figure, $var2'$ relates to the value of $var2$ after the assignment has taken place.

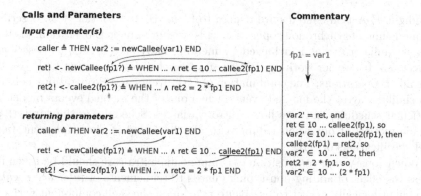

Fig. 3. Call parameters as guards

6 Discussion and Related Work

Much of our approach is comparable to the callable operations of the modularisation approach [2], which we describe in more detail in Sect. 6.1. But to summarize the differences briefly, we note that the underlying Event-B model is different. In the modularisation approach operation calls are modelled by separate events. The events model the steps of assigning actual parameters to formal parameters, evaluating the action, and then assigning a value to the return parameter. In our approach we model the call at a higher level of abstraction, in a single event. The modularisation approach makes use of pre- and post-conditions. In our *interface events*, we use guards to specify the types of the input and output parameters. Since, in an interface, we are only interested in the data crossing the components boundary, we do not refer to machine variables in the guards. The pre-conditions of the modularisation approach can be used to type operation parameters. However, they may also access machine variables, so they provide a more general mechanism for under-specification than our use of guards for typing.

Operation calls are an integral feature of the B-method [3], this is because the B method was designed as an approach for modelling software systems. Event-B is a direct descendant of the B method, but it was primarily devised as a means for modelling systems at a higher level of abstraction, so it does not have operations as an integral feature. Nevertheless, if the development is to proceed towards the implementation, it is necessary to introduce implementation level specifications, as we have done here.

Actions systems, are a precursor of the Event-B method, and were devised for the specification of parallel programs. Back and Sere describe the use of remote procedure calls, which use parameters for communication between parallel compositions of action systems modules, in [6]. This is similar to our use of parameters to share information between Event-B components, in *interface event* calls. Procedure-style calls were also introduced by Walden in [27], where they discuss a distributed load balancing algorithm, in the B-Action Systems paradigm. B-Action Systems are related to Event-B, also. Butler et al. describe the modelling of synchronous operation calls, within a single B operation, in [10]. This is similar to what is achieved by merging individual events, as described in Sect. 5.3. In further work [9], Butler and Leuschel describe using CSP [16] to schedule B operations. The combination of CSP events and B operations behave in a similar way to the merged events, when one of the merged events models a particular schedule, and uses flow control variables. Schedules of this kind, that include models of operation calling, can also be found in the implementation level specifications of [11].

When considering composition of components, extra care should be taken to assess the effect of adding non-typing guards to refinements of *interface events*. One might logically expect to be able to take an off the shelf component with an implementation, compose it with another machine, and make use of the existing implementation. At this stage we simply highlight that this may not be so straightforward, due to the effect of false guards in the called implementation. Now, *interface event* calls (including the nested calls) model a single, atomic operation call. But, if the translation makes use of a sequential implementation, some state updates may already have occurred before the operation call. In the event of a false guard in a call, this would require some form of roll-back, to undo any previous changes made before the call. This might be overcome by restricting the use of guards in the *interface events*, but this could be too restrictive to be useful. It could also be overcome by doing the automatic code generation using the composed machines (using the actual combined event clauses). This might negate any benefits of having a certified 'module', since composition may change its behaviour.

6.1 A Comparison with the Modularisation Approach – in More Detail

The work that we present here is an alternative to the existing modularisation approach [2], so we will provide a more detailed comparison of the two. The modularisation approach introduces a new interface module construct, which is based on specifying pre- and post-conditions. We do not introduce a 'separate' specification, as such, preferring to extend iUML-B class-diagrams to include the required detail. In our approach a syntactically-sugared version (a pretty-print view) of the interface specification could be shown to the user if required. This could indeed be presented as a pre- and post-condition specification, since these details can be derived from our specification. Our components can have events containing actions, and actions are a form of post-condition, so we consider that they do not require separate specification. We prefer the idea that interfaces (communication across component boundaries) should be kept separate from the behavioural aspects (that is, behaviour of the component). Modularisation contains the interface description in the pre-condition, and the behavioural description in the post-condition. Our interface approach is driven by the 'programming view' of an interface, one that describes the data flow across the component boundary, such as with Ada [7] or Java [14]. Our behavioural description is contained in the Event-B actions of the refinements of the *interface events*.

The pre-conditions that are introduced in the modularisation approach are not explicitly defined in our approach. Since we take the view that the interface specification should refer only to input and output parameters, we do not need a separate specification for them. This is because parameters are typed in guards, and are associated with direction annotations. We can then reason about the suitability of input-output ranges, as described in [13]. We can generate pre-style proof obligations, to show the feasibility of communication. We could also derive a pre-condition specification from this information, by interpreting input parameter guards as pre-conditions. We know that the corresponding output parameters would satisfy the pre-conditions. Generally, for any guard G and pre-condition P; when $G = P$, $G \implies P$ is true.

Modularisation is based on shared-variable style decomposition [5]. In this approach the shared variables can be exposed by the interface, to allow modification from outside the component. It could be argued that, in relation to the encapsulation techniques used in higher-level programming languages, this is a departure from the normal practice of component encapsulation through its interface, since direct modification of variables is usually prohibited. Our approach, using shared-event composition, is much more in keeping with the usual interpretation of encapsulation.

In the modularisation approach the underlying Event-B model is different in that they model three steps of an operation call in three separate events. The steps are those of assigning actual parameters to formal parameters, evaluating the action, and assigning a value to the return parameter. This requires special ordering guards, and variables, to ensure that no other event takes place while this sequence of events takes place. In our approach, this is specified by a merge of events, modelling the call in a single, atomic step – no additional guards and variables are required. It is also the case that modularisation operations allow side effects. We consider that this is acceptable when the call is not nested in an expression; but it is much less clear that this should be permitted when the calls are nested in expressions. It is usually advised against in programming circles, due to concerns about order of evaluation of terms. Our initial stance is to prohibit side effects in the *interface event* calls that are used in expressions, and acknowledge that it may warrant further investigation. We, therefore, consider it to be useful to distinguish between function-style *interface events*, and procedure-style *interface events*, using additional annotations.

7   Conclusions

The aim of the work described in this paper is to improve reuse of Event-B artefacts, as part of an effort to make Event-B more agile and easier to use in the development of safety-critical systems. In this paper we describe an extension of Event-B components and interfaces, that we introduced in [13]. Previous work relies on diagrammatic representations to facilitate instantiation of pre-existing components. Diagrams also describe machine and component inclusion, in a composition; and describes the communications between them. It is based on an abstract description of the interaction between communicating components, and models operation calling, using *interface events*, at a relatively high level of abstraction. Any machine with an interface, we can describe as an *interface machine*.

The extension, presented here, describes how a more concrete specification of communication can be provided. Using a programming-like notation, we introduce 'callable' *interface events*, a low-level description, facilitating the modelling of operations. These are further categorized as procedure-style or function-style *interface events*, where procedure-style *interface events* model operations that allow state updates (similar to Ada procedures). Function-style *interface events* model side effect free operations, for use as terms nested in expressions. We also introduce a new syntax for 'calling' the *interface events*.

In future work we would like to provide tool support for our approach. Then we could perform some experiments to evaluate the usability, and applicability, for solving various problems in an industrial setting. We are also interested in deriving a behavioural description from a component specification, and combining it with the interface specification, for the purposes of improving location and retrieval of relevant components from component libraries.

Acknowledgements. Many thanks to Sergey Ostroumov for insightful comments.

References

1. The Rodin User's Handbook. http://handbook.event-b.org/
2. Iliasov, A., Troubitsyna, E., Laibinis, L., Romanovsky, A., Varpaaniemi, K., Ilic, D., Latvala, T.: Supporting reuse in Event B development: modularisation approach. In: Frappier, M., Glässer, U., Khurshid, S., Laleau, R., Reeves, S. (eds.) ABZ 2010. LNCS, vol. 5977, pp. 174–188. Springer, Heidelberg (2010). doi:10.1007/978-3-642-11811-1_14
3. Abrial, J.R.: The B Book - Assigning Programs to Meanings. Cambridge University Press, Cambridge (1996)
4. Abrial, J.R.: Modeling in Event-B: System and Software Engineering. Cambridge University Press, Cambridge (2010)
5. Abrial, J.R., Hallerstede, S.: Refinement, decomposition, and instantiation of discrete models: application to Event-B. Fundam. Inform. **77**(1–2), 1–28 (2007)
6. Back, R.-J., Sere, K.: From action systems to modular systems. Softw. - Concepts Tools **17**(1), 26–39 (1996). http://dblp.uni-trier.de/rec/bib/journals/stp/BackS96
7. Barnes, J.: Ada 2012 Rationale, The Language, The Standard Libraries. LNCS, vol. 8338, 1st edn. Springer, Heidelberg (2013). doi:10.1007/978-3-642-45210-9
8. Butler, M.: Decomposition structures for Event-B. In: Leuschel, M., Wehrheim, H. (eds.) IFM 2009. LNCS, vol. 5423, pp. 20–38. Springer, Heidelberg (2009). doi:10.1007/978-3-642-00255-7_2
9. Butler, M., Leuschel, M.: Combining CSP and B for specification and property verification. In: Fitzgerald, J., Hayes, I.J., Tarlecki, A. (eds.) FM 2005. LNCS, vol. 3582, pp. 221–236. Springer, Heidelberg (2005). doi:10.1007/11526841_16

10. Butler, M., Petre, L., Sere, K.: Integrated Formal Methods. LNCS, vol. 2335. Springer, Heidelberg (2002)
11. Edmunds, A.: Providing concurrent implementations for Event-B developments. Ph.D. thesis, University of Southampton, March 2010
12. Edmunds, A., Rezazadeh, A., Butler, M.: Formal modelling for ada implementations: tasking Event-B. In: Brorsson, M., Pinho, L.M. (eds.) Ada-Europe 2012. LNCS, vol. 7308, pp. 119–132. Springer, Heidelberg (2012). doi:10.1007/978-3-642-30598-6_9
13. Edmunds, A., Snook, C., Walden, M.: On component-based reuse for Event-B. In: 5th International ABZ Conference ASM, Alloy, B, TLA, VDM, Z, 2016. Accepted paper - to be published
14. Gosling, J., Joy, B., Steele, G., Bracha, G., Buckley, A.: The Java Language Specification. Java (Addison-Wesley). Addison Wesley (2014)
15. Hallerstede, S.: Justifications for the Event-B modelling notation. In: Julliand, J., Kouchnarenko, O. (eds.) B 2007. LNCS, vol. 4355, pp. 49–63. Springer, Heidelberg (2006). doi:10.1007/11955757_7
16. Hoare, C.A.R.: Communicating Sequential Processes. Prentice Hall, Upper Saddle River (1985)
17. Abrial, J.R., et al.: Rodin: an open toolset for modelling and reasoning in Event-B. Softw. Tools Technol. Transf. **12**(6), 447–466 (2010)
18. Object Management Group (OMG). UML 2.0 Superstructure specification. http://www.omg.org/technology/uml/index.htm
19. Back, R., von Wright, J.: Refinement Calculus: A Systematic Introduction. Springer Science & Business Media, Heidelberg (2012)
20. Romanovsky, A., Thomas, M.: Industrial Deployment of System Engineering Methods. Springer, Heidelberg (2013)
21. Said, M.Y., Butler, M., Snook, C.: Language and tool support for class and state machine refinement in UML-B. In: Cavalcanti, A., Dams, D.R. (eds.) FM 2009. LNCS, vol. 5850, pp. 579–595. Springer, Heidelberg (2009). doi:10.1007/978-3-642-05089-3_37
22. Silva, R.: Towards the composition of specifications in Event-B. In: B 2011, June 2011
23. Silva, R.: Supporting development of Event-B models. Ph.D. thesis, University of Southampton, May 2012
24. Silva, R., Butler, M.: Shared event composition/decomposition in Event-B. In: Aichernig, B.K., Boer, F.S., Bonsangue, M.M. (eds.) FMCO 2010. LNCS, vol. 6957, pp. 122–141. Springer, Heidelberg (2011). doi:10.1007/978-3-642-25271-6_7
25. Snook, C.: Event-B Statemachines (2011). http://wiki.event-b.org/index.php/Event-B_Statemachines
26. The ADVICeS Team. The ADVICeS Project. https://research.it.abo.fi/ADVICeS/
27. Waldén, M.: Distributed load balancing. In: Sekerinski, E., Sere, K. (eds.) Program Development by Refinement. Formal Approaches to Computing and Information Technology FACIT, pp. 255–300. Springer, London (1999)

Algebraic Foundations for Specification Refinements

Pablo F. Castro[1,2(✉)] and Nazareno Aguirre[1,2]

[1] Departamento de Computación, FCEFQyN, Universidad Nacional de Río Cuarto,
Río Cuarto, Córdoba, Argentina
{pcastro,naguirre}@dc.exa.unrc.edu.ar
[2] Consejo Nacional de Investigaciones Científicas y Técnicas (CONICET),
Buenos Aires, Argentina

Abstract. In this paper we present a mathematical framework tailored for reasoning about specification/program refinements. The proposed framework uses formal concepts coming from Institution Theory and Category Theory, such as theories and morphisms, to capture the notion of specification/program refinement. The main benefits of the proposed mathematical theory are its generality and compositionality, that is, it is based on abstract concepts that can be used to reason about refinements in different formal settings (such as Z, B, VDM, Alloy, statecharts and others), as well as it heavily relies upon the notion of component, thus enabling modular reasoning over the process of specification/program refinement.

1 Introduction

Software Verification, i.e., the rigorous evaluation of a formal specification against a corresponding implementation, is perhaps the most widely acknowledged advantage of formal specification notations over their informal counterparts. Still, the task of formally verifying that a system correctly implements a specification is in general a complex task (although under certain restrictions, it can be algorithmically decided, e.g., via model checking), since systems and specifications are usually of a very different nature: the former are intrinsically operational and verbose, while the latter tend to be declarative and more concise.

An alternative to verification, strongly based on formal specification, consists of avoiding having to formally prove that an implementation complies with a specification, and instead *generate* a correct-by-construction implementation from a specification. Of course, this cannot be completely automated, but via a series of small, step by step, *sound* refinement steps, one may transform a declarative specification into an operational implementation complying with it. This has an obvious impact in scalability, since the "large" problem of system verification is modularised in a number of small sound steps, made by employing proved-correct *refinement rules*.

For most formal specification languages, such as Z [29], B [1] and VDM [19], the notion of refinement is usually a critical component. In effect, the B Method

© Springer International Publishing AG 2016
L. Ribeiro and T. Lecomte (Eds.): SBMF 2016, LNCS 10090, pp. 112–128, 2016.
DOI: 10.1007/978-3-319-49815-7_7

provides the possibility of *refining* a specification, until an implementation is reached. Each refinement step generates a set of proof obligations, whose validity guarantees the correctness of the refinement. Z does not provide a language for refinement within the Z notation, but "external" notations can be systematically employed for refining Z specifications, as is described for instance in [6,29]. In general, the approaches to refinement tend to be language/formalism dependent, since refinement rules depend on the specification language's constructs. In this work, we present an abstract categorical formulation of refinement, allowing us to capture the essentials of refinements in model based specification languages. Our approach, based on well known concepts from the theory of institutions, is defined at a level of abstraction that makes it formalism-independent, and enables us to capture what is the precise semantic relationship that must hold between a (structured) specification and its refinements, whatever the language these specifications and refinements correspond to. It also allows us to distinguish the more traditional refinement based on reducing nondeterminism, from an orthogonal kind of refinement, that of (abstract) state representation/implementation, and understand the relationship between them. We believe that an important aspect of the framework presented below is that its level of generality allows one to apply refinement over heterogeneous specifications, that is, specifications that are made using different formal languages; an example of this is CSP-Z [12] which uses Z for producing specification of states and operations and CSP for expressing the dynamic behavior of the systems; another important characteristic of our approach is that it enables compositional reasoning about refinements, that is, specifications that are structured in a collection of components can be refined by reasoning at the component level, simplifying in this way the task of refining.

The paper is structured as follows. In Sect. 2 we introduce the basic background assumed throughout this paper, we introduce the framework in Sects. 3 and 4, together with its properties. In Sect. 5 we present some conclusions and further work.

2 Preliminaries

In the following we use some basic notions of category theory. A *category* is a mathematical structure composed of two collections: a collection $a, b, c, \ldots$ of *objects*, and a collection $f, g, h, \ldots$ of arrows (or morphisms). Every arrow has two associated objects, its domain and codomain; we write $f : a \rightarrow b$ to indicate that a (resp. b) is the domain (resp. codomain) of arrow f. There are two basic operations involving arrows: the *identity*, that given an object a, it returns an arrow $id_a : a \rightarrow a$, and the *composition* which, given arrows $f : a \rightarrow b$ and $g : b \rightarrow c$, returns an arrow $f; g : a \rightarrow c$. Arrow composition is associative; identity arrows satisfy: $f; id_a = f$ and $id_b; f = f$, for every $f : a \rightarrow b$. A natural example of category is **Set**, made up of the collection of sets and the collection of functions between sets. A *functor* is essentially a homomorphism between categories. Given a category **C**, we denote by $|\mathbf{C}|$ its collection of objects, and by $\|\mathbf{C}\|$ its collection of arrows.

Given a category $\mathbf{C}$, a bicategory [5] is composed of: *(i)* a collection of objects, called 0-cells; *(ii)* a category $\mathbf{C}(A, B)$, for each pair of 0-cells A, B, whose objects are called 1-cells and whose arrows are called 2-cells; and *(iii)* a (bi)functor: $\mathbf{\mathring{,}} : \mathbf{C}(A, B) \times \mathbf{C}(B, C) \rightarrow \mathbf{C}(A, C)$, which satisfies some coherence properties: it must have an identity, and it must be associative. In bicategories, there are two kinds of arrows: the horizontal and the vertical ones. We refer the interested reader to [3], for an introduction to category theory. We will assume throughout the paper that the reader has some basic knowledge of category theory.

Since our main goal is to introduce the framework in an abstract language-independent manner, we do not use a particular logic to introduce the concepts; instead, we use the abstract setting of Institutions. It is useful to recall the definition of Institution:

Definition 1. *An institution* [13] *is given by:* (i) *a category* **Sign** *of signatures;* (ii) *a functor sen* : $\mathbf{Sign} \rightarrow \mathbf{Set}$, *that sends each signature to its set of formulas;* (iii) *a functor Mod* : $\mathbf{Sign}^{op} \rightarrow \mathbf{Cat}$, *that sends each signature to the category of its models[1]; and* (iv) *a collection of relations* $\vDash_\Sigma$ *(satisfaction relations relating models of a signature to formulas of the signature), that satisfies the following requirement:* $Mod(\sigma)(M') \vDash_\Sigma \phi \Leftrightarrow M' \vDash_\Sigma sen(\sigma)(\phi)$ *for any formula* $\phi \in sen(\Sigma)$ *and* $\sigma : \Sigma \rightarrow \Sigma'$.

Institutions are an abstract formulation of Model Theory. The last requirement in Definition 1 captures the fact that truth does not depend on notation.

Example 1 (Higher Order Logic). Let us give a standard example of Institution, Higher Order Logic (or simply **HOL**) is one of the basic institutions used in computer science. Here we follow the definition given in [9]. Given a set of sorts S, the set of *types* of S (denoted $\overline{S}$) is the least set such that: $S \subseteq \overline{S}$, if $s_1, s_2 \in S$ then $s_1 \rightarrow s_2$. A **HOL** signature is a tuple (S, F) where S is a set of sorts and F is a set of typed constants $\{F_s \mid s \in \overline{S}\}$. A morphism between signatures $\sigma : (S, F) \rightarrow (S', F')$ is a function $\sigma : S \rightarrow S'$, and a family of functions $\{\sigma_s : F_s \rightarrow F'_{\sigma^*(s)} \mid s \in \overline{S}\}$, where σ^* is the inductive extension of σ to $\overline{S}$. On the other hand, models in **HOL** are given by interpreting each type as a set. A model M of a signature (S, F) maps each type s to a set M_s (mapping types of the form $s \rightarrow s'$ to functions). A morphism between (S, F) models is a collection of functions $m_s : M_s \rightarrow N_s$, such that for any $f \in M_{s \rightarrow s'}$ (for $s, s' \in \overline{S}$) we have: $m_{s'} \circ f = m_{s \rightarrow s'}(f) \circ m_s$. Terms of HOL are defined as usual, any $f \in F_s$ is said to be a term of type s; and $t(t')$ is a term of type s_2, when t is of type $s_1 \rightarrow s_2$ and t' is of type s. Sentences of signature (S, F) are built up from equations by using the usual boolean connectives and quantifiers, the functor $sen : \mathbf{Sign} \rightarrow \mathbf{Set}$, sends each signature to the sets of its sentences. It is direct to define the relation $\vDash$. The institution **HOL** is the tuple $(\mathbf{Sign}_{HOL}, sen_{HOL}, Mod_{HOL}, \vDash)$ as defined above.

---

[1] $\mathbf{Sign}^{op}$ denotes the dual category of **Sign**, obtained by reversing arrows. This is so since reducts and translations go in different directions.

A restricted version of the institution **HOL** is obtained by requiring signature morphisms to preserve types. We have used this institution to capture constructions coming from the Z notation [7].

Example 2 (Z Notation). We describe briefly this institution, the technical details can be found in [7]. The institution $\mathbf{Z} = (\mathbf{Zign}, sen, Mod, \vDash)$ is as follows. Signatures in **Zign** are tuples (V, T) where V is a collection of typed variables, and T the basic types. A morphism $\sigma : \Sigma \to \Sigma'$ between signatures is defined as in Example 1, but we require that, for any variable v, the translated variable $\sigma(v)$ has the same type as v. The functor *sen* is defined as in **HOL**, we consider the standard mathematical operators usual in **Z** (see [29]), which can be defined in **HOL**. The models and the $\vDash$ relation are the same as Example 1.

We assume the reader is familiar with the **Z** notation, standard references are [26, 29]. Another interesting example is the institution of communicating sequential processes [23] (named **CSP**), let us introduce the basics of this formal construction which will be useful in the rest of the paper.

Example 3 (Communicating Sequential Processes). The category of CSP signatures (denoted $\mathbf{Sign}_{CSP}$) has as objects tuples (A, N), where A is an alphabet of communications, and $N = (\overline{N}, sort, param)$ contains the basic descriptions of processes: N is a collection of process names, *sort* is a function indicating the collection of possible communication in a given process (i.e., $sort(p) \subseteq A$); and *param*, for each process, returns the collection of its parameters. A morphism $\sigma : (A, N) \to (A', N')$ is given by functions $\alpha : A \to A'$ (translating alphabets) and $\nu : N \to N'$ (translating processes), respectively. Obviously, some coherence conditions are imposed over α and ν (e.g., preservation of parameters types, etc.) the interested reader is referred to [23]. There are different ways of giving semantics to CSP, one of them is to consider the set of possible traces of each process, this is called the *trace model*, model reducts can be defined directly over models, and model morphisms are captured as set inclusions; this gives rise to the category Mod_{CSP} of CSP models. On the other hand, sentences are given by standard CSP definitions by means of equations (see [15] for examples). The relation $M \vDash p(x_0, \ldots, x_k) = P$ holds when the interpretation of process p refines the set of traces defined by P^2. For the sake of clarity we omit the technical definitions here, but them can be consulted in [23].

3   A Category of Refinements

Before describing our formalization of refinement, let us we introduce the formal vehicle we use to express system specifications. The basic notion we employ to specify the states of a system is that of *theory presentation* [10].

---

^{2} In [23] this definition is stronger and the authors require that the sets of traces of both terms have to be the same, here we focus on refinement, and since that we only require an inclusion between the corresponding set of traces.

Definition 2. *Given an Institution* $\mathbf{I} = \langle \mathbf{Sign}, sen, Mod, \vDash \rangle$, *a theory presentation* $S = \langle \Sigma, \Phi \rangle$ *is made up of a signature* $\Sigma \in |\mathbf{Sign}|$ *and a set* $\Phi \subseteq sen(\Sigma)$ *of formulas (the axioms of the theory).*

Intuitively, a theory presentation is used to formally describe the states of the system. We have used the concept of theory presentation in [7] to capture the notion of *schema* employed in the Z notation; the generality of this concept allows us to give semantics to schema calculus through categorical constructions. Note also, that the given definition is independent of the logic used to described the state of the system, other logics can be used, some examples are show below. Let us give a simple example of how we can use theory presentation to express state specifications:

Example 4. Let us give a first example of theory and morphism in an Institution. Consider a simple specification of a memory, it can be written in the Institution of Z specifications (**Z**), as follows:

$$Mem = ((\{Data, Nat\}, \{mem : Nat \nrightarrow Data\}), \{\{true\}\})$$

which contains two types *Data* and *Nat* and a term of type *Nat* $\nrightarrow$ *Data*, representing a function that maps naturals to data; there is no axioms. From now on, we write Z specifications using Z notation, that is:

$$Mem \cong [Data : \mathbb{N}; \ mem : \mathbb{N} \nrightarrow \mathbb{N} \mid True]$$

On the other hand, a morphism between theory presentations is a translation of symbols that preserves properties:

Definition 3. *A theory morphism* $\tau : \langle \Sigma, \Phi \rangle \to \langle \Sigma', \Phi' \rangle$ *is a signature morphism* $\sigma : \Sigma \to \Sigma'$ *that satisfies the following condition:* $\forall \phi \in \Phi \bullet \Phi' \vDash sen(\sigma)(\phi)$.

Intuitively, a morphism between two specifications corresponds to two important concepts: specification embedding, that is, putting a specification into a wider system; and specification strengthening. Let us give an example in the Institution **CSP**, as presented in Sect. 2.

Example 5. Consider the following specification of a process:

$$\Gamma_0 = \{ VDM1 = coin \to (choc \to VDM1 \mid coffee \to VDM1) \}$$

a vending machine that, after receiving a coin, serves chocolate or coffee. The signature of this process is given by $A = \{coin, choc\}$, we have a unique process name: $VDM1$, where $sort(VDM1) = \{choc, coin\}$ and $param(VDM1) = ()$. Indeed, we can devise a more restrictive version of the vending machine:

$$\Gamma_1 = \{ VDM2 = coin \to choc \to VDM2 \}$$

where the functions *sort* and *param* are defined as above. As can be verified, The identity translation $\sigma : VDM1 \to VDM2$ is a morphism between these two specifications, it represents the refinement of $VDM1$ achieved by removing some internal non-determinism.

For any institution $\mathbf{I}$, it is direct to prove that specifications and morphisms are a category (see [10] for the technical details).

Definition 4. *Given an institution* $\mathbf{I} = \langle \mathbf{Sign}, sen, Mod, \vDash \rangle$, $\mathbf{Pres_I}$, *is the category composed of: 1. Theory presentations (see Definition 2) as objects, 2. Theory morphisms (see Definition 3) as morphisms.*

We just write $\mathbf{Pres}$ instead $\mathbf{Pres_I}$, when $\mathbf{I}$ is clear by context. Given any presentation s, we denote by $Ax(s)$ its sets of axioms, and $Sign(s)$ its signature. Note that, for any institution, $Sign : \mathbf{Pres} \to \mathbf{Sign}$ is a functor.

Another important concept when constructing software specifications is that of operation, usually operations are specified by stating their pre and post conditions. In our setting, operations are also logical theories, capturing their corresponding pre-post relations via formulas. Consider the following diagram in $\mathbf{Pres_I}$ (for any institution $\mathbf{I}$):

$$
\begin{array}{ccc}
 & Op & \\
 {}^{i}\nearrow & & \nwarrow{}^{j} \\
 S & & S'
\end{array}
$$

In this diagram, S is an state specification, $i : S \to Op$ is an inclusion (the embedding of S into the operation), while S' (denoting the states after the operation execution) is a theory obtained by priming the symbols in S, and $j : S' \to Op$ is the embedding of S' into the operation specification.

Let us give an example of operation for the specification of a memory given above.

Example 6. Given the state specification *Mem* the following is an operation over it:

$$Write \;\hat{=}\; [\Delta Mem;\; a? : \mathbb{N};\; i? : Data \mid Mem' = Mem \oplus \{a \mapsto d\}]$$

Here note that ΔMem means that the signature of *Mem* and its axioms are included as part of *Write* and similarly for *Mem'*, i.e., the inclusions $i : Mem \to Write$ and $j : Mem' \to Write$ are just the identity mappings.

In order to put together data domain and operation specifications, the latter understood as the above diagrams, the concept of *bicategory* [5] can be used. In effect, domain specifications (theories) correspond to 0-cells, whereas operations are diagrams of the form $S \to Op \leftarrow S'$, called cospans. The morphisms between cospans, that make the corresponding diagram commute, are the 2-cells. Cospans are in fact one of the typical examples of bicategories, where the two classes of arrows are the operations (horizontal arrows) and the morphisms between these operations (vertical arrows).

Let us see how we build this construction. Given any institution $\mathbf{I}$, we define the bicategory of states and operations over $\mathbf{I}$ as the bicategory of cospans over $\mathbf{Pres_I}$ (a proof that it is already a bicategory can be found in [5]).

Definition 5. *Spec* *is the* bicategory *of I-specifications, defined as the structure composed of:* (i) *the set* **|Pres|** *as its set of objects;* (ii) *for each pair of theory presentations S, S', the category $OP(S, S')$ of cospans between S and S' (called 1-cells), and morphisms between cospans (called 2-cells); and* (iii) *the composition between 2-cells is defined as usual by using the composition (i.e., pushouts) of cospans (denoted by $\mathring{,}$).*

A specification is a subcategory of **Spec**, the subcategory generated by the corresponding schemas and operations. We denote by $Op : S \Rightarrow S'$ the existence of operation Op from S to S', i.e., the cospan $S \rightarrow Op \leftarrow S'$. From now on, we assume that **Sign** is an *adhesive* category [20]. Roughly speaking, this means that pushouts (generalized unions) are *well-behaved*; this, for example, ensures us that **Sign** has nice properties that allow us to put together different parts of a specification. Examples of adhesive categories are the categories of sets, graphs, labelled graphs, trees, amongst others. We also assume that **Sign** has a strict initial object (that is, any arrow $\Sigma \rightarrow \emptyset$ is an isomorphism). This holds for most logics; for instance, in propositional logic, the empty set is the initial signature (which is strict). These basic assumptions imply, among other things, that **Sign** has finite colimits; this is important since the colimit is the standard construction to put together specifications [13].

Now, let us start dealing with the problem of refinement. Operation refinement is typically understood as a kind of *strengthening*. As we already mentioned, arrows in **Pres$_I$** capture the concept of specification strengthening. However, these morphisms are not adequate for formalizing the notion of operation refinement, since the strengthening associated with operations make a distinction between preconditions and postconditions: they correspond to weakening preconditions and strengthening postconditions. First, we need to distinguish preconditions from postconditions, thus we require that any operation Op has to be an *extension* of the coproduct $S + S'$ of S and S', that is, we assume the following situation regarding any operation Op:

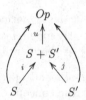

and we require that the arrow u be monic, i.e., symbols from S and S' are not mixed in Op. This will be useful for calculating pre and postconditions. An essential property that we must guarantee is that, under this characterization of operation specification, operations can be composed[3]. This is guaranteed by the following Theorem.

---

[3] Note that this is straightforward to prove for standard cospans when we have a finitely cocomplete category.

Theorem 1. *Given an institution* **I**, *if Sign* : **Pre** $\to$ **Sign** *is faithful, then, given operations* $Op_1 : S \Rightarrow S'$ *and* $Op_2 : S' \Rightarrow S''$, *the composition (denoted by* $Op_1 \,\Fcmp\, Op_2$) *exists, and is obtained by taking the colimit of the diagram composed by solid arrows below:*

$$Op_1 \,\Fcmp\, Op_2$$

$$Op_1 \qquad S + S' \qquad Op_2$$

$$S \qquad\qquad S' \qquad\qquad S''$$

Proof. *Since the category* **Pre** *is finitely cocomplete (Sign reflects colimits* [13]*), we know that the colimit of the diagram exists. We have to prove that the arrow* $u : S + S'' \to Op_1 \,\Fcmp\, Op_2$ *is mono. Since* **Sign** *is adhesive and has strict initial elements, the injection morphisms of a coproduct are monos, i.e., the arrows* $i : Op_1 \to Op_1 + Op_2$ *and* $j : Op_2 \to Op_1 + Op_2$ *are monos. Now, since* $Op_1 \,\Fcmp\, Op_2$ *is a colimit, we have an arrow* $Op_1 \,\Fcmp\, Op_2 \to Op_1 + Op_2$; *therefore, by properties of monic arrows, the morphisms* $Op_1 \to Op_1 \,\Fcmp\, Op_2$ *and* $Op_2 \to Op_1 \,\Fcmp\, Op_2$ *are monos. That is, the arrows* $f : S \to Op_1 \,\Fcmp\, Op_2$ *and* $g : S'' \to Op_1 \,\Fcmp\, Op_2$ *are monos (since they are compositions of monic arrows). Therefore, the arrow* $[f, g] = u$ *is monic (since* **Sign** *is adhesive and Sign reflects monos).*

As we explained, we need to factor the precondition and postcondition from an operation specification, to describe what a refinement is. Let us first deal with preconditions. A precondition is a predicate prescribing for which states an operation is correctly defined. Categorically, and given a component S, this concept of precondition over S corresponds to an arrow $pre : S \to P$. That is, pre is an extension of S which characterizes the states where the precondition is true. We require that pre preserves language; that is: $Sign(pre)$ must be iso in **Sign**. Now, preconditions can be weakened during the refinement of an operation. This corresponds to a construction called *coslice category*. The coslice category $S \downarrow \mathbf{Pres}^{op}$ has arrows $Pre : S \to P$ as objects; its morphisms are arrows $f : pre \to pre'$ that make the following diagram commute in **Pre**:

$$S$$
$$pre \swarrow \qquad \searrow pre'$$
$$P \xleftarrow{f} P'$$

Notice that we used **Pres**^{op}, since arrows go "in the opposite direction" for preconditions. We will denote by **pre(S)** the subcategory $S \downarrow \mathbf{Pres}^{op}$, of pre-conditions of S. The same observations that we made for preconditions can be extrapolated to postconditions. More precisely, a postcondition is an arrow $post : S + S' \to Q$ describing the correct final states of a given operation. Notice that, for postconditions, we include the language of the initial state (i.e., S). The reason for this is that, in model based specification languages, it is customary to often describe the "post states" in relation to the "pre states", i.e., to describe the transition relation of the operation as the postcondition of the operation. Using the (inclusion) arrows $i : S \to S + S'$ and $j : S' \to S + S'$, we obtain the cospan:

$$
\begin{array}{ccc}
 & Q & \\
\scriptstyle i;Post \nearrow & & \nwarrow \scriptstyle j;Post \\
S & & S'
\end{array}
$$

We require these two arrows to be extensions; furthermore, $i;$ $post$ must be conservative (see [11] for the definition of these concepts); intuitively this means that a postcondition does not add any restrictions on initial states.

The category $S + S' \downarrow \mathbf{Pres}$ gives us the base category to reason about postconditions of operations transforming S. We denote by $\mathbf{post}(S')$ the subcategory of $S + S' \downarrow \mathbf{Pres}$ of postconditions. Notice that, as opposed to the case of preconditions, in this case the arrows go in the usual direction.

As we mentioned previously, in order to be able to refine operations we need to express them as composed by preconditions postconditions. Notice that, given a precondition $pre : S \to P$ and a postcondition: $post : S + S' \to Q$ of an operation Op, we can compose these as follows:

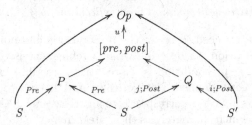

where $[pre, post]$ is the colimit of the above diagram. When the (unique) arrow $u : [pre, post] \to Op$ is conservative, we say that the operation $Op : S \Rightarrow S'$ can be factorized in $Pre : S \to P$ and $Post : S + S' \to S'$; in this case, we write Op as $[pre, post]$. The following theorem allows us to guarantee that every operation can be factorized, and therefore to treat operations as defined by pre and postconditions.

Theorem 2. *For any given institution* $\mathbf{I}$, *every operation in* $\mathbf{Spec_I}$ *can be factorized in a unique way (up to isomorphism).*

Proof. *Let us first prove that there is at least one factorization. Given* $Op :$ $S \Rightarrow S'$, *suppose that* $S = \langle \Sigma_S, \Phi_S \rangle$. *Let us define* $pre : S \to P$, *where* $P = \langle \Sigma_P, i^{-1}(\Phi_{Op} \cap i(\Phi_{\Sigma_S})) \rangle$, *where* $i : S \to Op$, i^{-1} *is the usual pre image over sets and* Φ_{Σ_S} *denotes the set of all formulas generated from* Σ. *Note that* $pre : S \to P$ *is mono, since Sign reflects monos. Let us prove that it is a morphism between presentations. If we have that* $\phi \in i^{-1}(\Phi_{Op} \cap i(\Phi_{\Sigma_S}))$, *then* $i(\phi) \in \Phi_{Op} \cap i(\Phi_{\Sigma_S})$ *but therefore* $\Phi_{Op} \vDash i(\Phi)$. *Now, let us define the postcondition* $post : \Sigma + \Sigma' \to Q$; *we define* Q *as* $\langle \Sigma_S + \Sigma_{S'}, j^{-1}(\Phi_{Op} \setminus i(\Phi_{Pre})) \rangle$. *By using the identity* $\Sigma_S +$

$\Sigma_{S'} \to \Sigma_S + \Sigma_{S'}$, *the proof that post* : $\Sigma + \Sigma' \to Q$ *is an arrow between theory presentations is similar to that of pre. Now, we need to prove that* $[pre, post]$ *is the unique (up to isomorphism) factorization. Consider the following diagram:*

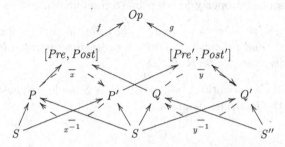

Let us show that there exist arrows x *and* y *as shown above. Note that, since* $Sign(pre) : Sign(S) \to Sign(P)$, *and* **Sign** *and* $Sign(pre') : Sign(S) \to Sign(P')$ *are iso in* **Sign**, *we can define the following arrow* $x = Sign(pre)^{-1}; Sign(pre')$: $P \to P'$. *Note that we have the following diagram which commutes, since* P *and* P' *are pre-conditions:*

The arrows $(f; pre) : P \to [P, Q]$ *and* $(g; pre')P' \to [P', Q']$ *are conservative. Furthermore, since* $Sign(pre)$ *and* (pre') *are iso, we have an arrow in* **Sign** $x : Sign(P) \to Sign(P')$ *which is iso. Let us prove that this arrow is a morphism between theory presentations: if* $\phi \in P$, *then* $(f; pre)(\phi) \in Op$. *Then, since these arrows commute (see the diagram above), we have that* $(g; pre')(\phi) \in Op$, *and therefore* $(g; pre')^{-1}(\phi) \in P'$. *So, by the commutativity of the diagram above, we get* $x(\phi) \in P'$. *Similarly, we can find a iso morphism* $y : Q \to Q'$. *Finally, by properties of colimit we get that* $[P, Q]$ *and* $[P', Q']$ *are isomorphic.*

We are now ready to define operation refinement. Given two operations Op and Op', factorized as $[pre, post]$ and $[pre', post']$, respectively, a *refinement* is composed of two arrows f and g, in the situation, involving the cospans of the two operations, captured in the following diagram:

$$
\begin{array}{c}
[pre, post] \\
\Big\downarrow {\scriptstyle [f,g]} \\
[pre', post'] \\
\end{array}
$$

$$
S \qquad\qquad S'
$$

Arrow f is in $\mathbf{pre}(S)$, while arrow g is in $\mathbf{post}(S')$. According to the definitions of these subcategories, an operation refinement is composed of a precondition weakening and a postcondition strengthening, precisely as we expected. The following result, stating that operations and operation refinements constitute a category, is an important one: it implies that operation refinements can be composed, an essential property for step by step refinement.

Theorem 3. *Given two theories S and S', the collection of operations $Op(S, S')$ between S and S', and refinement arrows between the corresponding factorizations, is a category, denoted by $\mathbf{Ref}(S, S')$.*

Furthermore, given factorizations $[pre, post] : S \to S'$ and $[pre', post'] : S' \to S''$, we can consider the following diagram:

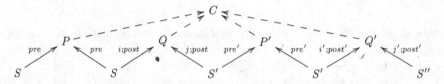

where C is the colimit of the base of the diagram (called cocone). Taking the factorizations of arrows $S \to C$ and $S'' \to C$, we obtain an object of $\mathbf{Ref}(S, S'')$. We can then define a bifunctor (composition) of factorizations $\mathbin{;} : \mathbf{Ref}(S, S') \times \mathbf{Ref}(S', S'') \to \mathbf{Ref}(S, S'')$. It is not hard to see that this bifunctor satisfies the coherence properties required for composition in bicategories (it is defined by using colimits in a similar way that it is done in cospan categories).

Let us present an example, illustrating our above construction. We have already introduced a specification of memories, with some operations. Consider an additional operation, called *Choose*, whose purpose is to nondeterministically choose an address, and returns the data stored in it. An implementation, or more concrete specification, of this operation may reduce nondeterminism, for instance by deterministically choosing a specific address to be read. A possible implementation would be to use the minimum of the addresses, and return the value read in it. This specification, called *MinChoose*, together with the more abstract *Choose*, their pre/postcondition factorizations and the refinement, are shown in the diagram below, together with the corresponding arrows. Notice that the arrows between schemas Q and Q' imply that any model of Q' would be a model of Q (semantic arrows go in the other direction).

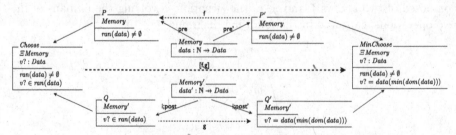

Let us finally put together specifications, operations, and operation refinements. Note that bicategory **Pres** is unsuitable to subsume refinement, since arrows between cospans (the vertical arrows) capture the notion of specification strengthening, not refinement. In order to deal with this issue, we define a new class of arrows between cospans: given operations Op, Op', with factorizations $[Pre, Post]$ and $[Pre', Post']$, respectively, we define the bicategory **Spec** of specifications as follows.

Definition 6. *The structure of specifications (called* **Ref***) and refinements is defined as follows:*

- *The collection of 0-cells is given by the collection of theory presentations.*
- *For each pair of theories S and S', we have the category* **Ref**(S, S') *as defined in Theorem 3, where cospans are the 1-cells, and refinements are the 2-cells.*
- *The composition $\mathbin{\mathaccent\cdot{,}} :$* **Ref**$(S, S) \times$ **Ref**$(S', S'') \to$ **Ref**(S, S'') *is as defined above.*

The following result shows the coherence of the above structure.

Theorem 4. **Ref** *is a bicategory.*

Proof. *That* **Ref**(S, S') *is a category follows from Theorem 4. The key of the proof is showing that $\mathbin{\mathaccent\cdot{,}}$ behaves as a composition. In order to show this, it suffices to take the factorization of the colimit of the factorizations.*

3.1 Heterogeneous Refinements

Let us give a simple example of how the framework described in the section above can be used to combine notions of refinements coming from different formal systems. Consider the combination of Z with CSP, this formal system can be defined in diverse ways, we take the definition of the institution **CZP** (that combines CSP with Z) specifications given in [7].

Definition 7. *The institution* **CZP** *is defined as follows:*

- *Signatures are tuples (Σ_Z, Σ_{CSP}), where Σ_Z is a Z signature, and Σ_{CSP} is a CSP signature, and signature morphisms are pairs of signature morphisms.*
- *sen is defined pointwise: $sen(\Sigma_Z, \Sigma_{CSP}) = (sen(\Sigma_Z), sen(\Sigma_{CSP}))$,*
- *Given a signature Σ_{CZP}, a model is this signature is a subset of the set:*

$$\{\langle a_0, \ldots, a_n \rangle, \langle \mathbf{I_0}, \ldots, \mathbf{I}_{n+1}, \rangle) \mid \langle a_0, \ldots, a_1 \rangle \in Mod(\sigma_Z) \wedge \mathbf{I}_j \in Mod(\Sigma_Z)\},$$

that is collection of traces together with a set of interpretations in **Z** *representing the state changes of the system during the given execution.*
- *The satisfaction relation is defined as follows: $M \vDash \langle \pi, \phi \rangle$ iff $\pi_1(M) \vDash \pi$ and for every $\langle \mathbf{I}_1, \ldots, \mathbf{I}_{n+1} \rangle \in \pi_2(M)$ we have $\mathbf{I}_i \vDash \phi$,*

In this institution, a theory presentation is defined as follows [7]:

Definition 8. *A theory in* **CZP** *is a tuple* $\langle \Sigma_{CSP}, \Sigma_Z, S, Ops, events, \pi \rangle$, *where:* *1.* $\Sigma_{CSP} = \langle A, N \rangle$ *is a signature in* **CSP**, *2.* Σ_Z *is a signature in* **Z**, *3.* S *is a collection of formulas, 4.* $OPS = \{ op_0 : S \Rightarrow S', \ldots op_n : S \Rightarrow S' \}$ *is a collection of operations over presentation* $\langle \Sigma_Z, S \rangle$. *5. event* : $A \rightarrow OPS$ *is a function mapping events to operations, 6.* π *is a set of* **CSP** *processes.*

Now, we can define the notion of refinement of specification in **CZP**:

Definition 9. *Given theories presentations* $P_i = \langle \Sigma_{CSP}^i, \Sigma_Z^i, S, Ops^i, events^i, \pi^i \rangle$, *for* $i \in \{0, 1\}$ *a* **CZP** *refinement* $r : P_0 \rightarrow P_1$ *is given by: 1. An arrow* $z : \langle \Sigma_Z^0, S^0 \rangle \rightarrow \langle \Sigma_Z^1, S^1 \rangle$ *in* **Pres**$_Z$, *2. An arrow* $p : \langle \Sigma_{CSP}^0, \pi^0 \rangle \rightarrow \langle \Sigma_{CSP}^1, \pi^1 \rangle$ *in* **Pres**$_{CSP}$, *3. A mapping* $i : Ops^0 \rightarrow Ops^1$, *such that, for each* $o \in Ops$, *there are arrows* $r : o \rightarrow i(o)$ *in* **Ref**$_Z$, *and the following holds:* $i \circ events^0 = events^1 \circ p$.

Roughly speaking, a refinement in **CZP** is composed of refinements of processes and refinements of schemas and operations satisfying certain coherence properties, basic properties of category theory imply that specifications and refinements in **CZP** conform a category.

4 Data Refinement

We have described a category of refinements that allows us to reason about the process of refining operations and strengthening state descriptions. Another mechanism for refining specifications is the so-called *data refinement* [14]. This form of refinement is achieved by adding details to the datatypes used in the specifications. In this way, specifications get closer to the data structures available in programming languages. Categorically, data refinements can be characterized by the so-called *institution representations*. Intuitively, a data refinement is a mapping between specifications that preserve basic properties. First, let us introduce the notion of institution representation, as presented in [27].

Definition 10 (*Institution representation*). *Let* $I = \langle \mathbf{Sign}, sen, Mod, \{\models_\Sigma \}_{\Sigma \in |\mathbf{Sign}|} \rangle$ *and* $I' = \langle \mathbf{Sign}', sen', Mod', \{\models'_\Sigma\}_{\Sigma \in |\mathbf{Sign}'|} \rangle$ *be institutions. The structure* $\langle \gamma^{Sign}, \gamma^{sen}, \gamma^{Mod} \rangle : I \rightarrow I'$ *is an* institution representation *if and only if:*

1. $\gamma^{Sign} : \mathbf{Sign} \rightarrow \mathbf{Sign}'$ *is a functor,*
2. $\gamma^{sen} : sen \rightarrow sen' \circ \gamma^{Sign}$, *is a natural transformation,*
3. $\gamma^{Mod} : Mod' \circ (\gamma^{Sign})^{op} \rightarrow Mod$, *is a natural transformation,*

Moreover, for any $\Sigma \in| \mathbf{Sign} |$, *the function* $\gamma_\Sigma^{Sen} : sen(\Sigma) \rightarrow sen'(\gamma^{Sign}(\Sigma))$ *and the functor* $\gamma_\Sigma^{Mod} : Mod'(\gamma^{Sign}(\Sigma)) \rightarrow Mod(\Sigma)$ *preserve the following satisfaction condition: for any* $\alpha \in sen(\Sigma)$ *and* $\mathcal{M}' \in| Mod(\gamma^{Sign}(\Sigma)) |$, $\mathcal{M}' \models_{\gamma^{Sign}(\Sigma)} \gamma_\Sigma^{Sen}(\alpha)$ *iff* $\gamma_\Sigma^{Mod}(\mathcal{M}') \models_\Sigma \alpha$.

An institution representation captures an embedding of a given logic in a richer logic. Data abstractions correspond to *endo* institutions representations, that is, they describe how a specification can be mapped into another one *within* the same formalism.

First, let us note that given a (endo) representation map such that γ^{Mod} is epi can be extended to a endofunctor between the corresponding categories of theory presentations.

Theorem 5. *Let* **I** *be an institution, and an institution representation* $abs = \langle \gamma^{Sign}, \gamma^{Sen}, \gamma^{Mod} \rangle : \mathbf{I} \to \mathbf{I}$, *with* γ^{Mod} *epi, then the mapping* $abs : \mathbf{Pres} \to \mathbf{Pres}$, *defined as follows:*

- *For any theory presentation* $\langle \Sigma, Ax \rangle$, $abs(\langle \Sigma, Ax \rangle) = \langle \gamma^{Sign}(\Sigma), \gamma_\Sigma^{Sen}(Ax) \rangle$
- *For any theory morphism* $\sigma : \langle \Sigma, Ax \rangle \to \langle \Sigma', Ax' \rangle$,

$$abs(\sigma) = \langle \gamma^{Sign}(\sigma), Sen(\gamma^{Sign}(\sigma)) \rangle$$

is a functor.

Proof. *The proof is straightforward by resorting to properties of institution representations, and the fact that abs is an endofunctor and* γ^{Mod} *is epi.*

Finally, the concept of data refinement can be formally defined using the notion of lax functor (homomorphisms between bicategories).

Definition 11. *Given specifications* $\mathbf{C_0}, \mathbf{C_1}$ *(subcategories of the bicategory* **Spec***) a data refinement is a lax functor* $a : \mathbf{C_0} \to \mathbf{C_1}$ *composed by:*

- *A mapping between the 0-cells (theory presentations), defined by an (endo) representation map* $\langle \gamma^{Sign}, \gamma^{Sen}, \gamma^{Mod} \rangle$ *such that* γ^{Mod} *is epi.*
- *Mappings between cospans (1-cells):* $f_{S,S'} : Op_{C_0}(S, S') \to Op_{C_1}(S, S')$. *For any operation* Op *we call* $abs(op)$ *its corresponding operation obtained by applying the data refinement.*

As in any lax functor, mappings $f_{S,S'}$ are subject to some coherence laws, roughly speaking, identity and composition must be preserved [5].

Intuitively, a data refinement is composed of a mapping between specifications (that preserves properties) and a mapping between operations. In this case the natural transformation γ^{Mod} can be thought of as the usual abstraction function [14]; the requirement that such mappings be surjective (epi) is standard for abstraction mappings.

Let us now present an example of data refinement. We use the Z notation to illustrate the above defined concepts, using an example of memories and memories with cache based on that described in [17]. A memory is, as we explained before, simply a mapping from addresses to data. A cache memory is composed of two memories: one smaller memory playing the role of the cache, and a main memory. The assumption is that the cache is faster, and thus can be used to speed up memory writing and reading. In Fig. 1 we have the specification of memories with cache, and their operations. In that figure, we can observe two specifications of a memory; the arrows between *Memory* (resp. *Memory'*) and *CacheMemory* (resp. *Memory'*) are obtained by mapping the function $data : \mathbb{N} \to Data$ to a

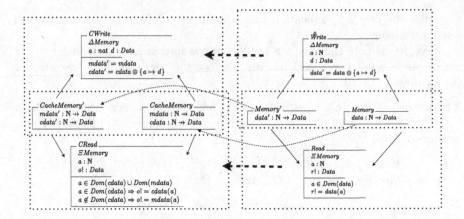

Fig. 1. An example of data refinement

pair of functions $mdata : \mathbb{N} \to Data$ and $cdata : \mathbb{N} \to Data$. The abstraction function in this case is obtained by the union of the two functions (see [17]). The mappings between the corresponding operations are represented by the big arrows between the squares.

5   Related Work and Conclusions

We have proposed an abstract, language independent, mathematical foundation for refinements. The abstract setting that we presented was developed using well established abstract notions of logical systems. Indeed, the notions that we used in this formalisation have been employed to structure concurrent system specification languages and algebraic specification languages, and other formalisms [10]; we think that one of the main benefits of this abstract framework is the possibility of combining different refinement calculi in a simple way by resorting to categorical constructions.

With respect to related work, various formalizations of refinement calculi have been previously presented. Most of these are concrete, language or formalism specific (e.g., [2,24,29]). In [2], there is a categorical treatment of refinement, but is restricted to the use of categories to capture semantic domains. In [4], a categorical framework of allegories is used to deal with program calculation, in the functional programming sense (as opposed to our case, where we consider the notion of state to be inherent to model based specification). In [25], an abstract treatment of refinement is presented, using the theory of π-institutions. However, [25] does not deal with the notions of operation or component, in the sense of component based specification, as we do in this paper. In [21], refinement is studied in comparison with composition, in the context of action-based systems; the treatment is categorical, but the approach is different from ours: [21] employs a category where objects are software components, and different arrows capture superposition and refinement between components. This work concentrates on action refinement, and does not deal with data refinement.

Unifying Theories of Programming (UTP) [16] provides a common notion of refinement for different programming paradigms, and it is used for providing the semantics of heterogeneous specification languages such as Circus [28]. It is worth noting that UTP mainly uses first-order logic and fixpoint constructions, whereas the framework described in this paper does not depend on any particular logic, it is based on the abstract notion of logical theory; thus, it can be employed to capture the notion of refinement in other settings, examples of this are specification languages using higher-order logics, infinitary logics, etc.

Finally, it is worth mentioning that there exist a broad literature on structuring algebraic specifications that may be applied to refinement as a particular case. For instance, [18] describes a categorical formulation of data refinement using lax transformations, this approach focuses on the semantics of an imperative language, even though the authors propose extensions to cope with more expressive languages. On the other hand, Institution theory has been used to provide heterogeneous specification formalisms, for instance, those described in [8, 22], although none of them particularly deal with specification refinements.

References

1. Abrial, J.-R.: The B-Book. Cambridge University Press, Cambridge (1996)
2. Back, R.J., von Wright, J.: Refinement Calculus: A Systematic Introduction. Springer, New York (1998)
3. Barr, M., Wells, C.: Category Theory for Computer Science. Centre de Recherches Mathématiques, Université de Montréal, Montreal (1999)
4. Bird, R., de Moor, O.: Algebra of Programming. Prentice-Hall, Upper Saddle River (1997)
5. Borceux, F.: Handbook of Categorical Algebra. Basic Category Theory, Encyclopedia of Mathematics and its Applications, vol. 1. Cambridge University Press, Cambridge (1994)
6. Cavalcanti, A.L.C.: A Refinement calculus for Z. Ph.D. thesis, Oxford University Computing Laboratory, Oxford, UK (1997)
7. Castro, P., Aguirre, N., Lopez Pombo, C., Maibaum, T.: Categorical foundations for structured specifications in Z. Form. Asp. Comput. 27(5–6), 831–865 (2015)
8. Diaconescu, R.: Grothendieck institutions. Appl. Categ. Struct. 10(4), 383–402 (2002)
9. Diaconescu, R.: Institution-Independent Model Theory. Birkhäuser Verlag, Basel (2008)
10. Fiadeiro, J.: Categories for Software Engineering. Springer, Heidelberg (2004)
11. Fiadeiro, J., Sernadas, A.: Structuring theories on consequence. In: Sannella, D., Tarlecki, A. (eds.) ADT 1987. LNCS, vol. 332, pp. 44–72. Springer, Heidelberg (1988). doi:10.1007/3-540-50325-0_3
12. Fischer, C.: Combining CSP and Z. Technical report, University of Oldenburg (1996)
13. Goguen, J., Burstall, R.: Institutions: abstract model theory for specification and programming. J. ACM 39(1), 95–146 (1992). ACM Press

14. He, J., Hoare, C.A.R., Sanders, J.W.: Data refinement refined resume. In: Robinet, B., Wilhelm, R. (eds.) ESOP 1986. LNCS, vol. 213, pp. 187–196. Springer, Heidelberg (1986). doi:10.1007/3-540-16442-1_14

15. Hoare, C.A.R.: Communicating Sequential Processes. Prentice Hall International, Upper Saddle River (1985)

16. Hoare, C.A.R., He, J.: Unifying Theories of Programming. Prentice Hall International Series in Computer Science. Prentice-Hall, Upper Saddle River (1998)

17. Jackson, D.: Data Abstractions. Logic, Language, and Analysis. MIT Press, Cambridge (2006)

18. Johnson, M., Naumann, D., Power, J.: Category theoretic models of data refinement. Electr. Notes Theor. Comput. Sci. **225**, 21–38 (2009)

19. Jones, C.B.: Systematic Software Development Using VDM, 2nd edn. Prentice Hall, New York (1990)

20. Lack, S., Sobociński, P.: Adhesive categories. In: Walukiewicz, I. (ed.) FoSSaCS 2004. LNCS, vol. 2987, pp. 273–288. Springer, Heidelberg (2004). doi:10.1007/978-3-540-24727-2_20

21. Lopes, A., Fiadeiro, J.: Superposition: composition vs refinement of non-deterministic, action-based systems. Form. Asp. Comput. **16**(1), 5–18 (2004). Springer

22. Mossakowski, T.: Heterogeneus specification and the heterogeneous tool set. Habilitation thesis (2005)

23. Mossakowski, T., Roggenbach, M.: Structured CSP – a process algebra as an institution. In: Fiadeiro, J.L., Schobbens, P.-Y. (eds.) WADT 2006. LNCS, vol. 4409, pp. 92–110. Springer, Heidelberg (2007). doi:10.1007/978-3-540-71998-4_6

24. Morgan, C.C.: Programming from Specifications. Prentice-Hall, Upper Saddle River (1990)

25. Rodrigues, C., Martins, M., Madeira, A., Barbosa, L.: Refinement by interpretation in π-institutions. In: Proceedings of the 15th International Refinement Workshop (2011)

26. Spivey, J.M.: The Z Notation: A Reference Manual. Prentice Hall, Upper Saddle River (1992)

27. Tarlecki, A.: Moving between logical systems. In: Haveraaen, M., Owe, O., Dahl, O.-J. (eds.) ADT/COMPASS -1995. LNCS, vol. 1130, pp. 478–502. Springer, Heidelberg (1996). doi:10.1007/3-540-61629-2_59

28. Woodcock, J., Cavalcanti, A.L.C.: The semantics of *Circus*. In: Bert, D., Bowen, J.P., Henson, M.C., Robinson, K. (eds.) ZB 2002. LNCS, vol. 2272, pp. 184–203. Springer, Heidelberg (2002). doi:10.1007/3-540-45648-1_10

29. Woodcock, J., Davies, J.: Using Z: Specification, Refinement, and Proof. Prentice Hall, Upper Saddle River (1996)

On Interval Dynamic Logic

Regivan H.N. Santiago[1], Benjamín Bedregal[1], Alexandre Madeira[2],
and Manuel A. Martins[3]([✉])

[1] Group for Logic, Language, Information, Theory and Applications—LoLITA,
Dep. de Informática e Matemática Aplicada—DIMAp,
Univ. Federal do Rio Grande do Norte—UFRN, Natal, RN, Brazil
[2] HASLab, INESC-TEC, Dep. Informática, Univ. Minho, Braga, Portugal
[3] CIDMA - Dep. Mathematics, Univ. Aveiro, Aveiro, Portugal
martins@ua.pt

Abstract. The wide number of languages and programming paradigms,
as well as the heterogeneity of 'programs' and 'executions' require
new generalisations of propositional dynamic logic. The dynamisation
method, introduced in [20], contributed on this direction with a systematic parametric way to construct Many-valued Dynamic Logics able to
handle systems where the uncertainty is a prime concern. The instantiation of this method with the Łukasiewicz arithmetic lattice over [0, 1],
that we derive here, supports a general setting to design and to (fuzzy-)
reason about systems with uncertainty degrees in their transitions.

For the verification of real systems, however, there are no *de facto*
methods to accommodate exact truth degrees or weights. Instead, the
traditional approach within scientific community is to use different kinds
of approximation techniques.

Following this line, the current paper presents a framework where the
representation values are given by means of intervals. Technically this is
achieved by considering an 'interval version' of the Kleene algebra based
on the [0, 1] Łukasiewicz lattice. We also discuss the 'intervalisation' of Ł
action lattice (in the lines reported in [28]) and how this class of algebras
behaves as an (interval) semantics of many-valued dynamic logic.

1 Introduction

Dynamic Logics (DL) are extensions of modal logic. They are recognised as the
most adequate logics to reason about computational systems in an assertional
way [12]. In its origin, DL was introduced by Pratt [26] as a modal logic suitable
to represent and reason about Hoare triples. Since then, DL assumed a central
role in the programs verification. Today, not only in response of the explosion
of programming and specification languages, but also in the emerging heterogeneous nature that a program can assume, a wide family of DL were defined to
be applied to more general complex behaviors. This ranges from the standard
versions for sequential imperative programmes (e.g. [12]) to other versions tailored for new computing paradigms, either probabilistic systems, following the
original work of Kozen [17], hybrid systems with the differential dynamic logic

© Springer International Publishing AG 2016
L. Ribeiro and T. Lecomte (Eds.): SBMF 2016, LNCS 10090, pp. 129–144, 2016.
DOI: 10.1007/978-3-319-49815-7_8

by Platzer [25] or even quantum versions due to Baltag and Smets [1]. Within this variety of dynamic logics, in [20], it is studied a method for a systematic construction of many–valued dynamic logics. The method is parametrised by an action lattice that supports both the computational paradigm and the truth space, combining in just one structure the underlying Kleene algebra for the computations and residuated lattices for the proposition assertions.

On the other hand, logics with many-valued semantics are applied in a variety of fields like Decision Making, Image Processing, Clustering, etc. One of such logics, which is a very important logic, is that of Łukasiewicz [8], which semantics is based on the residuated lattice $L = \langle [0,1], \rightarrow, 0, 1 \rangle$—where $a \rightarrow b = \min(1, 1 - a + b)$. In this logic the truth-values may be thought of as arising from normalized measurements of bounded physical observables, just as Boolean truth-values arise from yes/no-observables [24, Sect. 1.6]. In this context, it is worth to look into the instantiation of the 'dynamisation' parametrised by the Łukasiewicz action lattice $L = \langle [0,1], \max, \odot, 0, 1, *, \rightarrow, \min \rangle$. The space of values $[0,1]$ models exact measurements which is far from the real-world. In fact, any measurement presupposes an uncertainty which is not encoded by the elements of $[0,1]$. For instance, there is no machine representation of irrational numbers. This justifies the use of approximations to those practices. In order to capture and deal with such uncertainty the indicated approach is to **represent** the space $[0,1]$ by the space of closed intervals of its elements $\mathbb{I}([0,1]) = \{[a,b] \mid [a,b] \subseteq [0,1]\}$ (cf. [4]). Representation here means correction in the sense of interval mathematics [13,28] and can be summarised by the following expressions:

If $a \in A$ and $b \in B$, then:

1. $a^* \in A^*$, $a \rightarrow b \in A \rightarrow B$,
2. $\max(a,b) \in \max(A,B)$, $\min(a,b) \in \min(A,B)$ and
3. $a \odot b \in A \odot B$

Many interesting questions arise in the interval setting. Since $\mathbb{I}([0,1])$ extends $[0,1]$, what are the action lattices properties which are maintained or destroyed? Actually, we proved that the obtained interval structure is a Kleene Algebra (see Theorem 1). This paper's contribution can be useful on the specification and analysis of programs involving uncertainty degrees in the execution (transitions). Moreover, based on the Conway matrix constructions [9], we have a support for the composition under the Kleene operations (sequential composition, choice and *-closure) of transition systems weighed by intervals.

However, the notion of action lattice is not enough to abstract the resulting structure. Namely, the residuum property does not hold (see Proposition 3). Although, we still can derive a many-valued dynamic logic from such structure such that the semantics behaves as expected: the value of a sentence in the standard case belongs to the respective interval interpretation.

Outline of the paper. The paper is structured as follows: Sect. 2 introduces a Many-valued Dynamic Logic built on the L-action lattice, following the 'dynamisation' method of [20]. Then, Sect. 3 makes an overview on the interval arithmetics and applies it to the 'intervalisation' of L. It is also proved that this structure is, in fact, a Kleene algebra. In Sect. 4, we discuss the properties which are preserved and lost in this procedure. Finally, in Sect. 5 we present some direction for future work.

2   An Ł-Fuzzy Dynamic Logic

Many-valued versions of Modal Logics have been discussed in the literature along the times; the purposed logics vary in the focus where the many-valueless is presented: in accessibility relations, in propositions interpretation or in both. The latter is the case of the works [10,11] of M. Fitting suggest a logic with many-valueness evaluated in finite Heyting algebras. Later it was deeply investigated by Bou et al. in [6], who adopted the more generic truth support of finite integral commutative residuated lattices.

The literature is not so rich at respect of Many-Valued Dynamic Logics. Hughes et al. introduced in [14] a propositional dynamic logic over the continuum truth $(0,1)$-lattice with the standard fuzzy residues. However, from the perspective of dynamic logic, this formalism is quite restrictive, since it lefts behind both transitive closure and non deterministic choice. In the context of rational decision theory, Liau [19] introduced also another different many-valued dynamic logic w.r.t. the specific continuum truth $(0,1)$-lattice.

A systematic method to build Many-valued Dynamic Logics was then introduced in [20,21]. This method is parametrized by an action lattice [16], an algebraic structure that provides a generic support for computational space (as a Kleene algebra) and for truth space (as residuated lattice). The logic introduced in this section is based on this work and can be captured as an instantiation of this method.

2.1   The Łukasiewicz Action Lattice

The role or the Łukasiewicz residuated lattice, i.e., the algebraic structure

$$\textbf{Ł} = ([0,1], \max, \odot, 0, 1, \rightarrow)$$

with

- $x \rightarrow y = \min(1, 1 - x + y)$ and
- $x \odot y = \max(0, y + x - 1)$,

is taken as the standard fuzzy truth space [30]. Moreover, as stated above, we are looking for a structure suitable to support a fuzzy computational model. Whenever the max and the $\odot$ operators are used to model the choice and composition of atomic actions, we need to consider a Kleene operator to model the recursive iteration of programs. These constitute the components of an action lattice [16], the structure taken in [20,21] as a generic parameter for a many-valued logic definition. More precisely:

Definition 1. *An <u>action lattice</u> is a tuple*

$$\mathbf{A} = (A, +, ;, 0, 1, *, \rightarrow, \cdot)$$

where A is a set, 0 and 1 are constants, $*$ is an unary operation in A and $+, ;, \rightarrow$ and $\cdot$ are binary operations in A satisfying the axioms enumerated in Fig. 1, where the relation $\leq$ is induced by $+$: $a \leq b$ iff $a + b = b$.

$$a + (b + c) = (a + b) + c \qquad (1)$$
$$a + b = b + a \qquad (2)$$
$$a + a = a \qquad (3)$$
$$a + 0 = 0 + a = a \qquad (4)$$
$$a; (b; c) = (a; b); c \qquad (5)$$
$$a; 1 = 1; a = a \qquad (6)$$
$$a; (b + c) = (a; b) + (a; c) \qquad (7)$$
$$(a + b); c = (a; c) + (b; c) \qquad (8)$$
$$a; 0 = 0; a = 0 \qquad (9)$$
$$1 + a + (a^*; a^*) \leq a^* \qquad (10)$$

$$a; x \leq x \Rightarrow a^*; x \leq x \qquad (11)$$
$$x; a \leq x \Rightarrow x; a^* \leq x \qquad (12)$$
$$a; x \leq b \Leftrightarrow x \leq a \rightarrow b \qquad (13)$$
$$a \rightarrow b \leq a \rightarrow (b + c) \qquad (14)$$
$$(x \rightarrow x)^* = x \rightarrow x \qquad (15)$$
$$a \cdot (b \cdot c) = (a \cdot b) \cdot c \qquad (16)$$
$$a \cdot b = b \cdot a \qquad (17)$$
$$a \cdot a = a \qquad (18)$$
$$a + (a \cdot b) = a \qquad (19)$$
$$a \cdot (a + b) = a \qquad (20)$$

Fig. 1. Axiomatisation of action lattices (from [16])

Note that, by (19) and (20), the natural order $\leq$ can be equivalently defined by $a \leq b$ iff $a \cdot b = a$. Observe that by restricting the definition of $\mathbf{A}$ to the structure $(A, +, ;, 0, 1, *)$ axiomatised by (1)–(12) we obtain the definition of a *Kleene algebra* [9,18]. In the context of this work, this will be called the underlying Kleene algebra of $\mathcal{A}$. Moreover, by considering structure $(A, +, ;, 0, 1, \rightarrow, *)$ axiomatized by (1)–(15) we obtain the definition of (left-residuated) *action algebra* [27].

For the illustration of the structure with several examples and properties we suggest [20]. Just as example, we can consider a discrete 3-valued lattice underling the 3-valued logic:

Example 1 (3 - linear three-value lattice). The explicit introduction of a denotation for <u>unknown</u> gives rise to the the following three elements linear lattice

$$\mathbf{3} = (\{\top, u, \bot\}, \vee, \wedge, \bot, \top, *, \rightarrow, \wedge)$$

where

$\vee$	$\bot$	u	$\top$		$\wedge$	$\bot$	u	$\top$		$\rightarrow$	$\bot$	u	$\top$		$*$	
$\bot$	$\bot$	u	$\top$		$\bot$	$\bot$	$\bot$	$\bot$		$\bot$	$\top$	$\top$	$\top$		$\bot$	$\top$
u	u	u	$\top$		u	$\bot$	u	u		u	$\bot$	$\top$	$\top$		u	$\top$
$\top$	$\top$	$\top$	$\top$		$\top$	$\bot$	u	$\top$		$\top$	$\bot$	u	$\top$		$\top$	$\top$

It is easy to observe that, as a consequence of axiom (10), whenever $\top = 1$, we have that $x^* = 1$, for all x. Hence we have all the ingredients to introduced the Łukasiewicz arithmetic lattice, a structure that plays a main role in the theory developed in the sequel:

Definition 2 (Ł - the Łukasiewicz arithmetic lattice). *The Łukasiewicz arithmetic lattice is the structure*

$$\mathbf{Ł} = ([0,1], \max, \odot, 0, 1, *, \rightarrow, \min)$$

where

- $x \rightarrow y = \min(1, 1 - x + y)$,
- $x \odot y = \max(0, y + x - 1)$ *and*
- $x^* = 1$.

2.2   The Ł-Fuzzy Dynamic Logic

Signatures of $\mathcal{LDL}$ are exactly the same of the ones of Propositional Dynamic Logic: signatures are pairs (Π, Prop) of disjoint sets of atomic programs Π and of propositions symbols Prop.

Formulas of $\mathcal{LDL}$ consists in the positive fragment of Propositional Dynamic Logic: the set of Π -programs, denoted by $\text{Prg}(\Pi)$, consists of all expressions generated by

$$\pi \ni \pi_0 \,|\, \pi; \pi \,|\, \pi + \pi \,|\, \pi^*$$

for $\pi_0 \in \Pi$. Given a signature (Π, Prop), we define the $\mathcal{LDL}$-formulæ for (Π, Prop), denoted by $\text{Fm}^{\mathcal{LDL}}(\Pi, \text{Prop})$, as the ones generated by the grammar

$$\rho \ni \top \,|\, \bot \,|\, p \,|\, \rho \vee \rho \,|\, \rho \wedge \rho \,|\, \rho \rightarrow \rho \,|\, \rho \leftrightarrow \rho \,|\, \langle \pi \rangle \rho \,|\, [\pi] \rho$$

for $p \in \text{Prop}$ and $\pi \in \text{Prg}(\Pi)$.

Semantics. As expectable, the interpretation of atomic programs are Kripke structures with weighted transitions. For instance, atomic programs $\Pi = \{\pi, \pi'\}$ can be realized by the structures

$$\tag{21}$$

where that tags mention the uncertainty level of each states transitions. These weighted transition systems are usually represented by the underlying adjacency matrices

$$\mathcal{A}_\pi = \begin{bmatrix} 0 & \frac{\sqrt{2}}{3} \\ 0 & 0.7 \end{bmatrix} \qquad \mathcal{A}_{\pi'} = \begin{bmatrix} 0 & \frac{\sqrt{2}}{2} \\ \frac{\sqrt{3}}{2} & 0.5 \end{bmatrix}$$

Moreover, we need a mathematical framework to interpret composed programs, i.e., regular expressions of atomic programs. In other words, we need to consider a computational space for LDL where the programs are interpreted. Based on the classic matricial constructions over Kleene algebras (see [9,18]) we consider the structure

$$\mathbb{M}_n(Ł) = (M_n(Ł), \max, \odot, 0, 1, *) \tag{22}$$

as follows:

1. $M_n(Ł)$ is the space of $(n \times n)$-matrices over Ł
2. for any $A, B \in M_n(Ł)$, define $M = \max(A, B)$ by $M_{ij} \triangleq \max(A_{ij}, B_{ij})$, $i, j \leq n$.
3. for any $A, B \in M_n(Ł)$, define $M = A \odot B$ by taking

$$\max \left(A_{i1} \odot B_{1j}, \max(A_{i2} \odot B_{2j}, (\cdots, \max(A_{in} \odot B_{nj}) \cdots)) \right)$$

4. the matricial 1 and 0 are the $(n \times n)$-matrices defined by $1_{i,j} = \begin{cases} 1 & \text{if } i = j \\ 0 & \text{otherwise} \end{cases}$

   and $0_{i,j} = 0$, for any $i, j \leq n$.
5. for any $M = [a] \in \mathbb{M}_1(\mathbf{A})$, $M^* = [a^*]$;

   for any $M = \left[\begin{array}{c|c} A & B \\ \hline C & D \end{array}\right] \in M_n(\mathbf{A})$, $n > 1$, where A and D are square matrices,

   define

$$M^* = \left[\begin{array}{c|c} F^* & F^* \odot (B \odot D^*) \\ \hline (D^* \odot C) \odot F^* & \max(D^*, (D^* \odot (C \odot (F^* \odot (B \odot D^*))))) \end{array}\right]$$

where $F = \max(A, B \odot (D^* \odot C))$. Note that this construction is recursively defined from the base case (where $n = 2$) where the operations of the base action lattice $\mathbf{A}$ are used.

A classic result (e.g. [9,18]) establishes that Kleene algebras are closed under formation of matrices. This justifies the adoption of $\mathbb{M}_n(Ł)$ as a well behaved computational space for LDL.

Theorem 1. *The structure* $\mathbb{M}_n(Ł) = (M_n(Ł), \max, \odot, 0, 1, *)$ *defined above is a Kleene algebra.*

LDL-models for a set of propositions Prop and programs Π, denoted by $\text{Mod}^{LDL}(\Pi, \text{Prop})$, consists of tuples

$$\mathcal{A} = (W, V, (\mathcal{A}_\pi)_{\pi \in \Pi})$$

where W is a finite set (of states), $V : \text{Prop} \times W \to [0, 1]$ is a function, and $\mathcal{A}_\pi \in \mathbb{M}_n(Ł)$, with n standing for the cardinality of W.

The interpretation of programs in these models belongs to the space of the matrices over the underlying Kleene algebra of Ł. Each matrix represents the effect of a program executing from any point of the model. Formally, the interpretation of a program $\pi \in \mathrm{Prg}(\Pi)$ in a model $\mathcal{A} \in \mathrm{Mod}^{LDL}(\Pi, \mathrm{Prop})$ is recursively defined, from the set of atomic programs $(\mathcal{A}_\pi)_{\pi \in \Pi}$, as follows:

$$\mathcal{A}_{\pi;\pi'} = \mathcal{A}_\pi \odot \mathcal{A}_{\pi'}, \mathcal{A}_{\pi+\pi'} = \max(\mathcal{A}_\pi, \mathcal{A}_{\pi'}) \text{ and } \mathcal{A}_{\pi*} = \mathcal{A}_\pi^*.$$

together with the constants interpretations $\mathcal{A}_1 = \mathbf{1}$ and $\mathcal{A}_0 = \mathbf{0}$.

Returning to our running example, we are able to calculate the interpretation of the program $\mathcal{A}_{\pi+\pi'}$ by making

$$\mathcal{A}_{\pi+\pi'} = \max(\mathcal{A}_\pi, \mathcal{A}_{\pi'}) = \max\left(\begin{bmatrix} 0 & \frac{\sqrt{2}}{3} \\ 0 & 0.7 \end{bmatrix}, \begin{bmatrix} 0 & \frac{\sqrt{2}}{2} \\ \frac{\sqrt{3}}{2} & 0.5 \end{bmatrix}\right) = \begin{bmatrix} 0 & \frac{\sqrt{2}}{2} \\ \frac{\sqrt{3}}{2} & 0.7 \end{bmatrix} \quad (23)$$

that represents the following weighted transition system:

By considering the interpretation of the propositions $\mathrm{Prop} = \{p, q\}$ as $V(p, s_1) = 0.1$, $V(q, s_1) = 0.5$, $V(p, s_2) = \frac{\pi}{4}$ and $V(q, s_2) = 0.75$ we have a compete description of a concrete $(\{\pi, \pi'\}, \{p, q\})$-model $\mathcal{A} = (\{s_1, s_2\}, V, (\mathcal{A}_p)_{p \in \{\pi, \pi'\}})$.

Satisfaction. As mentioned above, the carrier of L corresponds to the space of truth degrees for LDL. Hence, the graded satisfaction relation for a model $\mathcal{A} \in \mathrm{Mod}^{LDL}(\Pi, \mathrm{Prop})$, consists of a function

$$\models : W \times \mathrm{Fm}^{LDL}(\Pi, \mathrm{Prop}) \to \mathrm{L}$$

recursively defined as follows:

- $(w \models \top) = 1$
- $(w \models \bot) = 0$
- $(w \models p) = V(p, w)$, for any $p \in \mathrm{Prop}$
- $(w \models \rho \wedge \rho') = \min\{(w \models \rho), (w \models \rho')\}$
- $(w \models \rho \vee \rho') = \max\{(w \models \rho), (w \models \rho')\}$
- $(w \models \rho \to \rho') = (w \models \rho) \to (w \models \rho')$
- $(w \models \langle \pi \rangle \rho) = \max\{\mathcal{A}_\pi(w, w') \odot (w' \models \rho) | w' \in W\}$
- $(w \models [\pi]\rho) = \min\{\mathcal{A}_\pi(w, w') \to (w' \models \rho) | w' \in W\}$

In order to illustrate the definition, the calculation of the truth degree of the formula $\langle \pi + \pi' \rangle(p \to q))$ in the introduced model $\mathcal{A}$ can be achieved as follows:

$$(s_1 \models \langle \pi + \pi' \rangle (p \to q)) = \max(0 \odot (0.1 \to 0.5), \tfrac{\sqrt{2}}{2} \odot (0.75 \to \tfrac{\pi}{4}))$$
$$= \tfrac{\sqrt{2}}{2} \odot (0.75 \to \tfrac{\pi}{4})$$
$$= \tfrac{\sqrt{2}}{2} \odot \min(1, 1 - 0.75 + \tfrac{\pi}{4})$$
$$= \tfrac{\sqrt{2}}{2}$$

Therefore, we conclude with a degree of certainty $\frac{\sqrt{2}}{2}$ that, after executing $\pi + \pi'$ from the state s_1, we have $p \to q$.

3   Ł-Interval Algebra

As stated before, the space of values $[0, 1]$ models exact measurements/truth values which is far from the real-world. In fact, any measurement presupposes an uncertainty which is not encoded by the elements of $[0, 1]$. Another situation arises whenever an expert is unable to supply an exact membership of an object in a fuzzy set, in this case he can provide a closed subinterval of $[0, 1]$ as an expression of his inability to supply an exact answer [7]. Such closed subintervals can also be used as the resulting abstraction of the exact values provided by various experts about the same membership. Therefore, assuming the **Łukasiewcz arithmetic lattice** $L = \langle [0, 1], \max, \odot, 0, 1, *, \to, \min \rangle$ as a natural space of measurements/truth values [24, Sect. 1.6] it is reasonable to investigate its interval counterpart. But what would be such interval counterpart? Before we proceed to answer this question, let's expose a little about the interval counterpart of real numbers algebra: $\langle \mathbb{R}; +, -, /, \times, 1, 0 \rangle$.

In the 50's Ramon Moore [22,23] and Teruo Sunaga [29] proposed the so called **interval arithmetics**. Interval arithmetics is a set of operations on the set of all closed intervals $[a, b] \subseteq \mathbb{R}$. They defined the arithmetic in the following way:

1. $[a, b] + [c, d] = [a + c, b + d]$
2. $-[c, d] = [-d, -c]$
3. $[a, b] \cdot [c, d] = [\min P, \max P]$—where $P = \{a \cdot c, a \cdot d, b \cdot c, b \cdot d\}$
4. $[a, b]^{-1} = [1/b, 1/a]$; provided that $0 \notin [a, b]$
5. $[a, b] - [c, d] = [a - d, b - c]$
6. $[a, b]/[c, d] = [a, b] \cdot ([c, d]^{-1})$

Observe what happens with each operation:

1. If $x \in [a, b]$ and $y \in [c, d]$, then $(x + y) \in [a, b] + [c, d]$,
2. If $x \in [a, b]$ and $y \in [c, d]$, then $(x \cdot y) \in [a, b] \cdot [c, d]$,
3. If $x \in [a, b]$ and $y \in [c, d]$, then $(x/y) \in [a, b]/[c, d]$, and
4. If $x \in [a, b]$, then $(-x) \in -[a, b]$.

The arithmetic on intervals reveals two desired properties: (a) **Correctness** and (b) **Optimality**.

"*Correctness.* ... when an expression is evaluated using intervals, it yields an interval containing all results of pointwise evaluations based on point values that are elements of the argument intervals.

...

Optimality. By optimality, we mean that the computed floating-point interval is not wider than necessary."

Hickey et al. [13, p. 1040]

The term *Correctness* connects n-ary interval operations F with n-ary real operations f and means that if F is *correct with respect to* f, then we can enfold any exact value $r \in \mathbb{R}$ in a closed interval $[a, b]$, such that $r \in [a, b]$, and then simply operate with such "envelopes" by using F, because the resulting interval $F([a, b])$ will enfold the desired result $f(r)$. Formally a function F is correct with respect to a real function f whenever:

$$r \in [a, b] \Rightarrow f(r) \in F([a, b]) \tag{24}$$

In practice, exact values are replaced by intervals which are operated with correct interval functions. Intervals enfold the exact values and provide a measure of impreciseness through its width.

Santiago *et al.* [2,28] investigated the notion of Correctness. Instead of correctness the authors used the term **representation**, since interval expressions could be faced not just as machine representations of an exact calculation, but also as an instance of a "mathematical representation of real numbers"[1]. Beyond correctness these interval operations are also optimum; namely the resulting intervals contain only the values of real operations. We could say that the proposed algebra of intervals is the **best interval representation for the arithmetic of real numbers**.

One side-effect of this process of intervalization is the loss of algebraic properties. The resulting structure is not an Euclidean field; for example $X - X$ is not always equal to $[0, 0]$. In this paper we will also lose some properties of Ł.

3.1   On the Interval Łukasiewicz Lattice

The Łukasiewicz arithmetic lattice $Ł = \langle [0, 1], \max, \odot, 0, 1, *, \rightarrow, \min \rangle$ contains non-finitely representable elements; e.g. irrational numbers. In a similar way we can think of an interval algebra for Ł. A piece of such algebra was introduced by Bedregal and Santiago in [4]. There, the authors proposed a correct interval implication for "$\rightarrow$". In what follows we propose the interval counterpart for $Ł = \langle [0, 1], \max, \odot, 0, 1, *, \rightarrow, \min \rangle$ in such a way that the resulting operations are correct and optimal, i.e. they are **best interval representations**.

Definition 3. *Consider the real unit interval* $U = [0, 1] \subseteq \mathbb{R}$ *and the set* $\mathbb{U} = \{[a, b] \mid 0 \leq a \leq b \leq 1\}$ *of subintervals of* U. *For any interval* $X \in \mathbb{U}$, $\underline{X}$ *is the*

---

[1] This idea is confirmed in some Representation Theorems of Euclidean continuous functions.

minimum of X and $\overline{X}$ the maximum of X; i.e. $X = [\underline{X}, \overline{X}]$. Given two intervals $X, Y \in \mathbb{U}$, let be the following partial orders on $\mathbb{U}$:

(i) *The **product or Kulisch-Miranker order** :*

$$X \leq Y \Leftrightarrow \underline{X} \leq \underline{Y} \wedge \overline{X} \leq \overline{Y}; \tag{25}$$

(ii) *The **set inclusion order**: for all $X, Y \in \mathbb{U}$,*

$$X \subseteq Y \Leftrightarrow \underline{Y} \leq \underline{X} \wedge \overline{X} \leq \overline{Y}. \tag{26}$$

Definition 4 [28]. *An interval $X \in \mathbb{U}$ is a **representation** of any real number $\alpha \in X$. Considering two interval representations X and Y for a real number α, X is said to be an interval representation of α better than Y, if $X \subseteq Y$. This notion can also be naturally extended for n-tuples of intervals. A function $F : \mathbb{U}^n \longrightarrow \mathbb{U}$ is said to be an **interval representation** of a real function $f : U^n \longrightarrow U$ if, for each $\boldsymbol{X} \in \mathbb{U}^n$ and $\boldsymbol{x} \in \boldsymbol{X}$, $f(\boldsymbol{x}) \in F(\boldsymbol{X})$. F is also said to be <u>correct</u> with respect to f. An interval function $F : \mathbb{U}^n \longrightarrow \mathbb{U}$ is said to be an interval representation of a real function $f : U^n \longrightarrow U$ <u>better</u> than an interval function $G : \mathbb{U}^n \longrightarrow \mathbb{U}$, if $F(\boldsymbol{X}) \subseteq G(\boldsymbol{X})$, for each $\boldsymbol{X} \in \mathbb{U}^n$. The **best interval representation** of a real function $f : U^n \longrightarrow U$ is the interval function $\widehat{f} : \mathbb{U}^n \longrightarrow \mathbb{U}$, defined by*

$$\widehat{f}(\boldsymbol{X}) = [\inf\{f(\boldsymbol{x}) \mid \boldsymbol{x} \in \boldsymbol{X}\}, \sup\{f(\boldsymbol{x}) \mid \boldsymbol{x} \in \boldsymbol{X}\}]. \tag{27}$$

In what follows we show the best interval representation for the Łukasiewicz arithmetic lattice $\mathbb{L} = \langle [0, 1], \max, \odot, 0, 1, *, \rightarrow, \min \rangle$. Almost all of the resulting interval representations comes from previous works. Before we go further it is noteworthy that **the following resulting structure is the best possible interval structure to represent the Łukasiewicz arithmetic lattice.**

Definition 5. *Given $X, Y \in \mathbb{U}$.*

1. $Max(X, Y) = [\max(\underline{X}, \underline{Y}), \max(\overline{X}, \overline{Y})]$
2. $Min(X, Y) = [\min(\underline{X}, \underline{Y}), \min(\overline{X}, \overline{Y})]$
3. $X \odot Y = [(\underline{X} \odot \underline{Y}), (\overline{X} \odot \overline{Y})] = [\max(0, \underline{X} + \underline{Y} - 1), \max(0, \overline{X} + \overline{Y} - 1)]$
4. $X \Rrightarrow Y = [(\overline{X} \rightarrow \underline{Y}), (\underline{X} \rightarrow \overline{Y})] = [\min(1, 1 - \overline{X} + \underline{Y}), \min(1, 1 - \underline{X} + \overline{Y})]$
5. $X^{\circledast} = [\underline{X}^*, \overline{X}^*] = [1, 1]$.

Proposition 1. *All of these interval operations are the best interval representations of the operations in L; i.e. $Max = \widehat{\max}$, $Min = \widehat{\min}$, $\odot = \widehat{\odot}$, $\Rrightarrow = \widehat{\rightarrow}$, and $\circledast = \widehat{*}$.*

Proof. The operations min and $\odot$ are T-norms on $[0, 1]$ and the interval representations of T-norms, according to [5, Theorem 4.3], is given by $\widehat{T}(X, Y) = [T(\underline{X}, \underline{Y}), T(\overline{X}, \overline{Y})]$. The max operation is a T-conorm on $[0, 1]$ and the interval representations of T-conorms, according to [3, Theorem 5.2], is given by $\widehat{S}(X, Y) = [S(\underline{X}, \underline{Y}), S(\overline{X}, \overline{Y})]$. According to [4, Proposition 4.4] $\Rrightarrow = \widehat{\rightarrow}$. Finally, it is trivial that $\circledast = \widehat{*}$.

Proposition 2. $X \leq Y$ iff $Max(X, Y) = Y$.

Proof. $X \leq Y$ iff $\underline{X} \leq \underline{Y}$ and $\overline{X} \leq \overline{Y}$ iff $\max(\underline{X}, \underline{Y}) = \underline{Y}$ and $\max(\overline{X}, \overline{Y}) = \overline{Y}$ iff $Max(X, Y) = Y$.

The structure $\langle \mathbb{U}, Max, Min, [0, 0], [1, 1] \rangle$ is a bounded lattice.

Theorem 2. *The structure* $K(\widehat{L}) = \langle \mathbb{U}, \widehat{max}, \widehat{\odot}, [0, 0], [1, 1], \widehat{*} \rangle$ *is a Kleene algebra.*

Proof. $\widehat{max}$ trivially satisfies Eqs. (1)–(4). According to [5, p. 3224] $\widehat{\odot}$ satisfies Eqs. (5)–(6). Equation (7) requires the result that every T-norm distributes over the maximum [15, Proposition 2.22], the rest of the proof is an exercise. Equation (8) comes from Eq. (7) and the commutativity of $\widehat{\odot}$. Equation (9) is also easily proved. Since for every $A \in \mathbb{U}$, $A^* = [1, 1]$, and $[1, 1]$ is the top element in $\mathbb{U}$, then inequation (10) is trivially satisfied. Again, since $A^* = [1, 1]$, then $A^* \widehat{\odot} x = x$ and implication (11) is satisfied. A similar argument applies to implication (12).

Since $K(\widehat{L})$ is a Kleene algebra, we can canonically construct, as in (22), the space of matrices $\mathbb{M}_n(K(\widehat{L}))$ (which is also a Kleene algebra).

Observation: According to Proposition 1 every operation of the Kleene algebra $K(\widehat{L})$ is the best interval representation of the respective operation of $K(L)$. Therefore, we can say that $K(\widehat{L})$ and $\mathbb{M}_n(K(\widehat{L}))$ are, respectively, **the best interval representation of the Kleene algebras** L and $\mathbb{M}_n(K(L))$.

Notation: In order to simplify the notation we use the same symbols for the operations of Łukasiewicz Kleene algebra: $L = \langle [0, 1], \max, \odot, 0, 1, * \rangle$, its interval representation $K(\widehat{L}) = (\mathbb{U}, \max, \odot, 0, 1, *)$ and the corresponding spaces of matrices: $\mathbb{M}_n(K(L)) = (M_n(L), \max, \odot, 0, 1, *)$ and $\mathbb{M}_n(K(\widehat{L})) = (M_n(K(\widehat{L})), \max, \odot, 0, 1, *)$.

The next automata are the interval representation of (21)

$$\mathcal{A}_\pi : \quad [0.7, 0.7] \quad [0.4, 0.5] \quad (s_1) \longrightarrow (s_2) \qquad\qquad \mathcal{A}_{\pi'} : \quad [0.5, 0.5] \quad [0.6, 0.8] \quad (s_1) \rightleftarrows (s_2) \quad [0.7, 0.9]$$

Their interval matrices are:

$$\mathcal{A}_\pi = \begin{bmatrix} (0, 0) & (0.4, 0.5) \\ (0, 0) & (0.7, 0.7) \end{bmatrix} \qquad \mathcal{A}_{\pi'} = \begin{bmatrix} (0, 0) & (0.6, 0.8) \\ (0.7, 0.9) & (0.5, 0.5) \end{bmatrix}$$

The interpretation of the program $\mathcal{A}_{\pi + \pi'}$ is

$$\max \left(\begin{bmatrix} (0, 0) & (0.4, 0.5) \\ (0, 0) & (0.7, 0.7) \end{bmatrix}, \begin{bmatrix} (0, 0) & (0.6, 0.8) \\ (0.7, 0.9) & (0.5, 0.7) \end{bmatrix} \right) = \begin{bmatrix} (0, 0) & (0.6, 0.8) \\ (0.7, 0.9) & (0.7, 0.7) \end{bmatrix}$$

which represents the following weighted transition system:

$$\mathcal{A}_{\pi+\pi'} : \quad \underset{[0.7,0.9]}{\overset{[0.6,0.8]}{\underset{\longrightarrow}{}}} \begin{array}{c} [0.7,0.7] \\ \end{array}$$

$$\mathcal{A}_{\pi+\pi'} : \quad (s_1) \; \underset{[0.7,0.9]}{\overset{[0.6,0.8]}{\rightleftharpoons}} \; (s_2) \; {}^{[0.7,0.7]} $$

4   The Price

Before we proceed, it must be clear why do we use intervals. Intervals are used in a variety of situations when it is not possible to use exact values. If the exact values can be used, then it does not make sense to use intervals.

Although it is possible to use a near exact value to represent a desired point; e.g. 3.14 would be used to represent π, the information about impreciseness is not codified by such exact value. Intervals provide such kind of information and the quality of such representation can be measured by the width of the interval: the tight is the interval the better is the representation.

Sometimes intervals are the only representation available to work with; e.g. (1) some magnetic resonance machines provide intervals for non-exact values (2) some applications in Fuzzy Systems provide intervals as inexact membership degree or as the abstraction of several membership degrees provided by different experts.

In any case, intervals are the entities provided instead of exact values. To deal with intervals a **price must be paid**; namely: not all properties of the space containing the exact values are preserved in the interval space. For example, in the case of real numbers, the respective interval representation does not satisfy the property: $x - x = 0$.

As we will see the same happens with the interval representation of the action lattice L. Some properties stated in Fig. 1 are satisfied by L, but are not by its interval representation $\widehat{L}$. Since these properties are connected with Dynamic Logics, there will be impacts of interval representation on the logical axioms. Some of these impacts are discussed below:

Observe that in the Lukasiewicz action lattice, L, the equation "$x \rightarrow x = 1$" is satisfied while this is not true in its interval representation: $\widehat{L}$. *But this is a crucial feature of* $\widehat{L}$! Take the following example: $[0.5, 0.6] \rightarrow [0.5, 0.6] = [0.6 \rightarrow 0.5, 0.5 \rightarrow 0.6] = [0.9, 1] \neq [1, 1]$. Although $1 \in [0.9, 1]$, what is happening here? Suppose that the interval $[0.5, 0.6]$ is the tightest machine interval which represents the non-finitely representable exact values in L: $\frac{\pi}{6} = 0.523598775\ldots$ and $\frac{\frac{\pi}{6}+0.6}{2} = 0.5617993875\ldots$. Then, in order to calculate the implications: $\frac{\pi}{6} \rightarrow \frac{\pi}{6}$, $\frac{\frac{\pi}{6}+0.6}{2} \rightarrow \frac{\frac{\pi}{6}+0.6}{2}$, $\frac{\pi}{6} \rightarrow \frac{\frac{\pi}{6}+0.6}{2}$ and $\frac{\frac{\pi}{6}+0.6}{2} \rightarrow \frac{\pi}{6}$, the only way is to calculate: $[0.5, 0.6] \mathbin{\widehat{\rightarrow}} [0.5, 0.6]$. In this case, $\frac{\pi}{6} \rightarrow \frac{\pi}{6} = 1$, $\frac{\frac{\pi}{6}+0.6}{2} \rightarrow \frac{\frac{\pi}{6}+0.6}{2} = 1$, $\frac{\pi}{6} \rightarrow \frac{\frac{\pi}{6}+0.6}{2} = 1$, $\frac{\frac{\pi}{6}+0.6}{2} \rightarrow \frac{\pi}{6} = 0.9617993875\ldots$, and $[0.5, 0.6] \mathbin{\widehat{\rightarrow}} [0.5, 0.6] = [0.6 \rightarrow 0.5, 0.5 \rightarrow 0.6] = [0.9, 1]$. Therefore, all the previous implications are contained in the implication $[0.5, 0.6] \mathbin{\widehat{\rightarrow}} [0.5, 0.6]$. In other words, unless an interval X has the form $[a, a]$, it does not make sense to impose $X \to X = [1, 1]$, since the same interval can be used to represent two different exact values. Therefore, the known logical laws of Dynamic Logic must be reviewed.

The price to be paid for using intervals does not stop here, in what follows we show that the structure $\widehat{L} = \langle \mathbb{U}, \max, \odot, 0, 1, *, \widehat{\to}, \min \rangle$ is not an action lattice. This means that to propose a Dynamic Logic which deals with interval values some properties of action lattices must be *generalized*.

Proposition 3. *1. Equation (13) $a; x \leq b \Leftrightarrow x \leq a \to b$ (Left-residuation) fails.*
2. Equation (15) $(x \to x)^* = x \to x$ fails, instead $x \to x \leq (x \to x)^*$.

Proof. 1. Make $x = [1, 1]$, then $a \odot x \leq b \Leftrightarrow x \leq a \to b$ becomes $a \leq b \Leftrightarrow a \to b = [1, 1]$ which is not true, since $x \leq x$, but, as we saw, $x \to x$ is not always equal to $[1, 1]$; make $x = [0.5, 0.6]$.
2. Make $x = [0.5, 0.6]$. By definition $(x \to x)^* = [1, 1]$, but $x \to x = [0.9, 1]$. More generally, since $\underline{x \to x} = \overline{x} \to \underline{x} \leq 1$ and $\overline{x \to x} = 1$, then $x \to x \leq [1, 1] = (x \to x)^*$.

Proposition 4. *Equations (16)–(20) are satisfied.*

Proof. It is well-known that the structure $\langle \mathbb{U}, \max, \min \rangle$ is a lattice.

However, it is possible to observe that some fragment of the logic generated by action lattices remains untouched and behaves as expected. For example, by considering the interpretation of the propositions $\mathrm{Prop} = \{p, q\}$ as $V(p, s_1) = [0.1, 0.1]$, $V(q, s_1) = [0.5, 0.5]$, $V(p, s_2) = [0.7, 0.8]$ and $V(q, s_2) = [0.75, 0.75]$ we have:

$(s_1 \models \langle \pi + \pi' \rangle (p \to q))$
$= \max([0, 0] \odot ([0.1, 0.1] \to [0.5, 0.5]), [0.6, 0.8] \odot ([0.5, 0.5] \to [0.7, 0.8]))$
$= \max([0, 0], [0.6, 0.8] \odot [0.5 \to 0.7, 0.5 \to 0.8])$
$= [0.6, 0.8] \odot [1, 1]$
$= [0.6, 0.8] \ni \frac{\sqrt{2}}{2}$.

5   Conclusion and Further Work

Dynamic logics are very important to specify and verify properties on programs' executions. Nowadays, Dynamic logics refers to a large family of logics that have been intensively used in the verification of computational systems, that have been able to evolve and adapt to new, and complex validation challenges.

In [20, 21] there was introduced a generic method to build propositional many-valued dynamic logics, parametrized by an action lattice. Moreover, it is shown that, from beyond of these generic constructions, only the ones parametrized by action lattices behave well, in the sense of the respect of the classic axiomatic of propositional dynamic logic [12].

We start this work by looking in a such special case, namely the Łukasiewski lattice over $[0, 1]$ (it is well known that it can be expanded to an Action lattice). This structure support a suitable framework to design and reason about systems with uncertainty degrees in transitions. However, for implementation purposes or in the verification of real systems, it is not possible to deal with exact degrees (for instance irrational numbers), being hence mandatory the use approximations. In this view we proposed in Sect. 3.1 an interval version of the Łukasiewski lattice. Also here, it can be defined a closure operations in order to obtain a Kleene Algebra and then the Conway's matricial constructions [9] can be applied. Although, not all works perfectly. Actually, the interval Łukasiewski Kleene algebra is not an action lattice (see Proposition 3).

This is the price to have intervals. In Sect. 4 we discuss some important questions related to this situation. In particular, we explain some non intuitive phenomena: for instance the implication $[a, b] \rightarrow [a, b]$ is not necessarily the top element of the lattice.

This work paves the way for an interesting research agenda. The next step will the generalization of the intervalising process to an arbitrary Kleene algebra and to find the axiomatisation for the abstract interval pseudo-action algebras. We have already worked on this subject and some weakening of the residuum adjunction must be considered. Another important question, that we shortly consider at the end of Sect. 4, is how these structures constitute a sound (interval) semantics for Dynamic Logic. It can be proved that this semantics is correct in the sense that the value of a sentence in the standard case belongs to the respective interval interpretation.

Acknowledgements. R. Santiago and B. Bedregal are supported by Marie Curie project PIRSES-GA-2012-318986 GetFun funded by EU-FP7 and by the *Brazilian National Council for Scientific and Technological Development* (CNPq, Portuguese: *Conselho Nacional de Desenvolvimento Científico e Tecnológico*) under the Projects 304597/2015-5 and 307681/2012-2. This work is also financed by the ERDF – European Regional Development Fund through the Operational Programme for Competitiveness and Internationalisation - COMPETE 2020 and by National Funds through the Portuguese funding agency, FCT-*Fundação para a Ciência e a Tecnologia* within project POCI-01-0145-FEDER- 016692. A. Madeira and M. Martins are also supported by the FCT BPD individual grant SFRH/BPD/103004/2014 and UID/MAT/04106/2013 at CIDMA, respectively.

References

1. Baltag, A., Smets, S.: Quantum logic as a dynamic logic. Synthese **179**(2), 285–306 (2011)
2. Bedregal, B., Santiago, R.: Some continuity notions for interval functions and representation. Comput. Appl. Math. **32**(3), 435–446 (2013)
3. Bedregal, B.C., Takahashi, A.: Interval valued versions of t-conorms, fuzzy negations and fuzzy implications. In: 2006 IEEE International Conference on Fuzzy Systems , pp. 1981–1987 (2006)
4. Bedregal, B.R.C., Santiago, R.H.N.: Interval representations, Łukasiewicz implicators and Smets-Magrez axioms. Inf. Sci. **221**, 192–200 (2013)
5. Bedregal, B.R.C., Takahashi, A.: The best interval representations of t-norms and automorphisms. Fuzzy Sets Syst. **157**(24), 3220–3230 (2006)

6. Bou, F., Esteva, F., Godo, L., Rodríguez, R.O.: On the minimum many-valued modal logic over a finite residuated lattice. J. Log. Comput. **21**(5), 739–790 (2011)
7. Bustince, H., Barrenechea, E., Pagola, M., Fernandez, J., Xu, Z., Bedregal, B., Montero, J., Hagras, H., Herrera, F., Baets, B.D.: A historical account of types of fuzzy sets and their relationships. IEEE Trans. Fuzzy Syst. **24**(1), 179–194 (2016)
8. Cignoli, R., d'Ottaviano, I., Mundici, D.: Algebraic Foundations of Many-Valued Reasoning. Trends in Logic. Springer, Netherlands (1999)
9. Conway, J.H.: Regular Algebra and Finite Machines. Printed in GB by William Clowes & Sons Ltd, London (1971)
10. Fitting, M.: Many-valued modal logics. Fundam. Inform. **15**(3–4), 235–254 (1991)
11. Fitting, M.: Many-valued model logics II. Fundam. Inform. **17**(1–2), 55–73 (1992)
12. Harel, D., Kozen, D., Tiuryn, J.: Dynamic Logic. MIT Press, Cambridge (2000)
13. Hickey, T., Ju, Q., Van Emden, M.H.: Interval arithmetic: from principles to implementation. J. ACM **48**(5), 1038–1068 (2001)
14. Hughes, J., Esterline, A.C., Kimiaghalam, B.: Means-end relations and a measure of efficacy. J. Log. Lang. Inf. **15**(1–2), 83–108 (2006)
15. Klement, E.P., Mesiar, R., Pap, E.: Triangular Norms, 1st edn. Springer, Berlin (2000)
16. Kozen, D.: On action algebras (manuscript). In: Logic and Flow of Information, Amsterdam (1991)
17. Kozen, D.: A probabilistic PDL. J. Comput. Syst. Sci. **30**(2), 162–178 (1985)
18. Kozen, D.: A completeness theorem for Kleene algebras and the algebra of regular events. Inf. Comput. **110**(2), 366–390 (1994)
19. Liau, C.-J.: Many-valued dynamic logic for qualitative decision theory. In: Zhong, N., Skowron, A., Ohsuga, S. (eds.) RSFDGrC 1999. LNCS (LNAI), vol. 1711, pp. 294–303. Springer, Heidelberg (1999). doi:10.1007/978-3-540-48061-7_36
20. Madeira, A., Neves, R., Martins, M.A.: An exercise on the generation of many-valued dynamic logics. J. Log. Algebraic Methods Program. **85**(5), 1011–1037 (2016)
21. Madeira, A., Neves, R., Martins, M.A., Barbosa, L.S.: A dynamic logic for every season. In: Braga, C., Martí-Oliet, N. (eds.) SBMF 2014. LNCS, vol. 8941, pp. 130–145. Springer, Heidelberg (2015). doi:10.1007/978-3-319-15075-8_9
22. Moore, R.E.: Interval arithmetic and automatic error analysis in digital computing. Ph.D. dissertation, Department of Mathematics, Stanford University, Stanford, CA, USA, November 1962. (Also published as Applied Mathematics and Statistics Laboratories Technical report No. 25)
23. Moore, R.E., Yang, C.T.: Interval analysis I. Technical document LMSD-285875, Lockheed Missiles and Space Division, Sunnyvale, CA, USA (1959)
24. Mundici, D.: Advanced Łukasiewicz Calculus and MV-Algebras. Trends in Logic. Springer, Netherlands (2011)
25. Platzer, A.: Logical Analysis of Hybrid Systems - Proving Theorems for Complex Dynamics. Springer, Berlin (2010)
26. Pratt, V.R.: Semantical considerations on floyd-hoare logic. In: 17th Annual Symposium on Foundations of Computer Science, Houston, Texas, USA, 25–27 October 1976, pp. 109–121. IEEE Computer Society (1976)
27. Pratt, V.: Action logic and pure induction. In: Eijck, J. (ed.) JELIA 1990. LNCS, vol. 478, pp. 97–120. Springer, Heidelberg (1991). doi:10.1007/BFb0018436
28. Santiago, R.H.N., Bedregal, B.R.C., Acióly, B.M.: Formal aspects of correctness and optimality of interval computations. Formal Aspects Comput. **18**(2), 231–243 (2006)

29. Sunaga, T.: Theory of an interval algebra and its application to numerical analysis [reprint of Res. Assoc. Appl. Geom. Mem. **2**, 29–46 (1958)]. Japan J. Ind. Appl. Math. **26**(2–3), 125–143 (2009)
30. Xu, Y., Ruan, D., Qin, K., Liu, J.: Lattice-Valued Logic: An Alternative Approach to Treat Fuzziness and Incomparability. Studies in Fuzziness and Soft Computing. Springer, Berlin (2012)

An Evolutionary Approach to Translate Operational Specifications into Declarative Specifications

Facundo Molina[1(✉)], César Cornejo[1], Renzo Degiovanni[1,3], Germán Regis[1],
Pablo F. Castro[1,3], Nazareno Aguirre[1,3], and Marcelo F. Frias[2,3]

[1] Department of Computer Science, FCEFQyN,
National University of Río Cuarto, Río Cuarto, Argentina
{fmolina,ccornejo,rdegiovanni,gregis,pcastro,naguirre}@dc.exa.unrc.edu.ar
[2] Department of Software Engineering,
Buenos Aires Institute of Technology (ITBA), Buenos Aires, Argentina
mfrias@itba.edu.ar
[3] National Council for Scientific and Technical Research (CONICET),
Buenos Aires, Argentina

Abstract. Various tools for program analysis, including run-time assertion checkers and static analyzers such as verification and test generation tools, require formal specifications of the programs being analyzed. Moreover, many of these tools and techniques require such specifications to be written in a particular style, or follow certain patterns, in order to obtain an acceptable performance from the corresponding analyses. Thus, having a formal specification sometimes is not enough for using a particular technique, since such specification may not be provided in the right formalism. In this paper, we deal with this problem in the increasingly common case of having an *operational* specification, while for analysis reasons requiring a *declarative* specification. We propose an evolutionary approach to translate an operational specification written in a sequential programming language, into a declarative specification, in relational logic. We perform experiments on a benchmark of data structure implementations, that show that translating representation invariants using our approach and verifying invariant preservation using the resulting specifications outperforms verification with specifications obtained using an existing semantics-preserving translation. Also, our evolutionary computation translation achieves very good precision in this context.

1 Introduction

Many software validation and verification activities, both formal and informal, require a description of the software under analysis, since many analyses typically consist in checking compliance of the software against some prescribed intended behavior [12]. In the last few decades, formal specifications have gained an important notoriety in such contexts, mainly due to their unambiguous interpretation and the increasing availability of technologies for their automated analysis, which are making them part of effective software analysis approaches.

© Springer International Publishing AG 2016
L. Ribeiro and T. Lecomte (Eds.): SBMF 2016, LNCS 10090, pp. 145–160, 2016.
DOI: 10.1007/978-3-319-49815-7_9

Among the broad variety of formal notations, some styles or specification paradigms can be identified. For instance, in the context of program specification via pre- and postconditions, representation invariants, and the like, two distinguishing styles are the *operational*, and the *declarative*. In the operational style, specifications are captured through code, e.g., via a routine that checks whether the internal representation of a given object is consistent [19]. On the other hand, the declarative style often uses a logical formalism for expressing the same kind of property. A well-established approach is based on using a first-order logic complemented with closure operators, as put forward by notations such as JML [3] and Alloy's relational logic [14].

A problem that arises with the proliferation of notations and, more importantly, with the above described different specification styles, is that different tools adopt different styles, and provide optimizations and enhancements that only become available for such particular notations or styles. For instance, the test generation tool Korat [2] requires a specification to be provided operationally (as a repOK routine) to automatically produce test inputs; it implements "perfect" symmetry-breaking and search pruning techniques that are particularly tied to such representation, and thus makes it very difficult (and ineffective) to generate tests for, say, an object-oriented program equipped with a JML contract. On the other hand, tools for verification based on declarative notations, e.g., TACO [10], can exploit mechanisms such as tight bounds [9], whose computation are also strongly tied to declarative notations, and cannot straightforwardly (nor effectively) be computed from operational specifications. This situation is combined with the increasing need for cross-usage of automated analysis tools. A sample scenario arises with current techniques for fault localization and program repair, that require tests for their application; combining such tools with automated test generation is an obvious approach that combines automated analysis technologies. This problem leads to a clear demand to be able to translate specifications across different styles and notations.

Notice that even when semantics-preserving translations are available between different formalisms, in many cases these produce translated specifications that, although "correct" in the sense that they preserve the semantics of the original specifications, are ineffective for the analysis mechanisms of the target notations, due to the violation of (many times implicit) patterns for optimal exploitation of analysis. For instance, Korat requires repOK methods to "fail as soon as possible", in the sense that these methods should try to decide when a structure does not satisfy the predicate visiting the least possible elements of the structure, for test generation to be effective. Similarly, the efficiency of tools like Alloy are in many cases very dependent on how specifications are written; analyzing specifications with large numbers of (existential) quantification often fails during preprocessing (e.g., in translation to CNF to use SAT-based verification), while expressing equivalent specifications through simple transformations (e.g., skolemizations) can have a drastic impact in analysis efficiency. Thus, in some cases the existence of semantics-preserving syntax-guided translations are still unsatisfactory.

In this paper, we deal with a particular instance of the above described situation, namely the translation from an operational specification of a representation invariant, written in an imperative sequential programming language, to a declarative invariant specification, in relational logic. While there exists a semantics preserving translation from one to the other, we show that the resulting specifications are inadequate for analysis. We then propose an evolutionary approach to produce relational logic specifications from imperative ones, based on a genetic algorithm especially designed for this purpose. We evaluate our approach on a benchmark of data structure implementations, translating their corresponding representation invariants for verification. As our experiments show, translating specifications using our approach and verifying invariant preservation using the resulting specifications outperforms invariant preservation verification directly with specifications obtained using the semantics-preserving translation, and our evolutionary computation translation achieves very good precision in this context.

The remainder of the paper is organized as follows. In Sect. 2, we motivate our approach by presenting an illustrating example, that in particular shows the need to translate across different specification styles. In Sect. 3 we present our evolutionary algorithm for learning declarative specifications from operational ones, including detailed descriptions of how candidate specifications are captured as chromosomes, and how these are evaluated during the genetic algorithm's search. In Sect. 4 we experimentally evaluate our approach, on a benchmark composed of various data structure implementations. Section 5 compares our technique with related work, and finally, in Sect. 6, we present our conclusions and lines for further work.

2   A Motivating Example

In order to motivate our approach, let us consider an analysis scenario involving a simple data structure, *singly linked lists*. This data structure is captured through classes SinglyLinkedList and Node, as defined in Fig. 1. Assume, for instance, that we would need to verify that a routine manipulating such data structure, e.g., an insertion routine, preserves the representation invariant of lists, i.e., inserting an element in a *valid* list retrieves also a *valid* list. In order to proceed with this verification, we then need a specification of what it means for singly linked lists to be *valid*. A particular specification, with a style put forward in [19], consists in capturing the *representation invariant* of the structure (i.e., the intended *validity* condition for singly linked lists) through a boolean routine, that checks whether the condition holds or not for a given structure. An example of such method, named repOK() as is usual, indicating that singly linked lists must be acyclic and their number of nodes must coincide with the value in the size field, is shown in Fig. 2.

A substantially different approach to the *operational* style of using code to write specifications, is based on the use of some suitable logical formalism, for the same task. This alternative approach has been extensively used, from the

```
public class SinglyLinkedList {        public class Node {
    private Node header;                    private int element;
    private int size;                       private Node next;
    ...                                      ...
}                                          //setters and getters
                                           //of the above fields
                                            ...
                                       }
```

Fig. 1. Java classes defining singly linked lists.

```
public boolean repOK() {
    Set<Entry> visited = new java.util.HashSet<Entry>();
    visited.add(header);
    Entry current = header;
    while (true) {
        Entry next = current.getNext();
        if (next == null) break;
        if (!visited.add(next)) return false;
        current = next;
    }
    if (visited.size() != size) return false;
    return true;
}
```

Fig. 2. Operational version of the representation invariant for singly linked lists.

seminal work of Hoare and Floyd, where first-order logic is used to express assertions regarding program states, to more modern languages such as JML [3] and Alloy [14], which due to further expressive power needs, have extended first-order logic with closure or reachability predicates. In particular, notice that first-order logic is not sufficiently expressive to capture the acyclicity on singly linked lists, in our example. A declarative predicate, expressed in Alloy's relational logic, and capturing exactly the same property as method repOK() in Fig. 2, is shown in Fig. 3. Notice how reflexive-transitive and transitive closures (denoted by operators * and ^, respectively) are employed to capture reachability and acyclicity.

To illustrate the need for effective translations across different specification styles, suppose that we only count with the *operational* invariant, specified through method repOK() in Java. While this specification is suitable for generating test inputs using Korat (in fact, this particular example is taken from Korat's set of case studies [17]), if we want to perform bounded verification using a tool like TACO [9,10], then this specification becomes unsuitable, since TACO expects a *logical* specification. However, it is possible to translate an operational specification into an equivalent declarative specification (equivalent in bounded contexts), e.g., using the translations embedded in tools like TACO [9,10] and CBMC [18]. The logical specification resulting from the translation

```
one sig Null { }

sig List { }

sig Node { }

pred repOK[thiz: List, header: List-> one Node+Null,
           next: Node -> one Node+Null] {
   (all n: thiz.header.*next | n !in n.^next) and
   (# thiz.header.*next = thiz.size)
}
```

Fig. 3. Declarative version of the representation invariant for singly linked lists, in Alloy's relational logic.

of the repOK() method shown in Fig. 2 is shown in Fig. 4. This specification, while correct with respect to the semantics of the original (again, for a particular bounded scope), is unsuitable for verification. For instance, verifying that method **insert** preserves the representation invariant for lists of size at most

```
pred repOK[thiz_0: List, header_0: List ->one (Node + Null),
     size_0: List ->one Int, next_0: Node ->one (Node + Null),
     result_0, result_1: boolean] {

nodesToVisit_1 = thiz_0.size_0 and
current_1 = thiz_0.header_0 and ((lt[thiz_0.size_0, 0] and
result_1 = false and current_1 = current_4 and
nodesToVisit_1 = nodesToVisit_4 ) or (not lt[thiz_0.size_0,0]
and  ((current_1 = current_4 and
nodesToVisit_1 = nodesToVisit_4 ) or
(gt[nodesToVisit_1, 0] and current_1 != Null and
nodesToVisit_2 = sub[nodesToVisit_1, 1] and
current_2 = current_1.next_0 and ((current_2 = current_4 and
nodesToVisit_2 = nodesToVisit_4 ) or (gt[nodesToVisit_2, 0]
and current_2 != Null and nodesToVisit_3 =
sub[nodesToVisit_2,1] and  current_3 = current_2.next_0 and
((current_3 = current_4 and
nodesToVisit_3 = nodesToVisit_4 ) or (gt[nodesToVisit_3, 0]
and current_3 != Null and nodesToVisit_4 =
sub[nodesToVisit_3, 1] and current_4 = current_3.next_0))))))
and not (gt[nodesToVisit_4, 0] and current_4 != Null ) and
((eq[nodesToVisit_4, 0] and current_4 = Null and
result_1 = true) or (not (eq[nodesToVisit_4, 0] and
current_4 = Null) and result_1 = false))))
}
```

Fig. 4. Declarative representation invariant for singly linked lists, obtained using a semantics-preserving translation from repOK in Fig. 2.

12 takes 3839 seconds when using the invariant in Fig. 2, whereas it takes 1648 seconds when using the invariant in Fig. 3. As we will show later on in this paper, such difference in efficiency becomes more notorious in more complex data structure invariants (see the Validation Section).

The above described problem is the motivation for our approach. As we explain in the following section, we will develop an evolutionary algorithm to translate from operational specifications into declarative ones, with the aim of obtaining better suited specifications, from the point of view of analysis. More precisely, our aim is to obtain, from operational specifications such as that in Fig. 2, declarative specifications closer to that in Fig. 3 (as opposed to that in Fig. 4), that would allow us to perform certain automated analyses more efficiently.

3   An Evolutionary Algorithm for Learning Declarative Specifications

As we mentioned in previous sections, our objective is to compute a declarative specification Φ in relational logic, from an operational specification Φ_{op}, written in a sequential programming language. To do so, we design a genetic algorithm, that we describe below. Genetic algorithms [13] are non-exhaustive guided search algorithms, based on a hill climbing strategy [24]. The search space is composed of a generally very large set of individuals (the candidates), and the search objective is to find an individual with sought-for features. As opposed to classic search algorithms, genetic algorithms maintain a *set* of individuals, called the population, and search progresses by iteratively selecting a number of individuals in the population, using these for evolution (building new individuals out of these), and leaving out some individuals of the whole set (the "old" ones and the "new" ones). Selection of individuals for population evolution, as well as individuals' removal, are guided by a *fitness function*, the heuristic function used to guide the search. This function applies to individuals, and its result is generalizable to the population too (e.g., the fitness of the population may be taken as the fitness of its "fittest" individual). This function captures the features sought for in the search, and thus can be used as a halting criterion (e.g., algorithm stops after finding an individual with fitness above a certain threshold). Finally, individuals are often called *chromosomes*, and represented as vectors of *genes* that capture their characteristics. This idea is strongly related to how new individuals are constructed: by representing candidates as vectors of independent characteristics, one can build new candidates by combining part of the characteristics of an individual with part of the characteristics of another, or by arbitrarily *changing* a characteristic of a given individual. These two forms of evolution are called *crossover* and *mutation*, respectively, and are the traditional mechanism to build new candidates out of existing ones in genetic algorithms. For further details, we refer the reader to [20].

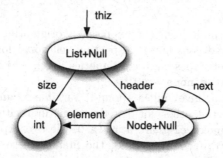

Fig. 5. Type graph for singly linked lists.

3.1 Genes and Chromosomes to Represent Candidate Specifications

In order to capture candidate specifications, we start by taking the structure's signature, i.e., its type description, and building a *type graph*. A type graph for a structure is automatically built from its fields and their types; nodes represent types, while arcs capture fields. As an example, consider the type graph for linked lists, as defined in Fig. 1, shown in Fig. 5.

Type graphs are used to form expressions, that will constitute the candidate specifications. Expressions are built out of paths in the graph. To make expressions finite, recursive fields are traversed at most once, and further "iteration" is represented through closure operators. For instance, from the type graph in Fig. 5, the following expressions are computed:

```
thiz
thiz.size
thiz.header
thiz.header.next
thiz.header.element
thiz.header.next.element
thiz.header.*next
thiz.header.*next.element
```

Moreover, in type graphs with multiple arcs connecting the same source and target nodes, their "union" is also considered for building expressions. Thus, for instance, for binary trees, there will be expressions of the form `thiz.root.left`, `thiz.root.right`, as well as `thiz.root.(left+right)`.

These expressions are complemented with constants, e.g., `Null`, `0`, `none` (empty set), to build expressions (integer expressions are also generated by applying the cardinality operator to non-singleton expressions). Also, the expressions cardinalities are taken into account (notice that the first 6 expressions above denote singletons, whereas the last two denote sets of any cardinality). Genes, the basic (independent) units that characterize chromosomes (in our case, representing candidate specifications) can be:

- boolean constant `true`,
- an atomic formula built from the expressions originating in the type graph (including considered constants), respecting relational logic's grammar and taking into account types and cardinalities (e.g., `thiz.header != Null`, `thiz.header.*next = none`, etc.),
- a quantified formula, involving a (bound) variable x, and two expressions, one for x's scope, the other for "predicating" in relation to x (e.g., `all n: thiz.header.*next.element | n != 0`, the two expressions here being `thiz.header.*next.element` and 0); the first of these expressions is constrained to be a "set" expression, not a singleton.

Notice that, according to Alloy's grammar, the second item above includes, for every atomic formula α, its negation ¬α. This is due to the fact that "boolean" operators in Alloy include their negated counterparts (e.g., `=` and `!=`, `in` and `!in`) [14].

Chromosomes are simply vectors of the previously described genes, and represent *conjunctions* of the corresponding genes. As opposed to what is common in genetic algorithms, our chromosomes have varying lengths, and genes' positions are disregarded (i.e., if a gene belongs to a chromosome, it is part of the corresponding conjunction, independently of whether it is at the beginning of the conjunction, or in any other position; this is of course due to the well known associativity and commutativity properties of conjunction). Genes' positions do play a role in crossover; we use one-point crossover to build new chromosomes, by randomly selecting points to "split" two chromosomes, and combining the initial (resp., final) part of one of them with the final (resp., initial) part of the other. If both chromosomes have size 1, then their crossover is the union of their genes.

Our genetic algorithm has a very rich set of mutations. The simplest changes a randomly picked gene to `true` (equivalent to removing the gene). The others include changing an operator by another (e.g., `=` replaced by `!=`), changing a quantifier (e.g., `all n: ...` changed into `some n: ...`), adding or substracting from an integer in an expression (e.g., changing `#thiz.header.*next` by `#thiz.header.*next+1` in an expression), and inserting/removing closure operators from expressions (e.g., changing `thiz.header.next` to `thiz.header.*next` and vice versa).

3.2   Fitness of Candidate Specifications

Our fitness function applies to chromosomes representing candidate specifications, and is meant to assess how close are the corresponding candidates to the desired specification. Of course, we do not have the desired specification (it is what we are trying to build), so a direct comparison is impossible. However, we do have the operational specification Φ_{op}, so we can (indirectly) compare candidate specifications against this one. In order to do so, we automatically generate from Φ_{op} a set of *positive* and *negative* examples. These are instances that satisfy and do not satisfy Φ_{op}, respectively. These instances can be generated using any test input generation mechanism that requires an operational specification, e.g. [2, 26]. We use an ad hoc variant of Korat, that generates inputs using a field-exhaustive approach [23]. Intuitively, this generation skips structures that cover the same values for fields than previously generated structures, and produces more variability with fewer inputs (cf. [23]). The number of generated positive and negative cases is limited to a provided bound k.

Fitness $f(c)$ for a chromosome c is computed as follows. First, we build the specification Φ_c corresponding to c (conjunction of its genes), and evaluate whether the positive and negative cases (recall that these are positive or negative according to Φ_{op}) satisfy Φ_c. If any positive case fails with Φ_c, meaning that there are cases that should be accepted but our specification rejects them, then $f(c) = 0$. Instead, if the candidate has only negative cases (cases that should not pass the specification but do so), fitness is defined as follows:

$$f(c) = (\mathsf{MAX} - \mathsf{neg}(c)) + \left(\frac{1}{\mathsf{len}(c) + 1} \right)$$

where MAX is a constant larger than k, the total number of negative cases; $\mathsf{neg}(c)$ is the number of negative cases that satisfy Φ_c; and $\mathsf{len}(c)$ is the length of c, i.e., its number of non-trivial genes (genes that are not the constant true).

The rationale for this definition of the fitness function has to do with the fact that we attempt to over approximate to the sought-for specification. This motivates also how we capture candidate specifications. Thus, when a positive case is not accepted by a candidate, we will simply consider it unfit. Fitness for other candidates has two parts. First, the fewer the "counterexamples", the better; second, the smaller the specification, the better. This last part can be thought of as a penalty related to formula length, that will make the genetic algorithm tend towards producing smaller formulas. Of course, this is a secondary issue, and this is why it contributes a fraction to the fitness value, as opposed to the actual driving acceptance criterion, namely, the number of counterexamples approaching to zero.

3.3 Overall Structure of the Genetic Algorithm for Learning Specifications

The previously described elements are the constituting parts of our genetic algorithm. These are put together following the general structure of a genetic algorithm, namely: producing the initial population, and then iteratively select individuals for evolution (crossover/mutation), produce the ampled population, and discard some individuals to control population size, until a maximum number of evolutions is reached, or a suitable individual is produced. The initial population is generated by producing size 1 chromosomes, covering combinations of the previously described expressions. Both the initial population and the succeeding ones are limited in size to 100 individuals.

The selection of chromosomes for crossover and mutation is based on a "fittest-first" policy. We select the fittest 10% for crossover and mutation, and randomly pick pairs from these for crossover; a small proportion of these, less than 10% (i.e., about 1% of the size of the population), are selected for mutation.

Finally, the algorithm stops after 20 evolutions, or generations, have been produced. Whenever a satisfying specification is generated (i.e., one that thas no counterexamples), it is stored and the time measured, but the algorithm is not stopped, in an attempt to produce shorter (i.e., more concise) specifications.

The rationale behind our selection of the above values for the genetic algorithm's parameters (population size, number of generations, percentage of individuals used for evolution, etc.) is not arbitrary. We learned adequate values for these parameters from trial-and-error runs of our genetic algorithm, on a single case study, namely singly linked lists. Trial-and-error is a common mechanism used, in the context of evolutionary computation, to appropriately set parameters of the evolutionary search. It is important to remark that, while we selected these values based on experimentation, a single case study was involved in the experiments leading to parameter selection, and the same selected values were employed on all cases of our experimental validation.

4   Validation

In this section we perform an experimental assessment of our evolutionary approach to learning declarative specifications from operational ones. All experiments were run on a workstation with Intel Core i7 2600, 3.40 Ghz, and 16 Gb of RAM. The genetic algorithm has been implemented using JGAP [15], running on Java OpenJDK 1.7, on an Ubuntu 16.04 LTS x86_64 operating system. The first part of our evaluation analyzes how fast our algorithm is able to learn a declarative specification from an operational one. We do so for data structure invariants, on a number of data structure implementations with increasingly complex invariants. These are implementations of

- singly linked lists;
- sorted singly linked lists;
- circular linked lists;
- binary trees;
- heaps;
- (binary) directed acyclic graphs; and
- red-black trees.

All these structures and their corresponding operational invariants have been taken from Korat's set of accompanying examples, or are simple variants of these. For each case study, we ran the algorithm 10 times, with a limit of 20 generations (evolutions of the genetic algorithm population). We report the minimum, maximum and average runs, indicating the number of generations that were necessary, and the time in seconds required for learning the corresponding invariant. We report the cost of computing the first invariant (the time and generations required to get a suitable invariant), and the cost of computing the "best" invariant (the algorithm continues running after an invariant has been

Table 1. Experimental results corresponding to learning declarative invariants from operational ones, using our evolutionary algorithm.

Data structure	First Invariant Found						Best Invariant Found					
	Min		Max		Avg		Min		Max		Avg	
	Gen	Sec.	Gen	Sec.	Gen	Sec.	Gen	Sec.	Gen	Sec.	Gen	Sec.
s. linked lists	0	1	2	8	1	4	0	1	2	10	1	4
s. linked sort. lists	1	10	4	27	2	15	2	13	5	35	3	23
s. circular lists	0	1	1	7	0	3	0	1	2	11	0	3
Binary trees	1	10	4	31	2	18	1	10	4	31	2	19
Heaps	2	27	7	73	4	44	2	27	11	105	5	55
Binary DAGs	0	2	2	15	1	7	0	2	2	15	1	7
Red-black trees	4	56	8	112	6	85	4	82	12	165	8	119

found, to try to optimize it, e.g., making it more concise). These results are summarized in Table 1.

The second part of the experiments compares our approach with a semantics preserving translation from operational specifications into declarative ones, in verification scenarios. More precisely, we verify, for increasingly larger scopes (i.e., maximum sizes of the corresponding structures), that the insertion routine of the corresponding structure preserves the structure's representation invariant. We use DynAlloy [8] for this task, using the original operational specification translated into relational logic as described in [8,9], and our learned declarative specification. Running times are reported in minutes:seconds, in Table 2. Notice that we used different scopes for different kinds of structures. In particular, linear data structures admit larger scopes for analysis, compared to tree-like structures.

Finally, we analyze the precision of the obtained invariants. We compare our learned invariants with automatically inferred ones using Daikon [7]. Daikon computes likely invariants from run-time information, and thus requires tests to exercise the program under analysis, and perform the inference. We fed Daikon

Table 2. Comparison of operational invariants vs our computed declarative invariants, verifying invariant preservation in bounded scenarios.

Data structure	Rel.Spec.	Op.Spec.	Rel.Spec.	Op.Spec.	Rel.Spec.	Op.Spec.	Rel.Spec.	Op.Spec.
Scopes	**5**		**12**		**15**		**20**	
s. linked lists	< 00:01	< 00:01	00:01	00:03	00:07	00:10	01:46	01:38
s. linked sorted lists	< 00:01	< 00:01	00:30	01:54	03:25	10:16	21:51	TO
s. circular lists	< 00:01	< 00:01	00:02	00:04	00:10	00:22	01:37	02:18
Scopes	**5**		**7**		**8**		**9**	
Binary trees	< 00:01	00:01	00:01	01:05	00:10	28:06	01:25	TO
Heaps	00:01	00:03	00:48	02:45	01:54	49:52	06:54	TO
Binary DAGs	< 00:01	00:03	00:01	00:54	00:06	07:14	00:43	50:15
Red-black trees	< 00:01	00:01	00:01	01:40	00:13	36:22	01:16	TO

with randomly produced tests, computed using Randoop [21]. Daikon computes invariants for all involved classes; when an invariant refers to an auxiliary class, e.g., Node, we report the inferred invariant as being a property of all nodes of the structure. Invariants inferred by Daikon are JML expressions. We show these as relational logic expressions for easier comparison. The obtained invariants are summarized in Table 3.

4.1 Assessment

Let us now evaluate our experimental results. First, consider the running times for our genetic algorithm. For most structures and in most runs, we are able to compute invariants in a few seconds. Our most complex data structure considered, red-black trees, takes in some cases a few minutes (about 2.5 min in the worst case) to compute an invariant. In general, our algorithm runs very efficiently.

Regarding the efficiency of our computed invariants as opposed to the operational ones for bounded verification, declarative invariants show a substantial profit in analysis, with the sole exception of our simplest case study, singly linked lists. In this case study, and for our largest considered scope, the operational invariant is actually better than the declarative one, in verification time (although very slightly). In all other cases, verification with the declarative invariant outperforms verification with the operational one. Notice that learning pays off exceedingly, comparing the time taken in learning and the speed up achieved when replacing the operational invariant with the declarative one.

Of course, neither of the first two parts of our analysis is meaningful if our invariants are imprecise. Our third part of the analysis confirms that our learned invariants are rather precise, compared to the expected outcome. Indeed, in all cases except red-black trees, we learn an invariant that is actually *equivalent* to the repOK. In order to check equivalence, besides manually inspecting the obtained invariants, we bounded-exhaustively enumerated instances satisfying repOK using Korat, for various selected bounds, and compared the number of obtained instances with the number of bounded instances satisfying our obtained Alloy specification, for the corresponding bounds. In the case of red-black trees, we are able to learn most of the expected invariant, except for the "black height" portion of it. This part of the invariant states that *"the number of black nodes in all paths from the root to a leaf is the same"*. Such constraint is not expressible with the expressions that our genetic algorithm considers, and thus constitutes a limitation of our approach. In relation to the alternative mechanism to learn invariants that we considered for comparison, namely the Daikon approach, our approach computes more precise specifications. Indeed, as our third table shows, Daikon is able to compute weaker invariants (sometimes erroneous ones, resulting from properties that consistently hold for the tests used for inference, but are not true in the general case), compared to our computed specifications.

Table 3. Comparison of our learned invariants with automatically inferred ones using Daikon.

Our approach	Daikon
s. linked lists	
(all n: thiz.header.*next | not (n in n.ˆ next)) and eq[#(thiz.header.*next - Null), thiz.size]	thiz.header != Null and thiz.size >= 0
s. linked sort. lists	
(all n: thiz.header.*next | not (n in n.ˆnext)) eq[#(thiz.header.*next - Null),thiz.size] (all n: thiz.header.*next-Null | (n.next != Null) => lte[n.element,n.next.element])	thiz.header!=Null and gte[thiz.size,0] and eq[thiz.header.element,0]
s. circular lists	
(all n: thiz.header.*next | (n in n.ˆnext)) and eq[#(thiz.header.*next), thiz.size]	thiz.header=Null and gte[thiz.size,0]
binary trees	
(all n : thiz.root.*(left + right) | (n .left.*(left + right)) & (n.right.*(left + right)) in Null) and (eq[thiz.size,#(thiz.root.*(left + right) - Null)]) and (all n : thiz.root.*(left + right) | n !in n .ˆ(left+right))	thiz.rootˆ(left+right)>=0 and gte[thiz.size, 0] and (all n:Node | #(n.ˆ(left+right)) >= 0) and (all n:Node | #(n.left.ˆ(left+right)) >= 0) and (all n:Node | #(n.right.ˆ(left+right)) >= 0) and (all n:Node | #(n.left.ˆ(left+right)) <= #(n.ˆ(left+right))) and (all n:Node | #(n.right.ˆ(left+right)) <= #(n.ˆ(left+right)))
heaps	
(all n: thiz.root.*(left+right)| n !in n.ˆ(left+right)) and eq[thiz.size, #(thiz.root.*(left + right) - Null)] and (all n : thiz.root.*(left+right) | n.left.*(left+right) & n.right.*(left+right) in Null) and (all n:thiz.root.*(left+right) | ((n.left!=Null) => gte[n.element,n.left.element]) and ((n.right!=Null) => gte[n.element,n.right.element]))	thiz.rootˆ(left+right)>=0 and gte[thiz.size, 0] and (all n:Node | #(n.ˆ(left+right)) >= 0) and (all n:Node | #(n.left.ˆ(left+right)) >= 0) and (all n:Node | #(n.right.ˆ(left+right)) >= 0) and (all n:Node | #(n.left.ˆ(left+right)) <= #(n.ˆ(left+right))) and (all n:Node | #(n.right.ˆ(left+right)) <= #(n.ˆ(left+right)))
binary DAGs	
(all n: thiz.root.*(left+right)-Null| n !in (n.ˆnext)) and eq[thiz.size,#(thiz.root.*(left+right)-Null)]	
red-black trees	
all n: thiz.root.*(left+right)| n !in n.ˆ(left+right)) and eq[thiz.size,#(thiz.root.*(left+right)-Null)] and (thiz.root.color != Red) and (all n : thiz.root.*(left+right) | n.left.*(left+right) & n.right.*(left + right) in Null) and (all n : thiz.root.*(left+right)-Null | n.color=Red => ((n.left.color!=Red) and (n.right.color!=Red)))	(thiz.root.color = Black) and (thiz.size >= 0)

5   Related Work

Translating between formal languages has a long tradition both in Logic and in Computer Science. There exist translations and mappings between logical systems that have been used for automated analysis purposes, as well as for complexity and decidability arguments (see, e.g., [4]). This kind of approach has been borrowed by formal methods, in particular heavyweight ones, whose associated analysis mechanism is in general deductive verification, with the aim of using a proof system for a given formalism to reason about specifications in a different one (see, e.g., [1]). In general, the emphasis has been in sound, many times partial, syntactic mechanisms to define semantics-preserving translations, that enable *conservative* analyses of the source specifications in the target formalism. With the advent of lightweight formal methods, the conservativeness requirement can sometimes be dropped, as is the case e.g., with the (incomplete) SAT-based checking of Alloy specifications [14]. In these works the use of imprecise search based techniques such as the one presented in this paper is not observed, as far as we are aware of. However, learning techniques associated with formal specification has been applied in the past. Some examples are the use of the L* algorithm to assist assume-guarantee reasoning [22] and the inference of loop invariants through a combination of mutation (as in genetic programming) and static checking [11]. The first attempts to learn specifications of a routine from calls it receives from the environment, while the second applies specifically to loop invariants, thus differing from our presented work. Model synthesis is also an active line of research related to our work. In the general case, synthesis techniques assume a specification, and work on synthesizing operational models that satisfy it (cf. [5,6,16,25]), thus working on a different direction compared to our presented work.

6   Conclusions and Future Work

The increasing availability of automated technologies based on formal methods is evidencing a lack of formal specifications accompanying software systems, while at the same time contributes to showing their necessity. Indeed, many tools for program analysis, including run time assertion checkers, and static analysis tools for verification, fault localization, test generation and bug finding, require formal specifications. In this paper, we argued about the fact that, even in cases in which one has a formal specification available, many times this specification is unsuitable for the kind of analysis, tool or technique, one is interested in. We studied this situation in the particular case in which an operational specification, represented as code, is available, but one requires such specification to be provided in a logical setting. We proposed an evolutionary algorithm that produces such declarative specifications from operational ones, and showed that, for a benchmark composed of data structures of varying complexities, the algorithm is able to learn adequate declarative representation invariants, from their operational counterparts. Moreover, we showed that these learned invariants are better suited for analysis, in particular bounded verification, than performing an existing semantics preserving translation of the operational ones and using those for the same analysis. We also showed that our algorithm produces, for the analyzed case studies, specifications that are significantly more precise than those generated by related specification inference tools.

The presented work opens several lines for future work. As we explained in the paper, we have concentrated on properties of linked structures, and the whole design of our algorithm and the expressions it supports makes it infeasible to learn some relevant properties (the color invariant for red-black trees is an example of this situation illustrated in the paper). An obvious line of research is work on a generalization of our approach, to enable learning a richer set of specifications. Our case studies are so far limited to data structure representation invariants, so analyzing our approach on other kinds of programs, is also part of our plans. In particular, in attempting to learn specifications from larger programs we will come into scalability issues, that will need to be tackled. Finally, our operational-to-declarative approach enables interconnecting analysis techniques and tools, some of which we have mentioned in the paper. We plan to take advantage of our evolutionary algorithm to implement such tool cross usages.

Acknowledgements. The authors would like to thank the anonymous referees for their helpful comments. This work was partially supported by the Argentinian Agency for Scientific and Technological Promotion (ANPCyT), through grants PICT 2012 No. 1298, PICT 2013 No. 2624 and PICT 2013 No. 0080.

References

1. Bicarregui, J., Bishop, M., Dimitrakos, T., Lano, K., Maibaum, T., Matthews, B., Ritchie, B.: Supporting co-use of VDM and B by translation. In: Proceedings of VDM in 2000! (2nd VDM workshop) (2000)
2. Boyapati, C., Khurshid, S., Marinov, D.: Korat: automated testing based on Java predicates. In: Proceedings of the 2002 ACM SIGSOFT International Symposium on Software Testing and Analysis, ISSTA 2002. ACM (2002)
3. Burdy, L., Cheon, Y., Cok, D.R., Ernst, M.D., Kiniry, J.R., Leavens, G.T., Rustan, K., Leino, M., Poll, E.: An overview of JML tools and applications. STTT **7**(3), 212–232 (2005). Springer
4. Cranen, S., Groote, J.F., Reniers, M.: A linear translation from CTL* to the first-order modal mu-calculus. Theor. Comput. Sci. **412**(28), 3129–3139 (2011). Elsevier
5. Demasi, R., Castro, P.F., Maibaum, T.S.E., Aguirre, N.: Synthesizing masking fault-tolerant systems from deontic specifications. In: Hung, D., Ogawa, M. (eds.) ATVA 2013. LNCS, vol. 8172, pp. 163–177. Springer, Heidelberg (2013). doi:10.1007/978-3-319-02444-8_13
6. Emerson, E.A., Samanta, R.: An algorithmic framework for synthesis of concurrent programs. In: Bultan, T., Hsiung, P.-A. (eds.) ATVA 2011. LNCS, vol. 6996, pp. 522–530. Springer, Heidelberg (2011). doi:10.1007/978-3-642-24372-1_41
7. Ernst, M.D., Perkins, J.H., Guo, P.J., McCamant, S., Pacheco, C., Tschantz, M.S., Xiao, C.: The Daikon system for dynamic detection of likely invariants. Sci. Comput. Program. **69**(1–3), 35–45 (2007). Elsevier
8. Frias, M.F., Galeotti, J.P., Pombo, C.L., Aguirre, N.: DynAlloy: upgrading alloy with actions. In: Proceedings of International Conference on Software Engineering, ICSE 2005. ACM (2015)
9. Galeotti, J.P., Rosner, N., López Pombo, C., Frias, M.F.: Analysis of invariants for efficient bounded verification. In: Proceedings of the 19th International Symposium on Software Testing and Analysis, ISSTA 2010. ACM (2010)

10. Galeotti, J.P., Rosner, N., Pombo, C.L., Frias, M.: TACO: efficient SAT-based bounded verification using symmetry breaking and tight bounds. IEEE Trans. Softw. Eng. **39**(9), 1283–1307 (2013). IEEE
11. Galeotti, J.P., Furia, C.A., May, E., Fraser, G., Zeller, A.: Inferring loop invariants by mutation, dynamic analysis, and static checking. IEEE Trans. Softw. Eng. **41**(10), 1019–1037 (2015). IEEE
12. Ghezzi, C., Jazayeri, M., Mandiroli, D.: Fundamentals of Software Engineering, 2nd edn. Prentice-Hall, Upper Saddle River (2003)
13. Goldberg, D.: Genetic Algorithms in Search, Optimization and Machine Learning. Addison-Wesley, Salt Lake City (1989)
14. Jackson, D.: Software Abstractions: Logic, Language, and Analysis. MIT Press, Cambridge (2006)
15. Web site of the Java Genetic Algorithms Package (JGAP). http://jgap.sourceforge.net
16. Klein, U., Piterman, N., Pnueli, A.: Effective synthesis of asynchronous systems from GR(1) specifications. In: Kuncak, V., Rybalchenko, A. (eds.) VMCAI 2012. LNCS, vol. 7148, pp. 283–298. Springer, Heidelberg (2012). doi:10.1007/978-3-642-27940-9_19
17. Home Page of the Korat test generation tool. http://korat.sourceforge.net
18. Kroening, D., Tautschnig, M.: CBMC – C bounded model checker. In: Ábrahám, E., Havelund, K. (eds.) TACAS 2014. LNCS, vol. 8413, pp. 389–391. Springer, Heidelberg (2014). doi:10.1007/978-3-642-54862-8_26
19. Liskov, B., Guttag, J.: Program Development in Java: Abstraction, Specification, and Object-Oriented Desig. Addison-Wesley, Salt Lake City (2000)
20. Michalewicz, Z.: Genetic Algorithms + Data Structures = Evolution Programs, Springer, Heidelberg (1996)
21. Pacheco, C., Lahiri, S.K., Ernst, M.D., Ball, T.: Feedback-directed random test generation. In: Proceedings of the 29th International Conference on Software Engineering, ICSE 2007. IEEE (2007)
22. Pasareanu, C.S., Giannakopoulou, D., Bobaru, M.G., Cobleigh, J.M., Barringer, H.: Learning to divide and conquer: applying the L* algorithm to automate assume-guarantee reasoning. Formal Methods Syst. Des. **32**(3), 175–205 (2008). Springer
23. Ponzio, P., Aguirre, N., Frias, M., Visser, W.: Field-exhaustive testing. In: Proceedings of International Symposium on the Foundations of Software Engineering FSE 2016, Seattle (WA), USA. ACM (2016, to appear)
24. Russell, S., Norvig, P.: Artificial Intelligence: A Modern Approach, 2nd edn. Prentice-Hall, Upper Saddle River (2003)
25. Uchitel, S., Brunet, G., Chechik, M.: Synthesis of partial behavior models from properties and scenarios. IEEE Trans. Softw. Eng. **35**(3), 384–406 (2009). IEEE
26. Visser, W., Pasareanu, C.S., Khurshid, S.: Test input generation with Java PathFinder. In: Proceedings of the ACM SIGSOFT International Symposium on Software Testing and Analysis, ISSTA 2004. ACM (2004)

A Refinement Repair Algorithm
Based on Refinement Game for KMTS Models

Efraim Machado and Aline Andrade[✉]

Distributed Systems Laboratory (LaSiD), Computer Science Department,
Federal University of Bahia, Salvador, Bahia 40170-110, Brazil
efraimmachado@gmail.com, aline@ufba.br
http://www.lasid.ufba.br

Abstract. In a perspective of an incremental and iterative formal development of software, models should preserve a refinement relation with already existing specifications models. In cases where a model is not a refinement of a specification model, it should be modified in order to create a refinement relation between them. This paper proposes a refinement repair algorithm guided through an analysis of the refinement game between a specification model and another model that is not related by a refinement relation. We are interested in models expressed as Kripke Modal Transitions Systems (KMTS) which are appropriate to represent partial information of systems.

Keywords: Model refinement · Model repair · Refinement game · KMTS · Partial information

1 Introduction

Nowadays, software can be developed in an incremental and iterative way so as to rapidly accommodate changing requirements and mitigate the risks of long development cycles. The user's knowledge about how the system should behave is initially partial and will hopefully evolve into stable and complete requirements as new versions are released.

Mechanisms to support software development in the presence of partial and incomplete knowledge are important in order to reduce the impact of changes in such scenario. The explicit representation of indeterminations in the models facilitates the analysis of the software requirements in relation not only to necessary but also possible requirements. This means not having to take hasty decisions very early in the development process.

KMTS is a Kripke structure that describes required and possible behaviors through indefinitions in states and modalities in transitions, enabling more accurate models regarding underdetermined software requirements.

A. Andrade—This author is supported by the grant # 447178/2014-8, Brazilian Research Council (CNPq).

L. Ribeiro and T. Lecomte (Eds.): SBMF 2016, LNCS 10090, pp. 161–178, 2016.
DOI: 10.1007/978-3-319-49815-7_10

In an incremental development new requirements can produce new models which should preserve a correctness relation with other models. Refinement concepts are used to guarantee a correctness relation between models, even partial behavior models, such as example in [10]. Most studies define and characterize refinement for various modal structures other than KMTS and use techniques, such as parity games, to analyse whether there is a refinement relation between two models as in [2–4]. The games used in these works are adaptations of the games presented in [8] or [9] which analyses whether there is a bisimulation relation between two models.

However, the presented works, as far as we know, do not focus on a common problem in software development: how to fix (or repair) a model in order for it to be a refinement of a specification. In this context, this paper proposes an algorithm to repair a model in order for it to be a refinement of a specification model, returning a set of repaired models as output. The algorithm is guided by the analysis of the refinement game in order to do the modifications by identifying the causes of the model not to be a refinement of another model. The refinement game presented in this work is an adaptation of [4] for KMTS models.

To the best of our knowledge the refinement repair as presented here, over KMTS partial models and based on refinement game, has not been proposed before.

This paper is organized as follows. Section 2 presents the main concepts related with this research which are important for understanding the refinement repair. Section 3 presents the refinement game approach. In Sect. 4, the theoretical foundation of refinement repair is developed and a refinement repair algorithm is presented. Section 5 presents the conclusions and future work.

2   KMTS Refinement

A KMTS is a modal Kripke structure that expresses required and possible behaviors by modalities in its transitions and indefinitions is its states.

Definition 1 (KMTS). *Let AP be a set of atomic propositions and $Lit = AP \cup \{\neg p \mid p \in AP\}$ the set of literal over AP and Act a finite set of action symbols. A Kripke modal transition system (KMTS) is a tuple $M = (AP, Act, S, s_0, R^+, R^-, L)$, where S is a set of finite sates, $s_0 \in S$ is the initial state, $R^+ \subseteq S \times Act \times S$ e $R^- \subseteq S \times Act \times S$ are transition relations such that $R^+ \subseteq R^-$, and $L : S \to 2^{Lit}$ is a label function, such that for all state $s \in S$ and $p \in AP$, at most one between p and $\neg p$ occurs.*

The transitions R^+ and R^- are called *must* and *may* transitions, respectively. From now on, for readability in some propositions, we define that $s \xrightarrow{a} s'$ represents $(s, a, s') \in R^+$ and $s \dashrightarrow^{a} s'$ represents $(s, a, s') \in R^-$.

The purpose of this paper is restricted to KMTS models where there is at most one outgoing transition for each action in a given state. We call this specific type of KMTS as Deterministic KTMS (DKMTS).

Definition 2 (Deterministic KMTS). *A KMTS is deterministic iff for every* $s \in S$ *and* $a \in Act$ *there is at most one* $s' \in S$ *such that* $s \overset{a}{\dashrightarrow} s'$.

From now on, all references to KTMS refers to DKMTS, except when explicitly defined.

Informally, the concept of refinement over partial models introduces the idea of model evolution by removing uncertainties. This relation ensures that relative to a specifitation model, a more refined model, i.e. the model with less unknowns, should preserve all the required behavior of the specification and can preserve or not possible behaviors, making them mandatory or removing them. Our definition of KMTS refinement is based on *Strong Modal Refinement* because this is the basis for all other existing refinement concepts.

Definition 3 (Strong Modal Refinement). *Given* $M = (AP_M, Act_M, S_M, s_{M0}, R_M^+, R_M^-, L_M)$ *and* $N = (AP_N, Act_N, S_N, s_{N0}, R_N^+, R_N^-, L_N)$ *two KMTS. N refines M iff there is a relation* $\mathfrak{R} \subseteq S_M \times S_N$ *such that* $(s_{M0}, s_{N0}) \in \mathfrak{R}$, *and for any pair* $(m, n) \in \mathfrak{R}$, *the following hold:*

1. $L_M(m) \leqslant L_N(n)$
2. *For all* $(m, a, m') \in R_M^+$, *there is* $(n, a, n') \in R_N^+$ *with* $(m', n') \in \mathfrak{R}$
3. *For all* $(n, a, n') \in R_N^-$, *there is* $(m, a, m') \in R_M^-$ *with* $(m', n') \in \mathfrak{R}$

where $L_M(m) \leqslant L_N(n)$ *iff for all* $p \in L_M(m)$ *then* $p \in L_N(n)$ *and the truth value of* p *in* m *is the same as the truth value of* p *in* n. *The symbol* $L_M(m) \nleqslant L_N(n)$ *is used when* $L_M(m) \leqslant L_N(n)$ *does not holds.*

We use $M \preceq N$ to denote that N is a refinement of M and $M \npreceq N$ to denote that N is not a refinement of M. In similar way, we define the refinement notion between states of two KMTS.

Definition 4. *Given* $M = (AP_M, Act_M, S_M, s_{M0}, R_M^+, R_M^-, L_M)$ *and* $N = (AP_N, Act_N, S_N, s_{N0}, R_N^+, R_N^-, L_N)$ *two KMTS,* $\mathfrak{R}$ *a refinement relation between them. A state* n *is a refinement of* m *(m $\preceq$ n) iff* $(m, n) \in \mathfrak{R}$.

We ilustrate the KMTS refinement through the following adapted example from [7]. In this example the behavior of a camera with three main behaviors is considered: shutter open or closed, flash on or off and auto focus or not. The following properties are considered: s - represents whether the shutter is opened (T) or closed (F); fo - represents whether the auto focus is being applied (T) or not (F); and fl - indicates whether the flash is on (T) or off (F). The camera has three actions: a - represents the user pressing a button to take a photo; b - represents the user pressing a button to start auto focus; c - represents the user pressing a button to cancel the photo shooting; and r - represents the automatic action to make the camera ready for shooting again.

Figure 1(A) shows the KMTS that represents the shutter behavior and the possibility of face focus, i.e., a feature that automatically focuses on the faces of people. Let's assume that stakeholders have decided that the face focus functionality will not be avaliable in the camera. Figure 1(B) shows a KMTS that is a possible refinement of the specification presented in Fig. 1(A).

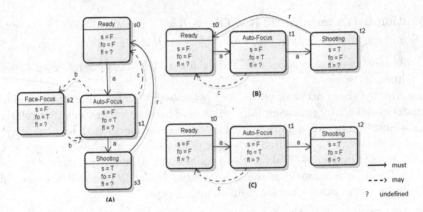

Fig. 1. KMTSs representing possible camera behaviors. In (A) the camera behavior specification. In (B) a possible refinement of the specification in (A). In (C) a camera behavior model that is not a refinement of the specification in (A).

The refinement relation is defined over two different models. In a same model it is more useful to identify which states are equivalent. Two states are equivalent if they have the same value for their propositions and achieve equivalent states from transitions of same modality (must or may).

Definition 5 (Equivalence between states). Let $M = (AP, Act, S, s_0, R^+, R^-, L)$ a KMTS. The states m and n of S are equivalent iff $(m, n) \in \mathfrak{E} \subseteq S \times S$ such that:

1. $L(m) = L(n)$
2. if $m \xrightarrow{a} m'$, there is $n \xrightarrow{a} n'$ with $(m', n') \in \mathfrak{E}$
3. if $n \dashrightarrow{a} n'$, there is $m \dashrightarrow{a} m'$ with $(m', n') \in \mathfrak{E}$
4. if $n \xrightarrow{a} n'$, there is $m \xrightarrow{a} m'$ with $(n', m') \in \mathfrak{E}$
5. if $m \dashrightarrow{a} m'$, there is $n \dashrightarrow{a} n'$ with $(n', m') \in \mathfrak{E}$

Proposition 1. Let $M = (AP, Act, S, s_0, R^+, R^-, L)$ a KMTS and $\mathfrak{E}$ the equivalence relation between states (Definition 5). Then $\mathfrak{E}$ is an equivalence relation.

Proof. The proof follows directly from Definition 5.

Proposition 2 shows that equivalent states of M are mapped in a same state of N by the refinement relation such that $M \preceq N$.

Proposition 2. Given $M = (AP_M, Act_M, S_M, s_{M0}, R^+_M, R^-_M, L_M)$ and $N = (AP_N, Act_N, S_N, s_{N0}, R^+_N, R^-_N, L_N)$ two KMTS, $\mathfrak{R}$ a refinement relation between M and N and $\mathfrak{E}$ an equivalence relation between states of M. If $(m, n) \in \mathfrak{R}$ and $(m, m') \in \mathfrak{E}$ then $(m', n) \in \mathfrak{R}$.

Proof. The proof follows directly from Definitions 3 and 5.   □

The concept of equivalent states is used to find out how many states are actually distinct in a specific partial model. In the present work this information is used to analyze how many states at least a model must possess in order to be a refinement of a specification. This information is obtained from the size of the quocient set defined by the equivalence relation $\mathfrak{E}$ over the set of states of the specification. The quocient set is denoted by $S/\mathfrak{E}$ where S is the set of states of the specification model.

2.1 Preserving Refinement Through KMTS Modifications

In general when there is not a refinement relation between a specification S and a model M it is possible to change M to generate a model M' such that M' refines S. Structural changes over the KMTS can be produced from some primitive changes such as removing a transition, adding a state or modifying the value assigned to a literal in a state.

Definition 6 (Primitive Change). *A primitive change x is a structural operation over a KMTS* $M = (AP, Act, S, s_0, R^+, R^-, L)$ *defined as:*

RT-(s, a, s'): *removes* (s, a, s') *from* R^- *and from* R^+ *(if* $(s, a, s') \in R^+$*);*
RT+(s, a, s'): *removes the transition* (s, a, s') *from the relation* R^+*;*
AT-(s, a, s'): *adds the element* (s, a, s') *in* R^-*;*
AT+(s, a, s'): *adds the element* (s, a, s') *of* R^- *in* R^+*;*
$AL(s, l)$: *assigns a literal l to the state s of the model if* $l \notin L(s)$*;*
$RL(s, l)$: *removes a literal l from the state s of the model if* $l \in L(s)$*;*
$CL(s, l, v)$: *changes a value of a literal l to v in the state s, where* $v \in \{true, false\}$*;*
$CT(s, a/b, s')$: *transforms the transition* (s, a, s') *into* (s, b, s')*;*
$AS(s)$: *adds the state s in M.*

The application of a primitive change x over M is represented by $x(M)$ and the application of a set of primitive changes X is represented by $X(M)$. In both cases a KMTS, that represents the model M modified, is the result of the application. For example, consider the addition of a must transition (s, a, s') in a KMTS M. This is performed by a change X that comprises two primitive changes: one of type $AT-$ to add a may transitition in M; and another of type $AT+$ to transform the may transition into a must transition. It is important to perform $AT-$ before $AT+$ although the notation $X(M)$ abstracts the execution order, but in the implementation it must be considered.

Given two primitive changes p_0 and p_1 we say that p_0 and p_1 are consistent with each other if one does not interfere in the modification of the other. For example $p_0 = RT + (s, a, s')$ and $p_1 = RT - (s, a, s')$ are not consistent with each other because p_1 removes the transition (s, a, s') added by p_0. As will be shown later, this consistency concept between primitives changes is important to prevent the repair algorithm from going to an infinite loop configuration.

The primitive changes can be use to modify a KMTS to satisfy the conditions of refinement relation. Proposition 3 shows that is possible to modify a KMTS to satisfy the condition (1) of Definition and Proposition 4 shows that always is possible to add a may/must transitions to satisfy the conditions (2) and (3) of Definition.

Proposition 3. *Given* $M = (AP_M, Act_M, S_M, s_{M0}, R_M^+, R_M^-, L_M)$ *and* $N = (AP_N, Act_N, S_N, s_{N0}, R_N^+, R_N^-, L_N)$, $m \in S_M$, $n \in S_N$ *and* $L_M(m) \not\leqslant L_N(n)$. *There is a set of changes* X *applicable over* n *such that* $L_M(m) \leqslant L_N(X(n))$.

Proof. By Definition 7, $L_M(m) \leqslant L_N(n)$ *is true iff for all* $p \in L_M(m)$ *and* $p \in L_N(n)$ *if* p *valuation in* m *is true or false the valuation of* p *in* n *must have the same value. It is possible to apply the primitive change of the type AL to add all literals* p *such that* $p \in L_M(m)$ *and* $p \notin L_N(n)$. *After applying these changes, the state* n *has all the literals that the state* m *has (and may even have more literals). Now just applying primitive changes type CL makes the valuation of all literals of* m *and* n *equal.*   □

Proposition 4. *Given* $M = (AP, Act, S, s_0, R^+, R^-, L)$, m *and* $m' \in S$ *such that* $(m, a, m') \notin R^+$ *(or* $\notin R^-$*). There is a set of primitive changes* X *such that* $X(M) = M' = (AP, Act', S, R'^+, R'^-, L)$ *and* $(m, a, m') \in R'^-$ *(or, if necessary,* $(m, a, m') \in R'^+$*).*

Proof. It is possible to apply primitive changes of type AT- (to add in R_M^-*) and AT+ (to add in* R_M^+*) to add the desired transition according to the desired modality. As the KMTS is deterministic, if there is a transition such that* $(m, a, m'') \in R'^-$ *and* $m' \neq m''$ *it is possible to remove it (with primitive changes of the type RT-) or change it (with primitive changes of the type CT).*   □

From Propositions 3 and 4 one of the main results of this paper can be shown: given M and N two KMTS such that $M \not\preceq N$, there is a set of primitive changes that can transform N into a refinement of M if the number of states equivalence classes in M is less than or equal to the number of states in N. The number of states equivalence classes represents the number of distincts states in M. Thus, this restriction guarantees that N can have at least one state corresponding to each distinct state of M, i.e., states of N can be used to represent every state of M.

In the proof of Theorem 1 there are cases (worst cases) where the primitives changes applied over N makes N to be a copy of M, while in better cases N is modified to $M \preceq N$ without N being a copy of M. It is worth mentioning that to ensure the refinement relation between M and N, in the proof of this theorem, states are only added in model N, complying with the limit of the number of equivalence classes over the states of M. The model M is not modified because M represents the specification and it is assumed to be correct.

Theorem 1. *Given* $M = (AP_M, Act_M, S_M, s_{M0}, R_M^+, R_M^-, L_M)$, $N = (AP_N, Act_N, S_N, s_{N0}, R_N^+, R_N^-, L_N)$ *and* $\mathfrak{E}_M$ *an equivalence relation between states of* M. *Let* $S_M/\mathfrak{E}_M$ *an equivalence classes set defined by* $\mathfrak{E}_M$ *over* S_M *and* $| S_M/\mathfrak{E}_M |$ *the number of equivalence classes of the quocient set* $S_M/\mathfrak{E}_M$. *Suppose that* $M \not\preceq N$ *and* $| S_M/\mathfrak{E}_M | \leqslant | S_N |$ *then there is a set* X *of primitive changes over* N *such that* $M \preceq X(N)$.

Proof. Let's create a relation RM that maps states of M in states of N (1) and modifies N by a set X of primitive changes generating N' (2). We show that RM is a refinement relation between M and N' (3).

1. *Let $RM = \{(s_M, s_N) \mid s_M \in S_M \text{ and } s_N \in S_N\}$ that relates every state of M with a state of N such that the initial state of M is mapped to the initial state of N and two states of M are mapped to a same state of N iff they belong to a same equivalent class. As $\mid S_M/\mathfrak{R}_M \mid \leqslant \mid S_N \mid$ then each element of $S_M/\mathfrak{E}_M$ is mapped in a different state of N.*

2. *Let $(m, n) \in RM$, by Proposition 3 it is possible to apply a set of changes X_p in n such that $L(m) \leqslant L(X_p(n))$. Based on Proposition 4 we can create a clone operation to copy transitions from R_M^+ to R_N^+ such that if $(m, a, m') \in R_M^+$ then the cloned transition in n is a transition $(n, a, n') \in R_N^+$ and $(m', n') \in RM$. It is noteworthy that when there is more one state of M mapped by RM in a state $n \in S_n$, any state of M can be taken to modify n leading to the same result because only equivalent states of M are mapped in a same state of N. Finally, it is possible to apply primitive changes to remove existing transitions in N which have not been created by the cloning operation. Let X be the set of all primitive changes used to modify N as described, then $X(N) = N' = (AP'_N, Act_N, S_N, s_{N0}, R_N^+, R_N^-, L_N)$.*

3. *RM is a refinement relation:*
   (a) *The initial states are mapped by RM, i.e. $(s_M0, s_N0) \in RM$;*
   (b) *Let $(m, n) \in RM$. We have $L_M(m) \leqslant L'_N(n)$; for all $(m, a, m') \in R_M^+$, there is $(n, a, n') \in R_N'^+$ with $(m', n') \in RM$; and for all $(n, a, n') \in R_N'^-$, there is $(m, a, m') \in R_M^-$ with $(m', n') \in RM$ by Item 1 and 2.* □

3   Refinement Game

A refinement game is a turn based game between two players whose goal is to find out whether a model N is a refinement of a specification M. The game players are the spoiler and the duplicator. The purpose of the spoiler is to execute a movement that the duplicator can not imitate. The aim of the duplicator is to imitate all movements performed by the spoiler.

A game represents all possibles matches, where a match is represented by one sequence of game configurations. A game configuration is a pair (s, t) where s and t are states of M and N, respectivelly. The current configuration of a match is represented by a game configuration (m, n) which means that m is the current state of M and n is the current state of N. If the spoiler/duplicator moves from a configuration (m, n) then we say (m, n) is a spoiler/duplicator configuration respectively. A match is composed of several turns until a player wins the match. In each turn the players modify the current state of the match, through a movement from transitions in M or N that leads them to other states of the models. A match is characterized by the following rules:

1. The match initial state is the pair (m_0, n_0) where m_0 and n_0 are the initial state of M and N, respectively;
2. If $L_M(m_0) \leqslant L_N(n_0)$ does not hold then the spoiler wins the match;
3. A match is composed of rounds which comprises two turns: a spoiler turn and a duplicator turn in this order;
4. In its turn, the spoiler must choose one of the models to execute his movement. If he chooses M then he must execute the movement represented by a transition $t = (m, a, m') \in R_M^+$. If he chooses N then he must execute the movement represented by a transition $t' = (n, a, n') \in R_N^-$;
5. After the spoiler's turn, the current match state is (m', n) if he moved in M or (m, n') if he moved in N;
6. In its turn, the duplicator must execute a movement in the model that was not chosen in the last spoiler movement. If he executes the movement in M then the movement must represent the transition $t = (m, a, m') \in R_M^+$ and $L_M(m') \leqslant L_N(n')$ must hold. If he executes the movement in N then the movement must represent the transition $t' = (n, a, n') \in R_N^-$ and $L_M(m') \leqslant L_N(n')$ must hold;
7. After the duplicator's turn, the new current state is (m', n') and the match continues to a new round.

The match ends in two situations: when it is infinite, i.e. all possible movements set the current game state to a previous game state, in this case the duplicator wins the match; or when one of the players cannot move, in this case the player who cannot move loses the game. As previously mentioned, a game can contain several matches. If the duplicator wins in all matches then there is a refinement relation between M and N. In the other case, there is no refinement relation between M and N. A game can be characterized by all possible matches in a graph.

Definition 7 (Refinement Game). *A refinement game between the models* $M = (AP_M, Act_M, S_M, s_{M0}, R_M^+, R_M^-, L_M)$ *and* $N = (AP_N, Act_N, S_N, s_{N0}, R_N^+, R_N^-, L_N)$ *is a graph* $RG_{M,N} = (V_S, V_D, E)$ *where* V_D *is the set of vertexes wherein the duplicator plays,* V_S *is the set of vertexes wherein the spoiler plays and* $E \subseteq (V_D \cup V_S) \times (V_D \cup V_S)$ *is the set of edges such that:*

$\qquad V_S = \{(m, n) \mid m \in S_M \land n \in S_N \land L(m) \leqslant L(n)\}$
$\qquad V_D = V_{D1} \cup V_{D2}$ *where:*

- $V_{D1} = \{(m, m', n) \mid m \in S_M \land m' \in S_M \land n \in S_N \land L(m) \leqslant L(n) \land m \xrightarrow{a} m' \land a \in Act_M\}$
- $V_{D2} = \{(m, n', n) \mid m \in S_M \land n' \in S_N \land n \in S_N \land L(m) \leqslant L(n) \land n \dashrightarrow{a} n' \land a \in Act_N\}$

$\qquad E = E_1 \cup E_1' \cup E_2 \cup E_2'$ *where:*

- $E_1 = \{[(m, n)_S, (m, m', n)_D] \mid m \xrightarrow{a} m' \land a \in Act_M\}$
- $E_2 = \{[(m, n)_S, (m, n', n)_D] \mid n \dashrightarrow{a} n' \land a \in Act_N\}$
- $E_1' = \{[(m, m', n)_D, (m', n')_S] \mid m \xrightarrow{a} m' \land a \in Act_M \land n \xrightarrow{a} n' \land a \in Act_N \land L(m') \leqslant L(n')\}$

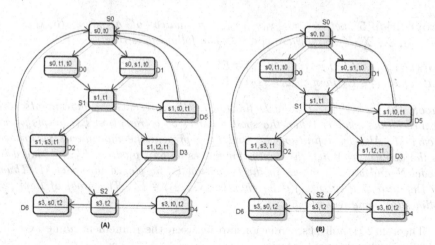

Fig. 2. Two refinement games: (A) between the models of Fig. 1(A) and Fig. 1(B); (B) between the models of Fig. 1(A) and Fig. 1(C)

- $E'_2 = \{[(m, n', n)_D, (m', n')_S] \mid m \overset{a}{\dashrightarrow} m' \wedge a \in Act_M \wedge n \overset{a}{\dashrightarrow} n' \wedge a \in Act_N \wedge L(m') \leqslant L(n')\}$

where $(i, j)_S$ represents spoiler vertices and $(w, x, k)_D$ represents duplicator vertices with $i, j, w, x, k \in S_M \cup S_N$.

Considering the refinement game $RG_{M,N} = (V_S, V_D, E)$, the spoiler movements are represented by the union of the subsets $E_1 \cup E_2$ such that $E_1 \subseteq E$ represents the movements of the spoiler in the model M and $E_2 \subseteq E$ represents the movements of the spoiler in the model N. In a similar way, the duplicator movements are represented by the union of the subsets $E'_1 \cup E'_2$ such that $E'_1 \subseteq E$ represents the movements of the duplicator in the model N and $E'_2 \subseteq E$ represents the movements of the duplicator in the model M. As $E = E_1 \cup E'_1 \cup E_2 \cup E'_2$ (Definition 7) we can refer the game $RG_{M,N} = (V_S, V_D, E)$ as $RG_{M,N} = (V_S, V_D, E_1, E'_1, E_2, E'_2)$.

A finite or infinite path in the refinement game graph represents a match and this satisfies the match conditions presented before in this section. For example, suppose the refinement game shown in Fig. 2(B). The path $S0 - D0 - S1 - D2 - S2 - D4$ is a finite match whereas the path $S0 - D0 - S1 - D3 - S0 - ...$ is an infinite match.

Definition 8 (Match). *A match ϕ of a refinement game $RG_{M,N} = (V_S, V_D, E)$ is a finite or infinite sequence $v_0 v_1 ... v_n ...$ of vertexes such that $(v_i, v_{i+1}) \in E$ and $v_0 = (m_0, n_0)$ where m_0 and n_0 are the initial states of M and N respectively.*

It is possible to deduce a set of properties relating a match and the type of transitions which connect the vertexes of this match. We can identify the type of transition that represents the movement of the duplicator in a round analyzing the type of transition that represents a movement of the spoiler in the same round.

Proposition 5. *Let* $\phi = v_0 v_1 ... v_n ...$ *a match of a game* $RG_{M,N} = (V_S, V_D, E_1, E_1', E_2, E_2')$ *where* $v_i \in V_S$. *The following is true:*

- *if* $(v_i, v_{i+1}) \in E_1$ *then* $(v_{i+1}, v_{i+2}) \in E_1'$;
- *if* $(v_i, v_{i+1}) \in E_2$ *then* $(v_{i+1}, v_{i+2}) \in E_2'$.

Proof. Let $(v_i, v_{i+1}) \in E_1$, *by Definition 7,* E_1 *represents the movements performed by the spoiler. When the spoiler moves by a transition* E_1, *he played in model* M. *Also by definition,* E_1' *and* E_2' *represent the movements performed by the duplicator. When the duplicator moves by an transition* E_1', *he played in model* N *and when it moves in the transition* E_2' *he played in model* M. *Thus, by Definition 7 if* $(v_i, v_{i+1}) \in E_1$ *then* $(v_{i+1}, v_{i+2}) \in E_1'$. *The proof of Item (2) follows the same reasoning.* □

Theorem 2 establishes a relationship between the refinement game and the existence of a refinement relation.

Theorem 2 (Relation between a refinement and a game). *Let* $M = (AP_M, Act_M, S_M, s_{M0}, R_M^+, R_M^-, L_M)$ *and* $N = (AP_N, Act_N S_N, s_{N0}, R_N^+, R_N^-, L_N)$, *N is a refinement of* M, $M \preceq N$, *iff the duplicator wins in all matches of the refinement game* $RG_{M,N} = (V_S, V_D, E)$.

Proof. ($\Rightarrow$) *Suppose by contradiction that there is at least one match where the duplicator loses. So, two cases can occur:*

(i) $L_M(m_0) \leqslant L_N(n_0)$ *does not hold. This case contradicts the hypothesis that* $M \preceq N$ *(where* $L_M(m_0) \leqslant L_N(n_0)$*); or*

(ii) *the duplicator cannot imitate the spoiler movement. Consider that the current state game in the spoiler's turn is* (m, n). *So, the spoiler can move from:*

(a) *a transition* $t = (m, a, m') \in R_M^+$; *or*

(b) *a transition* $t = (n, a, n') \in R_N^-$;

In both cases we get to a contradiction. Let's show the case (a) (case (b) is similar):

The spoiler moves from $(m, a, m') \in R_M^+$ *and there is no transition in* R_N^+ *such that the duplicator can imitate this movement. As* $M \preceq N$, *so there is a refinement relation* $\Re$ *between* M *and* N *and* $(m, x) \in \Re$ *for some* $x \in S_N$ *((m, x) there is because m is reachable from m_0 in the model M, otherwise (m, n) cannot be a game configuration (hypothesis)). By the refinement definition, if $(m, x) \in \Re$ then for all transition $(m, a, k) \in R_M^+$ exists a transition $(x, a, x') \in R_N^+$ such that $L_M(k) \leqslant L_N(x)$ where the duplicator can move, i.e., there is always a transition where the duplicator can imitate the spoiler movement* $\frac{1}{4}$.

($\Leftarrow$) *Suppose the duplicator wins in all matches of the refinement game* $RG_{M,N}$. *Let* $\Re = \{(a,b) | (a,b)$ *is a spoiler configuration}. Let's prove that* $\Re$ *is a refinement relation between* M *and* N. *Suppose by contradiction that* $\Re$ *is not a refinement relation, i.e., (a) $(m_0, n_0) \notin \Re$; or (b) for some pair $(m, n) \in \Re$ one of following items does not hold: (i) $L_M(m) \not\leqslant L_N(n)$; or (ii) exists $(m, a, m') \in R_M^+$ and there is no $(n, a, n') \in R_N^+$ with $(m', n') \in \Re$; or (iii) there is $(n, a, n') \in R_N^-$ and there is no $(m, a, m') \in R_M^-$ with $(m', n') \in \Re$.*

(a): By game def. (m_0, n_0) is the initial spoiler configuration, so $(m_0, n_0) \in \Re$, which contradicts (a);

(b)(i): By game def. if (m, n) is a spoiler configuration then $L_M(m) \leqslant L_N(n)$, which contradicts (b)(i);

(b)(ii) and (b)(iii): when the spoiler plays from configuration (m, n), there are two possible duplicator configurations: (m', n) or (m, n'). As the duplicator wins all matchs, in both cases the duplicator can imitate the spoiler movement, i.e., if the spoiler changes the configuration to (m', n) from any transition $(m, a, m') \in R_M^+$ then the duplicator will change the match configuration to (m', n') from a transition $(n, a, n') \in R_N^+$ with $L_M(m') \leqslant L_N(n')$ (according to game definition rules). So, for all transitions $t \in R_M^+$ that represents the changing of a match configuration from (m, n) to (m', n) in the spoiler turn, there is a transition $t' \in R_N^+$ that represents the changing of a match configuration from (m', n) to (m', n') in the duplicator turn with $L_M(m') \leqslant L_N(n')$ and $(m', n') \in \Re$ ((m', n') is a spoiler configuration), which contradicts the item (b)(ii). If we take the configuration (m, n') as the match configuration after the spoiler movement, it is possible to get to a contradiction with item (b)(iii) following a similar reasoning used to obtain the contradiction in item (b)(ii).

Figure 2 shows two refinement games between the specification of Fig. 1(A) and the other models. In Fig. 2(A) it is possible to see the refinement game where the duplicator wins (all matches are infinite) and in Fig. 2(B) it is possible to see the refinement game where the spoiler wins because the duplicator cannot move from state $D4$. The state (or configuration) where the duplicator cannot move is called *failure witness* (D_{wf}). For example, the state D4 of the game in Fig. 2(B) is a failure witness. The Proposition 6 affirms that if there is no refinement between two models then there is a spoiler movement such that in the next turn the duplicator cannot move.

Proposition 6. *Let $M = (AP_M, Act_M, S_M, s_{M0}, R_M^+, R_M^-, L_M)$ and $N = (AP_N, Act_N, S_N, s_{N0}, R_N^+, R_N^-, L_N)$ two KMTS such that $M \npreceq N$ and the refinement game $RG_{M,N} = (V_S, V_D, E)$. Then there is a failure witness $D_{wf} \in V_D$, $s \in V_S$ such that $(s, D_{wf}) \in E$ but there is no $s' \in V_S$ such that $(D_{wf}, s') \in E$.*

Proof. By Theorem 2 if $M \npreceq N$ then there is at least a finite match wherein the duplicator cannot move. If the duplicator cannot move then there is $D_{wf} \in V_D$ such that there is no a transition from D_{wf} to any vertex $s \in V_S$.

As shown above there is a pattern in the type of transitions of the game. The type of the transition responsible for a duplicator movement depends on the type of the transition of the last movement of the spoiler. Given two models M and N and a game $RG_{M,N} = (V_S, V_D, E_1, E_1', E_2, E_2')$. If the spoiler moves through an E_1 transition then the duplicator will move through an E_1' transition. If the spoiler moves through an E_2 transition then the duplicator will move throught a E_2' transition. Based on this, it is possible to obtain, according to the game definition, the transition that should exist to connect the failure witnesses with another vertice allowing the duplicator to keep playing.

Proposition 7. *Given M and N such that $M \not\preceq N$, the refinement game $RG_{M,N} = (V_S, V_D, E_1, E_1', E_2, E_2')$ and $(s, p) \in E$ where p is a failure witness vertice and $s' \in V_S$. It is true:*

- *If $f(s, p) \in E_1$ then there is no $(p, s') \in E_1'$;*
- *If $f(s, p) \in E_2$ then there is no $(p, s') \in E_2'$.*

Proof. This proof is a direct consequence of the Propositions 5 and 6.   □

4   Refinement Repair

Refinement repair should be applied when a model is not a refinement of the specification. Refinement repair is based on the refinement game and consists of modifying the model so that the duplicator can continue to play. The changes to be applied in the model are determined by information obtained from failure witnesses which characterize the causes for the duplicator loss in the failure witness configurations.

Definition 9 (Cause of Failure). *Given two models $M = (AP_M, Act_M, S_M, s_{M0}, R_M^+, R_M^-, L_M)$ and $N = (AP_N, Act_N, S_N, s_{N0}, R_N^+, R_N^-, L_N)$ such that $M \not\preceq N$, the refinement game $RG_{M,N} = (V_S, V_D, E_1, E_1', E_2, E_2')$, an edge $(s, p) \in E$ and a failure witness $p = (s_M, s_N)$. A cause of failure is defined by existent conditions in the models expressed by:*

1. *$(s_N, a, s_N') \notin R_N^+ \vee L(s_M) \not\preceq L(s_N')$ if $(s, p) \in E_1$; or*
2. *$(s_N', a, s_N) \in R_N^-$ if $(s, p) \in E_2$.*

   Where s_N' is any state of S_N.

The condition $(s, p) \in E_1$ in item (1) expresses that the spolier plays in M and it is in state s_M. So, the duplicator must play in N from state s_N to a state s_N' which is a refinement of s_M. However, there is no such a transition because (s_M, s_N) is a failure witness. The condition $(s, p) \in E_2$ in item (2) expresses that the spoiler plays in N from state s_N' to a state s_N. So, the duplicator must play in M. But there is not a possible movement in M because (s_M, s_N) is a failure witness. So, in this case the transition where the spoiler plays is the cause of failure.

Proposition 8. *Given M and N two KMTS. If $M \not\preceq N$ then there is at least one cause of failure in the refinement game $RG_{M,N}$.*

Proof. According to Proposition 6 if $M \not\preceq N$ then there is at least one failure witness in the refinement game between M and N and consequently by Definition 9 at least one cause of failure.

The negation of a cause of failure indicates what should be true to prevent the duplicator from losing the game in that configuration and can be used to define a set of primitive changes to be applied in the model to remove the cause of failure.

We denote the set of causes of failures of the refinement game $RG_{M,N}$ as $CF(M,N) = \{cf \mid cf$ is a cause of failure from the refinement game $RG_{M,N}\}$.

For any cause of failure it is possible to change the model through primitive changes to remove it as specified in Proposition 9.

Proposition 9. *Given* $M = (AP_M, Act_M, S_M, s_{M0}, R_M^+, R_M^-, L_M)$ *and* $N = (AP_N, Act_N, S_N, s_{N0}, R_N^+, R_N^-, L_N)$ *and a cause of failure* $cf \in CF(M,N)$ *such that* cf *follows from failure witness* (s,p) *where* $p = (m,n)$. *There is a set* X *of primitives changes such that* $X(N) = N'$ *and* $cf \notin CF(M,N')$.

Proof. *Take a* $cf \in CF(M,N)$. *It is suffice to apply primitive changes to* N *such that item 1 and 2 are satisfied (according Definition 9):*

1. $(n,a,n') \notin R_N^+ \vee L(m') \nleq L(n')$ *if* $(s,p) \in E_1$: *by Propositions 3 and 4 there is a set of primitive changes composed of types RT-, AT-, AT+, AL, CL, CT such that* $(n,a,n') \in R_N^+ \wedge L(m') \leqslant L(n')$ *is satisfied;*
2. $(n,a,n') \in R_N^-$ *if* $(s,p) \in E_2$: *it is possible to use a primitive change of type RT- to remove a transition from* R_N^- *such that* $(n,a,n') \notin R_N^-$ *is satisfied.*

Thus, for any $cf \in CF(M,N)$, *there is at least one set of primitive changes that applied in* N *make* cf *not satisfied.* □

From Proposition 9 it is possible to remove a cause of failure with a set of primitive changes. However, there are several possibilities for each primitive change. For example, suppose that the cause of failure has the form $(n,a,n') \notin R_N^+$. In this case, it is possible to create a state n' through a primitive change of type AS and add a transition to n' through primitive change of type AT+ or AT−. Another alternative is the application of a primitive change CT to modify the action of the transition and several actions in Act_N can be used. The refinement algorithm computes every possible change for every cause of failure.

4.1   Refinement Repair Algorithm

Given two models that do not satisfy a refinement relation, the algorithm proposed in this paper uses the refinement game to find out all possible causes of failures and for each one it explores all possible changes to remove the failure from the model. The algorithm returns a set of possible KMTS generated from the model which are the refinement of the specification.

Figure 3 shows a structure that represents the refinement repair algorithm execution between a specification M and a model N. Each cause of failure found $(CF_1, CF_2, \ldots, CF_n)$ can be removed by applying different sets of primitive changes $(X_1, X_2, \ldots, X_k)$. Every set of primitive changes is a possible change. The application of each set X_i over N generates models which can be a refinement of M $(X_1(N), X_2(N), \ldots, X_w(N))$. For each modified model, the algorithm checks if it is a refinement of M. If the modified model is not a refinement, the algorithm is repeated recursively. It is worth noting that each branch can produce a model that is a refinement of M.

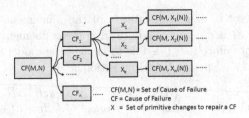

Fig. 3. Example of the execution of the repair algorithm for M and N

The pseudocode presented below shows the main part of the algorithm. The abstract data structures Set<X>, Pair<X, Y> and Vector<X> represent respectively: a set of elements of the type X; a pair of elements, where the first element is of type X and the second is of type Y; and a vector of elements of type X. The types CF and PC represent Cause of Failure and Primitive changes respectively.

The *RefinementRepair* function is initially called receiving as input the specification M and the model N. The first step of it is to find the causes of failure between M and N calling the function *findCausesOfFailure(M, N)* (line 3). This function returns all causes of failure from the refinement game.

The next step in the algorithm is to find the possible changes for each cause of failure (line 8). An important part of this step is that the algorithm must know what changes have been applied in the model to avoid undoing any changes with the new changes found, otherwise the algorithm can go into an infinite loop if it undoes any change. In this step, the concept of consistency is used to avoid undo applied changes. Another important aspect of this step is the use of primitive changes SA to add new states. The algorithm only adds new states while the restriction of Theorem 1 is false, i.e. the model N has fewer states than the number of equivalence classes of M.

Different changes can remove a single cause of failure. As it is not possible to figure out the best change to be applied, the algorithm processes every possible set of changes separately saving the resulting model as well as the applied changes in a pair (resulting model, applied changes) (line 10). For example, if it is necessary to add a transition, and model N has $|S_N|$ as the number of states, so the algorithm creates $|S_N|$ possibilities (one for each state).

Finally, *RefinementRepair* is called recursively (line 12), for each pair (resulting model, applied changes) receiving as input the specification M, the modified model (N') and all already applied changes over it $(X_{N'})$. If the modified model is a refinement of M this recursive call returns only the modified model (the expression in line 04 is false and go to line 14). Otherwise, the algorithm repeats the process.

Returning to the example in Fig. 2(B), the failure witness is the vertice D4. It is possible to show that the cause of failure is $(t2, t, t0) \notin R_N^+ \vee L(t2) \nleq L(t0)$ and one of the possible changes suggested by the algorithm to remove this cause of failure is AT-(t2, t, t0) and AT+(t2, t, t0) to add the transition in R_N^- and in R_N^+, respectively. From this change the algorithm returns a model equal to the model presented in Fig. 1(B).

Algorithm 1. RefinementRepair

Data: KMTS M and N such that $M \npreceq N$ and a set X_A of already applied primitive changes over N

Result: R = {N' | $M \preceq N'$ e $X(N) = N'$ for some set X of primitive changes}

```
 1  begin
 2  │   R ⟵ ∅
 3  │   causesOfFailure ⟵ findCauseOfFailures(M, N)
 4  │   if causesOfFailure ≠ ∅ then
 5  │   │   Set < Vector < PC >> possiblePrimitiveChanges ⟵ ∅
 6  │   │   Set < Pair < KMTS, Set < PC >>> modelsAndChanges ⟵ ∅
 7  │   │   for cf ∈ causesOfFailure do
 8  │   │   │   possiblePrimitiveChanges ⟵
 │   │   │     findPossiblePrimitiveChanges(N, cf, X_A)
 9  │   │   │   if possiblePrimitiveChanges ≠ ∅ then
10  │   │   │   │   modelsAndChanges ⟵
 │   │   │   │     applyPossibleChanges(N, possiblePrimitiveChanges)
11  │   │   │   │   for pair = (N', X_{N'}) ∈ modelsAndChanges do
12  │   │   │   │   │   R ⟵ R ∪ {RefinementRepair(M, N', X_{N'})}

13  │   else
14  │   │   R ⟵ R ∪ {N}
```

We can show that the algorithm terminates. This is because the algorithm does not try to repair a model infinitely because the changes already made can not be undone. So as the set of changes and the model are finite there is a situation where the set of possible changes is empty (the expression in line 09 is false). The number of changes is finite because the number of states is finite and the number of primitive changes that can be done in a state (without undoing any applied change) is finite. Suppose a state s of a model $N = (AP_N, Act_N, S_N, s_{N0}, R_N^+, R_N^-, L_N)$. Considering the state s it is only possible to apply at most two primitive changes (to add a proposition and assign a value to it) because if any other primitive change is done over the same proposition the primitive changes will not be consistent. Then, the number of primitive changes can be applied over s related to propositions is $2 \times |AP_N|$. Using the same reasoning it is possible to see that the maximum number of primitive changes related to transitions to the state s is $2 \times |S_N| \times Act_N$ which means adding a transition for every action in R_N^- and R_N^+ for each state in S_N. Then, the maximum number of primitive changes that can be applied in N is the sum of the maximum number of primitive changes applied over each state. The expression that represents the sum is $(|S_N|)^2 \times 2 \times (1 + Act_N)$. Also note that the algorithm only adds new states while the restriction of the Definition 1 is not satisfied. Thus, even adding states, the maximum number of primitive changes that can be applied into a model is finite.

Moreover, the models returned by the algorithm are always a refinement of the specification because it only returns refinement models when there is no failure witnesses in the refinement game (expression in line 04 is false then go to line 19). Therefore, according to Theorem 2 the algorithm only returns models that are refinements of the specification.

The implementation of the algorithm as well as several tests are available in [1]. A set of seventy test cases has been generated and each test was composed to one specification model M and another model N. All models in these tests have 10 states, 3 transitions per state and 4 propositions per state. These tests have been arranged in blocks according to the number of failure causes presented in the refinement game between M and N. The measured average (and standard deviation) of the algorithm execution time to solve the test cases per block is shown in Table 1.

Table 1. Average execution time (milliseconds) per number of causes of failures

	Number of cause of failures						
	0	1	2	3	4	5	6
Average	432,18	8512,65	11345,11	12987,65	15672,89	22463,11	35234,17
Standard deviation	774,17	1111,76	3000,22	600,12	5512,22	1233,55	4425

Figure 4 shows a graph of average execution time per number of causes of failures corresponding to Table 1. This graph shows an exponential growth in time in function of the number of failure causes.

The high value of the standard deviation can be explained due to the complexity (resulting in a high execution time) to solving some specific cases in which the size of the execution tree is increased because many changes are needed for the model repair. Although preliminary tests confirm the exponential nature of the algorithm, more tests should be performed, for example, the number of

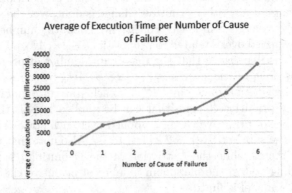

Fig. 4. Graph of average execution time (milliseconds) per number of causes of failures

states, transitions and propositions for examining the impact of these variables in the peformance of the algorithm.

Considering an exponential nature of the algorithm, there are several points which could be improved: (1) The algorithm finds solutions for each cause of failure, working with an in depth search and this process can be improved by identifying a minimum set of changes to remove all causes of failures at once, reducing the number of combinations to be analyzed by the algorithm; (2) It is possible to use dynamic programming techniques in order to reuse solutions already produced in relation to the cause of failures already considered in order to ensure a refinement relation.

5   Conclusions and Future Works

In this paper we propose an algorithm to modify a KMTS model in order to preserve a refinement relation with a specification represented also as a KMTS. To the best of our knowledge this is the first algorithm proposed to repair a KMTS model in the context of refinement between models. In [11] the authors define a repair algorithm for bisimulation relation. This algorithm is based on maximal bisimulation but this solution is not applicable to partial models. The proposed solution calculates the largest subgraph of a model that is bisimilar to the specification. Then the model elements that do not belong to this subgraph are removed from the model and the specification elements that are not mapped to a bisimilar subgraph are added from the specification subgraph. Unlike this our proposal treats refinement instead of bisimulation and is based on a refinement game considering the failure of the refinement game to find the changes to be applied to the model in order to ensure a refinement relation with the specification.

The works [5,6] propose algorithms to repair a KMTS in order to make it satisfy a required property specified as a temporal logic formula based on model checking. Unlike these works, our work aims to repair a model to ensure a refinement relation with another model, using an algorithm based on a refinement game. Thus, we belive that our work contributes to the perspective of incremental and iterative software modeling behavior in which a refinement relation is required between models of components with partial information.

Although we have not analyzed the complexity of the refinement repair problem we suspect that this problem is difficult in terms of complexity (possibly it is an exponential problem). We are interested in investigating some heuristics to improve the efficiency of the algorithm in some cases. In addition, we believe that there are cases where the set of changes used to guarantee refinement is not minimal, i.e., the algorithm can return two models N' and N" as output such that the set of changes used to generate N", for example, is contained in the set of changes used to generate N' then only N" should be considered as the solution. We are analysing this problem in order to improve the algorithm. Another line of research is to define the refinement game repair for other types of refinement such as weak and branching refinements.

We also believe that this work can be used to give support to the area of *change impact analysis* in the context of iterative and incremental software development. The impact of changes can be measured by assigning weight to each type of primitive change and calculating the cost of change in each model produced by refinement repair.

References

1. Refinement repair algorithm. https://sourceforge.net/projects/kmtsframework/. Accessed 10 Aug 2016
2. Beneš, N., Křetínský, J., Larsen, K.G., Srba, J.: On determinism in modal transition systems. Theoret. Comput. Sci. **410**(41), 4026–4043 (2009). Festschrift for Mogens Nielsens 60th birthday
3. Bozzelli, L., van Ditmarsch, H., French, T., Hales, J., Pinchinat, S.: Refinement modal logic. Inf. Comput. **239**, 303–339 (2014)
4. Bulychev, P., Konnov, I., Zakharov, V.: Computing (bi) simulation relations preserving ctl* x. for ordinary and fair kripke structures. Math. Methods Algorithms Inst. Syst. Program. Russ. Acad. Sci. **12** (2007)
5. Chatzieleftheriou, G., Bonakdarpour, B., Smolka, S.A., Katsaros, P.: Abstract model repair. In: Goodloe, A.E., Person, S. (eds.) NFM 2012. LNCS, vol. 7226, pp. 341–355. Springer, Heidelberg (2012). doi:10.1007/978-3-642-28891-3_32
6. Guerra, P.T., Andrade, A., Wassermann, R.: Toward the revision of CTL models through kripke modal transition systems. In: Iyoda, J., de Moura, L. (eds.) SBMF 2013. LNCS, vol. 8195, pp. 115–130. Springer, Heidelberg (2013). doi:10.1007/978-3-642-41071-0_9
7. Sabetzadeh, M., Easterbrook, S.: Analysis of inconsistency in graph-based viewpoints: a category-theoretical approach. In: 18th IEEE International Conference on Automated Software Engineering, pp. 12–21. IEEE (2003)
8. Stirling, C.: Local model checking games (extended abstract). In: Lee, I., Smolka, S.A. (eds.) CONCUR 1995. LNCS, vol. 962, pp. 1–11. Springer, Heidelberg (1995). doi:10.1007/3-540-60218-6_1
9. Thomas, W.: On the Ehrenfeucht-Fraïssé game in theoretical computer science. In: Gaudel, M.-C., Jouannaud, J.-P. (eds.) CAAP 1993. LNCS, vol. 668, pp. 559–568. Springer, Heidelberg (1993). doi:10.1007/3-540-56610-4_89
10. Uchitel, S., Kramer, J., Magee, J.: Synthesis of behavioral models from scenarios. IEEE Trans. Softw. Eng. **29**(2), 99–115 (2003)
11. Wang, F., Cheng, C.-H.: Program repair suggestions from graphical state-transition specifications. In: Suzuki, K., Higashino, T., Yasumoto, K., El-Fakih, K. (eds.) FORTE 2008. LNCS, vol. 5048, pp. 185–200. Springer, Heidelberg (2008). doi:10.1007/978-3-540-68855-6_12

Massive Open Online Courses and Monoids

Hugo Farias[1], Christiano Braga[1(✉)], and Paulo B. Menezes[2]

[1] Instituto de Computação, Universidade Federal Fluminense, Niterói, Brazil
hugofs@id.uff.br, cbraga@ic.uff.br
[2] Instituto de Informática,
Universidade Federal do Rio Grande do Sul, Porto Alegre, Brazil
blauth@inf.ufrgs.br

Abstract. Massive open online courses (MOOC) allows for distributed long-distance learning for extremely large student enrollment. Nowadays most universities throughout the world have their courses online. Web portals such as Coursera or edX join together courses from many of them. Even though there are many platforms to support the development of MOOC, such as Moodle or XBlock, it does not seem to be the case that there are many *languages* to help course descriptions. Moreover, we would like to allow the description of different *paths* to teach and learn a given subject. We propose Learn, a declarative language for course descriptions. The contribution of this paper is manyfold: (i) we exemplify Learn descriptions, (ii) formalize the meaning of Learn descriptions and teaching strategies, that allows for different teaching paths, and (iii) discuss the implementation of a toolkit to specify, analyze and generate a course in a MOOC platform from Learn descriptions.

1 Introduction

Massive open online courses (MOOC) portals such as Coursera [4] or edX [15] make it easy to access courses from the finest universities throughout the world. However, building, preparing and deploying a course in a platform such as Moodle [3] is not an easy task. It does not appear to be the case that there are many languages to ease this task so one can focus on preparing the lectures and not wasting time on the idiosyncrasies of a technology.

One such language is the eLesson Markup Language (eLML, [5,6,14]). A markup language for course descriptions with tools to transform eLML courses into DocBook, PDF, ODF and other document formats. Despite the apparent lack of support to MOOC platforms such as Moodle and XBlock [10], eLML does not support the description of different *paths* for teaching a given set of subjects, the so-called *learning objects* [13] in eLML terminology. They can only be viewed (or studied) in the way they are declared in a course, that is, there is no tool support to enable different paths to teach a subject. Moreover, to the best of our knowledge, eLML does not have a formal semantics. Of course, one can manually create teaching paths directly in a MOOC platform, through its visual interface or as HTML code to be imported by the MOOC platform,

© Springer International Publishing AG 2016
L. Ribeiro and T. Lecomte (Eds.): SBMF 2016, LNCS 10090, pp. 179–195, 2016.
DOI: 10.1007/978-3-319-49815-7_11

for instance, but this is clearly a laborious error prone task, as there can be a large quantity of such paths, with no support whatsoever from the underlying tool. A course description language language, with an associated generative process targeting MOOC platforms, appears to be a better and more robust approach than the manual one.

In this paper we propose Learn, a language to describe courses that allows for the description of different ways of teaching learning objects. Using Learn, one may teach learning objects in different ways. For instance, when teaching formal languages, one could start on the applications of regular languages, teach their formalization and then get a glimpse of computability. *In class* teaching of context-free grammars could perhaps benefit from a presentation of Greibach's normal form *right before* studying the equivalence between context-free grammars and push-down automata. A *book* presentation of these subjects, however, would gather both Chomsky's normal form and Greibach's with other properties of context-free grammars and only later on discuss the relationship between context-free grammars and push-down automata. The "in-class way" of presenting formal languages and the "book way" can be described in Learn as *teaching strategies* that constraint *all possible paths* of teaching a given set of subjects.

Perhaps it is clear from this example that a course in Learn has an automaton semantics. Moreover, it has a *monoidal* structure that may be constrained by a *partial order*. The states of such an automaton are given by a set of learning objects that may be taught in a given moment, depending on a chosen teaching path, that may fulfill the dependencies of learning objects and enable them to be chosen in a forthcoming state. A transition denotes a choice of a learning object to be taught from a given set. A computation then represents a path one may take to teach a given set of learning objects, as long as ordering constraints are fulfilled. The contributions of this paper are manyfold: (i) the language Learn, that supports teaching paths by means of *teaching strategies*, (ii) its monoidal semantics as partially-ordered monoids a new monoidal structure, and (iii) the Learn Maude Toolkit, a prototype execution environment in the rewriting logic language Maude [2,9] where computations are identified with rewritings in a suitable rewrite system.

Plan of the Paper. In Sect. 2 we give some examples of Learn descriptions, present Learn's monoidal semantics and prove that Learn languages, induced by Learn descriptions, are regular. In Sect. 3, we discuss the Maude language and its metaprogramming facilities. Section 4 introduces the Learn Maude Toolkit: how Learn's descriptions are represented as rewrite theories in Maude, a transformation from Learn to Maude using the latter's metaprogramming facilities and a transformation from Learn descriptions to HTML documents together with JavaScript. In Sect. 5 we discuss related work. We conclude our paper in Sect. 6 with our final remarks and future work.

2   Examples, Semantics and Chomsky Classification

In this Section we illustrate Learn descriptions and give them a formal semantics. Three examples are detailed in Sect. 2.1: (i) the simplest example is the most general one, from the teaching paths perspective, where a set of learning objects are declared and a course teaches it without any strategies - all possible combinations of learning objects are possible then; (ii) the second example declares an *order* among the learning objects taught in a course by means of **before** teaching strategy combinator; and (iii) finally, a course with a teaching strategy that makes use of **all-but**, a more elaborated teaching strategy combinator. In Sect. 2.2 we discuss a monoidal semantics for Learn descriptions.

2.1   Learn Syntax: Formal and by Example

In this Section we formalize Learn' syntax, illustrate its descriptions and its informal semantics with three examples using the teaching scenarios from the introductory Section.

Learn Grammar. The syntax of Learn descriptions is formalized by the following grammar, where *ID* is the syntactical class for identifiers, *STR* for strings, and ? denotes an optional syntactic class.

$$DESCR ::= \textbf{course on } STR \textbf{ teaches } ID^+ (\textbf{and } ID)^? STRAT^? LO^*$$
$$STRAT\text{-}DECL ::= \textbf{with teaching strategy } STRAT^+$$
$$STRAT ::= BASIC \mid COMB$$
$$BASIC ::= (ID \textbf{ before } ID)^* \mid (ID \textbf{ after } ID)^*$$
$$COMB ::= SET\ PREC \textbf{ all but } TSET$$
$$TSET ::= \textbf{the } SET \mid SET$$
$$SET ::= ID^* (\textbf{and } ID)^?$$
$$PREC ::= \textbf{before} \mid \textbf{after}$$
$$LO ::= \textbf{learning object } ID \textbf{ has } T\ I\ X$$
$$T ::= \textbf{title } STR$$
$$I ::= \textbf{image } STR$$
$$X ::= \textbf{text } STR$$

Course Without Teaching Strategies. A learning object is declared below using a homonymous keyword, it must be identified with a quoted identifier ('int3 in the example), has a title and optional attributes such as a text (body) and an image.

```
1    title "Introduction to Chapter 3"
2    image "auto.png"
3    text "The study of regular languages ..."
```

An example course entitled "Formal Languages" is declared in Listing 1.1. It states that the set of learning objects declared after keyword **teaches** are the ones to be studied. In this example, since no teaching strategies are declared, *all possible teaching paths are allowed*, that is, any combination (even infinite) of learning objects is possible. For instance, one may start with learning object 'ex3_2, which may as well be an exercise in the course's text book, then move on to learning object 'sec3_2 which may as well be the the section 3.2 of the course's text book, and only then read the introduction, possibly identified by 'int3.

```
1  course on "Formal Languages"
2      teaches <'int3 >, <'sec3_2 >, <'sec3_1 >, <'fig3_2 >, <'ex3_1 > and <'
           ex3_2 >
```

Listing 1.1. Course declaration example.

A Course with Two Teaching Strategies. A course with teaching strategies constraints the case with no teaching strategies by constraining it with a *partial order* among the learning objects. In Listing 1.2, when teaching strategy'class is chosen, learning object'int3, for instance, must be studied *before* learning object 'sec3_1, since the **before** combinator was used. Similarly, the **after** combinator can be used. *Therefore, if the path with chosen learning objects does not include 'int3 then learning object'sec3_1 may not be chosen.* If a course declares two or more teaching strategies, its semantics is the choice between them, that is, a teaching strategy must be chosen from the beginning and followed until the end. (In automata terms, is the disjoint union of the automata induced by each strategy.)

```
1   course on "Formal Languages"
2       teaches <'sec2_1 >, <'sec2_2 >, ... and <'ex3_2 >
3   with
4       teaching strategy <'class >
5           <'int3 > before <'sec3_1 >,
6           <'sec3_1 > before <'sec3_2 >, ...
7       teaching strategy <'book >
8           <'sec2_1 > before <'sec2_2 >,
9           <'sec2_2 > before <'sec2_4 >,
10          <'sec2_4 > before <'int3 >,
11          <'int3 > before <'sec3_1 >,
12          <'sec3_1 > before <'sec3_2 >, ...
```

Listing 1.2. Course with teaching strategies using **before** combinator.

*A course illustrating the use of **all-but** strategy combinator.* In Listing 1.3 we exemplify how new combinators can be used in Learn. Combinator **all-but** is a ternary combinator that defines a strategy where a set of learning objects, given by its first parameter, must be taught before or after a subset of the declared learning objects given as third parameter. In the example of Listing 1.3, the set **exercises** is defined to be $\{ex3\_1, ex3\_2\}$ and the teaching strategy ex makes use of it to define an order on the learning objects: it simply states that exercises come last, after all learning objects but the exercises.

```
1  course on "Formal Languages"
2      teaches <'int3 >, <'sec3_2 >, <'sec3_1 >, <'fig3_2 >, <'ex3_1 > and <'
           ex3_2 >
3  with
4      exercises <'ex3_1 > and <'ex3_2 >
5      teaching strategy <'ex > exercises after all but the exercises
```

Listing 1.3. Course with a teaching strategy using **after-but** combinator.

Finally, note that such a teaching strategy can be equivalently described as a strategy using the **before** combinator as in Example 1.2: we would simply list all possible orderings (since they form a finite set) using the **before** combinator.

2.2   Learn Descriptions Are Partially-Ordered Monoids

Definition 1 (Partially-ordered monoid). *The tuple* $(S, \cdot, \epsilon, \leq)$ *denotes a partially-ordered monoid where S is a finite set, $(S, \cdot, \epsilon)$ is a monoid, and $(S, \leq)$ a partial order such that, for all $x, y, w_i, 1 \leq i \leq 3$,*

$$(\text{ordered prefixing}) \quad x \leq y \implies w_1 \cdot x \cdot w_2 \cdot y \cdot w_3 \tag{1}$$

where $x, y \in S, w_i \in S^*$, x and y are not subwords of w_1.

Lemma 1. *The language whose elements are elements of a finite monoid is regular.*

Proof. Let $M = (\Sigma, \cdot, \epsilon)$ be a finite monoid, that is, $M = 2^\Sigma$. Every finite language is regular.

Lemma 2. *Any partially-ordered monoid is regular.*

Proof. A partially-ordered monoid $P = (S, \cdot, \epsilon, \leq)$ is a subset of the finite monoid $M = (S, \cdot, \epsilon)$. Order $\leq$ excludes the elements of M that do not satisfy (1). By Lemma 1, P is regular since finite regular languages are closed under inclusion.

Definition 2 (Non-stuttering partially-ordered monoid).   *A non-stuttering partially-ordered monoid is a partially-ordered monoid $P = (S, \cdot, \epsilon, \leq)$ such that for all $w \in P, \sigma \in S$,*

$$(\text{non-stuttering}) \quad w \cdot \sigma \cdot \sigma \notin P.$$

Corollary 1. *Non-stuttering partially-ordered monoids are regular.*

Proof. Every non-stuttering partially-ordered monoid is a subset of a partially-ordered monoids and both are finite sets.   □

Definition 3 (Learn descriptions and non-stuttering partially-ordered monoids).   *The teaching paths of a Learn description $L = (C, O, \uplus_i \varsigma_i)$, $i \in \mathbb{N}$, are the elements of a non-stuttering partially-ordered monoid $P_L = (O, \cdot, \epsilon, \uplus_i \leq_{\varsigma_i})$ such that for every declaration o_1 before o_2 in a teaching strategy ς_i in L there exists a pair $o_1 \leq_{\varsigma_i} o_2$ in P_L.*

Fact 1. *Learn descriptions are regular languages.*

3 Maude

Maude is a high-level language and high-performance system supporting both equational and rewriting computations. Rewriting Logic [9] is the underlying logical framework of the Maude system. Deduction rules for Rewriting Logic are given in Fig. 1. Given two states $[u], [v] \in T_{\Sigma/E,k}$, $[v]$ can be reached from $[u]$ by some possibly complex concurrent computation iff it can proven that $u \longrightarrow v$ in the logic. This provability is denoted by $R \vdash u \longrightarrow v$.

$$\frac{t \in T_\Sigma(\vec{x})}{(\forall \vec{x})t \longrightarrow t} \ Reflexivity \qquad \frac{(\forall \vec{x})t_1 \longrightarrow t_2 \quad (\forall \vec{x})t_2 \longrightarrow t_3}{(\forall \vec{x})t_1 \longrightarrow t_3} \ Transitivity$$

$$\frac{E \vdash (\forall \vec{x})t = u \quad (\forall \vec{x})u \longrightarrow u' \quad E \vdash (\forall \vec{x})u' = t'}{(\forall \vec{x})t \longrightarrow t'} \ Equality$$

$$\frac{f \in \Sigma_{k_1 \ldots k_n, k}(\forall \vec{x})t_i \longrightarrow t_i' \quad t_i, t_i' \in T_{\Sigma, k_i}(\vec{x}) \quad 1 \le i \le n}{(\forall \vec{x})f(t_1, \ldots, t_n) \longrightarrow f(t_1', \ldots, t_n')} \ Congruence$$

$$\frac{\begin{array}{c}(\forall \vec{x})\lambda : t \to t' \ if \ \bigwedge_{i \in I} p_i = q_i \wedge \bigwedge_{j \in J} w_j : s_j \wedge \bigwedge_{l \in L} t_l \to t_l' \in R \\ \theta : \vec{x} \to T_\Sigma(\vec{y}) \quad (\forall \vec{y})\theta(t_l) \longrightarrow \theta(t_l') \ l \in L \\ E \vdash (\forall \vec{y})\theta(p_i) = \theta(q_i) \ i \in I \quad E \vdash (\forall \vec{y})\theta(w_j) : s_j \ j \in J \end{array}}{(\forall \vec{y})\theta(t) \longrightarrow \theta(t')} \ Replacement$$

Fig. 1. Deduction rules for rewriting logic.

To specify a system in Maude its static part (state structure) and its dynamics (state transitions) are distinguished. The static part is specified by means of an equational theory (many-sorted, order-sorted or MEL), while the dynamics are specified by means of rules. Computation in a transition system is then precisely captured by the term rewriting relation using the given rules, where terms represent states of the given system.

The distinction between the static part and the dynamic part is realized in Maude by means of functional and system modules. Functional modules in Maude correspond to membership equational theories (Σ, E) which are assumed to be Church-Rosser (confluent and sort decreasing) and terminating. Their operational semantics is equational simplification. Rewriting is applied until a canonical form is obtained and a given term can not be further rewritten. Equations are used to define functions over static data as well as properties of states. The set of equations E is the union of a set A of structural axioms (such as associativity, commutativity, or identity), also known as equational attributes, for which matching algorithms exist in Maude, and a set E' of equations that are Church-Rosser and terminating modulo A.

System modules in Maude correspond to rewrite theories $(\Sigma, A \cup E', R)$ where rewriting with R is performed modulo the equations $A \cup E'$. Moreover, the rules R must be coherent with respect to the equations E' modulo A. Coherence means that the interleaving of rewriting with rules and rewriting with equations will not loose rewrite computations, that is, failing to perform a rewrite that otherwise would have been possible before an equational deduction step was taken. By assuming coherence, Maude always reduces to canonical form using E before applying any rule in R.

A Maude Example. In the following example, we illustrate the syntax of Maude modules by representing the computations of a non-deterministic automaton in terms of associative-commutative-identity rewriting. Module *AUTOMATON* in Listing 1.4 declares sort *Alphabet** for words in an alphabet with an homonymous sort, constructed with an associative-commutative juxtaposition operation (line 8) with identity given by constant empty of sort *Alphabet**. Configurations of an automaton are given by the current state of the automaton together with a subword of the input word. Configurations are constructed with an associative comma operator (line 9).

```
1  fmod AUTOMATON is
2      sort Alphabet Alphabet* InitialState FinalState State Configuration .
3      subsort InitialState FinalState < State .
4      subsort Alphabet < Alphabet* .
5      subsort State Alphabet* < Configuration .
6
7      op epsilon : → Alphabet* .
8      op __ : Alphabet* Alphabet* → Alphabet* [assoc id: epsilon] .
9      op _,_ : Configuration Configuration → Configuration [assoc comm] .
10 endfm
```

Listing 1.4. AUTOMATON functional module.

Listing 1.5 gives an example of a non-deterministic automaton that represents computations of an automaton that accepts words that have "aa" or "bb" as subwords of a given word over the alphabet $\{a, b\}$. After including the functional module *AUTOMATON*, module *AA-BB-SUBWORD* declares (in lines 4 and 5) 'a' and 'b' to be constants of sort *Alphabet*, and 'q0', 'q1', 'q2', and 'qf' to be constantes of sort *State*. Moreover, constants 'q0' and 'qf' are declared to be of sorts *InitialState* and *FinalState*, respectively, by means of membership equational axioms (in lines 7 and 8). Finally, rules (in lines 12 to 17) specify the transition rules of the automaton that check if a given word have "aa" or "bb" as subwords of a given word in an automaton configuration.

```
1  mod AA−BB−SUBWORD is
2      ex AUTOMATON .
3
4      ops a b : → Alphabet .
5      ops q0 q1 q2 qf : → State .
6
7      mb q0 : InitialState .
8      mb qf : FinalState .
9
10     var sigma : Alphabet . var W : Alphabet* .
```

```
11
12     rl q0 , sigma W ⇒ q0 , W .
13     rl q0 , a W ⇒ q1 , W .
14     rl q0 , b W ⇒ q2 , W .
15     rl q1 , a W ⇒ qf , W .
16     rl q2 , b W ⇒ qf , W .
17     rl qf , sigma W ⇒ qf , W .
18   endm
```

Listing 1.5. AA-BB-SUBWORD system module.

Now, given a term of sort *Configuration* representing the initial configuration of a given automaton, acceptance can be implemented by searching for a term of sort *Configuration* that contains a *FinalState* and the empty word epsilon. Listing 1.6 exemplifies that word "a b b a" is accepted by the automaton whose computations are specified in module *AA-BB-SUBWORD* since the final state 'qf' is reached with the empty word. (All symbols were read.) Since there is no solution for a search starting from configuration 'q0, a b a' it means that the word "a b a" is not accepted by the automaton.

```
1   ============================================
2   search in AA−BB−SUBWORD : q0,a b b a ⇒∗ epsilon,F:FinalState .
3
4   Solution 1 (state 10)
5   states: 11 rewrites: 17 in 0ms cpu (0ms real) (93406 rewrites/second)
6   F:FinalState ⟶ qf
7
8   No more solutions.
9   states: 11 rewrites: 17 in 0ms cpu (0ms real) (79812 rewrites/second)
10  ============================================
11  search in AA−BB−SUBWORD : q0,a b a ⇒∗ epsilon,F:FinalState .
12
13  No solution.
14  states: 7 rewrites: 10 in 0ms cpu (0ms real) (196078 rewrites/second)
```

Listing 1.6. Word acceptance as search.

An Example of Metaprogramming in Maude. Maude modules can be treated as terms in *META-LEVEL*, a predefined Maude module that represents an universal theory of meta-represented modules. The module *META-LEVEL* defines many data structures to manipulate terms and modules at the meta-level. The so-called descent functions in such data structures allow for performing different meta-level computations.

Listing 1.7 illustrates the same search done at object level (as opposed to meta-level) in Listing 1.6 for the initial configuration 'q0 , a b b a' calling *metaSearch* in the context of a module that includes modules *META-LEVEL* and *AA-BB-SUBWORD*. Function *metaSearch* has a number of parameters: (i) the meta-module where the meta-search will be performed, (ii) the meta-level representation of the initial state of the search, (iii) the meta-level representation of a pattern denoting the states to be reached, (iv) a condition for the meta-seach (which in Listing 1.7 is empty), (v) an identifier denoting the rewriting relation to be used ('* is used in Listing 1.7 denoting zero or more rewrites), (vi) a bound for the search, denoting the maximum depth of the search and (vii) the solution number. The result of metaSearch is a term of sort ResultTriple with a meta-term denoting a reachable state, its meta-represented type and a set of substitutions with respect to the pattern in parameter (iii).

```
1  mod META−LEVEL−EXAMPLE is
2      pr META−LEVEL . pr AA−BB−SUBWORD .
3  endm
4  ===============================================
5  reduce in META−LEVEL−EXAMPLE :
6  metaSearch(upModule('AA−BB−SUBWORD, false), upTerm(q0,a b b a),
7      upTerm(epsilon,F:FinalState), nil,'*, 4, 0) .
8  rewrites: 19 in 0ms cpu (0ms real) (34608 rewrites/second)
9  result ResultTriple:
10 {'_',_['epsilon.Alphabet*,'qf.FinalState],'Configuration,
11     'F:FinalState ←'qf.FinalState}
12 ===============================================
13 reduce in META−LEVEL−EXAMPLE :
14 downTerm(getTerm(metaSearch(upModule('AA−BB−SUBWORD, false),
15     upTerm(q0,a b b a), upTerm(epsilon,F:FinalState), nil,'*, 4, 0)),
16         error:[Configuration]) .
17 rewrites: 22 in 0ms cpu (0ms real) (194690 rewrites/second)
18 result Configuration: epsilon,qf
```

Listing 1.7. Word acceptance by an automaton as metaSearch.

Functions *upModule* and *upTerm*, also used in Listing 1.7 are also meta-functions. Not surprisingly, they produce the meta-level representations of a given module and a given term, respectively. The output of *metaSearch* can be brought to object level using functions *getTerm* and *downTerm*. The former projects the first component out of a *ResultTriple* (the output of *metaSearch*) and *downTerm* produces the object level representation of a meta-term or its second argument when it fails to produce the object level representation of the first argument.

Section 4 uses the meta-level API discussed in this Section to implement a transformer from Learn descriptions to Maude modules.

4   Learn Maude Toolkit

In this Section, we discuss a prototype executable environment for Learn in Maude. It is available for download at https://github.com/HugoFarias/learn/. We have implemented two transformers:[1] (i) Learn to Maude transformer

---

[1] A transformer from Learn descriptions to regular grammars is also available in Learn's Git Hub repository. It implements a formalization of Learn descriptions as right-linear grammars discussed in [12].

(see Sect. 4.2) produces a Maude system module implementing a mapping from Learn descriptions to rewrite theories as described in Sect. 4.1, and (ii) Learn to HTML describes a transformer (see Sect. 4.3) from Learn descriptions to HTML code with JavaScript that can be imported into Moodle, a MOOC platform.

4.1 Learn Descriptions as Rewrite Theories

Recall from Sect. 2.2 that a Learn description L is a triple $(C, O, \uplus_i \varsigma_i)$ where $i \in \mathbb{N}$.

Definition 4 (Learn strategies as rewrite theories). *A rewrite theory* $\mathcal{R}_{\varsigma_i} = (\Sigma, E, R)$ *is associated with a Learn strategy* ς_i. *The signature* Σ *includes: (i) a sort* State *with constructor* state : Strategy LOSet LOList $\rightarrow$ State, *where* Strategy *is the sort for strategy identifiers,* LOSet *is the sort for sets of learning objects identifiers, that is, terms of* LOSet *denote elements in* 2^O, *constructed by juxtaposition of learning object identifiers; (ii)* LOList *is the sort for lists of learning objects identifiers such that for every* $l_1 \cdot l_2 \cdot \ldots l_n \in$ LOList *we have* $l_i \in O, 1 \leq i \leq n$, *and operator* pred : Strategy LearningObject $\rightarrow$ LOSet *where terms in* LearningObject *denote elements of* O. *The set* E *of equations defines equalities for operator* pred *of the general form*

$$\textbf{ceq } pred(S, l) = L \ . \tag{2}$$

where $S \in$ *Strategy, denoting a teaching strategy* ς_i, l *is a* LearningObject, *and* L *is an* LOSet *representing the set* $\{o \mid o \leq_{\varsigma_i} l\}$, *that is, the set of predecessors of* l. *The set of rules* R *includes two conditional rules*

$$\textbf{crl } state(S, AS, \epsilon) \Rightarrow state(S, (AS - A), A) \ \textbf{if}$$
$$choose(AS) \Rightarrow A \wedge pred(S, A) = \emptyset \ . \tag{3}$$

$$\textbf{crl } state(S, AS, AL) \Rightarrow state(S, ((AS - A)B), (AL \cdot A)) \ \textbf{if}$$
$$(choose(AS) \Rightarrow A) \wedge (B := all - AS) \wedge (AL \neq \epsilon) \wedge$$
$$[\forall \sigma \in pred(S, A)(\sigma \ is \ subword \ of \ AL)] \ . \tag{4}$$

where S *is a strategy identifier,* AS *and* B *are a sets of learning objects identifiers,* A *is a learning object identifier,* AL *is a list of learning objects identifiers, constant* all *is declared in* Σ *with sort* LOSet *and is identified with set* O *in the equation set* E, ϵ *denotes the empty list of learning objects identifiers and* $\emptyset$ *denotes the empty set of learning object identifiers.*

Let ς_i be a teaching strategy of a given Learn description L, P_{ς_i} is the non-stuttering partially-ordered monoid of ς_i according to Definition 3, $\mathcal{R}^{\varsigma_i}_{State}$ the rewrite theory of ς_i given by Definition 4, $w \in O^*_L$, $o \in O_L$, $T^{\mathcal{R}_{\varsigma_i}}_S$ be the initial algebra of sort S induced by rewrite theory $\mathcal{R}_{\varsigma_i}$, $AS \in T^{\mathcal{R}_{\varsigma_i}}_{LOSet}$, $AL \in T^{\mathcal{R}_{\varsigma_i}}_{LOList}$, $\pi_3 : State \rightarrow LOList$ be the third projection of terms constructed with state : Strategy LOSet LOList $\rightarrow$ State, and $\hat{\pi}_3 : 2^{T^{\mathcal{R}_{\varsigma_i}}_{State}} \rightarrow 2^{T^{\mathcal{R}_{\varsigma_i}}_{LOList}}$ to be π_3 lifted to sets of terms of sort $State$.

Lemma 3 $(P_{\varsigma_i} \subseteq \hat{\pi}_3(T_{State}^{\mathcal{R}_{\varsigma_i}}))$.

$$\forall \varsigma_i \exists P_{\varsigma_i}, \mathcal{R}_{\varsigma_i}[(w \cdot o) \in P_{\varsigma_i} \implies state(\varsigma_i, pred(\varsigma_i, o) \cup AS, w \cdot o) \in T_{State}^{\mathcal{R}_{\varsigma_i}}]$$

Proof. By induction on the size n of words in P_{ς_i}. For $n = 0$, Definition 4 identifies $\epsilon \in P_{\varsigma_i}$ with $state(\varsigma_i, \Omega_{\varsigma_i}, \epsilon)$ where $\Omega_{\varsigma_i} = \{\omega \mid pred(\varsigma_i, \omega) = \emptyset\}$. When $n = 1$, every symbol word $o \in P_{\varsigma_i}$ is such that $\nexists o'(o' \leq_{\varsigma_i} o)$. Such words are obtained with $\mathcal{R}_{\varsigma_i}$ by a one step rewrite with Rule 3 applied to term $state(\varsigma_i, \Omega_{\varsigma_i}, \epsilon)$. The inductive case

$$w \cdot o \in P_{\varsigma_i} \implies state(\varsigma_i, AS, w \cdot o) \in T_{State}^{\mathcal{R}_{\varsigma_i}}$$

is proved assuming as induction hypothesis $w \in P_{\varsigma_i} \implies state(\varsigma_i, AS_1 \cup \{o\}, w) \in T_{State}^{\mathcal{R}_{\varsigma_i}}$ such that the rewriting relation $\Rightarrow_{\mathcal{R}_{\varsigma_i}}$ preserves ordered prefixing (Definition 1) and non-stuttering (Definition 2) up to w. The application of Rule 4 to $state(\varsigma_i, AS, w)$ produces the *set* of terms $T = \bigcup_{\forall a \in AS} \{state(\varsigma_i, (AS - \{a\}) \cup (O_L - AS), w \cdot a)\}$. Given a word $w \cdot o \in P_{\varsigma_i}$, we need to prove that: (i) $o \in AS$, (ii) T preserves ordered prefixing and (iii) T preserves non-stuttering. Property (i) holds by induction hypothesis. Property (ii) holds by condition $\forall \sigma \in pred(S, o)(\sigma$ is subword of $AL)$ of Rule 4. Finally, Property (iii) is proved the right-hand side of Rule 4, that is, $o \notin AS$ where $AS = AS_1 \cup (O_L - AS_1)$. $\square$

Lemma 4 $(\hat{\pi}_3(T_{State}^{\mathcal{R}_{\varsigma_i}}) \subseteq P_{\varsigma_i})$. *Given a Learn description* $L = (C, O, \biguplus_i \varsigma_i)$,

$$\forall \varsigma_i \exists P_{\varsigma_i}, \mathcal{R}_{\varsigma_i}(state(\varsigma_i, AS, AL) \in T_{State}^{\mathcal{R}_{\varsigma_i}} \implies AL \in P_{\varsigma_i}).$$

Proof. By induction on the length of rewrites of $\mathcal{R}_{\varsigma_i}$ from the initial term

$$state(\varsigma_i, T_{LearningObject}^{\mathcal{R}_{\varsigma_i}}, \epsilon)$$

where $T_{LearningObject}^{\mathcal{R}_{\varsigma_i}}$ denotes the initial algebra of sort *LearningObject* in $\mathcal{R}_{\varsigma_i}$, which is a finite set. Zero length rewrites reach terms of the same form of the initial term by reflexivity of the rewriting logic calculus and $\epsilon \in P_{\varsigma_i}$. Rewrites of length 1 reach terms of the general form

$$state(\varsigma_i, AS - \{A\}, A)$$

such that $pred(\varsigma_i, A) = \emptyset$, by application of Rule 3. Since ς_i and $\mathcal{R}_{\varsigma_i}$ share the set of learning objects, A is ς_i since A is trivially a non-stuttering and partially-ordered word. Rewrites with length > 1 reach terms of the general form

$$state(\varsigma_i, AS - \{A\}, AL \cdot A)$$

by Rule 4 and transitivity of the rewriting relation. By induction hypothesis, AL is non-stuttering and ordered prefixed. Pattern $AS - \{A\}$ on the right-hand side of Rule 4 guarantees that there is no such term as $AL \cdot A \cdot A$ thus preserving non-stuttering. Moreover, condition $\forall \sigma \in pred(S, A)(\sigma$ is subword of $AL)$ guarantees ordered prefixing. Therefore, $AL \cdot A \in P_{\varsigma_i}$. Rewritings are always on the top since there are no nested terms of sort *State*. Congruence is never applied. $\square$

Theorem 1 (Correctness of Learn strategies as rewrite theories).

$$P_{\varsigma_i} = \hat{\pi}_3(\mathcal{T}^{\mathcal{R}_{\varsigma_i}}_{State})$$

Proof. By Lemmata 3 and 4. □

Section 4.2 discusses the implementation of this translation in Maude.

4.2   Learn to Maude Transformer

This Section explains the structure and main aspects of the Learn to Maude transformer prototype.

The main modules of the transformer are: (i) *LEARN-SIG*, that defines the grammar for Learn descriptions as illustrated in Sect. 2.1, (ii) *STRATEGY*, that implements the set of rules described in Sect. 4.1, (iii) *TRANSFORM-LEARN*, that implements the meta-function that generates Maude system modules from Learn descriptions, and (iv) *CMD*, that allows for executing meta-level computations using Learn syntax. In what follows we exemplify some of the declarations of each module.

A Learn course is a course declaration followed by learning objects declarations.

```
1    op _ _ : CourseDecl LearnObjDecls → LearnCourse .
2    op course on_teaches_and_with_ : CourseID SetObj LearnID CourseSpecs →
         CourseDecl .
```

Terms such as

```
1    course on "Formal Languages"
2          teaches <'sec2_1 >, ... and <'ex3_2 >
3    with ...
4
5    learning object <'int3 > has ...
```

can be written due to these declarations.

As mentioned before, module *STRATEGY* essentially defines the rules described in Sect. 4.1. Apart from auxiliary declarations, it defines operation init declared with the following operator

```
1    op init : Strategy → State .
```

with an equation that identifies it with a state containing all learning objects identifiers.

```
1    eq init(S) = state(S, all, ε) .
```

The main declaration of module *TRANSFORM-LEARN* is perhaps function *transformLearnCourse* that given a term in sort *LearnCourse* produces a system module in Maude, a term of sort *SModule*, where *Cid* is a quoted identifier, *SObj* is a set of learning object identifiers, *Lid* is a learning object identifier, *CS* is a set of teaching strategies and *LOdecls* are learning object declarations. Note that the generated module includes module *STRATEGY*.

```
1   op transformLearnCourse : LearnCourse → SModule .
2   eq transformLearnCourse(course on Cid teaches SObj and Lid with CS
        LOdecls) =
3       (mod q(Cid) is
4           (including'BOOL . including'STRATEGY .)
5           sorts none
6           none
7           none
8           none
9           (eq'all.LOSet = transformOverSetObj(SObj, Lid) [none] .)
10            transformCourseSpecs(CS) transformLearnObjDecls(LOdecls)
11          none
12      endm) .
```

Finally, module *CMD* declares functions to help animate Learn declarations. Function search calls *metaSearch* composed with *getTerm* and *downTerm*, as in Listing 1.7, thus encapsulating the meta-representation of Learn modules from the user.

```
1   op search : LearnCourse Qid Bound Nat → State .
2   eq search(LC, Q, B, N) = downTerm(getTerm(metaSearch(transform(LC),
        'init['st[upTerm(string(Q))]], 'S:State, nil, '*, B, N)), st) .
```

Learn to Maude Examples. Let us consider now the Learn description in Listing 1.2. After loading module theory_transformer.maude into the Maude interpreter we may execute the command in Listing 1.8 where *eg3* is a constant of sort *LearnCourse* identified with the Learn description in Listing 1.2. It will return the meta-representation of the Learn description in Listing 1.2. (We have removed some of the equations for readability.)

```
1   Maude> red transform(eg3) .
2   reduce in TEST : transform(eg3) .
3   rewrites: 507 in 0ms cpu (0ms real) (1701342 rewrites/second)
4   result SModule: mod'Formal'Languages is
5     including'BOOL .
6     including'STRATEGY .
7     sorts none .
8     none
9     none
10    none
11    eq'all.LOSet ='__['__['lo['"'ex3_1".String],'__['lo['"'fig3_2".String],'__['lo['"'int3".
        String],'__['lo['"'sec2_1".String],'__['lo['"'sec2_2".String],'__['lo[
12    '"'sec2_4".String],'__['lo['"'sec3_1".String],'__['lo['"'sec3_2".String],'__['lo['"'sec3_3".
        String],'lo['"'sec3_7".String]]]]]]]]]]],'lo['"'ex3_2".String]] [none] .
13    eq'image['lo['"'fig3_2".String]] ='"'fig3.2.png".String [none] .
14    ...
15    ceq'pred['st['"'book".String],'LO:LearningObject] ='lo['"'ex3_1".String] if'
        _subset_['LO:LearningObject,'lo['"'ex3_2".String]] ='true.Bool [none] .
```

```
16   ceq'pred['st['"class".String],'LO:LearningObject] ='lo['"ex3_1".String] if'
          _subset_['LO:LearningObject,'lo['"ex3_2".String]] ='true.Bool [none] .
17   ...
18   none
19   endm
```

Listing 1.8. Meta-representation of the Learn description in Listing 1.2.

We may now use the search command from module *CMD* to animate the Learn description in Listing 1.2. Listing 1.9 displays the execution of command *search(eg3,'class, 4, 7)* which produces a path from learning object *'int3* to *'fig3_2* as the third projection of the resulting state.

```
1   Maude> reduce in TEST : search(eg3,'class, 4, 7) .
2   rewrites: 572 in 0ms cpu (0ms real) (1692307 rewrites/second)
3   result State: state(st("class"), lo("ex3_1") lo("ex3_2") lo("int3") lo("
         sec2_2") lo("sec2_4") lo("sec3_1") lo("sec3_2") lo("sec3_3") lo(
4      "sec3_7"), lo("int3") ; lo("sec3_1") ; lo("sec3_2") ; lo("fig3_2"))
```

Listing 1.9. Animating a Learn description with search.

4.3   Learn to HTML Transformer

Learn Maude Toolkit (LMT) provides a way to integrate course descriptions into MOOC by transforming Learn descriptions into HTML with JavaScript: HTML provides standard formatting and anchorage support while JavaScript code implements ordering prefix control. In this Section we describe this transformer.

LearnHTML generates HTML with JavaScript in the *single-page application* model from a Maude module as described in Sect. 4.2. Operator *convertHTML* is the one responsible for transforming a Maude system module into a string encoding its HTML representation which can then be saved into a text file.

```
1    op convertHTML : SModule → String .
2    eq html(LC) = convertHTML(transform(LC)) .
```

Module CMD offers a function that concatenates the output of operation *transformLearnCourse* and *convertHTML* and then generate HTML code from a Learn description.

```
1    op html : LearnCourse → String .
```

Figures 2a and b illustrate HTML pages representing the *class* and *book* strategies, respectively, declared in Example 1.2. We emphasize that different links are made available at each point depending on the chosen teaching path. Figure 3 shows an example page inside Moodle.

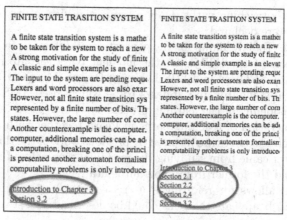

(a) Section 3.1 in teaching strategy *class*.

(b) Section 3.1 in teaching strategy *book*.

Fig. 2. HTML pages representing the *class* and *book* strategies.

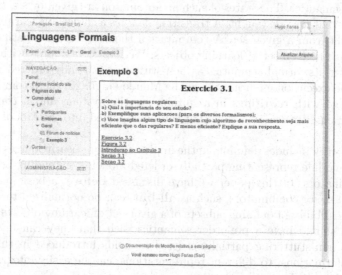

Fig. 3. A Learn course for formal languages in moodle.

5 Related Work

To the best of our knowledge, Learn's teaching strategies are unique. Moreover, there are not many languages that allows for course descriptions in a declarative way and none with a formal semantics.

The *eLesson Markup Language* [6] is a markup language that can be transformed into PDF, LaTeX, ODF, DocBook and other formats. It appears that it can not be integrated with MOOC platforms and does not provide any support similar to Learn's teaching paths. Only a sequential view of its constituents in the order they were declared.

Learn Maude Toolkit allows for the generation of different representations of Learn descriptions. Only HTML for the moment but there are no restrictions for other formats. SCORM and IMS Learning Design [11]. SCORM is actually a set of technical standards and appears to be widely used. IMS Learn Design allows for the modeling of the learning process as whole.

The free generation of teaching paths in Learn together with an automaton semantics for online courses are inspired by previous work of the third author and others. The latter came from studying the monoidal semantics of non-sequential automata [8] and the former from hyperautomata [7].

Duolingo [1] allows for referring a user to past exercises when one starts failing a subject. It appears that this could be described as a strategy in Learn.

6   Conclusions

We propose Learn, a language for course description. Learn courses have an automata semantics. The states of such an automaton are given by a set of learning objects that may be taught. A transition denotes a choice of a learning object to be taught from a given set. A computation then represents a path one may take to teach a given set of learning objects. We have contributed with the language Learn, its formal semantics as non-stuttering partially-ordered monoids, a prototype execution environment in the Maude language where computations are identified with rewritings in a suitable rewrite system, and a transformer from Learn descriptions into code that can be imported into the Moodle MOOC platform.

Future work includes defining, in the implementation, LearnCourses as extensions of a module representing partially-ordered monoids, extending Learn with new combinators. In this paper we have discussed **before**, a basic one, where a complete set of combinators, such as **all-but**, can be normalized to, together with the possibility of defining subsets of a given set of learning objects. Further extensions should have a pre-order semantics such that they can be incorporated into non-stuttering partially-ordered monoids introduced in this paper. New transformations, to different representations, can be easily integrated into the Learn Maude Toolkit.

Acknolwdgements. The authors would like to thank Bruno Lopes and the reviewers of SBMF 2016 for their constructive comments on a draft of this paper.

References

1. Duolingo. https://www.duolingo.com/
2. Clavel, M., Eker, S., Durán, F., Lincoln, P., Martí-Oliet, N., Meseguer, J.: All About Maude - A High-performance Logical Framework: How to Specify, Program, and Verify Systems in Rewriting Logic. Programming and Software Engineering, vol. 4350. Springer, Heidelberg (2007)

3. Dougiamas, M.: Moodle learning platform. https://moodle.org
4. Koller, D., Ng, A.: Coursera online courses portal. http://coursera.org
5. Lütolf, G.: eLML - eLesson Markup Language. http://www.elml.org
6. Lütolf, G.: Zugänglichkeit von geographischen E-learning-Kursen für Sehbehinderte und Blinde am Beispiel von GITTA. Master's thesis, University of Zurich (2006) http://www.gitta.info/website/en/download/gitta/luetolf/gluetolf_diplomarbeit.pdf
7. Menezes, P.B., Machado, J.P.: Web courses are automata: a categorial framework. In: Proceedings of 2nd Workshop of Formal Methods, pp. 79–88 (1999)
8. Menezes, P.B., Sernadas, A.S.C., Costa, J.F.: Nonsequential automata semantics for concurrent, object-based language. In: 2nd US-Brazil Joint Workshops on the Formal Foundations of Software System. ENTCS, vol. 14, pp. 245–273 (1997). doi:10.1016/S1571-0661(05)80239-7.
9. Meseguer, J.: Conditional rewriting logic as a unified model of concurrency. Theor. Comput. Sci. **96**(1), 73–155 (1992). http://www.sciencedirect.com/science/article/pii/030439759290182F
10. Open edX: Xblock: Open edx courseware components. https://xblock.readthedocs.org/en/latest/
11. Qu, K., He, W.: SCORM versus IMS-LD: discussion on development trends of e-learning. In: International Conference on Computational Intelligence and Software Engineering, CiSE 2009, pp. 1–4. IEEE (2009)
12. Silva, H.F.: Learn - a language for the declaration of online courses. Technical report, UFF (2016). http://www2.ic.uff.br/~cbraga/learn-monografia.pdf
13. Sosteric, M., Hesemeier, S.: When is a learning object not an object: a first step towards a theory of learning objects. Int. Rev. Res. Open Distrib. Learn. **3**(2) (2002). http://www.irrodl.org/index.php/irrodl/article/view/106
14. Weibel, R., Bleisch, S., Nebiker, S., Fisler, J., Grossmann, T., Niederhuber, M., Collet, C., Hurni, L.: Achieving more sustainable e-learning programs for GIScience. Geomatica **63**, 109–118 (2009)
15. xConsortium: edX on line courses portal. http://www.edx.org

Model Checking

A Bounded Model Checker for Three-Valued Abstractions of Concurrent Software Systems

Nils Timm$^{(\boxtimes)}$, Stefan Gruner, and Matthias Harvey

Department of Computer Science, University of Pretoria, Pretoria, South Africa
{ntimm,sgruner}@cs.up.ac.za

Abstract. We present a technique for verifying concurrent software systems via SAT-based bounded model checking. It is based on a direct transfer of the system and an LTL property into a formula that encodes the corresponding model checking problem. In our approach we first employ three-valued abstraction. The state space of the resulting abstract system is then logically encoded, which saves us the expensive construction of an explicit state space model. The verification result can be obtained via two SAT checks. Our work includes the definition of the encoding and a theorem which states that the SAT result for an encoded verification task is equivalent to the result of the corresponding model checking problem. We also introduce an extension of the encoding by fairness constraints, which facilitates the verification of liveness properties. We have implemented our technique in an automatic verification tool that supports bounded LTL model checking under fairness.

1 Introduction

Three-valued abstraction (3VA) [12] is a well-established technique in software verification. It proceeds by generating an abstract state space model of the system to be analysed over the values *true*, *false* and *unknown*, where the latter value is used to represent the loss of information due to abstraction. For concurrent software systems composed of many processes, 3VA does not only replace concrete variables by predicates. It also abstracts away entire processes by summarising them into a single approximative component [11], which allows for a substantial reduction of the state space. The evaluation of temporal logic properties on models constructed via 3VA is known as *three-valued model checking* (3MC) [2]. In 3MC there exist three possible outcomes: *true* and *false* results can be immediately transferred to the modelled system, whereas an *unknown* result reveals that abstraction refinement is necessary [15].

Verification techniques based on 3VA and 3MC typically assume that an *explicit* three-valued state space model corresponding to the system to be analysed is constructed and explored [2]. However, explicit-state model checking is known for its high memory demands in comparison to *symbolic* model checking techniques like BDD-based model checking [3] and SAT-based bounded model checking (BMC) [1]. The benefits of BMC are that its compressed state space representation allows to handle larger systems than explicit-state techniques, and

L. Ribeiro and T. Lecomte (Eds.): SBMF 2016, LNCS 10090, pp. 199–216, 2016.
DOI: 10.1007/978-3-319-49815-7_12

that its performance profits from the advancements in the SAT solver technology. Although there exist a few works on *three-valued bounded model checking*, these approaches are either solely defined for hardware systems [5], or they require an explicit state space model as input which is then symbolically encoded [16]. It is however not efficient to translate a given system first into an *explicit* state space model before encoding it symbolically for BMC.

In this paper we present an approach to the verification of *concurrent software systems* based on an immediate transfer of the input system and the property to be verified into a propositional logic formula that encodes the corresponding bounded model checking problem. Our approach first employs 3VA and thus profits from the state space reduction capabilities of this technique. The state space of the resulting abstract system is then directly encoded in propositional logic, which saves us the expensive construction of an explicit state space model. Finally, the verification result can be obtained via two satisfiability checks.

Our work includes the definition of the immediate encoding as well as a proven theorem which states that the SAT result for an encoded verification task is equivalent to the result of the corresponding model checking problem. Moreover, we introduce an extension of the encoding by *weak* and *strong fairness* constraints, which facilitates the verification of liveness properties of concurrent systems under realistic conditions. We have integrated the steps *abstraction*, *encoding* and *SAT solving* into a fully-automatic verification tool (available at www.cs.up.ac.za/cs/ntimm/tool.zip) that supports bounded LTL model checking under fairness. Preliminary experiments show promising performance results.

2   Concurrent Software Systems

We start with a brief introduction to the systems that we consider in our work. A *concurrent software system* Sys consists of a number of possibly non-uniform processes P_1 to P_n composed in parallel: $Sys = \|_{i=1}^{n} P_i$. It is defined over a set of variables $Var = Var_s \cup \bigcup_{i=1}^{n} Var_i$ where Var_s is a set of shared variables and $Var_1, \ldots, Var_n$ are sets of local variables associated with the processes $P_1, \ldots, P_n$, respectively. The state space over Var corresponds to the set S_{Var} of all type-correct valuations of the variables. Given a state $s \in S_{Var}$ and an expression e over Var, then $s(e)$ denotes the valuation of e in s. An example for a concurrent system implementing mutual exclusion is depicted below.

$$y : \texttt{semaphore where } y = 1;$$

$$P_1 :: \begin{bmatrix} \texttt{loop forever do} \\ \begin{bmatrix} \texttt{0: acquire } (y,1); \\ \texttt{1: release } (y,1); \end{bmatrix} \end{bmatrix} \parallel P_2 :: \begin{bmatrix} \texttt{loop forever do} \\ \begin{bmatrix} \texttt{0: acquire } (y,1); \\ \texttt{1: release } (y,1); \end{bmatrix} \end{bmatrix}$$

Here we have two processes operating on a shared semaphore variable y. Processes P_i can be formally represented as *control flow graphs* (CFGs) $G_i = (Loc_i, \delta_i, \tau_i)$ where $Loc_i = \{[0]_2, \ldots, [\|Loc_i\|]_2\}$ is a set of control locations given as binary numbers, $\delta_i \subseteq Loc_i \times Loc_i$ is a transition relation, and $\tau_i : Loc_i \times Loc_i \to Op$ is a function labelling transitions with operations from a set Op.

Definition 1 (Operations). *Let* $Var = \{v_1, \ldots, v_m\}$ *be a set of variables. The set of operations* Op *on these variables consists of all statements of the form* $assume(e) : v_1 := e_1, \ldots, v_m := e_m$ *where* $e, e_1, \ldots, e_m$ *are expressions over* Var.

Hence, every operation consists of a guard and a list of assignments. For convenience, we sometimes just write e instead of $assume(e)$. Moreover, we omit the *assume* part completely if the guard is *true*. The control flow graphs G_1 and G_2 corresponding to the processes of our example system are depicted below. G_1 and G_2 also illustrate the semantics of the operations $acquire(y, 1)$ and $release(y, 1)$.

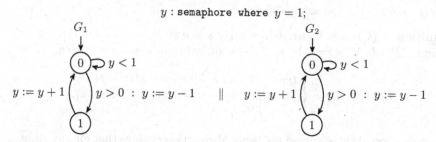

A concurrent system given by n individual control flow graphs $G_1, \ldots, G_n$ can be modelled by one composite CFG $G = (Loc, \delta, \tau)$ where $Loc = \times_{i=1}^{n} Loc_i$. G is the product graph of all individual CFGs. We assume that initially all processes of a concurrent system at location 0. Moreover, we assume that a deterministic initialisation of the system variables is given by an assertion ϕ over Var. In our example we have that $\phi = (y = 1)$. Now, a computation of a concurrent system corresponds to a sequence where in each step one process is non-deterministically selected and the operation at its current location is attempted to be executed. In case the execution is not blocked by a guard, the variables are updated according to the assignment part and the process advances to the consequent control location. For verifying properties of concurrent systems typically only *fair* computations where all processes infinitely often proceed are considered. We will discuss our notion of fairness in more detail in Sect. 5. The overall state space S of a concurrent system corresponds to the set of states over Var combined with the possible locations, i.e. $S = Loc \times S_{Var}$. Hence, each state in S is a tuple $\langle l, s \rangle$ with $l = (l_1, \ldots, l_n) \in Loc$ and $s \in S_{Var}$.

Control flow graphs allow to model concurrent systems formally. For an efficient verification it is additionally required to reduce the state space complexity. For this purpose, we use *three-valued predicate abstraction* [11]. Such an abstraction is an approximation in the sense that all definite verification results (*true*, *false*) obtained for an abstract system can be transferred to the original system. Only *unknown* results necessitate abstraction refinement [15]. In abstract systems operations do not refer to concrete variables but to predicates $Pred = \{p_1, \ldots, p_m\}$ over Var with the three-valued domain $\{true, unknown, false\}$. *Unknown*, typically abbreviated by $\perp$, is a valid truth value as we operate with the three-valued *Kleene logic* $\mathcal{K}_3$ [4] whose semantics is given by the following truth tables.

$\wedge$	$true$	$\bot$	$false$
$true$	$true$	$\bot$	$false$
$\bot$	$\bot$	$\bot$	$false$
$false$	$false$	$false$	$false$

$\vee$	$true$	$\bot$	$false$
$true$	$true$	$true$	$true$
$\bot$	$true$	$\bot$	$\bot$
$false$	$true$	$\bot$	$false$

$\neg$	
$true$	$false$
$\bot$	$\bot$
$false$	$true$

Operations in abstract systems are of the following form:

$$assume(choice(a,b)) : p_1 := choice(a_1, b_1), \ldots, p_m := choice(a_m, b_m)$$

where $a, b, a_1, b_1, \ldots, a_m, b_m$ are logical expressions over $Pred$ and $choice(a,b)$-expressions have the following semantics:

Definition 2 (Choice Expressions). *Let s be a state over a set of three-valued predicates $Pred$. Moreover, let a and b be logical expressions over $Pred$. Then*

$$s\left(choice\left(a,b\right)\right) = \begin{cases} true & iff\ s(a)\ is\ true\ (and\ s(b)\ is\ false), \\ false & iff\ s(b)\ is\ true\ (and\ s(a)\ is\ false), \\ \bot & else. \end{cases}$$

The application of three-valued predicate abstraction ensures that for any state s and for any expression $choice(a,b)$ in an abstract control flow graph the following holds: $s(a) = true \Rightarrow s(b) = false$ and $s(b) = true \Rightarrow s(a) = false$. In particular, this implies that $s(a)$ and $s(b)$ are never both $true$. Moreover, the following equivalences hold: $choice(true, false) \equiv true$, $choice(false, true) \equiv false$, $choice(false, false) \equiv \bot$, $choice(a, \neg a) \equiv a$, $choice(\neg a, a) \equiv \neg a$, $choice(a,b) \equiv (a \vee \neg b) \wedge (a \vee b \vee \bot)$, and $\neg choice(a,b) \equiv choice(b,a)$.

A three-valued expression $choice(a,b)$ over $Pred$ approximates a Boolean expression e over Var, written $choice(a,b) \preceq e$, iff a logically implies e and b logically implies $\neg e$. The three-valued approximation relation can be straightforwardly extended to operations as described in [11]. An abstract system Sys' approximates a concrete system Sys, written $Sys' \preceq Sys$, if the systems have isomorphic CFGs and the operations in the abstract system approximate the corresponding ones in the concrete system. An example for an abstract system that approximates the concrete system on the previous page is depicted below.

$$(y > 0) : \textbf{predicate where } (y > 0) = true;$$

For illustration: the abstract operation $(y > 0) := choice((y > 0), false)$ sets the predicate $(y > 0)$ to $true$ if $(y > 0)$ was $true$ before, and it never sets the predicate to $false$. This is a sound three-valued approximation of the concrete operation $y := y + 1$ over the predicate $(y > 0)$.

The state space of an abstract system is defined as $S = Loc \times S_{Pred}$ where S_{Pred} is the set of all possible valuations of the three-valued predicates in $Pred$. The state space corresponding to the abstraction of our example system is thus

$$S = \{ \; \langle (0,0), (y > 0) = true \rangle, \langle (0,0), (y > 0) = \bot \rangle, \langle (0,0), (y > 0) = false \rangle$$
$$\langle (1,0), (y > 0) = true \rangle, \langle (1,0), (y > 0) = \bot \rangle, \langle (1,0), (y > 0) = false \rangle$$
$$\langle (0,1), (y > 0) = true \rangle, \langle (0,1), (y > 0) = \bot \rangle, \langle (0,1), (y > 0) = false \rangle$$
$$\langle (1,1), (y > 0) = true \rangle, \langle (1,1), (y > 0) = \bot \rangle, \langle (1,1), (y > 0) = false \rangle \; \}.$$

So far we have seen how concurrent systems can be formally represented and abstracted. Next we will take a look on how model checking of abstracted systems is defined.

3   Three-Valued Bounded Model Checking

CFGs allow us to model the *control flow* of a concurrent system. The verification of a system additionally requires to explore a corresponding *state space* model. Since we use three-valued abstraction, we need a model that incorporates the truth values *true*, *false* and *unknown*. *Three-valued Kripke structures* are models with a three-valued domain for transitions and labellings of states:

Definition 3 (3-Valued Kripke Structure). *A three-valued Kripke structure over a set of atomic predicates AP is a tuple $M = (S, \langle l^0, s^0 \rangle, R, L)$ where*

- *S is a finite set of states and $\langle l^0, s^0 \rangle \in S$ is the initial state,*
- *$R : S \times S \to \{true, \bot, false\}$ is a transition function with $\forall \langle l, s \rangle \in S :$ $\exists \langle l', s' \rangle \in S : R(\langle l, s \rangle, \langle l', s' \rangle) \in \{true, \bot\}$,*
- *$L : S \times AP \to \{true, \bot, false\}$ is a labelling function that associates a truth value with each atomic predicate in each state.*

A simple example for a three-valued Kripke structure M over $AP = \{p\}$ is depicted below.

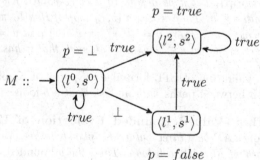

A path π of a Kripke structure M is a sequence of states $\langle l^0, s^0 \rangle \langle l^1, s^1 \rangle \langle l^2, s^2 \rangle \ldots$ with $R(\langle l^k, s^k \rangle, \langle l^{k+1}, s^{k+1} \rangle) \in \{true, \bot\}$. $\pi(k)$ denotes the k-th state of π, whereas π^k denotes the k-th suffix $\pi(k)\pi(k+1)\pi(k+2)\ldots$ of π. By Π_M we denote the set of all paths of M starting in the initial state. Paths are considered for the evaluation of temporal logic properties of Kripke structures.

As defined in [11], a concurrent system $Sys = \|_{i=1}^{n} P_i$ abstracted over a set of predicates $Pred$ can be represented as a three-valued Kripke structure M over $AP = Pred \cup \{(loc_i = l_i) \,|\, i \in [1..n], \, l_i \in Loc_i\}$ where the predicate $(loc_i = l_i)$ denotes that the process P_i is currently at control location l_i. The number of states of a Kripke structure corresponding to a given system is exponential in the number of its locations and variables. State explosion is the major challenge in software model checking. One approach to cope with the state explosion problem is to use a symbolic and therefore more compact representation of the Kripke structure. In SAT-based bounded model checking [1] all possible path prefixes up to a bound $b \in \mathbb{N}$ are encoded in a propositional logic formula. The formula is then conjuncted with an encoding of the temporal logic property to be checked. In case the overall formula is satisfiable, the satisfying truth assignment characterises a witness path of length b for the property in the state space of the encoded system. Hence, bounded model checking can be performed via SAT solving. We now briefly recapitulate the syntax and bounded semantics of the temporal logic LTL:

Definition 4 (Syntax of LTL). *Let AP be a set of atomic predicates and $p \in AP$. The syntax of LTL formulae ψ is given by*

$$\psi ::= p \,|\, \neg p \,|\, \psi \vee \psi \,|\, \psi \wedge \psi \,|\, \mathbf{G}\psi \,|\, \mathbf{F}\psi \,|\, \mathbf{X}\psi.$$

The temporal operator $\mathbf{G}$ is read as *globally*, $\mathbf{F}$ is read as *finally* (or *eventually*), and $\mathbf{X}$ is read as *next*. Due to the extended domain of truth values in three-valued Kripke structures, the bounded evaluation of LTL formulae is based on the Kleene logic $\mathcal{K}_3$ (compare Sect. 2). Based on $\mathcal{K}_3$, LTL formulae can be evaluated on b-bounded path prefixes of three-valued Kripke structures. Such finite prefixes $\pi(0) \ldots \pi(b)$ can still represent infinite paths if the prefix has a *loop*, i.e. the last state $\pi(b)$ has a successor state that is also part of the prefix.

Definition 5 (b-Loop). *Let π be a path of a three-valued Kripke structure M and let $r, b \in \mathbb{N}$ with $r \leq b$. Then π has a (b,r)-loop if $R(\pi(b), \pi(r)) \in \{true, \perp\}$ and π is of the form $v \cdot w^{\omega}$ where $v = \pi(0) \ldots \pi(r-1)$ and $w = \pi(r) \ldots \pi(b)$. π has a b-loop if there exists an $r \in \mathbb{N}$ with $r \leq b$ such that π has a (b,r)-loop.*

For the bounded evaluation of LTL formulae on paths of Kripke structures we have to distinguish between paths *with* and *without* a b-loop.

Definition 6 (Three-Valued Bounded Evaluation of LTL). *Let $M = (S, \langle l^0, s^0 \rangle, R, L)$ over AP be a three-valued Kripke structure. Moreover, let $b \in \mathbb{N}$ and let π be a path of M with a b-loop. Then the b-bounded evaluation of an LTL formula ψ on π, written $[\pi \models_b^k \psi]$ where $k \leq b$ denotes the current position along the path, is inductively defined as follows:*

$$[\pi \models_b^k p] \qquad\equiv L(\pi(k), p)$$
$$[\pi \models_b^k \neg p] \qquad\equiv \neg L(\pi(k), p)$$
$$[\pi \models_b^k \psi \vee \psi'] \equiv [\pi \models_b^k \psi] \vee [\pi \models_b^k \psi']$$
$$[\pi \models_b^k \psi \wedge \psi'] \equiv [\pi \models_b^k \psi] \wedge [\pi \models_b^k \psi']$$
$$[\pi \models_b^k \mathbf{G}\psi] \qquad\equiv \bigwedge_{k' \geq k}(R(\pi(k'), \pi(k'+1)) \wedge [\pi \models_b^{k'} \psi])$$
$$[\pi \models_b^k \mathbf{F}\psi] \qquad\equiv \bigvee_{k' \geq k}([\pi \models_b^{k'} \psi] \wedge \bigwedge_{k''=k}^{k'-1} R(\pi(k''), \pi(k''+1)))$$
$$[\pi \models_b^k \mathbf{X}\psi] \qquad\equiv R(\pi(k), \pi(k+1)) \wedge [\pi \models_b^{k+1} \psi]$$

If π is a path without *a b-loop then the* b-*bounded evaluation of* ψ *is defined as:*

$$[\pi \models_b^k \mathbf{G}\psi] \equiv false$$
$$[\pi \models_b^k \mathbf{F}\psi] \equiv \bigvee_{k'=k}^{b}([\pi \models_b^{k'} \psi] \wedge \bigwedge_{k''=k}^{k'-1} R(\pi(k''), \pi(k''+1)))$$
$$[\pi \models_b^k \mathbf{X}\psi] \equiv \text{if } k < b \text{ then } R(\pi(k), \pi(k+1)) \wedge [\pi \models_b^{k+1} \psi] \text{ else } false$$

The other cases are identical to the case where π *has a b-loop. The universal bounded evaluation of* ψ *on an entire Kripke structure* M *is* $[M \models_{U,b} \psi] \equiv \bigwedge_{\pi \in \Pi_M}[\pi \models_b^0 \psi]$. *The existential bounded evaluation of* ψ *on a Kripke structure is* $[M \models_{E,b} \psi] \equiv \bigvee_{\pi \in \Pi_M}[\pi \models_b^0 \psi]$.

Checking temporal logic properties for three-valued Kripke structures is what is known as three-valued model checking [2]. Universal model checking can always be transformed into existential model checking based on the equation $[M \models_{U,b} \psi] = \neg [M \models_{E,b} \neg \psi]$. From now on we only consider the existential case, since it is the basis of satisfiability-based bounded model checking. Bounded model checking [1] is typically performed incrementally, i.e. b is iteratively increased until the property can be either proven or a completeness threshold [7] is reached. In the three-valued scenario there exist three possible outcomes: *true*, *false* and $\perp$. For our example Kripke structure M we have that $[M \models_{E,0} \mathbf{F}p]$ evaluates to $\perp$ and $[M \models_{E,1} \mathbf{F}p]$ evaluates to *true*, which is witnessed by the 1-bounded prefix $\langle l^0, s^0\rangle\langle l^2, s^2\rangle$.

It was shown in [11] that for a three-valued Kripke structure M modelling a concurrent system Sys abstracted over $Pred$ and an LTL formula ψ the following holds: $[M \models_{E,b} \psi] = true$ implies that there exists an execution path of length b in Sys that satisfies ψ, and $[M \models_{E,b} \psi] = false$ implies that no execution path of length b in Sys satisfies ψ. Hence, all definite model checking results obtained under three-valued abstraction can be immediately transferred to the concrete system Sys modelled by M, whereas an *unknown* result tells us that the current level of abstraction is too coarse.

In the next section we define a propositional logic encoding of three-valued bounded model checking tasks for abstracted concurrent systems. Our encoding allows to immediately transfer verification tasks into a propositional logic formulae that can be then processed via a SAT solver. Thus, the expensive construction of an explicit Kripke structure is not required in our approach. The state space of the system under consideration as well as the property to be checked will be implicitly contained in the propositional logic encoding, and the model checking result will be equivalent to the result of the corresponding satisfiability test.

4 Propositional Logic Encoding

In our previous work [13] we showed that the three-valued bounded model checking problem $[M \models_{E,b} \psi]$, where M is given as an *explicit* Kripke structure, can be reduced to two classical SAT problems. Here we show that for a given system Sys abstracted over $Pred$, a temporal logic property ψ, and a bound $b \in \mathbb{N}$, it is not even necessary to consider the corresponding model checking problem. We can immediately construct a propositional logic formula $[\![Sys, \psi]\!]_b$ such that:

$$[M \models_{E,b} \psi] = \begin{cases} true & \text{if} \quad \text{SAT}([\![Sys, \psi]\!]_b[\bot/false]) = true \\ false & \text{if} \quad \text{SAT}([\![Sys, \psi]\!]_b[\bot/true]) = false \\ \bot & \text{else} \end{cases}$$

Here $[\bot/false]$ resp. $[\bot/true]$ denotes the substitution of all occurrences of $\bot$ with *false* resp. *true*. Hence, it is not required to construct and explore an explicit Kripke structure M modelling the state space of Sys. All we need to do is to construct $[\![Sys, \psi]\!]_b$ and check its satisfiability in order to obtain the result of the corresponding model checking problem.

The formula $[\![Sys, \psi]\!]_b$ is defined over a set of Boolean atoms and the constants *true*, *false* and $\bot$. We now give a step-by-step description on how $[\![Sys, \psi]\!]_b$ can be constructed for a concurrent system $Sys = \|_{i=1}^n P_i$ abstracted over a set of predicates $Pred$ and given by a number of control flow graphs $G_i = (Loc_i, \delta_i, \tau_i)$ with $1 \le i \le n$, a temporal logic property $\psi \in$ LTL, and a bound $b \in \mathbb{N}$. The construction of $[\![Sys, \psi]\!]_b$ is divided into the translation of the abstract system into a formula $[\![Sys]\!]_b$ and the translation of the property ψ into a formula $[\![\psi]\!]_b$.

We start with the encoding of the system, which first requires to encode its states as propositional logic formulae. Since a state of a concurrent system is a tuple $\langle l, s \rangle$ where l is a composite location and s is a valuation of all predicates in $Pred$, we encode l and s separately. First, we introduce a set of Boolean atoms for the encoding of locations. A composite location $(l_1, \ldots, l_n) \in Loc$ is a list of single locations $l_i \in Loc_i$ where $Loc_i = \{0, \ldots, |Loc_i|\}$ and i is the identifier of the associated process P_i. Each l_i is a binary number from the domain $\{[0]_2, \ldots, [|Loc_i|]_2\}$. We assume that all these numbers have d_i digits where d_i is the number required to binary represent the maximum value $|Loc_i|$. We introduce the following set of Boolean atoms:

$$LocAtoms := \{l_i[j] \mid i \in [1..n], \ j \in [1..d_i]\}$$

Hence, for each process P_i of the system we introduce d_i Boolean atoms, each referring to a distinct digit along the binary representation of its locations. The atoms now allow us to define the following encoding of locations:

Definition 7 (Encoding of Locations). *Let the location $l_i \in \{0, \ldots, |Loc_i|\}$ be given as a binary number. Moreover, let $l_i(j)$ be a function evaluating to* true *if the j-th digit of l_i is 1, and to* false *otherwise. Then l_i can be encoded in propositional logic as follows:*

$$enc(l_i) := \bigwedge_{j=1}^{d_i} ((l_i[j] \wedge l_i(j)) \vee (\neg l_i[j] \wedge \neg l_i(j)))$$

Let $l = (l_1, \ldots, l_n)$ be a composite location. Then $enc(l) := \bigwedge_{i=1}^{n} enc(l_i)$.

Note that since the function $l_i(j)$ evaluates to $true$ or $false$ an encoding $enc(l_i)$ can be always simplified to a conjunction of literals over $LocAtoms$. For instance, the initial location $(0,0)$ of our example system will be encoded to $\neg l_1[1] \wedge \neg l_2[1]$.

Next, we encode the predicate part of states. Let $s \in S_{Pred}$ where $Pred = \{p_1, \ldots, p_m\}$. We introduce the following set of Boolean atoms:

$$PredAtoms := \{p[j] \mid p \in Pred,\ j \in \{u, t\}\}$$

Hence, for each three-valued predicate p we introduce two Boolean atoms. The atom $p[u]$ will let us indicate whether p evaluates to $unknown$, and $p[t]$ will let us indicate whether it evaluates to $true$ or $false$:

Definition 8 (Encoding of States over Predicates). *Let* $p \in Pred$ *and let* $val \in \{true, \bot, false\}$. *Then* $(p = val)$ *can be logically encoded follows:*

$$enc(p = val) := \begin{cases} \neg p[u] \wedge p[t] & if \quad val = true \\ \neg p[u] \wedge \neg p[t] & if \quad val = false \\ p[u] & if \quad val = \bot \end{cases}$$

Let s be a state over $Pred$. Then $enc(s) := \bigwedge_{p \in Pred} enc(p = s(p))$.

For an overall state $\langle l, s \rangle \in S$ we consequently get $enc(\langle l, s \rangle) := enc(l) \wedge enc(s)$. Since $enc(\langle l, s \rangle)$ yields a conjunction of literals, there exists exactly one satisfying truth assignment $\alpha : LocAtoms \cup PredAtoms \rightarrow \{true, false\}$ for a state encoding. We denote the assignment characterising an encoded state $\langle l, s \rangle$ by $\alpha_{\langle l, s \rangle}$. For instance, the initial state $\langle (0,0), (y > 0) = true \rangle$ of our abstracted example system will be encoded to $Init = \neg l_1[1] \wedge \neg l_2[1] \wedge \neg p[u] \wedge p[t]$ where $p = (y > 0)$, i.e. we abbreviate $(y > 0)$ by p. The assignment characterising $Init$ is $\alpha_{\langle (0,0), (y>0)=true \rangle} : l_1[1] \mapsto false, l_2[1] \mapsto false, p[u] \mapsto false, p[t] \mapsto true$.

The encoding function enc can be extended to *logical expressions* in negation normal form (NNF), which we require for our later transition encoding:

Definition 9 (Encoding of Logical Expressions). *Let* $p \in Pred$ *and* e, e' *logical expressions in NNF over* $Pred \cup \{true, \bot, false\}$. *Let* $val \in \{true, \bot, false\}$. *Then the encoding of a logical expression is inductively defined as follows:*

$$
\begin{aligned}
enc(val) \quad &:= val \\
enc(\neg val) \quad &:= \neg val \\
enc(p) \quad &:= (p[u] \wedge \bot) \vee (\neg p[u] \wedge p[t]) \\
enc(\neg p) \quad &:= (p[u] \wedge \bot) \vee (\neg p[u] \wedge \neg p[t]) \\
enc(e \wedge e') \quad &:= enc(e) \wedge enc(e') \\
enc(e \vee e') \quad &:= enc(e) \vee enc(e') \\
enc(choice(e, e')) &:= enc((e \vee NNF(\neg e')) \wedge (e \vee e' \vee \bot))
\end{aligned}
$$

Next, we take a look at how the transition relation of an abstracted system can be encoded. We will construct a propositional logic formula $[\![Sys]\!]_b = Init_0 \wedge$

$Trans_{0,1} \wedge \ldots \wedge Trans_{b-1,b}$ that exactly characterises path prefixes of length $b \in \mathbb{N}$ in the system Sys abstracted over $Pred$. Since we consider states as parts of such prefixes, we have to extend the encoding of states by index values $k \in \{0, \ldots, b\}$ where k denotes the position along a path prefix. For this we introduce the notion of indexed encodings. Let F be a propositional logic formula over $Atoms = LocAtoms \cup PredAtoms$ and the constants $true$, $false$ and $\perp$. Then F_k stands for $F[a/a_k \,|\, a \in Atoms]$. Our overall encoding will be thus defined over the set $Atoms_{[0,b]} = \{a_k \,|\, a \in Atoms, 0 \leq k \leq b\}$. An assignment $\alpha_{\langle l, s \rangle}$ to the atoms in a subset $Atoms_{[k,k]} \subseteq Atoms_{[0,b]}$ thus characterises a state $\langle l, s \rangle$ at position k of a path prefix, whereas an assignment $\alpha_{\langle l^0, s^0 \rangle \ldots \langle l^b, s^b \rangle}$ to the atoms in $Atoms_{[0,b]}$ characterises an entire path prefix $\langle l^0, s^0 \rangle \ldots \langle l^b, s^b \rangle$. Since all execution paths start in the initial state of the system, we extend its encoding by the index 0, i.e. we get $Init_0 = \neg l_1[1]_0 \wedge \neg l_2[1]_0 \wedge \neg p[u]_0 \wedge p[t]_0$. The encoding of all possible state space transitions from position k to $k+1$ is defined as follows:

Definition 10 (Encoding of Transitions). *Let* $Sys = \|_{i=1}^n P_i$ *over* $Pred$ *be an abstracted concurrent system given by the single control flow graphs* $G_i = (Loc_i, \delta_i, \tau_i)$ *with* $1 \leq i \leq n$. *Then all possible transitions for position* k *to* $k+1$ *can be encoded in propositional logic as follows:*

$$Trans_{k,k+1} :=$$

$$\bigvee_{i=1}^n \bigvee_{(l_i, l'_i) \in \delta_i} (enc(l_i)_k \wedge enc(l'_i)_{k+1} \wedge \bigwedge_{i' \neq i} idle(i')_{k,k+1} \wedge enc(\tau_i(l_i, l'_i))_{k,k+1})$$

where $idle(i')_{k,k+1} := \bigwedge_{j=1}^{d_{i'}} (l_{i'}[j]_k \leftrightarrow l_{i'}[j]_{k+1})$

and $enc(\tau_i(l_i, l'_i))_{k,k+1} := \quad enc(choice(a,b))_k$
$$\wedge \bigwedge_{j=1}^m (\quad (enc(a_j)_k \wedge enc(p_j = true)_{k+1})$$
$$\vee (enc(b_j)_k \wedge enc(p_j = false)_{k+1})$$
$$\vee (enc(\neg a_j \wedge \neg b_j)_k[\perp/true] \wedge enc(p_j = \perp)_{k+1}))$$

assuming that $\tau_i(l_i, l'_i) = assume(choice(a,b))$: $p_1 := choice(a_1, b_1), \ldots, p_m := choice(a_m, b_m)$.

Thus, we iterate over the system's processes P_i and over the processes' control flow transitions $\delta_i(l_i, l'_i)$. Now we construct the k-indexed encoding of a source location l_i and conjunct it with the $(k+1)$-indexed encoding of a destination location l'_i. This gets conjuncted with the sub formula $\bigwedge_{i' \neq i} idle(i')_{k,k+1}$ which encodes that all processes different to P_i are idle, i.e. do not change their control flow location, while P_i proceeds. The last part of the transition encoding concerns the operation associated with $\delta_i(l_i, l'_i)$: The sub formula $enc(\tau_i(l_i, l'_i))_{k,k+1}$ evaluates to $true$ for assignments $\alpha_{\langle l, s \rangle \langle l', s' \rangle}$ to the atoms in $Atoms_{[k,k+1]}$ that characterise pairs of states s and s' over $Pred$ where the guard of the operation $\tau_i(l_i, l'_i)$ is $true$ in s and the execution of the operation in s definitely results in the state s'. The operation encoding evaluates to $\perp$ for states s and s' where the guard of the operation is $\perp$ in s or where it is $unknown$ whether the execution of the operation in s results in the state s'. In all other cases $enc(\tau_i(l_i, l'_i))_{k,k+1}$ evaluates to *false*. Our transition encoding requires that an operation $\tau_i(l_i, l'_i)$ assigns to all predicates in *Pred*: Thus, if a predicate p is not modified by the operation we assume that $p := p$ is part of the assignment list.

The encoding of the control flow transition $\delta_1(0, 1)$ of our abstract example system with $\tau_1(0, 1) = (assume(p) : p := choice(false, \neg p))$ (where p abbreviates $(y > 0)$) yields the following:

$$
\begin{aligned}
enc(0)_k \quad &= \neg l_1[1]_k \\
\wedge \quad &\qquad \wedge \\
enc(1)_{k+1} \quad &= l_1[1]_{k+1} \\
\wedge \quad &\qquad \wedge \\
idle(2)_{k,k+1} \quad &= (l_2[1]_k \leftrightarrow l_2[1]_{k+1}) \\
\wedge \quad &\qquad \wedge \\
enc(\tau_1(0,1))_{k,k+1} &= ((p[u]_k \wedge \bot) \vee (\neg p[u]_k \wedge p[t]_k)) \wedge \\
&\quad ((false \wedge (\neg p[u]_{k+1} \wedge p[t]_{k+1})) \\
&\quad \vee (((p[u]_k \wedge \bot) \vee (\neg p[u]_k \wedge \neg p[t]_k)) \wedge (\neg p[u]_{k+1} \wedge \neg p[t]_{k+1})) \\
&\quad \vee (((p[u]_k \wedge true) \vee (\neg p[u]_k \wedge p[t]_k)) \wedge (p[u]_{k+1})))
\end{aligned}
$$

The encoding of the operation only evaluates to *true* for assignments to the atoms in $Atoms_{[k,k+1]}$ that characterise a predicate state s at position k with $s(p) = true$ and a state s' at position $k + 1$ with $s'(p) = \bot$. An overall satisfying assignment for this encoding is $\alpha_{\langle(0,0),(y>0)=true\rangle\langle(1,0),(y>0)=\bot\rangle}$ characterising the definite transition between the pair of states $\langle(0,0),(y > 0) = true\rangle$ and $\langle(1,0),(y > 0) = \bot\rangle$. The assignments $\alpha_{\langle(0,l_2),(y>0)=true\rangle\langle(1,l_2),(y>0)=false\rangle}$, $\alpha_{\langle(0,l_2),(y>0)=\bot\rangle\langle(1,l_2),(y>0)=false\rangle}$, $\alpha_{\langle(0,l_2),(y>0)=\bot\rangle\langle(1,l_2),(y>0)=\bot\rangle}$ with $l_2 \in \{0, 1\}$ yield *unknown* for the encoding and hereby correctly characterise $\bot$-transitions in the abstract state space. All other assignments yield *false* indicating that corresponding pairs of states do not characterise valid transitions.

The encoding definitions now allow us to construct the propositional logic formula $[\![Sys]\!]_b = Init_0 \wedge Trans_{0,1} \wedge \ldots \wedge Trans_{b-1,b}$ that characterises all possible path prefixes of length $b \in \mathbb{N}$ in the state space of the encoded system. Each assignment $\alpha : Atoms_{[0,b]} \rightarrow \{true, false\}$ that satisfies the formula characterises a definite path prefix, whereas an assignment that makes the formula evaluate to *unknown* characterises a prefix with some $\bot$-transitions.

The second part of the encoding concerns the LTL property to be checked. The three-valued bounded LTL encoding has been defined in [13] before. Here we adjust it to our encodings of predicates and locations. Again, we distinguish the cases where the property is evaluated on a path prefix with and without a loop. The LTL encoding for the evaluation on prefixes with a loop is defined as:

Definition 11 (LTL Encoding with Loop). *Let p and $(loc_i = l_i) \in AP$, ψ and ψ' LTL formulae, and $b, k, r \in \mathbb{N}$ with $k, r \leq b$ where k is the current position, b the bound and r the destination position of the b-loop. Then the LTL encoding with a loop, $_r[\![\psi]\!]_b^k$, is defined as follows:*

$$_r[\![(loc_i = l_i)]\!]_b^k \equiv enc(l_i)_k \qquad\qquad _r[\![\neg(loc_i = l_i)]\!]_b^k \equiv \neg enc(l_i)_k$$

$$_r[\![p]\!]_b^k \equiv enc(p)_k \qquad\qquad\qquad _r[\![\neg p]\!]_b^k \equiv enc(\neg p)_k$$

$$_r[\![\psi \vee \psi']\!]_b^k \equiv _r[\![\psi]\!]_b^k \vee _r[\![\psi']\!]_b^k \qquad _r[\![\psi \wedge \psi']\!]_b^k \equiv _r[\![\psi]\!]_b^k \wedge _r[\![\psi']\!]_b^k$$

$$_r[\![\mathbf{G}\psi]\!]_b^k \equiv \bigwedge\nolimits_{k'=min(k,r)}^{b} {_r}[\![\psi]\!]_b^{k'} \quad _r[\![\mathbf{F}\psi]\!]_b^k \equiv \bigvee\nolimits_{k'=min(k,r)}^{b} {_r}[\![\psi]\!]_b^{k'}$$

$$_r[\![\mathbf{X}\psi]\!]_b^k \equiv _r[\![\psi]\!]_b^{succ(k)}$$

where $succ(k) = k+1$ if $k < b$ and $succ(k) = r$ else.

For a path prefix without a loop the LTL encoding is defined as:

Definition 12 (LTL Encoding without Loop). *Let ψ be an LTL formula and $b, k \in \mathbb{N}$ with $k \leq b$ where k is the current position and b the bound. Then the LTL encoding without a loop, $[\![\psi]\!]_b^k$, is defined as follows:*

$$[\![\mathbf{G}\psi]\!]_b^k \equiv false \qquad\qquad\qquad [\![\mathbf{F}\psi]\!]_b^k \equiv \bigvee\nolimits_{k'=k}^{b} [\![\psi]\!]_b^{k'}$$
$$[\![\mathbf{X}\psi]\!]_b^k \equiv \text{if } k < b \text{ then } _r[\![\psi]\!]_b^{k+1} \text{ else } false$$

The LTL encoding without a loop of the other cases is identical to the LTL encoding with a loop.

An example encoding is $[\![\mathbf{F}p]\!]_2^0 = enc(p)_0 \vee enc(p)_1 \vee enc(p)_2$ which expresses that a predicate p holds *eventually*, i.e. at position 0, 1 or 2 along a 2-prefix. Remember that a prefix $\langle l^0, s^0\rangle \ldots \langle l^b, s^b\rangle$ has a b-loop if there exists a transition from $\langle l^b, s^b\rangle$ to a previous state $\langle l^r, s^r\rangle$ along the prefix with $0 \leq r \leq b$. Hence, we can define a loop constraint based on our transition encoding: A prefix characterised by an assignment $\alpha_{\langle l^0, s^0\rangle \ldots \langle l^b, s^b\rangle}$ has definitely resp. maybe a b-loop if the loop constraint $\bigvee_{r=0}^{b} Trans_{b,r}$ evaluates to *true* resp. *unknown* under $\alpha_{\langle l^0, s^0\rangle \ldots \langle l^b, s^b\rangle}$. This now allows us to define the overall encoding of whether a concurrent system Sys satisfies an LTL formula ψ: $[\![Sys, \psi]\!]_b := [\![Sys]\!]_b \wedge [\![\psi]\!]_b$ with $[\![\psi]\!]_b := [\![\psi]\!]_b^0 \vee \bigvee_{r=0}^{b}(Trans_{b,r} \wedge _r[\![\psi]\!]_b^0)$. We have proven the following theorem that establishes the relation between the satisfiability result for $[\![Sys, \psi]\!]_b$ and the result of the corresponding model checking problem:

Theorem 1. *Let M be a three-valued Kripke structure representing the state space of an abstracted concurrent system Sys, let ψ be an LTL formula and $b \in \mathbb{N}$ Then:*

$$[M \models_{E,b} \psi] \equiv \begin{cases} true & \text{if} \quad SAT([\![Sys, \psi]\!]_b[\bot/false]) = true \\ false & \text{if} \quad SAT([\![Sys, \psi]\!]_b[\bot/true]) = false \\ \bot & \text{else} \end{cases}$$

Proof. See http://www.cs.up.ac.za/cs/ntimm/ProofTheorem1.pdf.

Hence, via two satisfiability tests, one where the constant $\bot$ is substituted by *true* and one where it is substituted by *false*, we can determine the result of the corresponding model checking problem. Our encoding can be straightforwardly built based on the concurrent system, which saves us the expensive construction of an explicit state space model. In the next section we show that our encoding can be also easily augmented by fairness constraints, which allows us to check liveness properties of concurrent systems under realistic conditions.

5   Extension to Fairness

Our approach allows to check LTL properties of concurrent software systems via SAT solving. While the verification of safety properties like mutual exclusion does not require any fairness assumptions about the behaviour of the processes of the system, fairness is essential for verifying *liveness* properties under realistic conditions. The most common notions of fairness in verification are *unconditional*, *weak* and *strong* fairness: An unconditional fairness constraint claims that in an infinite computation, certain operations have to be infinitely often executed. A weak fairness constraint claims that in an infinite computation, each operation that is *continuously* enabled has to be infinitely often executed. A strong fairness constraint claims that in an infinite computation, each operation that is *infinitely often* enabled has to be infinitely often executed. All these types of constraints can be straightforwardly expressed in LTL. We now define these constraints for characterising fair, i.e. realistic, behaviour of our concurrent systems $Sys = \|_{i=1}^{n} P_i$ over $Pred$. Our unconditional fairness constraint is defined as:

$$ufair \equiv \bigwedge_{i=1}^{n} \bigvee_{(l_i, l_i') \in \delta_i} \mathbf{GF}(executed(l_i, l_i'))$$

Hence, for each process some operation has to be executed infinitely often, i.e. each process proceeds infinitely often. Note that we model termination via a location with a self-loop. Thus, terminated processes can still proceed. The expression $executed(l_i, l_i')$ can be easily defined in LTL. For this we extend the set $Pred$ by a progress predicate for each process: $Pred := Pred \cup \{progress_i \mid i \in [1..n]\}$. Moreover, we extend each operation as follows: $\tau_i(l_i, l_i')$ sets $progress_i$ to *true* and all $progress_{i'}$ with $i' \neq i$ to *false*. Now $executed(l_i, l_i')$ is defined as follows:

$$executed(l_i, l_i') \equiv (loc_i = l_i) \wedge \mathbf{X}((loc_i = l_i') \wedge progress_i).$$

Thus, an operation associated with a control flow transition (l_i, l_i') is executed if $(loc_i = l_i)$ holds in the current state and $(loc_i = l_i') \wedge progress_i$ holds in the next state. Next, we define our weak fairness constraint:

$$wfair \equiv \bigwedge_{i=1}^{n} \bigwedge_{(l_i, l_i') \in \delta_i} (\mathbf{FG}(enabled(l_i, l_i')) \rightarrow \mathbf{GF}(executed(l_i, l_i')))$$

Hence, for each process, each continuously enabled operation has to be infinitely often executed. Instead of incorporating *each* operation in this type of constraint it is also possible to restrict the operations to crucial ones, which results in a shorter constraint and thus also restrains the complexity of model checking under fairness. For our running example it is for instance appropriate to just incorporate operations in $wfair$ that correspond to the successful acquisition of the semaphore. Note that $wfair$ can be easily transferred into negation normal form via the common propositional logic transformation rules such that it is conform with the definition of LTL. The expression $enabled(l_i, l_i')$ can be defined as an LTL formula over locations and $Pred$ as follows:

$$enabled(l_i, l_i') \equiv (loc_i = l_i) \wedge choice(a, b)$$

assuming that $\tau_i(l_i, l_i') = assume(choice(a, b)) : p_1 := choice(a_1, b_1), \ldots, p_m := choice(a_m, b_m)$. Thus, an operation associated with a control flow transition (l_i, l_i') is enabled if $(loc_i = l_i)$ holds and the guard of the operation holds as well. Finally, we define our strong fairness constraint:

$$sfair \equiv \bigwedge_{i=1}^{n} \bigwedge_{(l_i, l_i') \in \delta_i} (\mathbf{GF}(enabled(l_i, l_i')) \rightarrow \mathbf{GF}(executed(l_i, l_i')))$$

Hence, for each process, each operation that is enabled infinitely often has to be executed infinitely often. In model checking under fairness we can either check properties under specific constraints or we can combine all to a general one

$$fair \equiv ufair \wedge wfair \wedge sfair.$$

Existential bounded model checking under fairness is now defined as:

$$[M \models_{E,b}^{fair} \psi] \equiv [M \models_{E,b} (fair \wedge \psi)]$$

Thus, we check whether there exists a b-bounded path that is fair and satisfies the property ψ. Such a model checking problem can be straightforwardly encoded in propositional logic based on our definitions in the previous section. We get

$$[\![Sys, fair \wedge \psi]\!]_b := [\![Sys]\!]_b \wedge [\![fair \wedge \psi]\!]_b,$$

which can be fed into a SAT solver in order to obtain the result of model checking ψ under fairness. Next, we present the implementation of our encoding-based model checking technique and we discuss example verification tasks that illustrate the capability of our approach.

6 Implementation

We have implemented a SAT-based bounded model checker for three-valued abstractions of concurrent software systems. Our tool employs the abstractor 3Spot [11] that builds abstract control flow graphs for a given concurrent system Sys and a set of predicates $Pred$. 3Spot supports almost all control structures of the C language as well as int, $bool$ and $semaphore$ as data types. Based on the CFGs and an input LTL formula ψ, our tool automatically constructs an encoding $[\![Sys, \psi]\!]_b$ of the corresponding verification task. The model checker now iterates over the bound b starting with $b = 0$, until a definite result can be obtained or a predefined threshold for b is reached: In each iteration the two instances of the encoding are processed by a solver thread of the SAT solver Sat4j [9]. A $false$ result for $[\![Sys, \psi]\!]_b[\bot/true]$ and a $true$ result for $[\![Sys, \psi]\!]_b[\bot/false]$ can be immediately transferred to the corresponding model checking problem $[M \models_{E,b} \psi]$. In case of a $true$ resp. $unknown$ result, a witness path for ψ in the form of an assignment satisfying $[\![Sys, \psi]\!]_b$ is additionally returned. The tool chain of our model checker is depicted below.

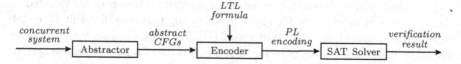

The abstractor 3Spot can construct finite abstractions of *fix-sized systems with non-uniform processes* as well as of *parameterised systems with an unbounded number of uniform processes* [14]. A finite abstraction of a parameterised system $Sys = \|_{i=1}^{n} P_i$ implementing a solution to the dining philosophers problem is depicted below. All processes continuously attempt to acquire the two resources p and q. Once a process has successfully acquired both resources it releases them in a single step and attempts to acquire them again. The order in which a process requests the resources is non-deterministically determined. 3Spot does not only use predicate abstraction, it also allows to abstract away entire processes by summarising them into a single approximative process $G_\perp$. The loss of information due to abstraction is modelled by the truth value $\perp$. In our example G_1 and G_2 are abstractions of two individual processes while $G_\perp$ approximates the behaviour of an unbounded number of additional processes.

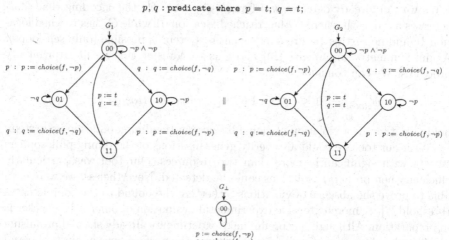

We now illustrate how our tool verifies properties of concurrent systems. We search for violations of desirable properties. For the dining philosophers the violation of mutual exclusion can be expressed as

$$\psi = \mathbf{F}((loc_1 = 11) \wedge (loc_2 = 11)).$$

Hence, we check whether the processes represented by G_1 and G_2 will be ever at their critical location 11 at the same time. Based on the abstract CFGs and ψ our encoder automatically constructs $[\![Sys, \psi]\!]_b$. Next, our tool iterates over b until a completeness threshold is reached[1]. Via SAT solving we obtain *false* results in

---

[1] Completeness thresholds for checking safety properties are linear in the size of the abstraction, i.e. in the number of abstract states [7].

all iterations, which allows to conclude that mutual exclusion is not violated for the processes abstracted by G_1 and G_2. Receiving this overall result takes 20 s on a 2.93 GHz Intel Core i3 system with 7 GB. The LTL formula ψ characterises a local property since it refers to particular processes of a parameterised system. However, as shown in [14] symmetry arguments allow us to transfer this result to arbitrary pairs of processes in the system. We can conclude that

$$\psi_{global} = \exists 1 \leq i, j \leq n, \ i \neq j : \mathbf{F}((loc_i = 11) \wedge (loc_j = 11))$$

does not hold as well for the dining philosophers, i.e. no pair of processes will be ever at their critical location at the same time. In the same manner, we can verify global liveness properties of concurrent systems under fairness assumptions. The formula

$$\psi' = \mathbf{F}((loc_1 = 00) \wedge \mathbf{G}\neg(loc_1 = 11))$$

characterises the violation of a liveness property. It states that eventually philosopher 1 is at its initial location and will never successfully acquire both resources. Our tool constructs $[\![Sys, fair \wedge \psi']\!]_b$. Within two iterations over b and a time of 0.37 s we can already detect a satisfying assignment for the encoding that characterises a fair path where G_1 has reached location 01 while G_2 has reached location 10 and no further progress in the entire system is possible (only self-loops). Again, symmetry arguments [14] allow us to transfer this result to arbitrary processes. We can conclude that

$$\psi'_{global} = \exists 1 \leq i \leq n : \mathbf{F}((loc_i = 00) \wedge \mathbf{G}\neg(loc_i = 11))$$

holds, i.e. there is a violation of global liveness in the dining philosopher system.

With our tool we could also verify generalisations of the dining philosophers system with significantly more than two resources. Our tool was particularly efficient when property violations could be detected. Nevertheless, we were even able to prove the absence of violations by setting the bound to the completeness threshold [7]. A more extensive experimental evaluation of our model checker is in preparation. Although our preliminary experiments already showed promising results, we expect that we can further enhance the performance of our tool based on optimisations that we mention in the conclusion of this paper.

7   Related Work

Our SAT-based software verification technique is related to a number of existing approaches in the field of bounded model checking for software. The bounded model checker CBMC [8] supports the verification of *sequential C programs*. It is based on a Boolean abstraction of the input program and it allows for checking buffer overflows, pointer safety and assertions, but not full LTL properties. A similar tool is F-Soft [6]. This bounded model checker for sequential programs is restricted to the verification of *reachability properties*. While CBMC and F-Soft support a wider range of program constructs like pointers and recursion, our approach focusses on the challenges associated with *concurrency* and the verification of *liveness properties* under fairness. The tool TCBMC [10] is an extension of CBMC for verifying *safety properties* of *concurrent programs*. TCBMC introduces the concept of bounding context switches between processes, which is a special abstraction technique for reducing concurrency. In our approach we use the process summarisation abstraction of 3Spot [11], which allows us to reduce the complexity induced by concurrency in a different way. In contrast to the above mentioned tools, we employ *three-valued abstraction*, which preserves *true* and *false* results in verification. *Three-valued BMC* is addressed in [5,16]. However, only in the context of *hardware verification* [5] resp. assuming that an *explicit three-valued Kripke structure* is given [16]. To the best of our knowledge, our approach is the first that supports software verification under fairness via an immediate propositional logic encoding and SAT-based BMC.

8   Conclusion and Outlook

We introduced a verification technique for concurrent software systems via three-valued abstraction and SAT-based BMC. We defined a direct propositional logic encoding of software verification tasks and we proved that our encoding is sound in the sense that SAT results can be straightforwardly transferred to the corresponding model checking problem. Hence, the expensive construction and exploration of an explicit state space model is not necessary. Our fully-automatic tool enables the verification of safety and liveness properties under fairness. Due to the efficiency of modern SAT solvers we achieve promising performance results.

As future work we plan to experimentally evaluate our approach based on case studies on concurrent software systems. Moreover, we intend to optimise our technique by integrating *incremental* SAT solving and by developing SAT solving *heuristics* tailored to the structure of our encodings. Finally, we want to extend our tool by a mechanism for *counterexample-guided abstraction refinement* [15].

References

1. Biere, A., Cimatti, A., Clarke, E.M., Strichman, O., Zhu, Y.: Bounded model checking. Handb. Satisf. **185**, 457–481 (2009)
2. Bruns, G., Godefroid, P.: Model checking partial state spaces with 3-valued temporal logics. In: Halbwachs, N., Peled, D. (eds.) CAV 1999. LNCS, vol. 1633, pp. 274–287. Springer, Heidelberg (1999). doi:10.1007/3-540-48683-6_25
3. Cimatti, A., Clarke, E., Giunchiglia, F., Roveri, M.: NuSMV: a new symbolic model checker. Int. J. Softw. Tools Technol. Transf. **2**(4), 410–425 (2000)
4. Fitting, M.: Kleene's 3-valued logics and their children. Fund. Inf. **20**(1–3), 113–131 (1994)
5. Grumberg, O.: 3-valued abstraction for (bounded) model checking. In: Liu, Z., Ravn, A.P. (eds.) ATVA 2009. LNCS, vol. 5799, p. 21. Springer, Heidelberg (2009). doi:10.1007/978-3-642-04761-9_2

6. Ivančić, F., Yang, Z., Ganai, M.K., Gupta, A., Shlyakhter, I., Ashar, P.: F-SOFT: software verification platform. In: Etessami, K., Rajamani, S.K. (eds.) CAV 2005. LNCS, vol. 3576, pp. 301–306. Springer, Heidelberg (2005). doi:10.1007/11513988_31

7. Kroening, D., Ouaknine, J., Strichman, O., Wahl, T., Worrell, J.: Linear completeness thresholds for bounded model checking. In: Gopalakrishnan, G., Qadeer, S. (eds.) CAV 2011. LNCS, vol. 6806, pp. 557–572. Springer, Heidelberg (2011). doi:10.1007/978-3-642-22110-1_44

8. Kroening, D., Tautschnig, M.: CBMC – C bounded model checker. In: Ábrahám, E., Havelund, K. (eds.) TACAS 2014. LNCS, vol. 8413, pp. 389–391. Springer, Heidelberg (2014). doi:10.1007/978-3-642-54862-8_26

9. Le Berre, D., Parrain, A.: The Sat4j library, release 2.2. J. Satisf. Boolean Model. Comput. **7**, 59–64 (2010)

10. Rabinovitz, I., Grumberg, O.: Bounded model checking of concurrent programs. In: Etessami, K., Rajamani, S.K. (eds.) CAV 2005. LNCS, vol. 3576, pp. 82–97. Springer, Heidelberg (2005). doi:10.1007/11513988_9

11. Schrieb, J., Wehrheim, H., Wonisch, D.: Three-valued spotlight abstractions. In: Cavalcanti, A., Dams, D.R. (eds.) FM 2009. LNCS, vol. 5850, pp. 106–122. Springer, Heidelberg (2009). doi:10.1007/978-3-642-05089-3_8

12. Shoham, S., Grumberg, O.: 3-valued abstraction: more precision at less cost. Inf. Comput. **206**(11), 1313–1333 (2008)

13. Timm, N.: Bounded model checking für partielle systeme. Master's thesis, University of Paderborn (2009)

14. Timm, N., Wehrheim, H.: On symmetries and spotlights – verifying parameterised systems. In: Dong, J.S., Zhu, H. (eds.) ICFEM 2010. LNCS, vol. 6447, pp. 534–548. Springer, Heidelberg (2010). doi:10.1007/978-3-642-16901-4_35

15. Timm, N., Wehrheim, H., Czech, M.: Heuristic-guided abstraction refinement for concurrent systems. In: Aoki, T., Taguchi, K. (eds.) ICFEM 2012. LNCS, vol. 7635, pp. 348–363. Springer, Heidelberg (2012). doi:10.1007/978-3-642-34281-3_25

16. Wehrheim, H.: Bounded model checking for partial Kripke structures. In: Fitzgerald, J.S., Haxthausen, A.E., Yenigun, H. (eds.) ICTAC 2008. LNCS, vol. 5160, pp. 380–394. Springer, Heidelberg (2008). doi:10.1007/978-3-540-85762-4_26

Model Checking Requirements

Sérgio Barza[✉], Gustavo Carvalho, Juliano Iyoda, Augusto Sampaio, Alexandre Mota, and Flávia Barros

Centro de Informática - Universidade Federal de Pernambuco,
Recife, PE 50740-560, Brazil
{sb,ghpc,jmi,acas,acm,fab}@cin.ufpe.br

Abstract. In software engineering, system requirements are written in a natural language such as English. Later in the design phase, these requirements are usually translated to a semi-formal language such as UML. This design model gives support to the development of the system in a programming language. Although natural language is easy to use, it is intrinsically ambiguous. Undesired effects may arise, as the errors generated by misinterpretation of the requirements can lead to a late discovery of a problem with a costly solution. In this paper, we propose the use of a Controlled Natural Language (CNL) (a subset of English that obeys a formal grammar) as a language for writing requirements. Moreover, we developed a translator from a CNL to the modelling language of the NuSMV model checker. In addition, we propose another CNL to describe properties in the style of a temporal logic. A second translator transforms this CNL into Computation Tree Logic. Therefore, our toolset allows the user to benefit from the user-friendliness of a natural language and to perform a formal analysis on the requirements using the NuSMV model checker. We are thus able to assert whether the requirements satisfy a property. The user only deals with CNLs as we hide all formal languages involved in the inputs of a model checker. Counter-examples are produced in the NuSMV notation, but they are fairly intuitive to understand. We illustrate our work in a case study.

1 Introduction

In software engineering, it is common to write system requirements in a natural language such as English, for example. Subsequently, these requirements are interpreted and refined in the design phase in semi-formal languages (like UML[1]) and then are implemented in a particular programming language. Occasionally, also in the design phase, a designer may use a formal model and tool such as Isabelle/HOL [20] depending on how critical the system is.

Natural language is user-friendly and is a widely used vehicle to communicate and describe requirements. Unfortunately, natural language is ambiguous and therefore susceptible to multiple interpretation. Due to this problem, a mechanical analysis of the requirements becomes infeasible. Moreover, the use of natural

---

[1] http://www.omg.org/spec/UML.

© Springer International Publishing AG 2016
L. Ribeiro and T. Lecomte (Eds.): SBMF 2016, LNCS 10090, pp. 217–234, 2016.
DOI: 10.1007/978-3-319-49815-7_13

language in the requirements phase also brings consequences to other stages of development: requirement misunderstanding leads engineers to produce incorrect designs and implementation. Late discovery of these problems has considerable impact on a system architecture and project schedule and budget.

In this paper, we propose the use of a Controlled Natural Language (CNL) to write requirements and perform model checking on them. CNLs are subsets of natural languages that obey a formal grammar [18]. As they are free from ambiguities, they can be compiled and, consequently, they can be analysed automatically while still preserving, to a great extent, the user-friendliness of a natural language. We propose requirements to be written in SysReq-CNL, previously developed by Carvalho et al. [12]. Here we develop a translator from SysReq-CNL to the modelling language of the model checker NuSMV [13]. In order to check properties concerning requirements, we also designed another CNL called Natural-CTL, and implemented a translator of it to Computation Tree Logic (CTL). With these two languages and two translators, we are able to write and formally verify properties of the requirements on the level of CNLs without the need of direct manipulation of the formal notation required by a model checker. Only when the model checker produces a counterexample the user has to deal with the native NuSMV counterexample notation. However, such notation is intuitive and easy to understand. Finally, a case study illustrates the use of our languages and translators.

Previous works reported by Aceituna et al. [1] and Cavada et al. [14] describe translations from description and specification languages to the NuSMV languages, while Holt [19] and Badger et al. [4] aim to translate temporal logic formulas from CNLs. The work done by Choi and Heimdahl [15] proposes and implements a tool that translates from a specific formal notation to NuSMV models. Our work is more complete than previous works in the sense that we provide solutions to translate requirements and desired properties both written in CNLs to the model and the temporal logic formula of NuSMV. This allows formal methods to be introduced very early in the software development process while preventing the user from learning formal notations.

The main contributions of this paper are listed below.

- We propose the use of two CNLs in the requirements phase: SysReq-CNL (introduced in our previous work [12]) and Natural-CTL, which was developed to write CTL-like properties. With this approach, requirements continue to be written in a language that is similar to a pure natural language in addition to allowing property specification to be used in fully automatic verification of the requirements;
- We developed two translators that hide from the user the need of learning and manipulating formal modelling languages (such as NuSMV) and property languages (such as CTL). In particular, the translators deal with constructions of the CNL that are not conventional for a model checker, like references to past states;

– A case study that illustrates all contributions of this work. In particular, we show that a subtle change in a property turns it false — such verification would be quite challenging to do by hand.

This paper is organised as follows. Section 2 briefly introduces the first two phases of our strategy, the syntactic and the semantic analyses of the SysReq-CNL. Section 3 explains how SysReq-CNL is translated to the NuSMV modelling language. Section 4 presents the Natural-CTL and how it is translated to CTL formulas. Section 5 illustrates our translators considering a Coffee Vending Machine as a case study. Section 6 presents the main related works and Sect. 7 concludes.

2 Syntactic and Semantic Analyses of Requirements

SysReq-CNL was created in the context of the NAT2TEST strategy [8] to generate test cases from natural-language requirements based on different internal and hidden formal languages. It provides a flexible structure to describe actions guarded by conditions. The grammar of this CNL is fully available in [12]. Here, we rely on the first two phases of the NAT2TEST strategy: the syntactic and the semantic analyses. The syntactic analysis phase receives as input the system requirements in order to verify whether these requirements are in accordance with the SysReq-CNL grammar, a CNL specially tailored for editing requirements of data-flow reactive systems [10].

Initially, we have designed and tested SysReq-CNL considering examples provided by our industrial partner Embraer[2] [11]. We have later also considered different examples provided by different companies. These include an example provided by Mercedes [9], a consolidation function, also in the aerospace domain, and the Ford car-alarm system reported by Aichernig et al. [3]. In all these cases the considered SysReq-CNL was basically the same. So, we have some evidence that, although the CNL has a controlled structure, it is not limited to particular examples; rather, it seems flexible enough to express requirements of reactive systems more generally. In order to illustrate the SysReq-CNL grammar, let us present a semaphore example written according to its grammar.

Example 1. **The Semaphore**

Requirement 1: *When the counter is 6 or the counter is lower than 3, the system shall assign green to the semaphore.*

Requirement 2: *When the counter is greater than or equal to 3, and the counter is lower than 5, the system shall assign yellow to the semaphore.*

Requirement 3: *When the counter is 5, the system shall assign red to the semaphore.*

Requirement 4: *When the counter is 6, the system shall reset the counter.*

---

[2] www.embraer.com.br.

Requirement 5: *When the counter is greater than or equal to 0, the system shall add 1 to the counter.*

The semantic analysis phase maps the syntax trees generated by the previous phase into an informal natural-language semantic representation based on the Case Grammar linguistic theory [17]. In this theory, a sentence is analysed in terms of the *thematic roles* (semantic roles) played by each word, or group of words in the sentence.

The verb is associated to a thematic role, which is aggregated into a structure named as case frame (CF). Each verb in a requirement natural language specification gives rise to a different CF. All derived CFs are joined afterwards to compose what we call a *requirement frame* (RF). The NAT2TEST strategy considers nine thematic roles: action (ACT) – the action performed if the requirement conditions are satisfied; agent (AGT) – the entity which performs the action; patient (PAT) – the entity which is affected by the action; and TOV – the patient value after action completion. Similar roles are defined for the verbs used in conditions (guards): condition action (CAC), condition patient (CPT), condition from value (CFV), condition to value (CTV), and condition modifier (CMD). Table 1 shows the requirement frame for Requirement 2.

Table 1. Requirement frame corresponding to the Requirement 2.

1	Condition #1 - main verb (CAC): is	
2	CPT: the counter	CFV: -
3	CMD: greater than or equal to	CTV: 3
4	Condition #2 - main verb (CAC): is	
5	CPT: the counter	CFV: -
6	CMD: lower than	CTV: 5
7	Action - main verb (ACT): assign	
8	AGT: the system	TOV: yellow
9	PAT: the semaphore	

3   CNL to NuSMV

In this section, we describe how requirement frames are translated to a NuSMV model. The translation process is introduced in terms of its main tasks: requirement frame pre-processing, variable mapping, type inference and transition building.

3.1   Requirement Frame Pre-processing

We are not able to use a requirement frame exactly as generated by the semantic analysis of the NAT2TEST strategy. Thus we apply two main pre-processing functions to a requirement frame. The first pre-processing function assigns the field TOV (the final value of a patient) to 0 whenever the action verb is *reset*. By making the meaning of the verb *reset* explicit, we are able to apply the remaining tasks of the translation uniformly regardless what the action verb is. The second main pre-processing function concatenates patient and agent names into a single word.

3.2   Mapping Variables

Once the pre-processing task is done, we map elements of a requirement frame to NuSMV variables. Firstly, let us define the sets that give support to the construction of the set of variables.

Definition 1. *Let CPTSET be the set of all CPTs (condition patients) associated with a condition, and PATSET be a set of all PATs (patients) affected by any action. Then VARSET is the set of all variables of the system requirements.*

$$VARSET = CPTSET \cup PATSET$$

Using Table 1 as reference, we have

$$VARSET = \{thecounter\} \cup \{thesemaphore\} = \{thecounter, thesemaphore\}.$$

3.3   Inferring the Types of the Variables

When a variable is declared in NuSMV, its type must be defined since a model checker expands all values that the variable might have. This section describes how we infer the type of variables and how we use data abstraction to reduce the set of values of a type. By reducing the set of values of a type, we avoid as much as possible the state explosion problem. In this paper, type inference and data abstraction are presented as a single procedure.

Definition 2. *Let $var \in VARSET$. Let $CFVSET_{var}$ be the set of all CFVs (conditions from value) of the variable var. Let $CTVSET_{var}$ be the set of all CTV (condition to value) values of the variable var. Let $TOVSET_{var}$ be the set of all TOV (patient value) values that are assigned to the variable var. Such values are constant integers, boolean values or enumeration values, i.e. they do not come from expressions involving addition and subtraction.*

The set of all values related to a variable var is defined as

$$VALUESET_{var} = CFVSET_{var} \cup CTVSET_{var} \cup TOVSET_{var}.$$

Let us illustrate the construction of $VALUESET_{thecounter}$ from Table 1. We have $CFVSET_{thecounter} = TOVSET_{thecounter} = \emptyset$, $CTVSET_{thecounter} = \{5, 3\}$. Hence, $VALUESET_{thecounter} = \emptyset \cup \emptyset \cup \{5, 3\} = \{5, 3\}$. This process needs to be done for all requirement frames related to all requirements of Example 1. So, the complete set of values for $thecounter$ is $\{0, 3, 5, 6\}$.

System requirements specification written in CNL are restricted to use a small number of verbs. Two of them, *"to add"* and *"to subtract"*, are different in the context of typifying: all the possible values of the variables that are operands of an addition and subtraction are not explicit in the requirements. Due to this fact, we need to define a superset of $VALUESET_{var}$ that includes values from additions and subtractions. We assume that additions and subtractions are of the form $var + k$ and $var - k$, where k is an integer constant. For instance, Requirements 5 in Example 1 shows the variable $thecounter$ being assigned to $thecounter + 1$.

Definition 3. *Let $v \in VALUESET_{var}$, where var is an operand of an addition or a subtraction (or both). Let a and b be the additive and subtractive constant terms, respectively, and min and max be the minimum and maximum values of an integer range, respectively (provided by the user), where $v, a, b, min, max \in \mathbb{Z}$, and $min \leq v \leq max$. The set of all possible values of var, $ADDSUBSET_{var}$, is defined below. The notation $gcd(a, b)$ denotes the greatest common divisor between a and b.*

$$
ADDSET_{var}(v) = \begin{cases} \emptyset, & if\, a = 0 \\ \bigcup_{k=0}^{\lfloor \frac{max-v}{gcd(a,\, b)} \rfloor} \{v + gcd(a,\, b) \cdot k\}, & if\, a \neq 0 \end{cases}
$$

$$
SUBSET_{var}(v) = \begin{cases} \emptyset, & if\, b = 0 \\ \bigcup_{k=0}^{\lfloor \frac{v-min}{gcd(a,\, b)} \rfloor} \{v - gcd(a,\, b) \cdot k\}, & if\, b \neq 0 \end{cases}
$$

$$
ADDSUBSET_{var}(v) = ADDSET_{var}(v) \cup SUBSET_{var}(v), \text{ and}
$$

$$
ADDSUBSET_{var} = \bigcup_{v \in VALUESET_{var}} ADDSUBSET_{var}(v)
$$

The set $ADDSET_{var}$ contains all values v that might be produced from an addition of a in the range $min \leq v \leq max$, where min and max are values provided by the user (not shown in Example 1 for conciseness). However, if the same variable var is also used in a subtraction from b, then the values must change over increments of $gcd(a, b)$. A similar reasoning is applied to $SUBSET_{var}$. For conciseness, this definition applies to a single addition and a single subtraction. If more than one addition or more than one subtraction takes place for the same variable (in different requirements), we can adopt the same reasoning except that the $gcd()$ is generalised to more than two arguments.

A variable var that has been assigned neither to additions nor to subtractions is of type $VALUESET_{var}$. Otherwise its type is $ADDSUBSET_{var}$.

In Example 1, by analysing all requirements, $VALUESET_{thecounter} = \{0, 3,$
$5, 6\}$. As it is added to 1 in Requirement 5, and assuming that $min = 0$ and $max =$
6, its type is $ADDSUBSET_{thecounter} = \{0, 1, 2, 3, \dots, 6\}$.

3.4   Building Transitions

A transition is the main constructor of the NuSMV description language. It is
characterised by a set of variables and how their values change. Here we define
a transition as relation between a variable *var*, and action over *var* and the
conditions (guards) for this action to happen.

In Table 1 the variable *thesemaphore* is assigned to the value *yellow* provided
two conditions are satisfied. For this particular requirement frame, the following
relation tuple is produced.

$$(thesemaphore, Action, \{Condition1, Condition2\})$$

Action, *Condition*1 and *Condition*2 refer to the rows 7–9, 1–3, 4–6, in Table 1,
respectively. The complete set of transitions of *thesemaphore* is produced by
constructing similar tuples from requirements 1, 3, 4, and 5.

As SysReq-CNL grammar allows the use of the actions *to become* and *to*
change in the requirements, our approach needs to capture which changes were
done for this statements. In this way, we are processing them before the construction of these transitions. In these cases, the field CFV (condition from value — a
guard of the action) is stored with an explicit condition that guarantees that the
assigned value is different from the previous value. For instance, suppose that a
requirement says that the variable *thesemaphore* must change to *yellow*. Then,
the CFV must hold the value *thesemaphore* $\neq$ *yellow*. If the requirements say
that the value must change from *green* to *yellow*, then the CFV must hold the
value *thesemaphore* = *green*. This guarantees that the new value is consistent
with the semantics of the verbs *to become* and *to change*.

3.5   NuSMV Code Generation

Once we have the set of all variables, their types, and the set of all transitions,
we can now produce the NuSMV model.

The general strategy is to transform each requirement variable into a NuSMV
module that contains the variables *past* and *value*. The NuSMV variable *past*
stores the previous value of the requirement variable, while *value* stores its current value. This approach allows us to build correct NuSMV models when verbs
such as *to become* and *to change* appear, as they need previous information.

Currently, our NuSMV automatic generated model is less efficient than a
manually produced model. For instance, the creation of the variables past and
value might not be needed in some domains. However, this is an intrinsic problem
of automatic code generation. As this project evolves, code optimisations will be
developed and the generated model can become as good as a model produced
by hand.

The translation algorithm starts from the set of variables and creates a module for each variable. Inside the module, the NuSMV variables *past* and *value* are declared. Finally the state transitions are defined in terms of the NuSMV *case* statements using the transitions built previously (Sect. 3.4). Code 1 shows the NuSMV code for the variable *thesemaphore*.

Code 1: The NuSMV module for the variable *thesemaphore*.

```
1   MODULE m_thesemaphore(thecounter)
2   VAR past : {green, yellow, red};
3       value : {green, yellow, red};
4   ASSIGN
5       next(past) := value;
6       next(value) := case
7                   ((thecounter.value = 6) ∨ (thecounter.value < 3)) : green;
8                   ((thecounter.value ≥ 3) ∧ (thecounter.value < 5)) : yellow;
9                   (thecounter.value = 5) : red;
10                  TRUE: {green, yellow, red};
11              esac;
```

It is important to note that if all conditions in the case block fail, the TRUE guard guarantees that the variable is assigned to either green, yellow, or red as NuSMV requires that all possible assignments for variables need to be explicit, even though this choice is done non-deterministically.

4   CNL to CTL

The task of translating properties in CNL to CTL formulas is different from the approach described in Sect. 3 as we can map CNL to CTL in a one-to-one mapping. For this, we use Syntax-Directed Translation (SDT) [2]. This section presents the grammar of Natural-CTL and shows the use of Syntax-Directed Translation in our strategy.

4.1   Natural-CTL

Natural-CTL allows the user to describe CTL-like sentences in a subset of English. Its grammar is illustrated in Fig. 1, where we can see the two types of CTL expressions: binary and unary expressions.

A *BinaryExpr* is either a *For All Until*, an *Exists Until*, any logical expression, or an arithmetic relation. A *For All Until* specifies a property that must be true for all paths in the future until something else becomes true. Similarly, *Exists Until* specifies a property that must be true to some paths in the future until something else becomes true. A *UnaryExpr* is either a *ForAllGloballyExpr*, an *ExistGloballyExpr*, a *ForAllFinallyExpr*, an *ExistFinallyExpr*, a *ForAllNextExpr*,

```
CtlSpec  ("check sentence:" CtlExpr ".")+
CtlExpr  BinaryExpr | UnaryExpr
BinaryExpr  ForAllUntilExpr | ExistUntilExpr | ImplicationExpr
 | BiImplicationExpr | OrExpr | AndExpr | EqualExpr | DifferentExpr
 | LessExpr | LessEqualExpr | GreaterExpr | GreaterEqualExpr
ForAllUntilExpr  CtlExpr ",for all paths, until" CtlExpr
ExistUntilExpr  CtlExpr ",for some path, until" CtlExpr
...

UnaryExpr  ForAllGloballyExpr | ExistGloballyExpr | ForAllFinallyExpr
 | ExistFinallyExpr | ForAllNextExpr | ExistNextExpr
 | NotExpr | Expr
ForAllGloballyExpr  "for all paths, globally," CtlExpr
ExistGloballyExpr  "for some path, globally," CtlExpr
ForAllFinallyExpr  "for all paths, in the future," CtlExpr
ExistFinallyExpr  "for some path, in the future," CtlExpr
ForAllNextExpr  "for all paths, in the next state," CtlExpr
ExistNextExpr  "for some path, in the next state," CtlExpr
NotExpr  "it is not true that" CtlExpr
Expr  Identifier | Constant | "(" CtlExpr ")"
...
```

Fig. 1. Extended BNF specification of the *Natural-CTL* grammar.

an *ExistNextExpr*, a *NotExpr*, or an *Expr*. A *ForAllGloballyExpr* states that a property must be true for paths in the model. An *ExistsGloballyExpr* states that a property must be true for some path in the model. A *ForAllFinallyExpr* states that a property is eventually true for all paths. An *ExistsFinallyExpr* states that a property must eventually be true for some paths. A *ForAllNextExpr* states that a property must be true for all paths in the next state. An *ExistsNextExpr* states that a property must be true for some paths in the next state. Finally, *Expr* is an expression and *NotExpr* is the negation of an expression.

To illustrate the use of Natural-CTL, let us write a sentence that describes a desired property about the Example 1 (the names of requirement variables like *the semaphore* must be written without spaces in the current version of the Natural-CTL translator).

check sentence: it is not true that for some path, in the future, thesemaphore is equal to red and thecounter is equal to 0.

4.2   Implementation of a Syntax-Directed Translation

Computation Tree Logic (CTL) is a branching-time logic in which the future is modelled as a tree-like structure. The CTL used in our work is the CTL accepted by NuSMV (for more detail about this CTL, see the NuSMV user manual [13]). In order to translate Natural-CTL to CTL we use a Syntax-Directed Translation. We embed semantic actions in the Natural-CTL grammar in order to parse input sentences to CTL specifications. In this section we rewrite the Natural-CTL grammar with some code snippets. Each piece of code is inserted between braces (we omit some grammar productions for conciseness).

Whenever "check sentence:" is found, the NuSMV keyword "CTLSPEC" is printed.

CtlSpec → ("check sentence:" CtlExpr "." {print "CTLSPEC" || BinaryExpr.str || "."})+

The symbol || denotes an infix operator for concatenation of strings. The expression *BinaryExpr.str* is a string of the top-level binary expression of the specification. The attribute *str* is present in all non-terminals of the grammar.

Let us see how this grammar handles a temporal logic operator. For example, a specification that states that, for all paths, p_1 must be true until p_2 becomes true inserts p_1 and p_2 in the string $A[p_1 U p_2]$.

ForAllUntilExpr → CtlExpr ",for all paths, until" CtlExpr {ForAllUntilExpr.str := "(A [" || CtlExpr.str || "U" || CtlExpr.str || "])"}

To illustrate the family of unary temporal logic operators, let us see the production of *ForAllFinallyExpr*, which is declared below.

ForAllFinallyExpr →"for all paths, in the future," CtlExpr {ForAllFinallyExpr.str := "(AF " || CtlExpr.str || ")"}

The CTL formula obtained from the property presented in Sect. 4.1 is shown below (the term *CTLSPEC* is the command of NuSMV to verify the CTL formula that follows).

$CTLSPEC\ (\neg(EF((thesemaphore.value = red) \wedge (thecounter.value = 0))))$

5   Case Study

In this section, we present a case study to illustrate the main steps required to generate NuSMV models from requirement frames. In addition to that, we illustrate the translation of properties written in Natural-CTL to CTL.

5.1   Example: The Coffee Vending Machine

A Coffee Vending Machine is an automatic coffee machine that produces either weak or strong coffee. The requirements listed below specify how this machine behaves. Table 2 illustrates the outcome of the requirement frame pre-processing applied to Requirement 2.

Example 2. The Coffee Vending Machine

Requirement 1: *When the system mode is idle, and the coin sensor changes to true, the coffee machine system shall: reset the request timer, assign choice to the system mode, assign 100 to the coffee counter.*

Requirement 2: *When the system mode is choice, and the coffee request button changes to pressed, and the request timer is lower than or equal to 30, the coffee machine system shall: reset the request timer, assign preparing weak coffee to the system mode, add 3 to the coffee counter.*

Requirement 3: *When the system mode is choice, and the coffee request button changes to pressed, and the request timer is greater than 30, the coffee machine system shall: reset the request timer, assign preparing strong coffee to the system mode, subtract 6 to the coffee counter.*

Requirement 4: *When the system mode is preparing weak coffee, and the request timer is greater than or equal to 10, and the request timer is lower than or equal to 30, the coffee machine system shall: assign idle to the system mode, assign weak to the coffee machine output.*

Requirement 5: *When the system mode is preparing strong coffee, and the request timer is greater than or equal to 30, and the request timer is lower than or equal to 50, the coffee machine system shall: assign idle to the system mode, assign strong to the coffee machine output.*

Requirement 6: *When the system mode changes to idle, the coffee machine system shall assign undefined to the coffee machine output.*

Table 2 illustrates the outcome of the requirement frame pre-processing applied to Requirement 2.

Lines 1–3, 4–6, and 7–9 describe conditions, while lines 10–12, 13–15, and 16–18 describe actions.

5.2 Retrieving the Variables

We are now able to retrieve all variables needed to build the NuSMV model. Recall that the set of all variables $VARSET$ is obtained from $CPTSET$ and $PATSET$. Thus, let us first produce the $CPTSET$ and $PATSET$ sets. The subscripts in each set range from 1 to 6 and are related to each requirement.

$CPTSET_1 = \{thecoinsensor, thesystemmode\}; CPTSET_2 = CPTSET_3 =$
$\{therequesttimer, thecoffeerequestbutton, thesystemmode\}$
$CPTSET_4 = CPTSET_5 = \{therequesttimer, thesystemmode\}$
$CPTSET_6 = \{thesystemmode\}$
$CPTSET =$
$\{thecoinsensor, thesystemmode, therequesttimer, thecoffeerequestbutton\}$

$PATSET_1 = PATSET_2 = PATSET_3 =$
$\{therequesttimer, thesystemmode, thecoffeecounter\}$
$PATSET_4 = PATSET_5 = \{thesystemmode, thecoffeemachineoutput\}$
$PATSET_6 = \{thecoffeemachineoutput\}$
$PATSET = \{therequesttimer, thesystemmode, thecoffeecounter,$
$\quad\quad thecoffeemachineoutput\}$

Table 2. Requirement frame corresponding to the Requirement 2 of Example 2.

1	Condition #1 - main verb (CAC): is	
2	CPT: therequesttimer	CFV: -
3	CMD: lower than or equal to	CTV: 30
4	Condition #2 - main verb (CAC): changes	
5	CPT: thecoffeerequestbutton	CFV: -
6	CMD: -	CTV: pressed
7	Condition #3 - main verb (CAC): is	
8	CPT: thesystemmode	CFV: -
9	CMD: -	CTV: choice
10	Action - main verb (ACT): reset	
11	AGT: the coffee machine system	TOV: 0
12	PAT: therequesttimer	
13	Action - main verb (ACT): assign	
14	AGT: the coffee machine system	TOV: preparingweakcoffee
15	PAT: thesystemmode	
16	Action - main verb (ACT): add	
17	AGT: the coffee machine system	TOV: 3
18	PAT: thecoffeecounter	

The set of all variables is the union of $CPTSET$ and $PATSET$.

$VARSET = CPTSET \cup PATSET = \{thecoinsensor, thesystemmode,$
$therequesttimer, thecoffeerequestbutton, thecoffeecounter, thecoffeemachineoutput\}$.

5.3 Inferring the Types of the Variables

Recall that the set of values of the variable var $VALUESET_{var}$ is defined as the union of $CFVSET_{var}$, $CTVSET_{var}$ and $TOVSET_{var}$. Below we illustrate how the values of $thesystemmode$ and $thecoffeecounter$ are produced.

For $thesystemmode$, the same notation concerning the subscripts ranging from 1 to 6 is considered here — and we omit the name of the variable in the subscript for clarity.

thesystemmode:

- $CFVSET_1 = CFVSET_2 = CFVSET_3 = CFVSET_4 = CFVSET_5 = CFVSET_6 = \emptyset$;
- $CTVSET_1 = \{idle\}$; $CTVSET_2 = CTVSET_3 = \{choice\}$; $CTVSET_4 = \{preparingweakcoffee\}$; $CTVSET_5 = \{preparingstrongcoffee\}$; $CTVSET_6 = \{idle\}$;
- $TOVSET_1 = \{choice\}$; $TOVSET_2 = \{preparingweakcoffee\}$; $TOVSET_3 = \{preparingstrongcoffee\}$; $TOVSET_4 = TOVSET_5 = \{idle\}$; $TOVSET_6 = \emptyset$;

We can now define $VALUESET$ for the variable $thesystemmode$.

$VALUESET_{thesystemmode} = \{idle, choice, preparingweakcoffee, preparingstrongcoffee\}$

As the variable $thecoffeecounter$ is assigned to an addition and subtraction, in order to generate a range of integers such that the result of addictions and subtractions are contained in this set, we need to compute $ADDSUBSET_{thecoffeecounter}$. We assume the following values.

- Additive term, a, is equal to 3 $(a \neq 0)$;
- Subtractive term, b, is equal to 6 $(b \neq 0)$;
- Minimum value, min, is equal to 80;
- Maximum value, max, is equal to 130.

As the $gcd(3,6) = 3$, we produce the following values.

$ADDSET_{thecoffeecounter}(100) =$
$\{100, 103, 106, 109, 112, 115, 118, 121, 124, 127, 130\}$.
$SUBSET_{thecoffeecounter}(100) = \{100, 97, 94, 91, 88, 85, 82\}$.
$ADDSUBSET_{thecoffeecounter} =$
$ADDSET_{thecoffeecounter}(100) \cup SUBSET_{thecoffeecounter}(100) =$
$\{82, 85, 88, 91, 94, 97, 100, 103, 106, 109, 112, 115, 118, 121, 124, 127, 130\}$.

5.4   Code Generation

The last phase in the translation is the generation of the transitions and the subsequently generation of the NuSMV model. Code 2 shows the final code generated by this phase for the variables *the coffee request button* and *the coffee machine output*.

Variable *the coffee request button* stores inputs from the user. Its module simply keeps its past and current value. The implementation of the variable *the coffee machine output* is more elaborate. In addition to storing the past and current value of the variable, it also specifies how the value of the variable changes in terms of the past and current states of the variables *the system mode* and *the request timer*.

5.5   Specifying Properties

Once the model has been created, we can now check some properties and verify whether the system requirements satisfy them. Let us see two examples of sentences written in Natural-CTL.

check sentence: for all paths, globally, thecoffeerequestbutton changes to pressed implies for some path, in the next state, therequesttimer is equal to 0.

check sentence: for all paths, globally, thecoffeerequestbutton changes to pressed implies for all paths, in the next state, therequesttimer is equal to 0.

Code 2: The NuSMV module for the Coffee Vending Machine.

```
1  MODULE m_thecoffeerequestbutton
2     VAR past : {pressed};
3        value : {pressed};
4     ASSIGN
5        next(past) := value;
6  MODULE m_thecoffeemachineoutput (thesystemmode, therequesttimer)
7     VAR past : {weak, strong, undefined};
8        value : {weak, strong, undefined};
9     ASSIGN
10       next(past) := value;
11       next(value) :=
12          case
13             ((therequesttimer.value ≤ 50) ∧
14             (therequesttimer.value ≥ 30) ∧
15             (thesystemmode.value = preparingstrongcoffee)) : strong;
16             ((therequesttimer.value ≤ 30) ∧
17             (therequesttimer.value ≥ 10) ∧
18             (thesystemmode.value = preparingweakcoffee)) : weak;
19             ((((!(thesystemmode.past = idle)) ∧
20             (thesystemmode.value = idle))) : undefined ;
21             TRUE : {weak, strong, undefined};
22          esac;
```

The difference between these sentences is subtle. The first one refers to some path in the next state, while the second one refers to all paths in the next state. Such analysis is not trivial to do manually with requirements written in natural language. Note that the user does not need to know that each variable is, in fact, a NuSMV module which contains two variables, called *past* and *value* (the translator is responsible for performing this task). The only minor inconvenience, in the current version of the translator, is that the user needs to concatenate each composite name, as occurred in *thecoffeerequestbutton*, for example. The specification, below, shows these sentences translated to the corresponding CTL formulas.

CTLSPEC (AG((((!(thecoffeerequestbutton.past = PRESSED)) & (thecoffeerequestbutton.value = PRESSED)) → (EX(therequesttimer.value = 0))))

CTLSPEC (AG((((!(thecoffeerequestbutton.past = PRESSED)) & (thecoffeerequestbutton.value = PRESSED)) → (AX(therequesttimer.value = 0))))

The Natural-CTL translators save these formulas in the same NuSMV model file. Once the model and the temporal logic properties are stored in the same file, the NuSMV model checker is able to check and verify if the model satisfies the set of temporal logic formulas written in CTL. A good way to see step-by-step what is happening to the model for each execution is to run the model checker interactively [13]. In particular, only the first property holds. Checking the second property produces the counter-example (partially) shown below.

```
-> State: 1.1 <-
thecoffeerequestbutton.past = PRESSED
thecoffeerequestbutton.value = PRESSED
thecoinsensor.past = FALSE
thecoinsensor.value = FALSE
...
-> State: 1.2 <-
thecoffeerequestbutton.value = PRESSED
thecoinsensor.value = TRUE
thesystemmode.value = CHOICE
...
```

In this case, the user has to interpret the output of the model checker as shown above. It is not so hard to read it and to understand how the states change before reaching an inconsistent state (with respect to the property provided). As we can see, it reveals implementation details like the *past* and *value* variables. It remains as future work to translate the counter-example notation of NuSMV back to a controlled natural language.

6   Related Work

Previous works have already addressed the generation of formal models from (controlled) natural languages. Some works do not impose any writing structure to the requirements, and thus require heavier user intervention to extract, categorise and provide additional information during the translation process. For instance, in [6], the translation from requirements to logical notation is assisted by the user. In approaches like this one, it is not required to (re)write the requirements according to the grammar of the adopted controlled, which is an advantage.

Differently, other studies impose a standardized (controlled) way for writing natural-language requirements that allow for automatic information retrieval to guide the translation process, and thus requiring less user intervention when deriving formal models. Some standards are more restrictive, whereas others provide a more flexible writing structure. For example, in [16], the requirements must adhere to a strict *if-then* sentence template. Similarly, the approach proposed in [7] rely on boilerplated requirements (text with placeholders to be filled in), from which Alloy specifications are generated. The SysReq-CNL is more flexible, since it does not consider predefined writing templates (boilerplated requirements), but at the same time still allowing for automatic generation of formal models.

Therefore, there is a trade-off between imposing writing standards and the degree of user intervention. Ideally, a compromise between these two possibilities should be sought to provide a useful degree of automation along with a natural-language specification feasible to be used in practice. Now, we compare our work with other studies that also generate NuSMV models or CTL/LTL formulae from natural-language requirements.

The work reported by Aceituna *et al.* [1] presents a systematic translation from requirements to the NuSMV model checker language by using a modelling scheme called CCM. The user has to provide information about the system variables, transitions and variable values, i.e., the user needs to detect all this information manually in order to define a Kripke structure needed to generate NuSMV code.

Holt presents how to translate a CNL to CTL specifications [19]. This is achieved through a parser that extracts a semantic representation from statements written in a restricted subset of English. However, there is no translation related to models, leaving to the user the task of producing the formal model. Similarly, Badger *et al.* addresses the use of CNL in order to generate LTL specifications. A tool called Requirements Conversion Engine automatically converts, via Natural Language Processing techniques, formalised requirements written in a CNL into LTL.

Cavada *et al.* [14] propose the use of a tool called EuRailCheck to formalise and analyse requirements using, in one of its steps, a model checker. In this approach, temporal logic formulas are derived from statements written in a CNL. In order to create models, the user has to categorise requirements fragments and create dependencies among them.

Choi and Heimdahl [15] describe how to translate automatically requirements written in a formal notation called $RSML^{-e}$ to the NuSMV model checker description language. An interesting fact is that this translator handles old values of variables. There is no mention about automatic translation to LTL or CTL formulas.

This work differs from previous works in the sense that it is more comprehensive (both the model and the properties are covered by controlled natural languages) and it is mechanised (the only user interaction is to provide minimum and maximum values of integer variables).

7   Conclusions

We propose the application of the model checking technology to the requirements phase of the software development without loss of the user-friendliness of a natural language description. We employ two controlled natural languages: SysReq-CNL for requirement specification, and Natural-CTL for property specification. Two translators have been developed for these languages: the NuSMV model generator and the CTL Translator. In combination, they allow us to automatically model check requirements written in SysReq-CNL. This work differs from previous works in the level of automation provided to the user and in the application of controlled natural languages to both modelling (SysReq-CNL) and analysis (Natural-CTL). The user has to interact with our translators only to provide minimum and maximum values for integer variables. No input from the user is needed with respect to the generation of the modelling language in

NuSMV or in the property description in CTL. The case study presented illustrates the main phases of the translation to NuSMV and CTL. More importantly, it illustrates how difficult it could be to analyse by hand requirements written in natural language. Subtle changes in the property to be verified ends up in producing a different answer from the model checker.

As future work, we intend to prevent the user to have to concatenate composite names of variables in the description of the properties in Natural-CTL. In addition to that, it would be interesting to advise the user whenever there are unspecified conditions associated to an specific system variable instead of representing this situation into TRUE guards. This goes better with the idea of using natural language to model and verify systems than to translate sentences from English to NuSMV. Concerning properties, the current Natural-CTL reflects too closely the syntactical structure of CTL. As future work we intend to devise a new version of it that abstracts away the logic from the language as much as possible. We will also design a controlled natural language to describe the counter-examples provided by NuSMV. Finally, we will investigate how a model checker like UPPALL [5] can be used in our strategy. As SysReq-CNL deals naturally with timing properties, it will be interesting to see how real-time systems could be modelled and verified in the context of our project.

Acknowledgements. This work was partially supported by the National Institute of Science and Technology for Software Engineering (INES), funded by CNPq and FACEPE, grants 573964/2008-4, 560256/2010-8 and APQ-1037-1.03/08.

References

1. Aceituna, D., Do, H., Srinivasan, S.: A systematic approach to transforming system requirements into model checking specifications. In: Companion Proceedings of the 36th International Conference on Software Engineering, ICSE Companion 2014, pp. 165–174. ACM, New York (2014)
2. Aho, A.V., Lam, M.S., Sethi, R., Ullman, J.D.: Compilers: Principles, Techniques, and Tools, 2nd edn. Addison-Wesley Longman Publishing Co., Inc., Boston (2006)
3. Aichernig, B., Brandl, H., Jöbstl, E., Krenn, W., Schlick, R., Tiran, S.: Killing strategies for model-based mutation testing. Softw. Test. Verif. Reliab. **25**(8), 716–748 (2015)
4. Badger, J., Throop, D., Claunch, C.: Vared: verification and analysis of requirements and early designs. In: 2014 IEEE 22nd International Requirements Engineering Conference (RE), pp. 325–326, August 2014
5. Behrmann, G., David, A., Larsen, K.: A Tutorial on UPPAAL 4.0. Department of Computer Science, Aalborg University, Denmark (2006)
6. Boddu, R., Guo, L., Mukhopadhyay, S., Cukic, B.: RETNA: from requirements to testing in a natural way. In: Proceedings of the RE, pp. 262–271 (2004)
7. Cadete, D., Cunha, A., Faria, J., Oliveira, J., Passos, A.: From boilerplated requirements to alloy: half-way between text and formal model. Technical report, Universidade do Minho (2012)

234   S. Barza et al.

8. Carvalho, G., Barros, F., Carvalho, A., Cavalcanti, A., Mota, A., Sampaio, A.: NAT2TEST tool: from natural language requirements to test cases based on CSP. In: Calinescu, R., Rumpe, B. (eds.) SEFM 2015. LNCS, vol. 9276, pp. 283–290. Springer, Heidelberg (2015). doi:10.1007/978-3-319-22969-0_20

9. Carvalho, G., Barros, F., Lapschies, F., Schulze, U., Peleska, J.: Model-based testing from controlled natural language requirements. In: Artho, C., Ölveczky, P.C. (eds.) FTSCS 2013. CCIS, vol. 419, pp. 19–35. Springer, Heidelberg (2014a). doi:10.1007/978-3-319-05416-2_3

10. Carvalho, G., Cavalcanti, A., Sampaio, A.: Modelling timed reactive systems from natural-language requirements. Formal Aspects Comput. **28**(5), 725–765 (2016)

11. Carvalho, G., Falcão, D., Barros, F., Sampaio, A., Mota, A., Motta, L., Blackburn, M.: Test case generation from natural language requirements based on SCR specifications. In: Proceedings of Symposium on Applied Computing, Coimbra, Portugal, vol. 2, pp. 1217–1222 (2013a)

12. Carvalho, G., Falcão, D., Barros, F., Sampaio, A., Mota, A., Motta, L., Blackburn, M.: NAT2TEST$_{SCR}$: test case generation from natural language requirements based on SCR specifications. Sci. Comput. Program. **95**(Part 3(0)), 275–297 (2014)

13. Cavada, R., Cimatti, A., Jochim, C.A., Keighren, G., Olivetti, E., Pistore, M., Roveri, M., Tchaltsev, A.: NuSMV 2.6 User Manual. FBK-irst - Via Sommarive 18, 38055 Povo (Trento), Italy (2010)

14. Cavada, R., Cimatti, A., Mariotti, A., Mattarei, C., Micheli, A., Mover, S., Pensallorto, M., Roveri, M., Susi, A., Tonetta, S.: Supporting requirements validation: the EuRailCheck tool. In: 24th IEEE/ACM International Conference on Automated Software Engineering, ASE 2009, pp. 665–667, November 2009

15. Choi, Y., Heimdahl, M.P.: Model checking RSML-e requirements. In: Proceedings of the 7th IEEE International Symposium on High Assurance Systems Engineering, pp. 109–118. IEEE (2002)

16. Esser, M., Struss, P.: Obtaining models for test generation from natural-language like functional specifications. In: International Workshop on Principles of Diagnosis, pp. 75–82 (2007)

17. Fillmore, C.: The case for case. In: Bach, E., Harms, R. (eds.) Universals in Linguistic Theory, pp. 1–88. Holt, Rinehart, and Winston, New York (1968)

18. Fuchs, N.: Controlled Natural Language. LNCS, vol. 5972. Springer, Heidelberg (2010). doi:10.1007/978-3-642-14418-9

19. Holt, A.: Formal verification with natural language specifications: guidelines, experiments and lessons so far. S. Afr. Comput. J., 253–257 (1999)

20. Nipkow, T., Paulson, L., Wenzel, M.: Isabelle/HOL – A Proof Assistant for Higher-Order Logic. LNCS, vol. 2283. Springer, Heidelberg (2002)

Refinement Verification of Sequence Diagrams Using CSP

Lucas Lima[1]([✉]), Juliano Iyoda[2], and Augusto Sampaio[2]

[1] Departamento de Estatística e Informática,
Universidade Federal Rural de Pernambuco, Recife, Brazil
lucas.albertins@deinfo.ufrpe.br
http://www.deinfo.ufrpe.br/
[2] Centro de Informática, Universidade Federal de Pernambuco, Recife, Brazil
{jmi,acas}@cin.ufpe.br
http://www.cin.ufpe.br/

Abstract. During the design of systems, models usually evolve from a conceptual level to a more concrete level that is close to how the implementation should be. In a stepwise development, it is required that lower-level models conform to the properties of higher-level models. In this work, we propose a strategy for verifying the refinement of UML sequence diagrams that uses a formal semantics defined in terms of CSP. In order to allow designers to benefit from this strategy we have implemented it in a modelling tool. Such a tool analyses if a sequence diagram is refined by another, that is, we check if the latter preserves the traces of the former sequence diagram. The main contributions of this paper are: (i) the definition of four different notions of sequence diagrams refinement; (ii) an approach to verify the refinement of sequence diagrams in CSP; and (iii) the development of a tool that allows our refinement notions to be verified without any knowledge of the underlying formal semantics. We illustrate our analysis with a text messaging case study.

Keywords: Sequence diagram · UML · Semantics · Refinement · CSP

1 Introduction

A stepwise design of a system starts from an abstract model and evolves to a concrete one as the system concepts mature. Such design task is usually carried out by producing a series of design models, where each model is a refinement of the previous. Design models can have informal or formal semantics. Whenever a design model has an informal semantics, it is up to the designer to judge whether a concrete model is a refinement of an abstract one. The designer relies solely on intuition and experience, which may lead to an error. Informal models like UML [14] are, however, easier to learn and adequate to capture initial ideas. Formal models are more difficult to learn as it requires the understanding and manipulation of mathematical concepts. But they are safer because they are

© Springer International Publishing AG 2016
L. Ribeiro and T. Lecomte (Eds.): SBMF 2016, LNCS 10090, pp. 235–252, 2016.
DOI: 10.1007/978-3-319-49815-7_14

unambiguous and allow tools to automatically verify whether one design is the refinement of another.

This work introduces an approach to put together the best of both worlds. A UML sequence diagram is a widespread informal design model used to describe interaction scenarios of a system. We propose four notions of refinement and describe how these notions are captured in terms of the Communicating Sequential Process (CSP) [7] refinement. For this, we make use of the formal semantics for sequence diagrams defined in our previous work [9,10].

We have also implemented a tool that provides a fully automatic refinement checker for sequence diagrams. If the refinement does not hold, our tool outputs a counter-example in terms of a sequence diagram that describes a scenario that captures where the refinement went wrong. This facility conceals from the designer the formal notation of CSP throughout the design phase. We illustrate our ideas in an industrial case study.

Concerning related work, broadly speaking, there are two kinds of approaches: (i) the definition of a semantic model to formalise Sequence Diagrams [16] and (ii) the translation to an existing formalism such as Z, B, CSP and Petri-Nets [2,3]. The main advantage of the latter is the reuse of existing tools. A few works also discuss refinement of the sequence diagrams, especially, from the point of view of system designers. Our work distinguish in defining a semantics that is supported by tools in order to translate the models to the formal notation and for providing refinement automated reasoning at the diagrammatic level that is based on the needs of the UML practitioners.

This paper is organised as follows. Section 2 presents sequence diagrams and CSP. Section 3 introduces the semantics of sequence diagrams in terms of CSP and four notions of refinement. Section 4 describes how our tool for sequence diagrams refinement checking works. Section 5 illustrates our refinement notions in a case study. Related works are presented in Sect. 6 and Sect. 7 concludes.

2 Background

This section introduces both sequence diagrams [14] and Communicating Sequential Processes [7].

2.1 Sequence Diagrams

Interactions are the abstract syntax elements in UML used to represent communications between several entities. The most common kind of interaction diagram is the sequence diagram, which focuses on the message interchange between a number of lifelines, which are the lifespans of every object in the diagram.

Figure 1 shows the main syntactical elements of sequence diagrams. Each diagram is called an *interaction* as it describes relationships along the *lifelines* of the participants: Classes and Objects. Such elements communicate with each other through *messages*. A message is classified according to the type of communication: synchronous communication (*synch call*), reply (the return of a *synch call*) or

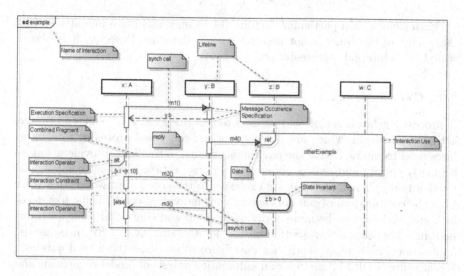

Fig. 1. Concrete Syntax of a Sequence Diagram.

asynchronous communication (*asynch call*). A synchronous communication may refer to an *operation* call of a block, while an asynchronous message may be a *signal*. An *occurrenceSpecification* is the basic semantic unit of *interactions*. Its specialisations determine the meaning for the main tasks in sequence diagrams. For example, the duration of an execution fired by a message call is delimited by the two *ExecutionOccurrenceSpecifications* (start and finish), where both are associated with an *ExecutionSpecification*. *MessageOccurrenceSpecifications* delineate the act of sending or receiving a message. The order of these occurrences determines the traces of the diagram and must conform with the following restrictions:

- Occurrences on the same lifeline must preserve the order they are specified.
- The act of receiving a message must always occur after the sending of the same message.

In addition to the events of sending and receiving messages, the flow of execution may be further elaborated with the use of *combined fragments*. Their use allows behaviours such as parallel execution, alternatives (typically, if-then-else constructions), loops and other facilities. Each one possesses an *interaction operator* from an *interaction operator kind* that specifies the behaviour of the fragment. They may have one or more *interaction operands*, which may be guarded by *interaction constraints*. *InteractionUse* allows us to reuse other interactions as part of a diagram. They may have parameters and the *lifelines* used in the *interactionUse* must match the ones contained by the enclosing *interaction*. Messages exchanged by the *interactionUse* and the enclosing *interaction* are connected through *gates*, which link two parts of a message. Finally, *state invariants* are constraints attached to *lifelines* that check a particular property during runtime. When such a property is evaluated to false the generated trace is invalid. More details will be presented on demand.

Each element of a particular diagram (like a message) has a unique identifier that, most of the time, is not depicted on the diagram. However, it is always stored in its internal representation.

2.2 CSP

A process algebra like CSP can be used to describe systems composed of interacting components, which are independent self-contained processes with interfaces used to interact with the environment. Such formalisms provide a way to explicitly specify and reason about interactions between different components. Furthermore, phenomena that are exclusive to the concurrent world, that arise from the combination of components and not individual components, like deadlock and livelock, can be more easily understood and controlled using such formalisms. Tool support is another reason for the success of CSP in industrial applications, and consequently, for our choice to use it as the formal notation. For instance, FDR3 [4] provides an automatic analysis of model refinement and of properties like deadlock and divergence.

A process is the basic unit for describing behaviour. It is defined in terms of events and other processes. The function $\alpha(P)$ returns the alphabet of a process, that is, the events that this process may communicate. A process may have its events renamed using the rename operator $P[\![^b/a]\!]$, which means that all occurrences of a in P are renamed to b. The parallel composition $P1 \parallel_{cs} P2$ synchronises $P1$ and $P2$ on the channels in the set cs; events that are not in cs occur independently. Processes composed in interleaving $P1 \ ||| \ P2$ run independently. The event hiding operator $P \setminus cs$ encapsulates the events that are in the channel set cs, which become no longer visible to the environment.

In this work, we use the traces denotational model of CSP ($\mathcal{T}$). Let Σ be the alphabet of all possible events, and Σ^* the set of all possible finite sequences of events in Σ. Then, a trace of a process P is a member of Σ^*, and $\mathcal{T}(P)$ denotes the set of all finite traces of P. For example $\mathcal{T}(\text{e1 -> e2 -> STOP}) = \{\langle\rangle, \langle e1\rangle, \langle e1, e2\rangle\}$. It is possible to compare the trace semantics of two processes by set inclusion: process Q refines process P, in the traces model, denoted $P \sqsubseteq_T Q$, if, and only if, $\mathcal{T}(Q) \subseteq \mathcal{T}(P)$. This can be mechanically checked using FDR [4]. In case the refinement does not hold, FDR yields a trace (the shortest counterexample), say ce, such that $ce \in \mathcal{T}(Q)$ but $ce \notin \mathcal{T}(P)$. We can also check equivalence between two process in the traces model. Thus, $P \equiv_T Q$ verifies if $\mathcal{T}(P) \equiv \mathcal{T}(Q)$.

3 Semantics and Refinement

This section overviews the semantics of sequence diagrams in terms of a CSP process and introduces four notions of sequence diagrams refinement.

3.1 Semantics

A sequence diagram is defined in terms of a CSP process. Figure 2 shows an example of how the semantics of a sequence diagram is captured by CSP elements. Each lifeline is represented by a CSP process defined by the sequential composition of other processes that represent fragments that happen in the lifeline: message occurrences, combined fragments, state invariants and interactionUse elements. Each type of fragment has a corresponding translation in our semantics. And the environment where the messages flow is the process MessagesBuffer. The lifelines that exchange messages synchronise in parallel among themselves and the environment.

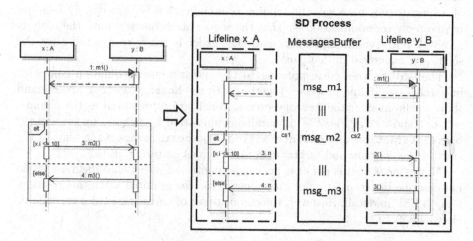

Fig. 2. Semantic representation of sequence diagrams in CSP.

The CSP process that models a sequence diagram is parameterised by the identifiers (of type ID) of the class instances that either are used in a lifeline or send messages through gates. This makes the model of the diagram as generic as the diagram itself, which is valid for any instances of the types used in the diagram.

Each message exchange is represented in CSP by two events: one corresponding to the moment when the message is sent and another to the moment when it is received. The channels used are mOP and mSIG, which correspond to operations and signals, respectively. For simplicity, we assume that operations and signals are synchronous and asynchronous messages, respectively. The mOP and mSIG channels communicate a data structure with five fields: (i) a unique identifier of the message; (ii) the event type of the message, which can be either s for a sending event, or r for a receiving event; (iii) the sender identifier; (iv) the receiver identifier; and (v) the contents of the message itself including any arguments needed.

The asynchronous nature of the sending and receiving of the messages requires an intermediate component to model the environment through which the messages flow. The CSP process `MessagesBuffer` plays the role of the environment and coordinates the message exchanging between lifelines by relaying messages from one lifeline to another. For each message there is a CSP process that synchronises on a sending event of the sender and then communicates the receiving event with the receiver. The behaviour of the `MessagesBuffer` is the interleaving of all these message communications.

Each message exchange is coordinated by an internal process that is part of `MessageBuffer`. Such message exchange process (for example, `msg_m1`, `msg_m2` and `msg_m3` in Fig. 2) synchronises on the sending communication with the sender lifeline and then on the receiving communication with the receiver lifeline. In case of a synchronous message, the sending communication is immediately followed by the reply communication, so that the sender stays blocked until the reply is received. For asynchronous messages, the sender is ready to proceed after the sending communication happens.

The CSP process corresponding to the entire sequence diagram composes in parallel the lifeline processes together with the `MessagesBuffer` process and they synchronise on the message events, which are represented in the channel sets `cs1` and `cs2` in Fig. 2. This parallel composition is enclosed by two events: `beginInteraction` and `endInteraction`. The `beginInteraction` signals the start of the diagram and `endInteraction` signals its termination.

As the focus of this paper is not the semantics of a sequence diagram we do not describe the translation of each constructor, for example, operation parameters, to CSP in detail. However, the complete set of translation rules is available elsewhere [9, 10].

3.2   Refinement

Engineers usually perform refinements on artefacts along the development process. However, depending on the semantic domain we are working, the term *refinement* can have different meanings. For instance, CSP formally defines what is a refinement between two specifications according to the semantic model used, which can be traces, failures, and failures-divergence. Considering the traces model, a specification P is refined by a specification Q, whose notation is $P \sqsubseteq_T Q$, if, and only if, the traces of Q are a subset of the traces of P.

UML determines refinement as a relationship between model elements at different semantic levels, e.g. analysis and design, and uses a stereotype constructor ≪ refine≫ to visually link the refined elements. However, the semantics of such a refinement is not clear. Assuming that a sequence diagram $SD1$ is refined (in UML) by another sequence diagram $SD2$, we do not know what would be the precise relation among the traces of such diagrams. Therefore, in order to precisely characterise different interpretations for refinement, we have defined four refinement notions for sequence diagram based on industry practices. They are all mapped to the CSP traces model refinement in order to benefit from the automated reasoning provided by FDR. Next, we detail each one of these notions and their correspondence to CSP refinement.

Strict Behaviour Incrementing Refinement. This is the most common refinement where a conceptual sequence diagram displays some high-level scenario and a more concrete sequence diagram displays another scenario closer to the implementation. The latter must preserve the traces of the former, however, it usually adds new messages that are relevant at this point because it shows features of how the system should be implemented. Nevertheless, apart from these new messages, the refined version should not have any trace that differs from those of the specification. For instance, consider the following scenario displayed in Fig. 3. It illustrates a specification behaviour from a text messaging application for mobile phones where a user simply sends a text message to another mobile phone.

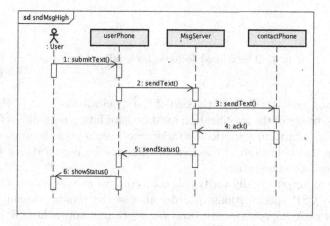

Fig. 3. The scenario for sending a message.

In this scenario, the user sends a text message to one of his contacts using his mobile phone (`submitText()`). In turn, the mobile phone requests the messaging server to send the message (`sendText()`) to the contact's mobile phone. Then, the server processes the request and sends the message to the desired phone, which replies with an acknowledgement (`ack()`). Afterwards, the server sends the message status to the user phone (`sendStatus()`), which can be viewed by the user in his mobile phone (`showStatus()`).

Next, we show how this specification can be refined by the introduction of implementation details. Figure 4 illustrates the same scenario with more details that are needed for the implementation of this scenario.

The refined scenario adds the message identifier that must be sent to the mobile phone once the server receives the request for sending the text message (`sendMsgId()`) and the message status request that must be made by the sender phone prior to receiving any message status (`requestStatus()`). This is a typical case where a specification scenario is refined by an implementation scenario. Although more implementation details were added, the flow of events of the

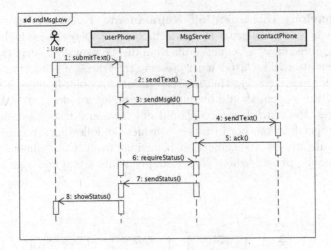

Fig. 4. The refined scenario for sending a message.

refined version must conform to the one of the specification, that is, the order of events of the traces of the specification must be kept intact regardless of what was added. The specification scenario abstracts away events from the implementation scenario (i.e. the behaviour of the specification can be regarded as a projection of that of the implementation).

In order to automatically verify this conformance we translate both sequence diagrams to CSP specifications in order to use the tooling capability of this language for verifying refinements. However, we cannot apply the CSP refinement directly because, as stated earlier, it checks if the traces of the refined diagram are a subset of the set of traces of the specification, which is not true in this case. The trace of the refined diagram might include more events than the traces of the specification diagram. Therefore, we propose a refinement notion, which is shown in Definition 1, for this specific case using the CSP notation.

Let $t\_sd()$ be a translation function that takes a sequence diagram and returns its corresponding CSP process. We say that a sequence diagram $SD1$ is refined by a sequence diagram $SD2$, written $SD_1 \sqsubseteq^{SIR}_{Interaction} SD_2$, if, and only if, $t\_sd(SD1)$ has the same traces as $t\_sd(SD2)$ after hiding all events that are present only in $SD2$ but not in $SD1$. The intuition here is that when we hide the events related to the new messages in the refined sequence diagram, it has the same traces of the specification diagram.

Definition 1 (Strict increment refinement). *Let $SD1$ and SD_2 be sequence diagrams, then*

$$SD_1 \sqsubseteq^{SIR}_{Interaction} SD_2 \Leftrightarrow$$

$$t\_sd(SD_1) \equiv_T (t\_sd(SD_2) \setminus \mathit{diff}(\alpha(t\_sd(SD2)), \alpha(t\_sd(SD1))))$$

The function *diff* returns the difference between two sets. We consider only the traces model because we cover only what the interaction can indeed perform. We do not deal with invalid traces in this approach. We are aware that the hiding operator of CSP may introduce nondeterminism, however, as our analyses are on the traces model this is not a concern. We only hide the additional behaviour of the refined diagram and this part is not relevant because we just want to make sure that the traces of the specification are still present in the refined version.

Weak Behaviour Incrementing Refinement. In addition to conforming to the traces of the specification diagram, sometimes the refined diagram also includes new traces that were not predicted in the specification, for instance, due to technological issues that only appeared in the design phase, to cover alternative and exception flows of a use case or to cover error handling situations. Thus, the refined diagram must still conform to the traces of the specification, however, it can add new traces. Figure 5 illustrates another refined scenario of Fig. 3.

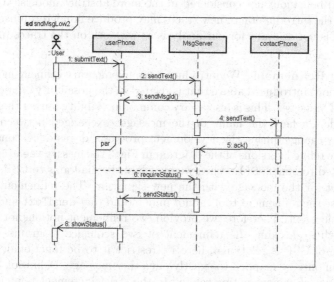

Fig. 5. The refined scenario adds new traces.

The scenario depicted in Fig. 5 has the same traces of the specification diagram in addition to some new traces that are not present in the high-level diagram of Fig. 3. In this case, the parallel combined fragment interleaves the messages of its operands. Therefore, this diagram has a trace where the message `ack()` happens before the message `sendStatus()` (conforming with the specification diagram) but it can also have a trace where the opposite happens (due to the interleaving of the parallel combined fragment).

This is another possible type of refinement considered by development teams. The implementation satisfies the specification according to the Strict Behaviour Incrementing Refinement in some traces, but it also creates new behaviours that are relevant only during the design phase. Thus, we have defined another refinement notion to cover this case. We consider it weak due to the relaxation of the restriction of not adding any new traces.

Definition 2 (Weak increment refinement). *Let $SD1$ and SD_2 be sequence diagrams, then*

$$SD_1 \sqsubseteq_{Interaction}^{WIR} SD_2 \Leftrightarrow$$

$$t\_sd(SD_2) \setminus diff(\alpha(t\_sd(SD2)), \alpha(t\_sd(SD1))) \sqsubseteq_T t\_sd(SD_1)$$

Note that the formal notion captured by Definition 2 is trace refinement in the inverse direction. The intuition here is that we want to assure that the traces of the specification are present in the traces of the refined diagram, however, the latter may have new traces that can capture, for instance, alternative (or exceptional) behaviour not considered in the more abstract models. We also are aware that the introduction of new traces may produce nondeterminism in CSP. Again, this is not relevant for our analysis as we work on the traces model.

Renaming Refinement. We introduce a complementary refinement notion to the two notions introduced above that is related to the possibility of updating the signature of messages. This is also a very common possibility during the evolution of the models, where the name of the messages exchanged between different entities may change during the development process. For instance, consider that in one of the refined versions of the diagram in Fig. 3 the message sendText() has been updated to sendSMS(). When we translate the diagrams to CSP we create a new event for the message with the new signature. The refinement checking fails because the refinement tool cannot understand that sendText and sendSMS are the same event. Therefore, we provide two refinement notions for renaming messages when checking the refinement of two sequence diagrams. Although the rename of CSP is relational, here we restrict it to be functional, that is, a message can only be mapped to exactly one other message. Definition 3 presents the renaming refinement notion related to the strict increment refinement. The refinement has a set of pairs of elements (a, b) that must be renamed where a is a message in $SD1$ and b is a message in $SD2$.

Definition 3 (Strict renaming refinement). *Let $SD1$ and SD_2 be sequence diagrams, then*

$$SD_1 \sqsubseteq_{Interaction}^{SRR\{(a,b)|a \leftarrow b, a \in \alpha(SD1), b \in \alpha(SD2)\}} SD_2 \Leftrightarrow$$

$$t\_sd(SD_1)[\![^b/a]\!] \equiv_T t\_sd(SD_2) \setminus diff(\alpha(t\_sd(SD2)), \alpha(t\_sd(SD1)))$$

This refinement in CSP is the direct application of the CSP renaming operator. Therefore, the process of the specification sequence diagram $SD1$ has its events passed as arguments (represented by a) renamed to the ones present in the process of $SD2$ (represented by b). Definition 4 is the analogous rename refinement considering now the weak increment refinement.

Definition 4 (Weak renaming refinement). *Let $SD1$ and SD_2 be sequence diagrams, then*

$$SD_1 \sqsubseteq^{WRR\{(a,b)|a \leftarrow b, a \in \alpha(SD1), b \in \alpha(SD2)\}}_{Interaction} SD_2 \Leftrightarrow$$

$$t\_sd(SD_2) \setminus \mathit{diff}(\alpha(t\_sd(SD2)), \alpha(t\_sd(SD1))) \sqsubseteq_T t\_sd(SD_1)[\![^b/a]\!]$$

Overall, the Renaming refinement notion described in Definition 3 follows the same trace refinement of Definition 1, but further allowing message renaming. The same happens between Definitions 2 and 4, respectively.

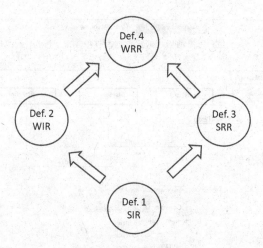

Fig. 6. The relationships between the refinement notions.

Figure 6 illustrates how the different refinement notions are related. Definition 1 is the strongest notion, that is, the more restrictive one. This definition implies Definitions 2 and 3. On the other hand, Definition 4 is the weakest notion, which means that it covers more cases than the others, and it is implied by Definitions 2 and 3, and by transitivity it is also implied by Definition 1.

4   Tool

In order to automate the refinement checking of sequence diagrams we have implemented a tool that, given two diagrams, verifies if one is refined by the other according to the refinement notions presented in Sect. 3.2. It has been developed as a plug-in of a modelling tool in order to allow the users to check refinements in the same environment they create diagrams. The Astah modelling environment [6] has been chosen due to several facts: its extension capabilities that facilitates the creation of modelling plug-ins, UML models can be created using several diagrams that allow us to extend our approach to other model elements in the future, and it has a large community of active users. Also, our plug-in requires the installation of the FDR3 tool, which is a CSP refinement checker. Once the plug-in is installed the user gets the capabilities to inform the FDR3 installation directory.

We do not describe how to create models using Astah; however, this task is considerably intuitive for UML practitioners. Once the models are created, the user has a view where the refinement of two sequence diagrams can be verified. Figure 7 depicts this view where the modeller must select the refinement notion to be used (either *Strict* or *Weak*), and must select the abstract sequence diagram and its refined version.

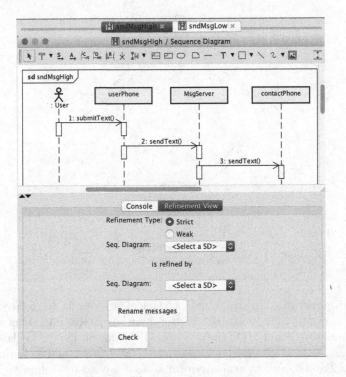

Fig. 7. The refinement plug-in.

In the case of refinement involving renaming, the user needs to press the *Rename messages* button to provide a mapping between messages of the two sequence diagrams chosen. Finally, by pressing the *Check* button the tool verifies the refinement. If the refinement is valid the tool presents a success message, otherwise, the tool generates a counterexample in terms of a sequence diagram to make it easier to understand the trace that invalidates the refinement. This way, the CSP notation is concealed from the user.

Internally, the *Check* button generates the CSP specifications related to each of the sequence diagrams according to the semantics discussed in Sect. 3.1, and then invokes the FDR3 tool to verify the refinement according to the notions described in Sect. 3.2. If no counterexample is returned, then the refinement is valid, otherwise the tool collects the generated counterexample and translates it to a sequence diagram that can be viewed in the Astah tool. Hence, all four notions described so far are supported in the tool.

This way the UML practitioners can check the evolution of their models in an automated way and without any knowledge of the underlying formal language.

5   Case Study

In order to evaluate the refinement approach we have performed some case studies using the example described in Sect. 3.2 regarding the text message application for mobile phones. First we have checked all the refinements previously described regarding the *strict increment*, the *weak increment* and the *renaming* notions, and all of them indeed hold.

In order to evaluate the scenarios where refinements were not valid we have used variations of those scenarios. For instance, assume that the order of the messages whose indexes are two (sendText()) and three (sendMsgId()) in Fig. 4 are swapped. When we check if this new diagram refines the one in Fig. 3 using the strict notion, a counterexample is returned. This happens because the trace that goes up to the new message 2 (sendMsgId()) is not part of the trace of Fig. 3. Therefore, this counterexample is generated as a sequence diagram, which is displayed in Fig. 8.

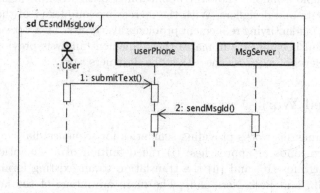

Fig. 8. The generated counterexample for the strict increment refinement.

Regarding the weak increment refinement notion, assume that the designer has forgotten to add the message seven (sendStatus()) in Fig. 5. When we check if this new diagram refines the one in Fig. 3, the counterexample in Fig. 9 is generated.

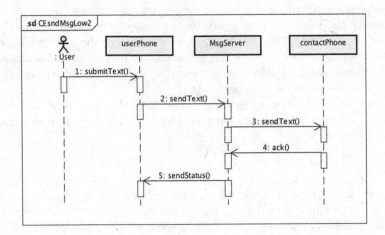

Fig. 9. The generated counterexample for the weak increment refinement.

Recall that, in the weak increment refinement, the refined version must preserve the traces of the specification or add new traces. In this case, the counterexample shows a trace that goes up to the message sendStatus, which is not part of the refined version, hence, this trace is not part of the traces generated by the refined version and should be considered in order to make the refinement valid. If the user adds the forgotten message at the correct point, then the refinement is successfully verified.

These simple examples show the applicability of the tool in the activities of system analysts and designers. With the increasing complexity of the diagram, the difficulty in identifying refinement problems also grows. Therefore, such a tool becomes useful because it automates the refinement analysis providing results at the same level of expressiveness that the designers work.

6   Related Work

There are numerous works providing semantics for sequence diagrams. Usually there are two kinds of approaches: (i) the definition of a semantic model to formalise diagrams [16] and (ii) the translation to an existing formalism such as Z, B, CSP, and Petri-Nets [2,3]. The main advantage of the latter is the existing tool support used to apply reasoning on the translations. Some related works discuss the refinement of the diagrams. However, they usually describe refinements from the point of view of the formal notation without leveraging it to the graphical level. In addition, few works provide tools to automate the refinement verification process.

Storrle presents an exhaustive work on formalising sequence diagrams using trace semantics [16]. Many constructs used in UML 2, including combined fragments, are covered. Storrle's semantics briefly discuss some interpretations for refinement using his semantics but no concrete definition is proposed, besides for refinement time elements. This work reports the problem of dealing with negative traces when considering refinement because the set of invalid traces is not clearly defined in UML.

Haugen et al. present another work that covers some of the Sequence Diagram elements we are interested in [5]. They also propose an approach based on a trace semantics in which refinement is used as a foundation for compositional analysis, verification and testing. However, only one notion of refinement is given, which is similar to our strict increment refinement. Lund gives an operational semantics for the Haugen's denotational semantics [11], which is implemented in the Maude language [1].

Although the approaches by Storrle and by Haugen et al. do not use a semantic model similar to CSP, they are inspiring works as they provide some important discussions over complete and partial traces, global versus local view, besides discussing strategies for refinement.

Dan and Danning [2] present an approach to semantic mapping specified using the language QVT [13] relations to CSP [7]. As their approach uses the CSP notation we could benefit from some of the ideas of their work. However, very few constructs of UML 2 are covered and they do not provide advances regarding refinement nor automated reasoning.

Kaizu et al. [8] provides a formal sequence diagrams semantics in CSP and tool support to translate the corresponding model to CSP. Also, the proposed approach uses FDR to check refinement of the diagrams. However, it is not clear what is the refinement notion at the diagrammatic level and how FDR is used to verify the models.

Shen et al. propose a formalisation using template semantics for UML 2 Sequence Diagrams [15]. The approach gives an operational semantics for which the basic computation model is hierarchical transition systems (HTS), however, the work does not provide any refinement strategies nor tool support for the semantics.

Most of these works differ regarding three main aspects: the number of constructions they cover, the semantics of constructions whose official meaning is vaguely defined, and the semantic domain used to formalise the semantics. The interesting aspect to notice is that when defining a semantics for sequence diagrams, some semantic decisions must be taken in order to allow its use. Micskei and Waeselynck have provided an excellent survey on these semantic choices [12]. We developed our work according to their classification and categorisation of semantic meanings for sequence diagrams. Whenever the meaning of an operator is vaguely defined, we have chosen one that is more convenient for modelling and for checking diagram consistency. For instance, the choice on synchronisation before evaluating guards of combined fragments in order to avoid inconsistency, and the unique identification of the messages.

Table 1. Comparison with related work.

	Formalism	Ref. notions	Tool support	Automated analysis
[16]	Traces semantics	2	×	×
[5,11]	Maude	1	✓	✓
[2]	CSP	0	×	×
[8]	CSP	1	✓	✓
[15]	HTS	0	×	×
Our work	CSP	4	✓	✓

Table 1 presents a comparison of the coverage of our formalisation and strategy with some of available literature. The works are compared according the formalism used to represent sequence diagrams, the number of refinement notions, and whether they provide tool support for the semantics and the analysis process is automated. The ✓ indicates that the feature is covered by the work on the column, and × indicates it is not.

As can be seen, only two of the works provide a mechanised translation, automated analysis and discuss refinement notions. However, most of the refinement notions discussed are not provided according to the needs of designers. Our work is distinctive not only for the automated strategy, but also for providing refinement approaches that are relevant for system modellers.

7   Conclusion

Sequence diagrams are widely used in industry during the development of a system. During the design phase, many versions of a sequence diagram are produced, where each version is a refinement of the previous. These versions reflect how our understanding of the system evolves. Unfortunately, there is no standard definition for what a sequence diagram refinement is. UML provides the ≪ refine≫ constructor, but its meaning is not clear.

We have proposed four notions of refinement for sequence diagrams. They are defined based on two foundational concepts: (i) the CSP traces model refinement; and (ii) the CSP semantics for sequence diagrams [9,10]. Strict Behaviour Incrementing refinement states that a sequence diagram $SD2$ is a refinement of $SD1$ whenever a projection of some of $SD2$ events result in $SD1$. (i.e. $SD2$ adds new events to the traces of $SD1$). Weak Behaviour Incrementing refinement allows traces of $SD2$ to be either projections of $SD1$ or new traces that implement new features not explicitly specified by $SD1$. Finally, the renaming refinements allow $SD2$ to rename events of $SD1$.

We have developed a refinement checker as a plugin of the Astah modelling environment [6] that makes use of the CSP FDR3 refinement checker. If a refinement does not hold, the tool produces a counter-example as a sequence diagram. This way, we conceal from the user all the formal concepts underlying the verification.

As future work, more industrial case studies will be carried out together with experiments to evaluate the performance and scalability of our tool. We also plan to allow the renaming of a message to a sequence of other messages in the future. Finally, another perspective of future work is to handle data, for instance, attributes of blocks and arguments of messages, when used in guards of combined fragments. We envision the usage of solvers to provide a minimum set of values to be used in these guards in order to avoid state space explosion.

Acknowledgement. This work was partially supported by the National Institute of Science and Technology for Software Engineering (INES (http://www.ines.org.br)), funded by CNPq and FACEPE, grants 573964/2008-4, 560256/2010-8 and APQ-1037-1.03/08.

References

1. Clavel, M., Durán, F., Eker, S., Lincoln, P., Martí-Oliet, N., Meseguer, J., Talcott, C.: All About Maude - A High-performance Logical Framework: How to Specify. Program and Verify Systems in Rewriting Logic. Springer, Berlin (2007)
2. Dan, L., Danning, L.: Towards a formal behavioral semantics for UML interactions. In: Proceedings of 2010 3rd International Symposium on Information Science and Engineering, ISISE 2010, pp. 213–218. IEEE (2010)
3. Eichner, C., Fleischhack, H., Meyer, R., Schrimpf, U., Stehno, C.: Compositional semantics for UML 2.0 sequence diagrams using Petri Nets. In: Prinz, A., Reed, R., Reed, J. (eds.) SDL 2005. LNCS, vol. 3530, pp. 133–148. Springer, Heidelberg (2005). doi:10.1007/11506843_9
4. Gibson-Robinson, T., Armstrong, P., Boulgakov, A., Roscoe, A.W.: FDR3 — a modern refinement checker for CSP. In: Ábrahám, E., Havelund, K. (eds.) TACAS 2014. LNCS, vol. 8413, pp. 187–201. Springer, Heidelberg (2014). doi:10.1007/978-3-642-54862-8_13
5. Haugen, O., Husa, K.E., Runde, R.K., Stolen, K.: Stairs towards formal design with sequence diagrams. Softw. Syst. Model. **4**(4), 355–367 (2005)
6. Hiranabe, K.: Astah. http://astah.net/. Accessed 09 Aug 2016
7. Hoare, C.A.R.: Communicating Sequential Processes. Prentice-Hall Inc., Upper Saddle River (1985)
8. Kaizu, T., Isobe, Y., Suzuki, M.: Refinement and verification of sequence diagrams using the process algebra CSP. IEICE Trans. **96**–**A**(2), 495–504 (2013)
9. Lima, L.: Formalisation of SysML design models and an analysis strategy using refinement. Ph.D. thesis, Universidade Federal de Pernambuco, Recife, March 2016
10. Lima, L., Iyoda, J., Sampaio, A.: A formal semantics for sequence diagrams and a strategy for system analysis. In: Proceedings of International Conference on Model-Driven Engineering and Software Development (MODELSWARD) (2014)
11. Mass Soldal Lund: Operational analysis of sequence diagram specifications. Ph.D. thesis, University of Oslo (2007)

12. Micskei, Z., Waeselynck, H.: The many meanings of UML 2 sequence diagrams: a survey. Softw. Syst. Model. **10**(4), 489–514 (2011)
13. OMG: MOF QVT Final Adopted Specification. OMG, June 2005
14. OMG: OMG Unified Modeling Language (OMG UML), superstructure, version 2.3. Technical report, OMG (2010)
15. Shen, H., Virani, A., Niu, J.: Formalize UML 2 sequence diagrams. In: Proceedings of 2008 11th IEEE High Assurance Systems Engineering Symposium, HASE 2008, Washington, DC, USA, pp. 437–440 (2008)
16. Storrle, H.: Trace semantics of interactions in UML 2.0 abstract (2004, preprint)

Author Index

Printed in the United States
By Bookmasters